942.5CABE...ABC

THE PARNELL TRAGEDY

THE PARNELL
TRAGEDY

JULES ABELS

THE BODLEY HEAD
LONDON · SYDNEY
TORONTO

© Jules Abels 1966
Printed and bound in Great Britain for
The Bodley Head Ltd
9-12 Bow Street, London, WC2
by Lowe & Brydone (Printers) Ltd, London
First published in Great Britain 1966

ILLUSTRATIONS

These photographs will be found following page 152.

PROLOGUE

From an interview with former Prime Minister William Ewart Gladstone by R. Barry O'Brien in 1898.

GLADSTONE: Parnell was the most remarkable man I have ever met. I do not say the ablest. I say the most remarkable and the most interesting. He was an intellectual phenomenon. . . .

O'BRIEN: He suffered terribly the last year of his life. The iron had entered his soul. I saw the agony of his mind though he tried to keep it a secret from us all.

GLADSTONE: Poor fellow. Ah, if he were alive today, I would do anything for him. Had Parnell lived and had there been no divorce proceedings, I do solemnly believe there would be a Parliament in Ireland now. . . . Oh, it was a terrible tragedy . . . dear, dear, what a tragedy. I cannot tell you how much I think about him and how much I am interested in everything about him. A wonderful man, a terrible fall.

From *Life of Charles Stewart Parnell*
by R. Barry O'Brien (1899)

PROLOGUE

BETWEEN 1846 and 1849 a catastrophe from natural causes occurred in Ireland of a magnitude paralleled only by the Black Death of the Middle Ages and the Biblical plagues of Egypt. The bulk of the population of Ireland was dependent for sustenance on the potato, and the potato crop was half destroyed by a mysterious blight in 1845, and was a total loss in 1846 and again in 1848. What ensued was a hideous chronicle of wholesale death known among the Irish as the Great Famine.

The Famine, when it came, was superimposed on a normal condition of abject poverty for the mass of peasants, with a large percentage existing in a state of chronic semistarvation. Under the union with Great Britain in 1801 English manufactures poured into Ireland, so there was little or no manufacturing there. The Irish therefore were flung on the land not as proprietors but as tenants, mostly tenants at will, of English landlords who held title under successive confiscations by Elizabeth I, James I and Cromwell. The population had soared to over nine million people, and land holdings had been minutely subdivided, with tenants bidding against each other so that even in good times only a bare existence could be eked out of the soil. A few years before the Famine, a French traveler, Gustave de Beaumont, commented, "I have seen the Indian in his forest and the Negro in his chains and I thought then I beheld then the lowest term of human misery but I did not know the lot of Ireland."

The 1846 crop debacle, after the partial failure of the previous year, caught everybody—the Irish farmers and English Government alike—entirely by surprise. The people, already impoverished and badly weakened, fed on whatever they could forage—cabbage leaves, weeds, thistles. They borrowed among themselves, begged from travelers, besieged food depots and workhouses—and then like sere leaves in the October wind fell to the ground and died in their hovels, in the fields and strewn along the roads.

3

On highway side where oft was seen
The wild dog and the vulture keen
Tug for the limbs and knaw the face
Of some starved child of the Irish race.

Death became only a "statistic," to use the phrase of a mass executioner of the twentieth century, and, indeed, due to the lack of
records, it did not achieve even that dignity. We have only rough
estimates that of the nine million inhabitants, at least a million died
and another million and a half, before they reached exhaustion,
scrambled onto boats, often "coffin ships" to seek survival elsewhere
—England, Canada, Australia and, mostly, the United States—in
a gigantic diaspora like that of the Jews in an earlier age.

A grave indictment can be brought against the English Government. It is certainly true that in the face of the emergency the
Government was neither indifferent nor inert. The Prime Minister,
Sir Robert Peel, actually wrecked his Conservative party in order to
bring about the repeal of the Corn Laws putting duties on imports
of agricultural products. It is also true that the Government was
staggered and bewildered by the enormity of the disaster and was
inhibited by the laissez-faire theories of economics, then considered
sacrosanct, under which governmental interference with normal
business was considered profane. It was hampered too by an abys-
mal ignorance about the economy of Ireland—it was said that the
English bureaucracy was better informed about West Africa.

Yet, with generous due for allowances, the legacy of lasting bitterness on the part of the Irish has good foundation. By the end of
1847 the Government had practically thrown up its hands and
abandoned all relief to the Poor Laws. Up to that time all relief
plans were hamstrung by restrictions which made them ineffective.
The Irish felt that under the Act of Union they were entitled to
be treated other than as stepchildren. If it had been the English
who were starving, they asked, would there have been so much
folderol in what was a life-and-death emergency? Would not all
inhibitions in the way of feeding the hungry have been thrown to
the wind? Would there have been bother and pother with unpro-
ductive work relief projects? Would there have been a requirement
that corn be imported only in English ships; a requirement that
ordinary channels of trade be relied on, which resulted in enormous
profiteering; or a requirement that no relief should go to owners
of a quarter acre of land, which resulted in their starvation?

Most important of all, would not all ports have been closed to the export of farm products? The Famine was only a famine in the potato—the other crops in Ireland were bumper ones—and corn, oats, barley, butter, eggs and livestock left Irish ports, bound for England, while the Irish were starving. In 1846 total exports of farm commodities amounted, according to official figures, to 44,958,000 pounds.

Irish historians are able to point to statements which indicate that considerations other than maintaining life in Ireland were on the minds of the English overlords. Thus, in the Queen's speech of 1847 concern over law and order was paramount: "It is satisfactory for us to observe that in many of the most distressed districts the patience and resignation of the people have been most exemplary. . . ." Charles Edward Trevelyan, Assistant-secretary to the Treasury and the administrator of relief, worked himself to the bone but at the same time seemed always most concerned that there should be no inordinate drain on the resources of Great Britain, or, as he put it, "to transfer the famine from one country to another." In 1847, the Prime Minister, Sir John Russell, defended the policy of not selling food cheap in Ireland because "it should have been increasing the price to our own consumers in England and Scotland." The next year, Sir John gave the Irish the gratuitous advice to use "the intelligence which they enjoy in a remarkable degree [to] fix their minds on the advantages which they might enjoy than upon the evils which they suppose themselves to suffer."

The curse of Ireland which multiplied the toll of the Famine manyfold was the iniquitous land system under which the tenant was at the mercy of the landlord and had to pay an exorbitant rack rent in competition with other tenants or face eviction, which was a more certain sentence of death. In the words of a Catholic bishop in a letter of 1847, "scores of persons are dying of starvation and fever, but the tenants are bravely paying their rent." To pay that rent "bravely" they had to sell all other crops they grew and depend for life on the potato, being left without any money to buy food no matter how cheaply it was priced by the Government when it was made available at food depots.

After the ravages of the Famine were over, the plight of the tenants became worse in many instances. Levies by the Government to help pay for the cost of relief had ruined many of the landlords, and the Encumbered Estates Act was passed to facilitate sale of their lands. The new owners were often more unreasonable than the landlords of the "old stock," and evictions were at a high level— 316,000 persons in the years 1848–1852. Then the repeal of the Corn Laws reduced agricultural prices and encouraged the wholesale conversion by large landowners of tillable land into pasture.

A generation after the Famine a land system—to all intents and purposes serfdom—was brought to an end. This was accomplished by the work of two men from Ireland of widely disparate backgrounds, personality and character. It is a remarkable coincidence that these men came into being at the very time that the Famine was commencing, when the worst evils of the land tenure were to afflict Ireland. Both were born in 1846, a few months apart.

One was a person of saintly character who became the intellectual of the land-reform movement after spending years of martyrdom because of his struggle against English rule. A man of the people, Michael Davitt was born in Straide, County Mayo, on March 25, 1846, the son of a poor tenant farmer. As a child he was told of the Famine and how, near Straide, over 300 bodies were thrown coffinless into a huge pit without a funeral service of any kind. When he was seven years old his family was evicted and thrown onto the roadside under one of the huge "clearances" into grazing ranches taking place. A priest found temporary refuge for the family in a barn. As the family trudged away to a seaport they could see their home burning. When they reached England, the father became ill and was confined to a hospital. To feed herself and her son, his mother worked days in a field and spun flax at night. At ten, Michael left school and went to work in a mill at Bexanden in Lancashire. He was told to tend a machine which by law was supposed to be worked by an adult; when he protested he was given a cuff and a kick. His right arm was crushed in the machine and had to be amputated. We shall follow his career later.

The second man was made of quite different clay. He was neither saintly nor intellectual. He was not a man of the people, but a member of the landowning class. He was not Catholic, like the bulk of the population, but Protestant. His family had settled in Ireland after the Restoration, and he was a member of the invading and ruling class of English so much hated by the Irish.

Nonetheless, he was the greatest leader the Irish have ever had. His public life was short. He entered Parliament when not quite twenty-nine and died at forty-five. He flashed across the sky like a comet, or, as it has been put in a change of simile, "His career was a success as lightning is a success." Under his leadership the shackles were struck from the feet of the tenant farmers and the Irish nation was led to the brink of Home Rule. But within sight of the Promised Land he faltered, was set upon by his followers and was destroyed in a macabre, Kafkaesque finale to his own life and to his nation's hopes. One of his most bitter foes at the end was his former friend and comrade Michael Davitt, who ten years later wrote of him, "To deny his greatness would be like denying the existence of a mountain."

This was Charles Stewart Parnell, born on June 27, 1846, in the family estate at Avondale in County Wicklow, Ireland. We give the official place of his birth, although Parnell himself once said to his Parliamentary colleague T. P. O'Connor that "he thought that he had been born in Brighton [England]." It is strange, indeed, —particularly for one of high rank in this modern age—to "think" that he was born in this place or that. It is even stranger if Parnell, knowing full well that he was born in Avondale, should have said that he "thought that he had been born in Brighton.' This peculiar note, however, is an appropriate opening for our story since Charles Stewart Parnell was an enigma in his lifetime, as he remains an enigma today. He baffled his contemporaries, and all that was written in later years about him by both those who knew him best and those who did not know him well at all has not solved the mystery.

Part One

THE YOUTH

I

IF CHARLES STEWART PARNELL had not been a Stewart *and* a Parnell, he would not have been the Parnell known to history. He was an aristocrat and was always conscious that he was to the manner born. He knew little of the past of Ireland, but he always bore in mind his own past. From this sprang his overtowering pride, the pride that was to be his chief asset, perhaps the secret of his power, and the pride that bore the seeds of his destruction.

His high lineage added to a possibly inherited instinct for command—his will to command. Then, too, in highly class-conscious Ireland, the common people, even his more intellectually gifted plebian associates, automatically looked up to him for command.

Another consideration is that the distinguished Parnells who were his ancestors had achieved renown as Irish patriots fighting for the interests of the Irish against the English. Parnell and his contemporaries were conscious of that inherited mandate. He was expected to fight as a champion of freedom, as was Brutus against Caesar because of the tradition of an earlier Brutus who had fought against the tyrant Tarquin.

There also was a patriotic inheritance from his mother, an American, who was violently—if not pathologically—anti-English. She was the descendant of Ulster Presbyterians who had fought against England in the Revolutionary War. Her father was Admiral Charles Stewart, who commanded the famous American warship *Constitution* in the War of 1812. Shortly before leaving Boston harbor in the refitted vessel, he married Delia Tudor, the daughter of a Boston judge. When she asked for a British frigate as a wedding gift, he promised her two. He almost kept the promise. On February 19, 1815, he engaged the *Cyane* and the *Levant* off the coast of Spain and captured both. In his cabin the two British captains poured recriminations upon each other for the disaster. "Gentlemen," said Captain Stewart, "there is no use getting warm about it. It would have been the same no matter what you had done. If you doubt that

I will put you all on board again and you can try over again." On the way back to the United States the *Levant* was recaptured by a British squadron, but Stewart brought the *Cyane* to port. For his feats in the war he was honored, banqueted and decorated by Congress and state legislatures. He was known for the rest of his days as "Old Ironsides," and he retired as a rear admiral. At the time of Fort Sumter he was eighty-three, but he wrote letters to newspapers demanding an assignment. "I am as young as ever to fight for my country."

There was a great deal of disagreement about the qualities of his grandson Charles Stewart Parnell, but there was a unanimity of opinion shared even by his bitter enemies that he was a tremendous fighter. Perhaps the fighting spirit of his doughty, seafaring grandfather filled his veins.

His father, John Henry Parnell, while touring America when he was twenty, met the daughter of the Admiral, then living in Bordentown, New Jersey. Delia Tudor Stewart was a striking beauty—vivacious, self-assured and very talkative. It was a love match, and in 1834 he brought her home to the estate at Avondale, which his sister turned over to him for a mortgage of £10,000.

The paternal line is far more important. The first Parnell we know of is Thomas Parnell, Mayor of Congleton, in Cheshire, England. After the Restoration his grandson, also Thomas Parnell, became a landlord in Queen's County, Ireland—probably as a safe haven after his connection with the Cromwellian cause. His son was the poet Thomas Parnell, who was an archdeacon in the Irish church but nonetheless managed to spend a great deal of time in London. He was a good friend of Alexander Pope, who once wrote to him urging his return, "You are a generous author, I a hackney scribbler. You are a Grecian and bred at a University, I a poor Englishman of my own educating." Samuel Johnson once wrote of Thomas Parnell, "He is sprightly without effort and always delights although he never ravishes."

The next distinguished Parnell, and the one whose career set the greatest example for Charles Stewart Parnell, was Sir John Parnell (1744–1801), who was Chancellor of the Exchequer in the Irish Parliament between 1785 and 1799. In this connection we must narrate some history which has a vital connection with the later fight for Home Rule.

Charles I established a Parliament in Ireland which had only fictitious independence since it was under the thumb of the English Government and was ruled by corruption. In the lower house, two-thirds of the 300 seats were controlled by 100 persons who sold them or manipulated them through Irish borough owners known as "undertakers." The pension list, used for boodle, included the Queen Dowager of Prussia and the mistresses of George I. When the American Revolution erupted, England's difficulty became, as it often did, Ireland's opportunity: Ireland was stripped of English redcoats for the greatest expeditionary force that Britain had ever mobilized. The Irish Volunteers were organized and a move was started for independence on a Dominion basis. Under Henry Grattan the revolt was successful, and with ranks of Volunteers drawn up before the House of Parliament, the English gave in.

In this Parliament, Sir John Parnell was Chancellor of the Exchequer for fifteen years. A man of unshakable integrity, he was most unusual in being free of any imputation of irregularity in the conduct of his office during an age when venality was rampant.

The Irish Parliament made some reforms, such as cutting the pension list, and passed a law lifting the ban in force against trade between Ireland and British colonies, but it lacked real control over the executive branch. Believing the battle won, Grattan made the fatal move of disbanding the Irish Volunteers. After the Peace Treaty with the colonies, British troops returned in force to Ireland, but in a few years there was new trouble—this time with Revolutionary France—which dovetailed into the Napoleonic Wars. There was always the threat of invasion from France, which necessitated a large English army in Ireland. One attempt was actually mounted, for which the patriot Wolfe Tone paid with his life.

In 1798 there was a general uprising in Ireland, which was put down by Lord Cornwallis (the same man who had surrendered to General George Washington at Yorktown), who proclaimed: "The minds of the people are in such a state that only blood will satisfy them." Loyal Orangemen from Ulster and Hessian mercenaries were loosed on the people in a savage bloodletting.

Now the British decided that only the privilege of complete union with Great Britain would settle the Irish problem and that the Irish Parliament must therefore vote for its own extinction. All officeholders who refused to go along were dismissed, and Sir John Parnell, who refused all bribes and blandishments offered him, was forced out. The ruthless Viscount Castlereagh was put in charge of the campaign of persuasion and the buying of votes began. The first vote was adverse to union by 109 to 105, so the "Bank of Persuasion" was made larger and the bribery became so flagrant that even Lord Cornwallis gagged. In addition to money bribes, forty-eight new peerages were created. In 1800 the Parliament finally voted its own abolition. To secure the assent Prime Minister William Pitt made many pledges which were not kept. One such was the emancipation of the Catholics, who were deprived of the normal privileges of citizenship. The excuse for not fulfilling that pledge was that to broach the subject to George III, then of unsound mind, would be to unduly upset him. Catholic emancipation did not come until 1828 through the efforts of the Duke of Wellington.

In a final speech on June 15, 1800, Henry Grattan delivered a moving threnody over the grave of Irish independence: "Identification is extinction, is dishonour, is conquest. Yet I do not give up on my country. I see her in a swoon, but she is not dead. Though in her tomb she lies helpless and motionless, still there is on her lips a spirit of life and on her cheek a glow of beauty."

Charles Stewart Parnell knew well this phase of Irish history and he often spoke of Grattan and the Irish Parliament with which his greatgrandfather was so intimately associated. In the spirit of Grattan, he saw as his mission the awakening of the sleeping Juliet lying apparently lifeless in her tomb.

The second son of Sir John was Henry Brooke Parnell (1776–1842), an extremely able man who was Secretary of State for War in the ministry of Lord Grey and a privy councilor. He was dismissed when he was unable to get along with Lord Grey, but in the Melbourne administration he was Paymaster General of the Forces and then was elevated to the peerage and sat in the House of Lords as Lord Congleton. He was a liberal on many issues, advocating an extension of the ballot and the abolition of flogging in the armed forces. Most notably, he was a friend of Ireland and an ardent advocate of Catholic emancipation in Parliament. He wrote *A History of the Penal Laws Against the Irish Catholics,* considered by many the best book on the subject.

The third son of Sir John was William, the grandfather of Charles Stewart Parnell. He too was a champion of the Irish and wrote a pamphlet, *An Historical Apology for the Irish Catholics,* which claimed that persecution was the real cause of Irish disaffection and recommended elimination of the grievances. It was a continuation of the argument begun in his earlier pamphlet, *An Enquiry Into the Causes of Popular Discontents in Ireland.* There was a good deal of witty illustration, such as comparing the Union to a grenadier selling the teeth of his child. When the child had a toothache the grenadier said to him, "All the rest will decay in turn and give you pain so have them all out." The child said, "How will I chew my victuals?" To which the father replied, "That is easy, I will chew them for you."

His son, John Henry, the father of Charles Stewart, was strictly nonpolitical and was loyal to the English establishment, as a justice of the peace, a grand juror and the chairman of the Board of Guardians under the Poor Law. He enjoyed life. He was fond of shooting, and as a Master of the Hounds he kept large stables and kennels and entertained the local gentry in great style. He was a fine cricketeer who had his own club maintained at his expense.

There is another aspect to the genetic inheritance of Charles Stewart Parnell that must be mentioned. There is some evidence of mental instability in his family. According to the *Dictionary of National Biography,* the poet Thomas Parnell "was always in a state either of elation or depression," which fits the description of a manic-depressive. Oliver Goldsmith said he "was the most capable man in the world to make the happiness of those he conversed with, and the least able to secure his own." After the death of his wife, he was mentally deranged until his own death at the age of thirty-eight. Lord Congleton hung himself during a period of melancholia. His older brother, John Augustus, was a deaf and dumb imbecile, and a younger brother, Thomas, was an eccentric who devoted his life to his obsession that the texts of the Bible could be arranged in a mysterious order that would give an infallible answer to all human problems.

The question of Parnell's sanity was raised in his lifetime, as we shall see. It was not absent from his own mind, and he once spoke to Davitt of his fear that he might go mad, saying that this was a subject "not treated lightly in my family."

II

One afternoon in the summer of 1857, a boy of eleven could be seen climbing to the coping of a roof, the highest point of a large manor house at Avondale. He hauled a pot customarily used for boiling potatoes, but which he had turned into a brazier for melting lead. The boy had heard that the best way to make bullets was to drop molten lead from great heights, so he was going to try it. The experiment was unsuccessful, so the boy hauled the brazier down.

This was Charles Stewart Parnell, a miniature of the man to be. His independence in consulting no one, his resourcefulness, calm security and daring in dragging the brazier to the rooftop already foreshadowed the mature man. In examining the child we shall see evidence of other traits.

The estate at Avondale, in which the boy grew up and which he was to inherit, was beautifully situated at the top of a high hill with meadows sloping down gently to the Avonmore Valley. Two miles from the home was the celebrated meeting of the waters described by Thomas Moore in a popular poem:

> There is not in the wide world a valley so sweet,
> As that vale in whose bosom the bright waters meet.

The terrain was beautifully wooded and an avenue of beech trees led up to the mansion, a squarely built house dating from 1777, which had a granite porch surrounded by pillars. The vestibule opened into a great square hall "capacious enough to drive a coach and four around." Log fires roared and revelry often took place, accompanied from the musicians' gallery at one end of the hall. All rooms on this floor entered into each other, and the doors could be opened to create a spacious atmosphere for balls and parties. Heads of elk and perhaps the largest antlers in existence hung on the walls. Also on the walls were the colors of the Irish Volunteers, which remained there until they were removed to drape the coffin of Charles Stewart Parnell.

Avondale was not the original family estate but was an adventitious acquisition. Samuel Hayes, a barrister who greatly admired Sir John Parnell, had willed it to him if his only daughter did not choose to live there. He had stipulated that the holder of the estate should add "Hayes" to his name, and in fact, Sir John's son William, the grandfather of Charles Stewart, had borne the name William Parnell-Hayes. The "Hayes" was dropped when his daughter Catherine inherited the property; she later transferred the estate to her brother John Henry upon his marriage.

On these sylvan grounds Charles romped with his brothers and sisters. Throughout his life he felt a close bond with his brother John Howard, born three years before him. There was a younger brother, Henry Tudor, who seemed to have played no part in his life. An older brother, William Tudor, had died eight years before his birth and another brother, Hayes, died in a hunting accident when Charles was sixteen. There were sisters in profusion: Delia, eight years older, whom Charles greatly resembled; Emily, five years older; Sophia Katherine, one year older; Fanny, his favorite sister, three years younger; Anna Catherine, six years younger; and Theodosia Tudor, seven years younger.

From infancy Charles was a headstrong and domineering child, determined to have his own way and impose it upon others, fractious to the point of being almost unmanageable. He acquired the nickname "Butthead" from his habit of charging into others who incurred his displeasure. The children's nurse, with the delightful name of Mrs. Twopenny (called by the children "Tuppy"), once exclaimed, "Charlie is born to rule." How fitting a characterization of his life, how fitting an epitaph for his tomb: "Charlie is born to rule."

In every game of "Follow the Leader," little Charlie had to be the leader. Moreover, in every contest, Charlie had to win. In a game of soldiers he played with his younger sister Fanny, the object was to bowl over opposing lines of soldiers. After one game his sister found that he managed to win by gluing down his soldiers before the shooting started.

He was an extremely nervous child, a somnambulist who had to take precautions against sleepwalking throughout his adult life. His older brother John Howard recalled how Charlie's fingers used to twitch nervously as he watched cricket matches as a child. Certainly the development of equilibrium was not aided by the influence of a mother who was somewhat étourdie. Once, while she was nursing Charles, she heard someone approaching and put him into a drawer, which she closed without thinking, and hurried to the drawing room. When the visitor left a half hour later, she had completely forgotten what she had done with Charles. A frantic search was made until muffled yells from the drawer where he was imprisoned were heard.

Educating this unruly child was no easy matter. To separate him from John, whose stammer he imitated, he was sent to England to a girls' school at Yeovil in Somersetshire. It was not a sound idea to send a nervous child away from his home and parents at such an early age. He was homesick and objected to being surrounded by girls who made a great fuss about his being the only boy. He had a bout with typhoid fever and was brought home, where he was put under the tutelage of his sisters' governess. But he objected to being taught by a woman and incessantly argued with her. His temper continued to be as violent as ever. When a housemaid accidentally broke some of his bird eggs he flew into such a tantrum that the frightened girl ran away and hid in the servants' quarters.

He was sent off again to England when he was eight for private tutoring with the Rev. Mr. Barton at Kirk Langley in Derbyshire, where he spent a brief period of time, terminated by his intractability and his inability to mingle with the other students. He returned to Avondale for haphazard instruction for the next few years. His education by fits and spurts under different teachers was inadequate, a fact which he recognized and deplored in later years. He never acquired great facility in reading, and the number of books he read in childhood were few indeed. He was alone during much of his boyhood. He did a good deal of wandering alone around Avondale, his mind engaged in projects like making bullets by dropping lead from high places or making gold by washing out the particles of real gold from the streams. There was a gold vein in Wicklow. Lord Byron had been acquainted with it and had said that it had "just enough ore to gild a bad guinea." He was right, though Parnell in years to come was to waste untold time and money to try to prove otherwise.

Within a few miles of Avondale was the shooting lodge where the boy learned marksmanship. Originally it had been a barracks built for soldiers in the insurrection of 1798, and nearby there was a granite stone on which the rebels had sharpened their pikes. The boy listened hungrily as the old men regaled him with tales of the fight for freedom which had occurred within their lifetime and even within their personal remembrance. The old gamekeeper,

Hugh Gaffney, told him a hair-raising tale of a rebel named Byrne, who was flogged in the belly so hard that his bowels protruded and he died shrieking, "For love of God, have mercy on me, Colonel Yeo." The boy listened in terror, and the image of the flogging haunted him for years. It filled him with hatred of flogging, and part of his life's work was to help abolish the practice.

When Charles was thirteen, his father died suddenly. As stubborn and self-willed as his son Charles was to be, John Henry Parnell had disregarded his doctor's advice and had gone to Dublin to take part in a cricket match in spite of having "rheumatism of the stomach." He caught a chill and died, at forty-eight, the day after the match, at the Shelbourne Hotel. At the time, Charles was alone at Avondale his brothers and sisters being either at school or with his mother in Paris. The boy went alone to the hotel to view the body and alone followed it to its final resting place. It was a very depressing experience. The next year his paternal grandmother died suddenly in her chair while visiting the family. From this time, Charles hated death, talk of death and all evidences and reminders of it. As an adult he would avoid all funerals where his presence was not mandatory.

By his father's will Charles inherited Avondale. The oldest son, John Howard, inherited the estate at Armagh, and the younger brother the property at Clonmore, Carlow. John seems to have been discriminated against because, in addition to his property's being a lesser estate than Avondale, he had to pay out of the rents a head rent of £1000 a year to Trinity College, as well as annuities to each of his sisters except Emily, whom her father cut off in the will because he feared that she would marry a man who was wastrel in his eyes, Captain Arthur Dickinson—who was indeed a wastrel and whom indeed she did later marry. The father had not intended disfavor to his oldest son; an uncle, Sir Ralph Howard, had intended to make John Howard Parnell his heir, and the father was trying to equalize the inheritances between the sons. But by inheriting Avondale with a rent-roll of £4000 a year Charles' certainly was left the choicest part of the estate.

The guardians of the children recommended that they be made wards in chancery, which was done. A solicitor, Mr. Alfred McDermott, who was appointed to manage the estate, took advantage of the proximity his assignment gave him to woo Emily, without success since her heart was pledged to Captain Dickinson. He then turned to Sophia Katherine, with complete success, though at the time she was only sixteen years old. They were married secretly at Gretna Green and she returned to the household, posing as an unmarried maid for the next five years, at the end of which time the couple went through another marriage ceremony. The estate was heavily burdened with debts that John Henry Parnell had piled up and Mr. McDermott recommended that Avondale be let and the livestock sold. The family lived for a time in a house named Khyber Pass in Dalkey, then near Clarinda Park in Kingstown, and finally on Upper Temple Street in Dublin, which most suited Mrs. Parnell, who enjoyed the bustle of city life.

The children were given the education best designed to equip them for their future lives. The girls were taught the best manners and social poise, then were given maximum exposure so that they could marry rich husbands. After some schooling they had a whirl in Paris, a "finishing education," then stayed with their uncle and aunt, Sir Ralph and Lady Howard, who walked them in the park, took them to balls and presented them to the Queen at Buckingham Palace, thus giving them "exposure."

The girls, with the exception of Anna, who was somewhat bony-faced, were beauties and attracted considerable attention wherever they were displayed. However, the girls were not lucky in love, either making indifferent matches or not marrying at all. Delia, the oldest, and a rare beauty, married an American millionaire, James Livingston Thomson, whom she told frankly she was marrying not for love but for money. She lived with him in misery in Paris; he drove her to distraction with his insane jealousy, finally restricting her from even going riding, which was her main recreation. Her beauty had become more of a curse than a blessing. The marriages that Emily and Sophia made, as we have stated, were not brilliant matches in pecuniary terms, though they were reasonably content. Fanny and Anna Catherine never married. The youngest, Theodosia, as unusually beautiful as Delia had been at her age, was married in 1880 to Commander Claude Paget, R.N.

III

When Charles was fifteen he was sent with his older brother John to a school, the Rectory, kept by a Rev. Mr. Wishaw in Chipping Norton, Oxfordshire, to prepare them for Cambridge University. As soon as they arrived Charles looked at the graveyard facing the Rectory and said, "I say, John, I don't quite like this." Already he was the prey of omens which were to make him as superstitious as a jungle medicine man.

His student life there was marked by his usual contentiousness. He would not accept even Scripture at face value if he disagreed. Once when he was called to book on an error, his tutor citing the Liddell and Scott Greek lexicon, Charles was not vanquished. He replied, "You must have gotten hold of a wrong edition."

Although he knew little Latin and less Greek, Charles entered Magdalene College as a pensioner when he was nineteen. John Howard did not join him, preferring to go to a technical school where mining was taught. Of the four years Charles spent at Cambridge we know practically nothing. Charles certainly absorbed little learning or love of learning. Even while enrolled at Cambridge he was in Ireland for a substantial part—if not most—of the year.

Charles was already developing toward the English an icy reserve stemming from hypersensitivity because he was Irish and thus might be treated as a person of a lower caste. He would say to John, "These English despise us because we are Irish, but we must stand up to them. That's the way to treat an Englishman—stand up to him." From this early contact with the English his later political attitudes were being molded. Because of this sensitivity he kept the English at arm's length during his university career and made no friends.

After Charles' death, his sister, Mrs. Emily Dickinson, wrote a biography entitled *A Patriot's Mistake* (which the *Irish Times* said should have been entitled *A Patriot's Sister's Mistake*). In the book she recounts an incident from his University days which seems like a page from a novel of the *Pamela* genre. While boating on the Cam when he was nineteen, Charles came upon the lovely daughter of a fruit farmer, Daisy, age sixteen, and became enamoured of her beauty. He contrived to establish a friendship and then seduced her. In typical *droit du seigneur* fashion with a girl of a lower class, he abandoned her after he had tired of her. One day while boating down the river he rounded the bend to her father's farm at the moment when the body of the drowned girl was being fished out of the river.

Pursuing Mrs. Dickinson's account—Charles testified at the inquest but his responsibility for the tragedy was carefully shielded.

Nonetheless the event terminated his University career since he was sent down. Thereafter he was subject to frequent fits of nervous depression. He claimed that Daisy's image would appear before him in the dead of night, standing at the foot of his bed, a dripping white-clad form. One night Captain Dickinson shared a room with him at Avondale and the next day told his wife, "He disturbed me half the night, moaning and calling out about some Daisy, and at one time he got so frenzied with a vision he said was at the foot of his bed that I had to hold him."

Aside from the ring of fiction, the most glaring defect in the story is that Charles was sent down from Cambridge a good deal later than in this account and because of something quite different. Another element that lends improbability is that John Howard Parnell in his biography of his younger brother does not mention it. A Parliamentary follower and worshiper of Parnell, Henry Harrison, who wrote in defense of Parnell's reputation decades after his death, claimed that he had looked into the coroners' records in the general area for the period and had found no such suicide and inquest.

Yet, the story cannot be rejected out of hand. Mrs. Dickinson had no conceivable motive to besmirch the reputation of her brother, and John Howard would have had every desire to protect it. The nature of her book tends to give credence to her story since it is a wooden, factual account obviously written by an unimaginative woman. The mistake about the cause of sending down Charles from Cambridge appears to be a spontaneous recollection which happens to be mistaken, not a studied fabrication. Moreover, the story does give some explanation of the nightmares to which Parnell, from the testimony of his wife, Katherine, was subject in his adult life.

The incident which actually caused his departure from the academic life occurred when Charles was twenty-three. One night he and two other students ate in an inn and the other two went off on the fly. Two men came along, probably under the influence of liquor, and tried to push Parnell off the footpath, whereupon he knocked them both down. He was arrested on the charge of assault and in a civil action was ordered to pay damages of 20 guineas. This was followed by a meeting of college authorities on May 26, 1869, which resulted in his being sent down two weeks before the end of the term.

Years later, while on a train journey with Michael Davitt, Parnell mused about the vagaries of chance in human lives. He told Davitt that when the policeman came along after he had knocked the men down, he had reached into his pocket and fished out what he thought was a sovereign and handed it to him. The policeman examined the coin under the light and when he saw that it was only a shilling he arrested him. If it had been a sovereign, he would not have been arrested, he would not have been rusticated, he would have stayed to take his degree at Cambridge and might well have stayed on in England as an absentee landlord. And thus history is made—"for want of a nail," for a shilling that felt like a sovereign in the dark.

IV

There had always been political talk at the Parnell table, emanating from Mrs. Parnell, who continued to fight the English as her forebears had done in the War for Independence and the War of 1812. The hatefulness of the English was an *idée fixe* with her and made her presence an explosive liability at every social gathering. Once, while she was visiting her sons when they were under the tutorship of the Rev. Wishaw, he tore himself away from her and said to a friend, "I say, I have met one of the most extraordinary women. She is a regular rebel. I never heard such treason in my life. Without a word of warning she opened fire on the British Government and by Jove she gave it to us hot."

To what extent she transmitted the anti-English virus to her children is problematical. Fanny became fanatically anti-English and pro-Irish and was the stuff that martyrs are made of. Anna had the same bias, though she was more intellectually and less emotionally charged up. Charles, in his youth, seemed completely disinterested and apathetic about politics. None of the other children then or later caught the virus.

Mrs. Parnell's peculiar inconsistency was that while she hated the English—that is politically—she liked and adopted all things English (reminding us of Kaiser Wilhelm, who, though the sworn enemy of the English, insisted on speaking English and wearing English tweeds). She educated her children in England, she had her daughters presented at the Royal Court. She adored the Queen, and once wrote to her son John: "The Queen is wise and good. Find out her opinions. Her ministers are not infallible." Her son Charles, when he became the dedicated antagonist of the English Government, was to be nevertheless all English in his tastes, accent, demeanor, clothes, class snobbery, etc.

In 1858, the Fenian movement, advocating armed revolt, had been started. Named for a legendary band of warriors (*féinne*), it was formed first in the United States and then in Ireland. One of its leaders, James Stephens, founded a revolutionary journal, the *Irish People,* in Dublin in 1862. It was a secret society in which the members took an oath of "allegiance to the Irish Republic now virtually established." After the American Civil War the movement acquired more impetus, since it now had a cadre of officers who were skilled in killing and in feats of daring and who were loathe to return to the quiet life. In 1866, some 800 Fenians under John O'Neill crossed the Niagara River and staged an abortive invasion of Canada. As a prelude to armed revolution, they started gunrunning into Ireland and infiltrating the Irish in the British armed forces.

In Ireland the Fenian movement came to be known as the Irish Republican Brotherhood (a name which continued long after Fenianism was dead). In the United States it was known as the Clan-na-Gael. This foreign revolutionary movement for Irish freedom, financed and launched from an inviolable sanctuary, was to plague England from that time on. The Irish abroad, particularly those in the United States, were more prosperous and upgraded in status than those who remained in the old country and thus furnished vigor and backbone to the revolutionary movement. (An analogy can be drawn with the American support for a Jewish homeland in Palestine.) The foreign branches often tended to be oblivious of practical difficulties in resistance to England and therefore tended to radicalism in their program.

As a young girl, Fanny Parnell was heart and soul in the movement, and when only fourteen she visited the offices of the *Irish People* to contribute her poems to the editor, John O'Leary. Fanny was a genuinely talented poetess, and her poems were to appear in later Irish anthologies. In the revolutionary cause which spurred with Fenianism she was considered the poet of highest rank, supplying ardor as Julia Ward Howe had done in the American Civil War. Her mother was also a fighter in the cause. When the finan-

cial situation had eased, Avondale had become the family home of
the Parnells again, but Mrs. Parnell preferred to remain in Dublin
in the Upper Temple Street home, which became a headquarters
for Fenians, whom she fed and helped financially. Fenianism got
most of its recruits at this time from young men of the laboring
class who struck Charles as a bunch of drunken ruffians. He objected to having his home contaminated by their presence. He
often waited for them behind the hall door, then would emerge to
rush them down the steps and into the street. One day it would
be the Fenians who would make him Ireland's leader, one of the
many ironies in his career.

Despite the vitality Fenianism gave to the Irish cause, the Fenians at their height probably had no more than 75,000 members.
The Catholic clergy, consistently conservative, condemned them,
and because of this clerical influence Fenianism never made deep
inroads among the tenant farmers. Then, too, secret oaths did not
go too well with the outspoken Celtic temperament. When armed
revolt instigated by Fenians broke out in 1867, few rifles had been
smuggled in. The British Government, alerted as always by informers, shifted disaffected regiments to India, suspended habeas
corpus and sent large numbers after mock trials to penal servitude.
An informer betrayed the *Irish People,* and in 1865 John O'Leary,
Charles Kickham and O'Donovan Rossa were tried and sentenced
to long years of penal servitude; James Stephens escaped to France.
Fanny, a girl of sixteen, attended every day of the trial and shed
copious tears. The calm fortitude of the accused made a deep impression on all the onlookers.

JUDGE FITZGERALD: You ought to have known that the game you
    entered upon was desperate and hopeless.
O'LEARY: Not hopeless.
JUDGE FITZGERALD: You ought further to have known that insurrec-
    tion in this country meant not insurrection alone but a war of
    extermination.
O'LEARY: No such thing.
JUDGE FITZGERALD: You have lost.
O'LEARY: For the present.
JUDGE FITZGERALD: It is my duty to announce that the sentence of
    the court is such as to deter others.
O'LEARY: I hope not.

c

In a drive by the Government to wipe out all the warrens of Fenianism, Mrs. Parnell's home was raided and Fanny had to take refuge for the night in a hotel. When Charles, at Cambridge, received a letter from Fanny describing the raid, he was enraged at the English for their impudence in searching his mother's bedroom and in turning his sister out onto the street. He was equally annoyed by a gross trespass on his personal property—thinking that they were Fenian uniforms, the raiders had taken Charles' and John's Wicklow Rifles uniforms. The two boys were proud of these uniforms and proud of being in the service of the Queen. It rankled Charles all the more since he could not attend the vice-regal balls of the Irish Viceroy, Lord Carlisle, who was a great friend of the family. Charles refused to attend in court dress because he said it looked too much like footman's livery. He paid a visit to the Viceroy, who retrieved the uniform for him and thus enabled Charles to resume his cherished social life.

On September 18, 1867, a dramatic event occurred in the history of Irish resistance to English rule. In Manchester, England, a prison van carrying two Fenians from court back to jail was stopped by a band of armed men who were bent on releasing the prisoners. A sledge and crowbar had been inadvertently left behind so one of the band, named Rice, had to shoot the lock off. The bullet hit and killed a Sergeant Brett, who by unhappy chance was looking through the keyhole. Rice was not found, but others of the gang were arrested and tried for first-degree murder under the felony-murder rule though there had been no premeditation.

Five prisoners, Maguire, Allen, Larkin, O'Brien and Condon were found guilty and sentenced to hang. (Maguire was later pardoned and Condon's sentence commuted.) Addressing the court the convicted men made statements which stirred the soul of Ireland. Allen said, "No man in the court regrets the death of Sergeant Brett more than I do. I positively say in the presence of the Almighty and ever-living God that I am innocent, aye, as innocent as any man in court. I do not say this for the sake of mercy. I want no mercy. I'll have no mercy. I'll die as many thousands have died for the sake of the beloved country or in defence of it."

Condon said, "I was not even present when the rescue took place. We are not afraid to die. I only trust that those who will be tried after us will have a fair trial and that our blood will satisfy the craving that exists. You'll soon send us before God and

I am perfectly prepared to die. I have nothing to regret or retract. I can only say 'God save Ireland.' "

"God save Ireland." T. D. Sullivan immediately wrote the words of an Irish song that was sung at Irish patriotic meetings from that time on.

On the cold morning of November 23, the three hapless men, Allen, Larkin and O'Brien, were hung. A howling English mob outside Salford jail turned the hanging into a Jubilee singing exultantly "Rule Britannia." In Dublin there was a different scene depicting again the wide gulf between the two nations. There was a commemorative funeral with three hearses, each bearing the name of one of the men. All was still in the crowd of 150,000 except for the strains of the "Dead March," all heads were bared and when the hearses passed, all fell to their knees.

The heroism of the Fenians was not in vain. In English liberal circles widespread sympathy for the Irish was aroused, together with a dawning realization that the oppression of which the Irish complained had real foundation. The noted liberal John Bright, protesting against the executions as a "mistake," said, "I believe that the three men were hanged because it was a political offence and not because it was an ordinary murder."

The executions aroused in the mind of one, who had been hitherto politically immature and indifferent, a first consciousness of the Irish problem. He was hotly indignant about the fate of the "Manchester Martyrs." It was his first identification with the Irish nation and the beginning of the political awakening of Charles Stewart Parnell.

V

At this time Michael Davitt, despite his youth (he was twenty-one at the time of the Manchester executions), was a prominent figure in the Fenian conspiracy. He had joined it when he was nineteen and had been one of the band who had planned to attack Chester Castle, a plan betrayed by an informer and thus frustrated. Davitt then became organizing secretary of the Fenians for England and Scotland. For his job of smuggling firearms into Ireland, he assumed the role of a commercial traveler dealing in firearms. Rifles sent to Ireland were packed in barrels to make them look like soap or some other harmless commodity and then intercepted at the railroad station by Fenian agents purporting to come from the consignees.

Davitt was arrested at Paddington Station in London in May, 1870. He had £152 on him and was to meet a gunsmith who had fifty revolvers. The usual police informer, one Corydon, testified against him and he was sentenced to fifteen years in jail. After he was arrested, he was kept in an almost totally darkened cell with neither bed nor bedding. At the first prison after sentencing, Margate, he was chained by the ankles so that he could only step 14 inches and had to hold the chain at all times. He next was taken to Millbank, where no detail calculated to bestialize the victim was omitted. His cell was 10 feet long and 8 feet wide with no table or chairs; the bed was raised 6 inches at the head and 3 inches at the foot. He had to sit on a covered bucket 14 inches high ten hours a day and pick oakum. When he complained to the warder about the difficulty of picking oakum with one hand, the warder replied that many one-armed "blokes" picked oakum very well with their teeth. One hour's exercise a day was permitted if the weather was good. In ten months he was allowed only twenty minutes' conversation with other prisoners. The food was putrid meat and decayed vegetables, and black beetles in the soup and bread was a common occurrence. Madness seemed inevitable under this treatment and many prisoners did go mad.

Davitt was told that he was to be freed and he fell to his knees in joy, but it was a cruel trick. When he reached the gate he found that he was to be transferred to Dartmoor prison. There he was put to work breaking stones or, in the terrible stench of a charnel house, breaking bones from the prison's meat supply, or, like a dray animal, he was harnessed to a cart hauling coal, stones and manure. For being unable to haul a load beyond his strength he was thrown into a punishment cell, and for answering a call with "Here" instead of "Sir" he was put into a cell on bread and water for four days. From the day of his imprisonment to the day of his discharge seven years later he was not allowed to receive a single visitor.

This especially cruel treatment was reserved for political prisoners. It did not break Davitt's spirit, and all during his confinement he was planning a program for Ireland's salvation after his release.

VI

In his salad days, life's main problem for the young Parnell was how most enjoyably to spend his days. When he reached twenty-one, he was feted with a three-day carnival and drinking binge. After he left Cambridge he spent almost all his time at Avondale, mostly fishing and hunting, a lonely youth wandering over hill and dale with his dog and gun. He made no friends. Throughout his life, Parnell was to make no friends, his brother John being the only person who could claim a close relationship. Unable to give of himself, he kept all others at a distance. He captained a cricket eleven, and once, when he had a tiff with the opposing captain, he pulled his team off the field even before the game had begun. As a leader, where he went he expected all others to follow.

The matrix of his personality formed and hardened. He was cold and reserved, unwilling to give his confidence to anyone, deliberate about all decisions, talking little—and then only if the subject interested him. Always present was the pride of an Irish aristocrat. His sister Fanny was wooed by an artist, but he ended it by deciding that the artist had not yet proved his talent to an extent that would make him worthy of his sister—thereby doing a great disservice to Fanny, who never married.

He attended all the balls at the viceregal lodge in Dublin, and John recalled that he never missed a ball at the British Embassy in Paris. The young squire was surpassingly handsome. He was tall and lean, with sandy hair, delicate features and reddish brown eyes that all who knew him found peculiarly magnetic and compelling. A myriad of small fires seemed to flicker in his unusual eyes and make them strangely alive.

He was a top matrimonial catch, but none in the parade of Irish girls caught his eye. He had no romances, illicit or otherwise, to our knowledge at this time. An old parish priest told a writer, Michael MacDonagh, that though there was much gossiping about the young squire at that time, there was never a breath of scandal attached to him, whether of carousing or lovemaking. In fact, aside from poor, disputed Daisy we know of only two loves in Parnell's entire life, and by coincidence they were by name arboreally the same—Miss Woods (first name unknown) and Katherine Wood, in

marriage Mrs. Katherine O'Shea. The first romance, which wilted
before it bloomed, is now at hand.

VII

Charles stayed for periods of time in Paris with his mother's
brother, Colonel Stewart. While there in 1870 he met an American
beauty, Miss Woods, who was an heiress of sorts—a not inconsid-
erable factor in her favor since Charles was spending a great deal
of his income from Avondale to supplement the slim annuities
that his brother John was able to give his sisters, and besides, he
needed capital for a pet project: to develop the mineral resources of
his estate. What is more important is that he was genuinely smitten
and the young lady was attracted to him.

The two spent their time constantly with each other, riding or
walking hand in hand down the Paris boulevards. Though no
pledges were made, Charles considered himself engaged. When the
girl went on to Rome with her family, he followed her there. Miss
Woods was as affectionate as ever though her parents were notice-
ably cool. He cut short his stay in Rome because of a warning from
Colonel Stewart of "Roman fever" in the summer, but he joined
her later in Paris and they seemed well-nigh united. In the transport of love he returned to Avondale to prepare it for the arrival
of a new mistress, but he received a curt letter from her saying that
she was returning to the United States. There was no intimation
at all in the letter that she felt that there was anything enduring
between them.

Parnell, to nouveau-riche American eyes, did not shape up as a
top matrimonial find, as Miss Woods' parents advised her. Although
he was an aristocrat he did not have a title which would bear
warranty to it and dazzle American eyes. He had no profession,
and the idleness of a country squire was not considered a virtue
in the American Puritan ethic. He lacked even an abundance of
his own money.

Charles was dismayed, but he did not give up hope. The next
year he crossed the Atlantic, the first of three trips he was to make
there, and visited the young lady in her home at Newport, Rhode
Island. There she told him quite frankly that she would not have

him because she wanted a husband who promised some achievement and distinction, and he obviously did not qualify.

From there Charles went south to Alabama, where John had established a farm at West Point growing cotton and peaches. The manager's wife told John that, in his early days on the farm, Charles had fits of brooding and dejection, that often when coming unexpectedly into the living room she found him crouching before the fire, his face cupped in his hands.

The long-range effects of his jilting by Miss Woods on the life of Charles Stewart Parnell are conjectural, but they were probably minimal. It has been speculated that the deep trauma led him to seek greatness in compensation, but if so, it is strange that he did not think about politics for another three years. He was, moreover, not the type to "trouble deaf heaven with bootless cries" and also was too proud to react for long to a rebuff by a young woman.

From John's account, it seems clear that, contrary to one published version, he did not see her again. John recounted that in 1882 he and his sister Theodosia did meet the former Miss Woods, now married to a lawyer, in Newport. "Do tell me, how is your great brother Charles? How famous he has become!" She stopped and then, bursting into tears, exclaimed, "Oh, why did I not marry him? How happy we should have been together."

Far from moaning and mooning, Charles seemingly in buoyant mood threw himself into the enjoyment of this new land and helping his brother with his projects. On one occasion, when a man for whom John was building a house complained about it, the terrible-tempered Charles knocked him down, saying that the house was far too good for him. There was a comical incident which remained always in John's memory. Their house was built on poles five feet high, leaving an open space underneath. Pigs .broke in to warm themselves in the recesses. One night, while in bed, Charles said to his brother, "I say, John, I can't sleep with that infernal noise." John suggested that he take his gun and have a shot at them. Charles did so and at the report of the gun the terrified animals bolted out, dumping Charles on the ground, gun and all. That image of Charles, *boulversé*, in his nightshirt, amused John often in recollection.

At this time, during the period of Reconstruction, with the abandonment of the slave and cotton economy, the foundations

were being built of the industrialized New South. Northern capital
was coming in and explorations were being made of the natural
mineral resources of the South hitherto neglected. John was conscious of this burgeoning industrial movement and tried to exploit
the new opportunities it presented.

By railroad the brothers traveled to the new city of Birmingham,
mostly bare fields which had been a cotton field the previous year
and were now laid out in sites by a land company. The location
was chosen because it was the junction of two railroads, the North
and South Railroad and the Chattanooga and Alabama Railroad,
and because it was overlooked by the Red Mountain, which had
iron ore cropping out of it, and there were coal fields nearby. With
the consummate confidence of which only Americans are possible,
the promoters had named a village of a few wooden houses Birmingham, for the great iron center of England. Their confidence was to
prove justified.

There was one small hotel, at which the brothers stayed, full of
adventurers of one sort or another. No property was safe unless it
was on one's person. Five or six strangers would be dumped into a
room without notice. In this hotel, dinner could consist of several
mouthfuls of bacon, and the greasy Southern cooking revolted
Charles.

They were introduced to a Colonel Powell, a pioneer of Birmingham, and here again Charles exhibited his supersensitivity
about his class status. "For God's sake, John, don't tell him we are
from Ireland, since they have never seen real Irish gentlemen and
wouldn't know one if they did." He was afraid of being lumped
with the Irish canaille who had emigrated from Ireland since the
Famine.

The three went to inspect the new Warrior coal field a few
miles away, and Charles became enthusiastic about the possibilities
of getting rich from the new Alabama industry. He made many
expeditions around the area by railroad, and on one occasion he
wired his brother to meet him at a certain station. John misread
the wire and reached the station a day early, but Charles had
himself changed his plans and arrived the same day. From his
sleeping car, to his surprise, Charles saw John on the platform
and joined him in the day coach. Soon afterward the train jumped
the tracks and the sleeping car was completely destroyed, together
with all its occupants. The mischance of John's misreading the

telegram had saved Charles' life. The incident helped to imprint on Charles' mind the strong streak of fatalism it would bear for the rest of his life. Whatever fate had in store for him, he could not argue whether it was for his ultimate good or ill.

In the accident John was seriously injured, and Charles nursed him tenderly back to health. Charles had been engaged in negotiations for the purchase of the Warrior mine, which was owned by two dentists who got their operating capital by extracting Negroes' teeth. Charles wanted to invest £3000, but he insisted on full control—which the dentists would not give him—so he abruptly concluded the negotiations. The mine became one of the great coal fields of Alabama, and if Charles had invested in it he would have become a millionaire. It was John's belief that the accident had badly jolted Charles and that, as one often does, Charles had linked the mishap with the physical environment and had lost enthusiasm for Alabama altogether. Had it not been for the wreck, John believed, Charles would have made a deal, would have stayed in the United States, and, again, history would have been different.

The next stop for the brothers was the Clover Hill coal mine in Virginia, in which they owned stock, where Charles again had a close shave: a protruding ledge almost decapitated him during the descent into the mine. John predicted, on the basis of his mining knowledge, that the veins in the mine would soon give out, and, in fact, the investment Charles had in the mine did prove to be a sour one. On New Year's Day of 1872 the brothers departed from New York for Ireland on the *City of Antwerp*.

VIII

A new national movement was in its early life in Ireland, and in contrast to Fenianism it hoped to use constitutional methods. In Ireland's history there had been a cycle of alternating constitutional and physical-force movements. There was the Repeal (of the Union) Association, headed by the great leader Daniel O'Connell, which came to an end in 1843 when the monster meeting at Clontarf was broken up by armed government forces, and O'Connell was sent for a time to prison. Then there was the Young Ireland movement headed by Smith O'Brien, Charles Gavan Duffy (who founded the newspaper *The Nation,* which was the organ for Young Ireland), Thomas F. Meagher and John Mitchel. In 1848, the Young Irelanders led an armed rebellion that was put down by the Government. Then there was a constitutional movement, the Irish Tenant League, which got nowhere, and Charles Gavan Duffy left for Australia declaring that there was no more hope for Ireland than there was for a corpse on a dissecting table. Then came Fenianism which had inspirited the Irish but brought no concrete results.

By a strange quirk, a new infusion of strength for Irish nationalism came as a result of a concession that England made to the great mass of the Irish people who were Catholics, in 1869, under Prime Minister William Ewart Gladstone. The Anglican Church, which served only the small minority of Anglicans in Ireland, was disestablished. This withdrawal of what was viewed as a legal recognition of the Protestant ascendancy enraged many Protestants and made many of them, particularly Ulsterites, ready to join in a legal revolutionary movement.

On May 19, 1870, at the Bolton Hotel, on Upper Sackville Street in Dublin, a meeting resulted in the formation of the Home Government Association. Prof. Galbraith of Trinity College had the happy thought that while "Repeal" was an ugly word to the English, having the effect of waving a red flag in front of a bull, "Home Rule" would sound less harsh. The euphemistic name was used from that time on. A resolution was passed that the organization would seek and support candidates for Parliament who supported Home Rule for Ireland.

The moving spirit was a distinguished barrister, Isaac Butt, a Protestant born in 1813 who had attended Trinity College, where he was a fine classical scholar, having translated Vergil's *Georgics* into English as a student. He had been a professor of political economy, then a member of the bar. In May, 1848, he had made a brilliant defense of the Young Irelanders Smith O'Brien and Thomas Meagher when they were tried for sedition and had secured their release. Between 1856 and 1859 he had neglected his rich law practice to defend the Fenian prisoners and had won fame and the nation's gratitude. In 1869 he had become President of the Amnesty Association seeking the release of the convicted Fenians, a group which united Irishmen of all shades of political thinking.

In 1873 there was a Home Rule Conference attended by 900 members. Three members of Parliament by their presence showed their adherence to the new cause. Among those present whose names would appear prominently later were John Dillon, then a young medical student, son of John Blake Dillon, a Young Irelander; Thomas Sexton, a young journalist for *The Nation;* Frank Hugh O'Donnell, an intellectual who was a journalist in London; Richard Pigott, a journalist of Fenian sentiments who owned *The Irishman* and *The Flag of Ireland.*

Among the members of the new group were two Fenians, John O'Connor Power and John Barry, but Fenians by and large stayed apart and condemned the new movement. To produce results it would be necessary to be in league with Englishmen, and in Fenian thinking "to say anything good about an Englishman is to say something good about poison." Moreover, if a newly elected member took the required oath to Queen Victoria it would contravene his oath taken to the Irish Republic.

In the Fenian viewpoint, too, there was little to hope for from hypocrites who proclaimed themselves patriots, went to Parliament and then bargained away their honor and pledges for places. There were so many discreditable cases to point to for confirmation. There was, for example, the notorious William Keogh, who as an M.P. from Athlone had said to the voters that he would never accept office or preferment from any government "which did not bring in a Land Reform Bill to stay the plunder and evictions which are bleeding Ireland to death." He nonetheless broke all his pledges to accept legal office in Ireland, became Attorney General and later sat as a judge in the trials which condemned Fenians to long terms of penal servitude.

IX

Although there was an influx of Protestants into the new movement, Parnell seemed completely unconcerned about Home Rule. Once, John asked him about it and he replied with his typical hauteur, "I would not have anything to do with that set"—meaning grubby politicians. Since his return from the United States he had spent his time living the life of a rich squire. He had become sheriff of Wicklow County, which made him a magistrate, and he also became a synod of the disestablished church, which made him a kind of church warden. He hunted and fished, he raised prize cattle which he exhibited at county fairs, he improved Avondale's sawmills and tried to exploit its mining properties. He was less of a bon vivant than in previous days and no longer dashed over to Paris to savor its gaiety, probably less because of the heart wound administered by Miss Woods than the fact that in the aftermath of the Franco-Prussian War and the Commune, Paris was still drab and grim.

The family's fortunes fluctuated. Sir Ralph Howard had died, and contrary to his pledge to John Henry Parnell he had not made his son John Howard Parnell his heir, but instead had left him shares of companies engaged in iron and coal in Wales bringing in £4000 a year. Unfortunately, the companies were unlimited in shareholder liability and shareholders were liable for calls, so that when the companies went into bankruptcy, John had to give them up. But then Mrs. Parnell's brother, Colonel Stewart, died leaving a huge estate in American railroad stocks to his sister, so money was plentiful—for a while. John no longer had to pay the annuities to his sisters, and Mrs. Parnell and her daughters Fanny, Anna and Theodosia flounced from Europe to America and back. Captain Dickinson, Emily's spouse, had proved to be an incompetent drunk, had mismanaged John's estates as his agent and was now largely supported by Charles' generosity. Mrs. Parnell was an inveterate gambler on the New York Stock Exchange and in the Panic of 1873 lost heavily, so family circumstances became straitened again.

One evening, in early 1874, Charles was to join John for dinner in the home of the Dickinsons in Lower Pembroke Street in Dublin. Charles arrived in an unusually jocose mood. Arriving at Kingsbridge Station from Cork, he had offered the driver of a jaunting car half a crown if he got him to the address by seven o'clock but nothing at all if he missed the time target. The jarvey was late by a couple of minutes, and Charles turned down his plea for a settlement by stating that a wager was sacrosanct. He was gay at dinner and discussed with some emphasis the rectitude of the position he had adopted with the jarvey. The discussion turned to politics and the coming elections for Parliament. Suddenly Charles said, "By Jove, it will a grand opening for me to enter politics."

His family could not have been much more surprised if he had announced his intention to become a missionary in Africa. The astonishment deepened when he announced that he was not interested in running as a Conservative or even as a Liberal but as a Home Ruler in the Isaac Butt movement. John replied very hesitantly, "Yes, indeed, Charles, it would be a very splendid opportunity." "Well, it is settled," Charles said, "will you and Dickinson come with me to the office of the *Freeman?*"

At the office of the newspaper the *Freeman's Journal,* the publisher, Sir John Gray, a fellow Protestant, was gratified by Charles' adhesion to the cause and his desire to publish an announcement to that effect, but reminded him that unfortunately he was overlooking the fact that as sheriff of Wicklow he was ineligible, having, in fact, important duties to perform in the election. So the next morning Charles went to see the Viceroy in person to ask for an immediate release from his duties; the answer was a regretful "no"—it would take some time to find a successor and by then it would be too late for him to run.

Charles was dismayed by this unexpected rebuff to his ambitions. The next night at dinner, Charles said to John, "You must run, John, now that I cannot." John protested that he was an Armagh man and not a Wicklow man and, besides, he had been away too long in America fruit farming. Charles had always been able to impose his will on his older brother and in this case too he was able to overcome his recalcitrance.

John became a candidate, and Charles wrote out his election manifesto and managed his campaign. He went off to Rathdrum, where he mounted a barrel and delivered a speech while surrounded by sheep and cattle. He organized a committee of priests for John (almost a sine qua non for election), then went off electioneering in West Wicklow. He had a fine time and joshed John, "What in the world are you picking up such a row for?" The astonished John replied, "It's you." With a straight face, disregarding his answer, Charles replied, "And you are very right to do so."

After the poll, Charles as sheriff had to announce the melancholy news that his brother had come in last in the group of candidates. This did not faze John a whit, and he set out with great relief for his Alabama peach farm. He blamed his low vote on the fact that he was the first to import frozen fruits and vegetables from America into Ireland, which made him unpopular with the Irish farmers.

The decision of young Parnell to seek office as a Home Ruler is the first question in the enigma of his personality. He had never been outspokenly patriotic and gave no indication that he had ever brooded over his country's misfortunes. He had attended no public meetings. He was volubly indignant about the Manchester Martyrs, which seemed to have awakened a feeling in his breast as an Irishman and not as an Englishman, but his partisanship for the Fenians subsided and he had no more to say on the subject of politics. He did not join the Amnesty Association, which attracted members from every layer of society in Ireland.

The perplexity of his family as to Charles' newly discovered interest is evident in the colorful explanation given by John in his biography of his brother. He says that he became a fighter for Irish freedom because his visit to the American South fired his mind with the sacrifices the Southerners had made for freedom in the Civil War—which is at least a new twist to the accepted version of the Civil War as a fight for the Negro's freedom.

X

Parnell's mind was set on this new career, whatever the inspiration and incentive may have been. He resigned as sheriff. He paid a visit to Isaac Butt in Dublin and solicited from him Home Rule support. Butt was impressed and told an associate, "I have got a splendid recruit, young Parnell . . . and, unless I am mistaken, the Saxon will find him an ugly customer, though he is a damned good-looking fellow." He was to be an ugly customer, indeed, for Isaac Butt, whom he would drive from leadership within five years.

A vacancy arose in county Dublin since the holder of a seat, Colonel Taylor, had been appointed to a government post and would therefore have to be reelected. Butt proposed Parnell to oppose him, but the committee to sift candidates had some doubts about him and asked to inspect him. His fine looks and, more important, his renowned name made a good impression on them, although his entire intellectual grasp of the Irish problem seemed to be limited to the injustice done to the Manchester Martyrs, which Parnell kept repeating was "cruel." As an aristocratic Protestant landowner, he was an asset to a party which wanted to boast the support of the best elements of the population. However, since his family ties with the English were so close would he not be susceptible to backsliding, which, alas, was a chronic problem with the nation's representatives at Westminster? John Martin, a patriot who had served in penal servitude with the Young Irelander John Mitchel, in Australia, vouched for him. "I would trust him. I would trust any of the Parnells." That was testimony enough, and he was approved as the candidate. There was another factor that undoubtedly played some part: the party treasury was exhausted and Parnell could pay his own election expenses.

The political debut of the young aristocrat was most inauspicious and unpromising. On March 9, 1874, he rose in the Rotunda in Dublin to make his adoption (acceptance) speech in an afternoon meeting chairmaned by the old soldier of fortune the O'Gorman Mahon and was introduced by A. M. Sullivan of *The Nation*. The audience gave him an enthusiastic greeting. He started, "Gentlemen, I am a candidate for the representation of the County of Dublin . . ." and stopped. He tried again, repeated what he had said, then choked up, could say no more and sat down amid a murmur of surprise and embarrassment. The audience gave him a sympathetic cheer, but there was widespread doubt about the new candidate. In the campaign he managed to give a few speeches —massive will power overcoming his nervousness—but the nails of his clenched fists, held behind his back, lacerated his palms until they bled. He was defeated by Colonel Taylor by a vote of 2112 to 1141.

Could anyone have anticipated that within a few years this shy, callow, politically naïve youth would be Ireland's great leader and that his power of speech would be able to enthrall and command? That would have seemed a wild notion indeed at the time. A. M. Sullivan expressed the belief that if he ever got to Parliament he would, at the very best, be known as "Single-Speech Parnell." A journalist in Dublin recalled, "He was a nice, gentlemanly fellow but he was hopelessly ignorant and seemed to have no political capacity whatever."

His defeat did not daunt the determined youth. An old cabman who drove him from Rathdrum station to Avondale after the defeat recalled, "That was a regular divil of man. He talked about nothin' the whole way but fightin' thim agin and batin' thim, an' he looked rale wild and fierce."

His opportunity did not come until a year later. In 1874 John

Martin had been elected a member from Meath, and in 1875 the famous John Mitchel had been elected from Tipperary. But when Mitchel had gone to Westminster to be seated, he had been barred by the new Prime Minister, Benjamin Disraeli, on the ground that he was an escaped convict, though that conviction had occurred a quarter of a century before. There was a writ for a new election, and Mitchel stood again as a candidate. Parnell, now immersed in the cause, announced a contribution of £25 to his campaign in the *Freeman's Journal*, which did Parnell no harm politically. But then Mitchel died. Martin, married to Mitchel's sister, attended the rain-swept funeral, caught a cold there and died too. Thus there was a vacancy from Meath, for which the Home Rulers decided to back Parnell as a candidate.

He was now a more confident speaker and at least was able to say what he had to say, though it cost him some nervous exhaustion. He was shrewd enough to put less emphasis on himself than on his illustrious ancestors. "My ancestor, Sir John Parnell, was an advocate of the old Irish Parliament and of the removal of the disabilities which afflicted his Catholic fellow-countrymen and in the evil days of corruption which destroyed the independence of Ireland he lost a great office and refused peerage to oppose the fatal measure of Union."

He was elected on April 19, 1875, the poll showing that he had received 1771 votes against 902 for his closest opponent. Bonfires were lit, and he was carried on the shoulders of his supporters in the town of Trim.

On April 22 he took his seat in Parliament, and as he walked down the aisle he was given an enthusiastic greeting by Irish members, as some English members looked with curiosity on the handsome, cool young man, not yet twenty-nine, with the historic name of Parnell. On that night the second reading of a coercion bill for Ireland took place, and an elfish-looking member from Ireland with an elfish humor spoke for three hours and forty-five minutes on matters far afield from the bill, a delaying tactic that went for naught. By a peculiar coincidence, it was on the very night he took his seat that the policy of "obstruction" was born, the policy with which the name of Charles Stewart Parnell would be always associated.

Part Two

THE ASCENSION

D

I

A LATER ASSOCIATE of Parnell, William O'Brien, wrote of the feeling of awe he experienced when, as a humble Irishman, he took a seat in the Imperial Parliament, the most powerful law-making body on earth, holding sway over 400,000,000 humans in the empire girdling the earth. He recalled his "consciousness of awful presences in the background, shades of the patriots of the Long Parliament, of the men who measured themselves with kings, echoes of the undaunted words that struck Charles' head off, that arraigned Warren Hastings, of the spirit that raised England from a rude island to the primacy of the world."

Such was the feeling of humility that Irish members felt in this hallowed hall filled in larger part with aristocratic English gentle-men, mostly retired on wealth, who regarded themselves as joined in an exclusive club which did not admit Irishmen. The Irish found it hard to shake off a feeling of not belonging, of being outsiders. T. P. O'Connor, who entered Parliament in 1880, said that of the 560 English members, he was not on speaking terms with more than three.

Charles Stewart Parnell had no such qualms or feeling of in-feriority. As an aristocrat and an Englishman, he felt that he was now in his proper habitat and did not even need to acclimate him-self to it. The confidence of equality with the English which he exuded would be one of the assets in his rise to leadership. Four days after he was seated he rose to make this proud declaration: "I trust that England will give to Ireland the right which she claims, self-government. Why should Ireland be treated as a geo-graphical fragment of England as I heard an ex-Chancellor of the Exchequer call her some time ago? Ireland is not a geographical fragment. She is a nation." Ten times more he was heard from during the session of 1875.

He did not attract attention of any kind during that first year. The rules of the House were intricate, and he was trying to master them. He asked questions freely of his colleagues, not hesitating to show his ignorance. He asked one how he got the material for questions he asked of the ministry. The colleague, amused by his naïvete, answered, "From the newspapers, from our constituents." Parnell replied, "Ah, I must ask a question myself some day."

In his early days in Parliament, Parnell became acquainted with a journalist who was foreign editor for the *Morning Post,* Frank Hugh O'Donnell. Three years younger than Parnell, he had been elected to Parliament for Galway in 1874, but had been unseated in a judicial contest because of some election tactics he had used, such as the distribution of placards reading VOTE FOR JOYCE AND KEOGH, Joyce being his opponent and Keogh being, of course, the traitor of ill-repute in Irish history. Tall and athletic looking, beetle-browed, wearing an eyeglass through which he viewed the world in supercilious fashion, he was a vain, fussy eccentric who was so crochety that Tim Healy labeled him "Crank" O'Donnell. In politics he was an adventurer, a figure out of Balzac, pitting his talents against the world, who claimed noble origins in *Tir-Condill* and connections with noble families in Europe. T. M. Healy claimed that he was an impostor—not the aristocratic O'Donnell he claimed to be, but the penniless son of a Scotch army officer stationed in India—and that his real name was Francis MacDonnell.

O'Donnell, who had great ability, in later years bitterly resented Parnell's ascension, claiming that Parnell climbed up on his shoulders, and labeled the ingrate Parnell as "my runaway apprentice." Even though O'Donnell's impressions of Parnell are admittedly tinctured with prejudice, nonetheless he was one of the few close to him in those early days and his incisive opinions are worth something.

From his talks with Parnell, he saw him as a dissatisfied, malcontent aristocrat, a *grand seigneur manqué,* and compared him with "those *cidevants* in the train of Mirabeau who had quarrelled with their order and thirsted to humiliate it." He saw Parnell as a fanatic of the honor and dignity of his family. His circumstances were modest (O'Donnell claimed they were straitened), and he felt scorned by the English aristocracy. He was thus face to face with a hostile, unfriendly world and "in his family pride he possessed the reserve of power and the incitement to distinction which was to carry him to a bold and overbearing ambition. There is no revolutionist like a malcontent aristocrat."

Is this shrewd insight into the psyche of Parnell? As many were to note through his career, his pride, an overweening pride, was at the core of his being. His sensitivity to his station in life and his fear of being humiliated were always present. Had his sense of pride in being a Parnell and his sense of duty as a Parnell brought him to Parliament? And was it the customary disdain and contemptuousness that the English aristocracy showed for all things Irish that drove the barb into his soul and determined him on a course of revenge?

In 1876 the House of Commons was going through the ritual of debating the annual Butt motion for an inquiry into the practicability of Home Rule for Ireland—the debate being granted on the understanding that nothing would come of it. The Irish Secretary, Sir Michael Hicks Beach, was talking to an almost empty House, since the subject was regarded by the English as a stupid waste of time necessitated by the need of the Irish members to justify themselves to their constituents. "Black Michael" (so called from his black temper and swarthy complexion, not his character, since he was an intellectual squire regarded as a fairly decent sort) came to the statement "Of all the extraordinary delusions which are connected with the subject the most strange appears to me the idea that Home Rule can have the effect of liberating the Fenian prisoners, the Manchester murderers."

"No, no," a cry rang out from the Irish bench. Hicks Beach looked surprised and aggrieved at the unexpected interruption and scanned the ranks of the Irish. In a tone of pained disappointment he said, "I regret that there is any Hon. member in this House who will apologise for murder."

Parnell rose. "The Rt. Hon. member looked at me so directly when he said that he regretted that any member should apologise for murder, that I wish to say . . . publicly . . . that I do not believe, and I never shall believe, that any murder was committed at Manchester."

Hicks Beach gazed at him intently, harrumphed and went on.

This forthright declaration on an issue that was an emotional pivot for them riveted the attention of the Fenian element on Parnell. This young aristocrat was no milksop, he did not fear to speak out to the English, he was different from the usual place hunter and timeserver who filled the ranks of the Irish representation. Was it not this young man who had shown coolness and daring at the Centenary Celebration for Daniel O'Connell the year before in Dublin? When the amnesty car with the legend "Freedom for the Political Prisoners" had been cut away from the horses and the horses led away, had he not taken the lead, enlisted some others, seized the traces of the car and dragged it to the head of the procession?

II

By 1876 the Fenian element and all those who favored action and not talk were convinced that the Butt movement and Butt himself were a failure. Contrary to Butt's prediction that sweet reasonableness would win over the English, from session to session Butt pleaded the case with eloquence and legal shrewdness and at most he had succeeded in winning only a dozen English votes for an inquiry into the subject. The whole cause seemed an incredible *ignis fatuus* foisted on the Irish people by politicians for their own ends. Among those sharing that belief was the leading Irish cleric, Cardinal Cullen, who called it "A bubble of the moment."

The demand for Home Rule was regarded by the English as at best a farce, at worst a piece of insolence. When the customary motion was made, Prime Minister Benjamin Disraeli bantered with it in his most roguish style. The discontent of the Irish could have only one cause: since they were farther out in the Atlantic Ocean, the dampness and gales of the Atlantic had depressed their spirits and infected them with discontent. How were the Irish conquered? he asked. Had they been conquered by Cromwell? What of it? Had not Cromwell also conquered the English? Why extract a peculiar grievance out of a common misfortune?

He prattled on as the House guffawed. He had always been surprised that a people like the Irish, with so much sentiment, so much genius, such winning qualities, should be so deficient in self-respect as to admit that they had been conquered. Then in simulated indignation his voice rose, "I deny that the Irish people are conquered. They are proud of it. I deny that they have any ground for that pride . . ."

Parnell soon saw the ludicrousness and hollowness of the sham performance. Once, when an Irish member had finished speaking in behalf of the motion, Butt patted him on the back of his head.

Parnell greeted the member in the lobby, patted him on the back of his head mimetically and said, "You have been a good boy and you may go home now and you won't hear about it again for another twelvemonth."

Completely ineffective in promoting legislation of any kind for Ireland, the Irish members could indulge in their pixyish sense of humor. Once they actually succeeded in overthrowing the Government by a triumph over new technology. The Conservatives used to go from the House by an underground passage to St. Stephens Club. On a call for a division, electric bells would summon them. One day an Irish M.P., Phil Callan, engaged in foul play. He snipped the electric wires to the club, and when the vote was called the Conservatives failed to show up and the Government lost by two votes. There was a recount.

The Irish were a dispirited, sorry lot. Some of them were museum pieces like James Delehunty, eighty years old, who wore a wig in which he kept his notes, his comb, his brush and other toilet articles. Joseph P. Ronayne, one of the few high-minded M.P.'s said, "Those of my colleagues whom you do not find dishonest, you will find drunk—and ready to play the extreme patriot until they can dispose of their seats to the Government for fifth-rate office."

Irish members groveled before the Government. There were successive coercion bills designed to throttle Irish freedom, and any slight concession was greeted with expressions of abject gratitude. "Like a condemned criminal shaking hands with the hangman," said Ronayne in disgust.

Those who stooped to sycophancy had a sober end in view—they were looking for good jobs for themselves. Careerism was an insidious weapon in subversion. In Ireland, government jobs had always been regarded in high esteem. It was said that at a peasant birth, admiring wives would say, "God bless the fine boy. Sure, it's a grand post-office sorter he'll make when he grows up." The high-echelon jobs were really worth having, since the emoluments were staggering compared to those of similar positions in the United States Government. Approximately, cabinet ministers received $25,000 a year; the Lord Chancellor, $50,000 and a $25,000 pension; the Lord Lieutenant of Ireland, $100,000 a year; the Irish Attorney General, with fees, a minimum of $50,000; the Chief Justice of Queen's Bench, $25,000, and lesser justices, $19,000; the governor of a colony, $25,000. All other jobs were paid on a similarly high scale. This helps to explain a chronic problem for Irish representation in Parliament: Members were upaid, and Irish members, generally impecunious, saw their chief objective that of ingratiating themselves with their supposed enemy to angle for his favor. In the early 1850s the Irish Tenant League counted on fifty members favorable to their program but awarding of places by the English Government cut their support to ribbons.

Daniel O'Connell had taken a stand in the 1840s in favor of members taking government jobs, since he felt that it was one way to ease their dependence on Irish largesse and it would help to obtain for Ireland the most sympathetic administration of justice. The Young Irelanders had squarely opposed him on this. After 1850, Irish members were looked on by the English as a group of hungry job applicants. The bait was the more attractive, of course, since election expenses ran quite high, as much as £2000, which might be regarded by an ambitious man as an investment in a career.

Butt himself was immune from the call of the siren song, although he was always in money trouble. In the election of 1874 he had to absent himself from Ireland most of the time to stay out of the clutches of the bailiffs. He was a genuine patriot who gave up good fees in a lucrative law practice for his public duties. His finances went steadily downhill, but he refused to accept from the English Government the post of Chief Justice of Ireland since he felt that acceptance would be betrayal.

He was a rotund, rubicund man who embraced all and sundry with a hearty "How are you, dear boy." No one visiting him could escape without a libation. His style was florid, as his election appeal of 1874 gives evidence: "Arise, awake. Put on thy glorious apparel. Lift thyself from the dust. Arise, cast off the chains of slavery from they neck, for oh, captive daughter of Erin, long enslaved and oppressed, seven centuries of your slavery gone and surely, oh surely indeed, the day of deliverance is at hand, the day of your redemption draweth nigh. Arise and rejoice in your liberty."

Butt not only loved the bottle but was an inveterate wencher. Once, at a political meeting, he was interrupted by a woman demanding that he support her illegitimate child, and once he was interrupted by a child calling for "Father." In ways of money he was totally improvident. A typical story is that after a law case he had a large wad of bills but, after spending the night with a friend, he found them gone in the morning. He was about to call the police, but the friend found that in the middle of the night Butt had stuffed them all in the window sash to keep it from rattling. A moody man, he believed in omens, and though not a Catholic, he had Masses said for the success of his law cases and on the way to the court could be heard reciting "Ave Marias."

As time passed, Butt sank into a state of innocuous desuetude. The English would some day see the light. Meanwhile, he was a convivial, anecdotal dinner companion, a great favorite of the English hostesses and a frequent guest in the great country houses, an experience which has softened sturdier wills than Isaac Butt's. A Parliamentary observer, Sir Henry Lucy, wrote, "Mr. Butt is fat and sleek and sleeps of night, which indeed he does in full view of the House."

The English, for their part, thought that Ireland was pretty well in tow and subdued. The Dublin correspondent for the London *Times* wrote, "The present circumstances of Ireland may be briefly summed up in the statement that at no prior time in her history did she appear more tranquil, more free from serious crime, more prosperous and contented."

III

Nemesis for Butt and the Butt way of life cropped out in an unlikely form: a pork butcher from Belfast who had become wealthy (about £100,000) and had become the member from Cavan. The first time he rose to speak Disraeli turned to the Irish Solicitor General and asked, "Is that what in your country is called a leprechaun?" He was only five feet tall and was a little hunchbacked. He loved glittering clothes and had a fine sealskin waistcoat and cut his trousers short to display high Wellington boots.

Joseph G. Biggar had been greatly influenced by discussions he had had with the shrewd J. P. Ronayne, who had said to him that the Butt policy was not only futile but brought the Irish membership into disrepute. Said Ronayne, "Butt says, 'Hear, hear,' when he should be saying, 'No, no.' We shall never make any impression on the House until we interfere in English business. When we want to get our business through, they stop us. We ought to show them that two can play at the game of obstruction."

Butt had told Biggar that he should speak "awhile" on an Irish coercion bill, and Biggar went to it. He spoke endlessly from blue books and government documents. When the Speaker complained that he could not hear him, Biggar moved closer on the Opposition bench and apologetically said that since the Speaker had not heard him, "Perhaps I had better begin again." In reading a blue book he did not miss a line, not even the end "London, Printed for Her Majesty's Stationery Office by Eyre and Spottinswoode, Printers of the Queen's Most Excellent Majesty."

After nearly four hours of this in his Belfast rasp, Biggar sat down. The House was somewhat astonished at the performance, not being accustomed to what in the United States Senate acquired the name of "filibustering." Since there was no one to follow Biggar (Ronayne was a sick man and soon afterward died), his effort bore no fruit insofar as the legislation on hand.

The impish Biggar was set on mischief. Five days later the Prince of Wales was in the gallery to watch the servants of the Crown at work and to listen to a debate on horse raising. Biggar rose and said, "I espy strangers." Under this traditional formula, the galleries must be cleared at once for security.

Amazement furrowed the brow of the Speaker. "Do I understand the honourable member to take notice of the presence of strangers in the House?" Biggar replied undaunted, "I do." The Speaker had no choice but to say, "That being so I must ask strangers to withdraw." The galleries were cleared, and His Majesty the Prince of Wales was whisked out.

The Prime Minister, Disraeli, was rushed into the House and asked for a suspension of the ancient rule. "I think that the course proposed by the honourable member tends to the discredit of the House and if the proceedings are resorted to, the country will cease to believe that the House is, notwithstanding one or two exceptions, an assembly of gentlemen." The House concurred and the Prince was able to resume his seat.

The servile Irish members begged the pardon of the House for the impudence of this reprobate member. One said, "I think that a member should be a gentleman first and a patriot afterward," and another, "The honourable member for Cavan seems to forget that he is now admitted to a society of gentlemen."

Biggar was now launched, let the English squirm as they may, on a one-man campaign of obstruction of legislation, which he called "an intelligent interest in English affairs." As a sympathetic neighbor to England, now residing in the country, he felt called upon to take this interest. Repeatedly, in the midst of debate on a bill, he would rise to speak his piece at great length. He would say sometimes that he was no orator (which was an understatement) but that he would try to entertain the House, and he then would read for hours copious dry-as-dust extracts from Hansard's Parliamentary Debates. He would badger the Irish Secretary with nuisance questions. He would call his attention to the fact that the postmaster at Paddywhackum had the measles and "in view of the epidemic of infectious diseases rendering the inhabitants unfit for their callings" did Sir Michael have any plans for remitting taxation there?

The temerity of Biggar in obstructing the work of the House brought down on him a torrent of abuse by the press. At that time and since, if a man was in trade his social status was not too high. Within trade there was a hierarchy of status, with manufacturing at the top, then wholesaling, then retailing at the bottom. Status was graduated within retailing according to the commodity being sold—in Biggar's case he was at the very, very lowest rung, as the press did not hesitate to remind him in pointed terms. A writer for the *World* wrote, "When he rose to address the House, which he did at least ten times tonight, a whiff of salt pork seemed to float upon the gale and the air is heavy with the odor of peppered herring."

During the sessions of 1876 and 1877, Parnell watched with growing interest these needling efforts by Biggar, which is all they were. He saw Biggar's efforts multiplied by the help of a Major O'Gormon, member from Waterford, and Biggar now had the two tellers required for making a motion for a division.

IV

In the summer of 1876 a group of "Advanced Nationalists" meeting in Dublin passed a resolution that a message of congratulation be sent to President Grant of the United States on the occasion of the Centenary of American independence. To present the address, two were chosen from Parliament, the noted Fenian John O'Connor Power and Parnell, then little known, but probably chosen because of his distinguished name and the fact that he was half American. The recognition was important in putting the spotlight on him and was the first step in his ascension.

Thus Parnell came to America for the second time. The two reached Washington in October and met with the Assistant Secretary of State, J. C. Bancroft Davis, in the absence of the Secretary, Hamilton Fish. In his diary Davis recorded his report to Grant: "The President spoke about the Irish address. I explained the custom and what they ought to do . . . and I was satisfied that I could not assist in presenting it without the knowledge of the British Minister." President Grant agreed and Davis so informed the emissaries. Parnell was filled with indignation. A people trying to escape from the British yoke were seeking to congratulate a people who had gotten free of the British yoke—and this message had to be communicated through the British Ambassador! But having no choice, the two left the address with the British Embassy for transmittal.

Parnell returned from Washington to New York, where he met his mother and his sister Fanny, and denounced Grant to them as a "vulgar old dog." He then went on to Philadelphia to the Centennial Exhibition, where he studied stonecutting machinery he could apply to his Wicklow quarries, went to inspect his Clover Hill investment in Virginia and then went home. O'Connor Power remained in the United States and presented an illuminated address to Congress, which on March 3, 1877, by resolution voted "grateful recognition for the Irish feeling."

V

Lord Palmerston once said of an Irish M.P., Cornelius O'Brien, "He was the best Irish M.P. we ever had. He didn't open his mouth in twenty years." Irish members were expected to be seen, not heard, except on matters purely Irish. It was therefore with some perturbation that the English saw, at the beginning of the 1877 session, the icy aristocrat at whom they could not sneer condescendingly, Charles Stewart Parnell, join forces with the misshapen, Quasimodo plebian, Biggar, to put their two noses into a multitude of subjects that were purely English and therefore ipso facto none of their business. There followed endless delaying motions—for adjournment and "to report progress"—which demanded divisions. Biggar and Major O'Gormon would act as tellers and Parnell would vote "aye." The vote would be 200 to 1 (the vote of Parnell), but Parnell would be satisfied if it resulted in holding up the legislation.

Isaac Butt, puzzled, asked Parnell what his intentions were, and he replied, "The English do not give me an opportunity to concern myself with the affairs of my country. I mean to concern myself with theirs." To his colleagues, Parnell explained why he was working havoc with the Government's time schedule. "Butt is hopeless. He is too much under the English influence. You may be sure when you are pleasing to the English we are not winning. The first thing you've got to do with an Englishman on the Irish question is to shock him. Then you can reason with him right enough."

Parnell had declared war on the English House of Commons and had adopted Biggar's four maxims: 1) Work only on Government time; 2) Aid anyone to spend Government time; 3) Whenever you see a bill, block it; 4) Whenever you see a raw, rub it.

This policy was first called the Biggar-Parnell policy, later the Parnell-Biggar policy, and finally, when it gained more adherents, the Active Policy.

In later years, Frank Hugh O'Donnell claimed that it was he who had planned the tactics of obstruction and, with Sheridan Knowles and Baker Greene of the *Morning Post,* had tutored Parnell—who he admits was a bright pupil—in the substantive amendments to put forward. He added that Parnell took over command, caught the public eye and stole the credit. It is true that O'Donnell did share in the obstruction program and that Parnell, who had blossomed overnight into a skilled parliamentarian, seemed to have been tutored in his criticism of bills and very well informed on the amendments he offered.

Parliament considered itself a gentlemen's club for gentlemen, and it had never before seen the tactics it was witnessing on this scale. The House of Commons had developed not as a legislative body but as a checkrein on the Executive under the Crown, and, as no thought had been given to suppressing the privilege of members to speak their piece, debate was unlimited. The House normally assembled in the beginning of February and sat until the second week of August. The Imperial Parliament was legislating for 400,-000,000 people, and the calendar was full; the last few months usually were an attempt to secure a victory in the race against time.

Except on Wednesday, when the hours were from 12 to 6 P.M., the House assembled at 4 P.M. Dinner was from half past seven until ten, and it was not considered etiquette to do anything important in those hours.

Monday and Thursday were Government nights, Tuesday and Wednesday were private nights for members and Friday was for consideration of Supply. When money was asked for Supply, discussion of grievances came first and might be extended. The long weekend was unknown then, and cabinet meetings, as well as sessions of the House, were held on Saturdays near the close of the session.

At the time, the rules laid the road wide open for obstructive tactics. Under the half-past-twelve rule, if a member were still talking at that hour on a private night it was not possible to introduce a Government bill. Debate did not have to be germane to the subject at hand except in a general sense. After the second reading of a bill it went into the committee stage. The House became a Committee of the Whole to consider amendments, and motions could be made to "report progress," which if approved automatically adjourned debate.

On April 12, the Mutiny Bill was being discussed. Each year Parliament had to pass a Mutiny Bill, otherwise discipline in the armed forces would revert to that governed by the common law. Parnell was loading the bill with amendments, forcing divisions on motions to "report progress," and he and Biggar were badgering the War Minister, Mr. Gathorne-Hardy, with questions. It was early morning and Hicks Beach sent out a call to Butt—would he not do something to halt these rowdy proceedings? Butt came into the House from the smoking room to hurl his Jovian shaft at these mischief-makers. "I regret," Butt said pontifically to the House, "that the time of the House has been wasted in this miserable and wretched discussion. If at this hour of the night any member really wished to propose a serious amendment I would support the motion to report progress and so also I think would the Secretary of War. But when there was no amendment to a number of clauses, I must express my disapproval of the course taken by the honourable member of Meath. It is a course of obstruction and one against which I must enter my protest. I am not responsible for the member for Meath and cannot control him. I have, however, a duty to discharge to the great nation of Ireland and I think I should discharge it best when I say I disapprove entirely of the conduct of the honourable member for Meath."

The House rang with loud cries of "Hear, hear." Parnell was always superb in the pithy, succinct statement conveying the exact nuance, and this time he uttered one sentence, a devastating riposte, which cut the ground out entirely from under Butt. "The Hon. and learned gentleman was not in the House when I attempted to explain why I was putting down notice of my amendments."

The meaning for the Irish was clear. Butt had chosen to reprimand a fellow Irish member on a matter of which he had only hearsay knowledge, and he did so obviously at the instigation of others—who could be only the English. It was the first step in Butt's downfall.

Parnell was now becoming a subject of interest to the English. The London *Times* first took note of him as "A slender and rather good-looking young man with a determined cast of features." Another paper described him as "having the modest exterior of a Methodist minister on his first circuit," which made his unruly conduct the more inexplicable.

When he rose to speak, howls from the English members sometimes prevented him from being heard for ten minutes. He stood with fists clenched and pale face, waited for the ebullitions of rage to subside, then hissed out words over the roar. Since he could scarcely be heard, it gave him the opportunity to talk without having to worry much about what he said, and this experience is given some credit for fashioning Parnell into an excellent public speaker.

To all pleas that he desist, to all objurgations, he was deaf. He had determined on his policy. England was in the habit of bullying weaker nations, he said, "much in the same way as I am subject to the menace of members of the House." He would repeat a story he had heard about one Nicholas Codd, who got into a dispute with his neighbor. No settlement could be made, so an intermediary took over and asked Codd if an alternative were possible. "Yes," said he, "he can go to hell." And so Parnell said, "They can always have the Nicky Codd alternative."

"Oh, he was a bonny fighter," wrote Frank Hugh O'Donnell years later, a concession in a recollection filled with acid references to an intellectual illiterate who, he claimed, had euchred him from the place of glory.

During June, the Prisons Bill came up, calling for the transfer of authority for prisons from local authority to the Home Office. This gave Parnell an opportunity to oppose the bill clause by clause, while at the same time attacking the Government for its cruel treatment of political prisoners. Parnell was gradually building a nucleus of support among the Irish members. O'Donnell himself had been elected as a member from Dungarvan in June, 1877, and now actively participated in obstruction. Also, there were Captain Nolan; Edmund Dwyer Gray, who had succeeded his deceased father, John Gray, as owner of the *Freeman's Journal*; Harley Kirk and John O'Connor Power.

John Barry, a prominent Fenian and a founder of the Home Rule Confederation of Great Britain, was one of the first to recognize the potential leadership of Parnell not only of a Parliamentary faction but of the Irish nation. "He is so much like the English," Barry confided to an associate, "Cold, callous, unexcitable, always going straight to the point and not caring much how he gets there as long as he gets there."

The Home Rule Confederation was the organization of Irish residents of Great Britain to promote Home Rule. Under Isaac Butt as President, it gave its support to English candidates for Parliament who pledged to support the motion for an inquiry into Home Rule. To whip up support for his obstruction policy, Barry offered to arrange meetings of Confederation branches in various cities for Parnell to address. Parnell accepted the offer, but when the schedule was presented to him he said that one city would have to be dropped. Why? There were thirteen, and he could never associate himself with that number. This was the first occasion in which Irish leaders encountered Parnell's pathological superstitions.

Parnell, in his speaking tour, found the Irish in Britain wildly enthusiastic about the man who was twisting the lion's tail in Parliament and making John Bull sit up. He was greeted everywhere with cries of "Pull down their ould Parliament!" "Don't let them sleep a wink!" Obstruction, and English fury about it, was some compensation for the degraded condition of the Irish, who were treated as helots and second-class citizens in England, the butt of anti-Catholic as well as anti-Irish feeling.

On July 2, Parnell forced the House to sit from 4 P.M. until 7:30 A.M. the following morning in a vain attempt by the Government to pass the Army Reserve Bill with members.on the march from one division to another.

After that bill was finally passed, obstructive tactics were employed again by the Parnell group against the South African Bill, calling for a confederation to include the Transvaal. It would have been better if wise statesmen had foreseen the troubles with the Boers and had opposed it on that ground. As it was, the English of both parties were fairly well united behind that bill. But Parnell announced that he was opposed. "As an Irishman coming from a country that has experienced to its fullest extent the results of English interference in its affairs, and the consequences of English tyranny and cruelty, I feel a special satisfaction in preventing and thwarting the intentions of the Government with respect to this Bill."

In a scene of turmoil, the Chancellor of the Exchequer, Sir Stafford Northcote, who was acting as Government leader in the House, moved that the words be taken down. The Committee dissolved and the Speaker was sent for. Parnell was asked by the Speaker if he had anything to say in explanation, and Parnell replied impudently, "I was saying that it is unnecessary to go into historical examples to prove that successive British governments have been utterly regardless of those weaker races and countries with which they have come into contact." He was then ordered to withdraw while the House debated the motion of Sir Stafford that "the honourable member for Meath be suspended from his functions of speaking and taking part in the debate of the House until Friday next."

When the words of Parnell were read and examined it was clear that he had vowed not to thwart the intentions of the House but of the Government, which was not inconsistent with his responsibilities as a House member. Sir Stafford admitted that his motion was based not "on the words used as taken by themselves but upon the words taken in connection with Mr. Parnell's conduct generally." The motion was withdrawn when it was decided to consider changes in the rules two days later. So Parnell, escorted by Biggar, descended from the gallery to the floor and resumed talking, imperturbable as ever, as if he had not been interrupted at all.

On July 29, the House made only very minor changes in the rules, the majority remaining jealous of the prerogative of un-

E

limited debate. Parnell explained to the House that his tactics were designed to promote more thorough consideration of legislation. The *Times* fumed at this cheek, "The House of Commons with its venerable traditions, its splendid victories and achievements is to be sent to school in this year of 1877 by a few ignorant Irishmen."

Of the wild session two days later, on July 31, the *Times* commented, "In all the centuries which the House of Commons has existed, no such scene has ever been witnessed." Parnell and Frank Hugh O'Donnell, with some assistance from other Irish members, kept the House in continuous session from 4 P.M. until 6:30 P.M. the following day to pass the South African Bill through committee, the longest session until then in the history of Parliament. At the very outset of the debate Parnell moved to "report progress" before anything was done. Sir William Harcourt, a Liberal member, said that Parnell was making a travesty of the rules, was engaged in wilful obstruction, and appealed to the House to control him. Parnell, unruffled, replied, "Sir, I will now continue my observations," and then warned the House that it was engaging in personal quarrels instead of sticking to the bill. The whips organized relays of members to stay on the floor and supplied weary members with food and drink. Parnell announced, "As for the threat of physical endurance held out to me, I can assure the House that if the members divide themselves into relays, my friends and I can divide ourselves into relays too," a piece of bravado, since his total force was a half dozen.

At 2 A.M., Harcourt read an excerpt from a Parnell speech in which he said, "My policy is not a policy of conciliation, but . . . of retaliation." O'Donnell defended it, saying that the Government was being paid back in its own coin. Butt rose and repudiated the right of the obstructionists to speak for Ireland. O'Donnell replied, "Sir, what I said was that I speak not for the Irish party but for the most advanced or if you please the most disaffected portion." Butt replied that if he did represent Ireland "I would retire from Irish politics as from a vulgar brawl in which no man can take part with dignity to himself or advantage to his country." There were cheers as he swept from the floor. O'Donnell rose, adjusted his monocle and in mock irony acknowledged the cheers as if they were directed to his rising on the floor.

All Parliamentary process broke down as Parnell and O'Donnell made a stream of motions to "report progress," and in a continuous

uproar members for hours were forced to march from one division
to another, fifteen times in all; the active group never mustered
more than five votes on these moves for adjournment. All pretense
of debate ceased between these divisions while Parnell and O'Donnell exchanged taunts, charges and insinuations with the English
members.

This continued throughout the night. At 7 A.M. Parnell announced that the "Hon. member for Cavan [Biggar] is peacefully
asleep and will soon return like a giant refreshed." Biggar, sleeping
at the time, for economy's sake, sprawled across three chairs in the
Library, was awakened by heavy calf volumes dropped beside him.
He entered the House at 8 A.M. "Mr. Chairman, I am better able
to go on having had a long sleep and a good breakfast." Parnell
then left for a few hours' sleep while O'Donnell continued in his
seat directing the fight. At noon, Harcourt threatened the obstructionists with expulsion, and O'Donnell decided that he would allow
the House to consider the bill.

When Parnell returned soon afterward he found the obstruction
ended. He was livid with anger and hissed to O'Donnell, "Why did
you haul down the flag?" To which the proud O'Donnell, his vanity
wounded, replied, "My dear Parnell, go to the devil and inquire."
It was not until six hours later that the debate ended. One who sat
all through the twenty-six hours was Fanny Parnell, her breast
swelling with pride for her brother.

VI

As the detestation of the English for Parnell had mounted, the
admiration of the Irish for him had correspondingly increased. No
one could see where obstruction could lead, but at least it proved
to the world and to the Irish themselves that they were a force to
be reckoned with. To the radical wing of the party, specifically the
Fenian element, it was clear that a new star had risen in the
heavens. As for Parnell's own ambitions, the extent to which leadership was thrust on him and the extent to which he reached
for it himself is a moot point. It is probable that he thirsted for
leadership power. However, thirteen years later, at the fateful meeting at Westminster when Parnell was himself deposed from leadership, he accused John Barry of wielding the poniard and being

the "leader killer," saying, "I never by word or deed counseled attacks on him [Butt], I allowed the old man to go down honoured to his grave."

At any rate the battle lines between Butt and Parnell were now drawn. The "Seven Champions of Obstruction" were heroes in Ireland, and at a meeting in the Rotunda in Dublin on August 21, Parnell, who had the place of honor, said defiantly, "I care nothing for the English Parliament and its outcries. I care nothing for its existence if that existence is to continue a source of tyranny and destruction to my country." Soon afterward, at a reception in County Limerick, he said, "It is our duty not to conciliate, not to beg, not to crave from England. It is our duty to demand and if we cannot get what we ask by demanding, it is our duty to show that England must give it." Then, using strong language, he inferentially indicted the leadership, "I do say to the people that their cause has been degraded by their representatives in Ireland."

The debate between Parnell and Butt was carried on in the columns of the *Freeman's Journal.* Butt's main thesis was stated: "No man can damage the authority of the House of Commons without damaging the cause of representative Government and of freedom all over the world. . . . [Obstruction] must tend to alienate our truest and best English friends. It must waste in aimless and objectless obstruction the time which we might obtain in some form or other for the discussion of Irish grievances. It must expose us to the taunts of being unfit to administer even the form of representative Government."

Parnell replied, "If Englishmen insist on the artificial maintenance of an antiquated institution, if the continued working of this institution is constantly attended with such wrong and hardship to my country, as frequently it has been the source of gross cruelty and tyranny, I cannot consider it my duty to connive in the imperfect performance of these functions.

"I should have been only too pleased to follow you in anything had you led in anything. I am denounced because I have not joined the majority in doing nothing in inactivity or absenteeism, because I have shown the country that they have a power which they little knew of, to use if they desire for the enforcement of just claims.

"I intended to do nothing more than to show that if two members can do so much, hampered in the choice of methods and weapons by the fact of their being only two, how vast and powerful might be the influence of a party of sixty."

Butt's argument was a fine legalistic argument, but only in the abstract since the Irish had few friends among the English to lose, and time saved from obstruction would obviously not be devoted to Irish affairs. On the other hand, Parnell's was a weak argument, too. Parliament was not such an antiquated institution that the rules could not be changed to block unlicensed speech, and, in fact, they soon were to be changed. Moreover, obstructiveness was not constructiveness, and Parnell did not demonstrate how being nasty to the English would help the Irish cause.

Yet the policy did pay invisible dividends in morale. It had raised the self-respect of the Irish, given a focus for their fighting spirit, given them some purpose and promoted cohesiveness. It had shown the English that the Irish were a force to be respected since they held seats in Parliament. By a strange paradox, what Parnell would eventually succeed in doing was, by playing on the hatred of the Irish for the English Parliament, to turn their thoughts to accomplishing their ends in that very Parliament, and Parnell's great success was to be as a Parliamentary leader.

For Parnell himself, in the first instance, obstruction elevated him to a post of leadership of the Irish. When the Home Rule Confederation of Great Britain met in early September, 1877, only one nomination was made, that of Parnell, and he was elected President. Isaac Butt, who had expected to be reelected President as usual, was not even nominated. Realizing that there was dissatisfaction with his leadership he had announced that he would give up the post, but this was a gesture he had not expected to be taken seriously. The sixty-four-year-old leader was crushed with grief and left the hall in tears. "I never dreamt that the Irish in England would do this to me." Only two months before, an Irish M.P. had said to him, "That young man will be the death of you," and Butt had replied, "Nonsense, I can drive him out of public life with a word."

The hurt and humiliation of the wound inflicted on the leonine old warrior was sounded by O'Donnell in his later history. "Was ever meaner reward or more brutal ingratitude than this? And remember. This venerable statesman and patriot, scholar, historian, economist, university professor, great lawyer, winning and eloquent advocate, who had defended the Young Ireland prisoners of 1848, who had defended the Fenian prisoners of 1866 and 1867, who had made and led the revival of self-government; this Irish Déak and Cavour, standing white-haired on the brink of the grave, was hustled out of his honours. And by whom? By a rusticated undergraduate, by an insolvent young squire, without a profession or education, who had been brought into public life by Butt, who owed to others the whole of his knowledge of politics and Parliament—and that was not much—who had literally done nothing but interpolate big talk about Ireland into irrelevant subjects and situations, and who never meant a word of his big talk; a young man of 31 who had done little and knew less. . . ."

VII

To many Irish the rising star of Parnell represented hope, and Butt and his movement were waves that had broken on the beach and had washed away. Butt lingered only a while longer on the political scene, nominally a leader of the Irish Home Rulers in Parliament, but revered only as a relic of a past era. Broken in spirit, Butt refused requests for a strategy conference of Home Rule members, fearing that the occasion might be used to depose him.

Parnell was laying the groundwork of a new party to be headed by himself. To a friend he said, "The Irish party consists not only of do-nothings but know-nothings. Anyone will be better than the miserable duffers most of these Home Rulers are." In 1878 Parnell backed George Delany for a vacancy in New Ross, Wexford, who was beaten by a candidate put up by Butt. However, Parnell was fixed on his course.

Parnell's leading rival in the radical faction was John O'Connor Power, who was a Fenian and had joined Parnell's obstruction movement. He was a powerful-looking man and a fine orator. The antithesis of the aristocratic Parnell, he reeked of the common clay—part of his childhood had been spent in a workhouse, and his ugly face was pockmarked, a sign of class inferiority those days since only the children of the very poor retained the traces of smallpox.

Parnell had a deep aversion for him, and they openly quarreled, Parnell calling him a "dirty scoundrel," to which Power made an unprintable reply which Parnell never forgave. Power remained a member of the radical faction, but from that time on, Parnell was determined to drive him from public life.

To build support among the militants, Parnell talked blood and fire, although he inwardly abhorred violence. Thus, in a speech at Meath he said, "No amount of eloquence could achieve what the fear of an impending insurrection, what the Clerkenwell explosion and the shot into the police van had achieved." At County Limerick he said, "We shall show them that with the Irish people at our backs we shall meet the English threats with deeds."

It must be borne in mind that Butt's "party" was not a party as we know it. It was only a loose confederation of members who were pledged to fight for Home Rule and other issues of interest to the Irish. Otherwise they went their own way. Though they had pledged to stay aloof from party combinations, most were considered Liberals and were contacted on party votes by Liberal party whips. Only one or two labeled themselves Nationalist.

Parnell would build a party of the Irish members which would be a more disciplined unit than the existing Liberal and Conservative parties. This was to be a totally different type of leader from any the Irish had ever had. Cold, reserved, sparse of words, abstemious, he was in another world from the gregarious, garrulous and bibulous Butt or Daniel O'Connell. "Imagine everything a stage Irishman is and you have everything that Parnell is not," wrote Sir Henry Lucy about him. When a member visited Butt in his chambers he could always expect to be embraced with a "My dear boy" and then to receive the inevitable libation. A visitor to Parnell could expect only a few chilly words and then a good-bye. Yet his very aloofness and remoteness set him apart and above the throng, somehow inspiring confidence in a superior being. The hypnotic quality of Parnell's personality was evident even in the early years.

A great asset for leadership was his aristocratic background. William O'Brien once wrote, "Unquestionably rank and brilliancy and chivalry and all the qualities that appertain to a privileged and leisured class have always had a fascination for the Irish." Davitt once said, "The Irish would never accept me as a leader because I come from the ranks of the people."

Frank Hugh O'Donnell said that in 1877 he often heard in reference to Parnell, "We want the county gintleman." There was some practical basis for this preference, since a patrician like Parnell could command more respect from a House of Commons made up of aristocrats than a man of mean birth. The fact that he was a Protestant was, by the same token, another qualification for leadership, since the great Irish patriots who had died for the Irish cause—Robert Emmet, Wolfe Tone and Lord Edward Fitzgerald—had been Protestants.

Beneath Parnell's shell, there were some who found a little warmth. He never attended dinners given by the English or socialized with them, but he attended dinners given by his Irish colleagues, occasionally giving one of his own, where he sat smiling and apparently having a good time, although he said nothing since he had no stock of small talk. Once, an M.P. asked him to go to the theater, and he declined, saying that he would like to go to the Agricultural Hall to see a walking match between an American and an Irishman. There Parnell tried to get the bandleader to play "God Save Ireland" without success, but was amused when the bandleader consented to play "Tramp, Tramp, Tramp, the Boys are Marching"—which has the same music.

At this time Parnell became acquainted with Justin McCarthy, a journalist for the *Daily News* who had written two novels and was at work on *A History of Our Own Times,* which was to make him famous. Sixteen years older than Parnell, he lived on Gower Street not far from Parnell's lodgings on Keppel Street. Parnell liked to visit McCarthy's happy home, particularly enjoying the companionship of his children. In his delight with the children his face would light up with a sweet, winsome smile. McCarthy recalled, "He was very tall, very handsome, wth finely moulded, delicate features. His eyes were especially remarkable. I have not seen others like them. Their light was peculiar, penetrating and to use aptly a hackneyed term, magnetic." McCarthy found him a gentle person. As for statements that were made that he was brusque and rude, he said, "I have seen him in all sorts of companionship, tried by all manner of provocation, beset by bores, perplexed by worries and I have never seen anything in his manner that did not belong to the character of a thorough gentleman."

VIII

In the session of 1878 Parnell resumed the policy of obstruction. In January, 1878, to the Home Rule Confederation, he said "I do not promise anything by Parliamentary action but I said I would punish the English and I predict the English will soon get afraid of punishment." On April 12 he took part in a disorderly debate in the House on the murder of an Irish landlord, Lord Leitrim, in Donegal, who, with his agent, was shot while driving on a country road. The word in Ireland was that he was not murdered because of his tenant policy, but for revenge by a farmer's son whose sister had been dishonored by Lord Leitrim, who had acted toward her in accord with *droit du seigneur*. The murderer was not caught, even though it was said that the whole county of Irish knew who he was. Parnell lifted the veil on the character of Lord Leitrim during the debate. O'Donnell backed up Parnell and was again rebuked by Butt, and Parnell for the second time was accused in the House of apologizing for murder. Biggar, with wry humor, deplored such attacks—since an innocent agent of the estate had been killed. He feared, he said, that bad markmanship in these cases might result in the death of innocent people.

The angriest attack in the 1878 session was made by Parnell on the Army Discipline Bill because it permitted flogging, which Parnell, influenced by his recollection of the tale he had heard as a child of flogging the rebel in 1798, opposed on humane grounds. Despite all the Irish could do, the provision was retained in the law. But the next year, when the bill came up again, Parnell had allies among the English for the first time. The radical Liberal Joseph Chamberlain, with his close associate Sir Charles Dilke, came to his support. To his colleagues Chamberlain said, "What does it matter who has begun it, if it is the right thing to do." John Bright also joined in the clamor against man's inhumanity to man. He urged that the maximum number of lashes be reduced from 50 to 25, which the Government accepted though it refused further concessions.

Parnell insisted that the "cat" should be exhibited. "I should like to know that the Government knows about the cats. I have a shrewd suspicion that they know very little. Let the cats be produced." At first the Government refused, but they finally agreed and the cats went on view in the library. The sight of them was fatal to the cause of the strict disciplinarians. The members shuddered when they saw that the "cat" had nine tails and each tail had hard knots in it. The Government defeated an amendment for total abolition of flogging but had to agree that flogging was to be used only when the alternative was the death penalty. Two years later flogging was abolished altogether.

It was a notable victory for Parnell, who had spoken 150 times on the bill, offering innumerable amendments. Obstruction in this case had not been used negatively but constructively to accomplish a change in legislation, a humane change which had won sympathy and gratitude for the Irish members. Chamberlain rose in the House to say, "I will only add before I sit down that the friends of humanity and friends of the British Army owe a debt of gratitude to the member for Meath for standing up alone against this system when I myself and other members had not the courage of our convictions."

Butt, although nominally the leader of the Home Rulers, was taking less part in Parliamentary affairs, as his physical powers as well as his memory were fading fast. Close to impoverishment, he tried to resume his law practice in Dublin, but without success. Some friends tried to launch a popular subscription to help him, but it was a miserable failure. When the Irish have used up a leader, they have no further use for him. All attempts to secure a reconciliation with Parnell on the "active policy" were without fruit.

He last appeared in public on February 5, 1879, at a meeting in Leinster House in Dublin. There he approached many of his friends who now supported Parnell with outstretched hands, saying, "Won't you speak to me?" Genuine friends avoided him since they grieved to see the mark of death on his face. Aware of his heart trouble, he himself knew that the end was near. "Is this not the curfew bell warning us that the light must be put out and the fire extinguished?" Alone and nearly destitute, he died on May 5, 1879, at the age of sixty-six.

A year later Parnell related to T. P. O'Connor the story of Butt's last miseries, and O'Connor later wrote, "I confess that Parnell seemed to tell the tragic story of the dark end of a once great Irishman with a frigidity that chilled and almost shocked me." To Parnell, in his roseate youth and rising greatness, death was a subject of remote interest. Little could he know that in only a decade death would beckon him to an end equally dark and tragic.

The choice of a successor to Butt lay between William Shaw and Mitchell Henry. Parnell, with too little support at this time for himself, supported Shaw, probably because he thought he would be easier to supplant. Shaw, a former Nonconformist minister, suffered the handicap of being known in Ireland only as chairman of the Munster Bank.

In July, 1879, Parnell had his first success in electing a member from Ireland under his own banner. Lysaght Finegan defeated William O'Brien, a Whig who had seemed to be a shoo-in to fill a seat in Ennis in County Clare. Parnell campaigned for Finegan while the *Freeman's Journal* supported O'Brien. Just before the voting day, the *Freeman* published a purported speech by Parnell at Limerick Junction in which Parnell supposedly referred to his opponents as "Papist rats," a favorite Orangeman epithet. No one had ever heard Parnell use the term, and it was considered an invention of Edmund Gray, the *Freeman* owner, with whom Parnell had had a recent dispute over an Irish University bill. Parnell's supporters rushed to his defense in a denial which was published in the *Freeman,* and the incident blew over. If credence had been put in the charge, it would have been fatal to Parnell's hopes of ascendancy in Catholic Ireland.

IX

In life there is always death and spiritual rebirth. At the time of Butt's death, Ireland was caught up in a regeneration of hopes and energies called the New Departure. This took form early in 1878, after the release of Michael Davitt from prison on a ticket-of-leave (a parole) in December, 1877. Since 1876, through underground channels in prison, Davitt had heard of Parnell, and was eager to meet him, which he did, in London, a few days after his liberation. "Mr. Parnell appeared to me to be much superior to his recommendation. He struck me at once with the power and directness of his personality. There was the proud and resolute bearing of a man of conscious strength with a mission, wearing no affectation, but without a hint of Celtic character or a trait of its enthusiasms."

Parnell saw a man six feet tall, his hair and beard coal-black, who looked more Spanish than Irish, more like a half-starved poet than a revolutionary. He was filled with admiration for this man who had borne such sufferings for his beliefs and by the strength of his character had emerged unscathed, who had such nobility of mind that he felt no bitterness toward the Egnlish for his imprisonment but rather felt that he had a gospel for the oppressed Englishman as well as the Irish. This was not a mean, self-seeking politician but a human being of a higher order. How had he endured it? Parnell asked Davitt, adding, "I would not face it. It would drive me mad. Solitude and silence are too horrible to think of. I would kill a warder and get hanged rather than endure years of such agony and possible insanity."

Davitt, with three other Fenians released at the same time— Sergeant McCarthy, Corporal Chambers and John P. O'Brien— traveled to Dublin on January 12 for a passionate greeting from the people, organized by Patrick Egan, a quiet, unobtrusive man who was a leading Fenian while holding a respectable position as head of the City Bakery. Parnell, as head of the reception committee, led a delegation to the pier of Kingstown and met the group as they descended from the mail boat. A small parade escorted the heroic four through Dublin from Westland Row to Morrison's Hotel.

Two days later Parnell invited the four to have breakfast with him at Morrison's Hotel. As they sat down to dine, McCarthy fainted and died on the spot, a tragedy which profoundly moved Parnell—it was a display of the sacrifices that men make for country, a spectacle accentuated in Parnell's mind by his own morbid fear of death. The Catholic churches of Dublin refused to receive the body of McCarthy because he belonged to a society condemned by the Church. In Davitt's will he left instructions that his remains should be conveyed to the one church that took McCarthy's body —the Church of the Carmelite Friars in Clarendon Street.

X

While in prison, Davitt had had the opportunity to spend as much time as he wanted thinking. The problem he pondered was whither Ireland and the revolutionary movement? Why had Fenianism been a failure? The first mistake he saw in it was its secrecy, which prevented it from obtaining the support of the people. Then, a second error was in thinking that the common man would be ready to fight for freedom in the abstract when he was more absorbed in fighting against the immediate tyranny under which he suffered daily. The tenant farmers absorbed in their daily struggle with their landlords had given Fenianism the cold shoulder for years. The farmer could never become a torchbearer for freedom unless a revolutionary movement could show him that it could stand between him and the power which a single Englishman wields over him. If the tenant farmer could be won over, it would pave the way for bringing the Church into the movement and thus lead to an agglutination of all elements of Irish society in the fight against the common enemy. This would include the Irish abroad, whose emigration had been due to the oppressions of the Land System.

The idea that the revolutionary movement should pivot on the land question was not new. A remarkable intellectual of Young Ireland days, James Finton Lalor, had seen the same thing. Repeal of the Union, he said, had too thin an appeal and had to be linked to some other question "like a railway car to an engine." This was the land problem, the heart of Ireland's future, compared to which in urgency, Repeal "dwarfs down to a petty parish question."

The roots of the New Departure started growing before Davitt's release from prison. The participation of Fenians in the Home Rule movement in Parliament was in itself a "New Departure," since it previously had been a tenet of Fenianism that Parliament was a "school for Anglicizing Irishmen." But now in Parliament, John O'Connor Power was a Fenian and Joseph Biggar was on the Supreme Council of the Irish Revolutionary Brotherhood.

In America, a leading figure of the Clan-na-Gael looked on Parnell with increasing interest. John Devoy, an editor of the New York

Herald, had been the chief organizer of Fenianism among British troops with James Stephens; and in 1866 he had been sentenced to fifteen years imprisonment, but was released in 1871.

In August, 1877, a colleague of Devoy on the *Herald,* James J. O'Kelly, while a correspondent in Europe, had two interviews with Parnell and wrote to Devoy: "He has an idea I held at the starting of the Home Rule organization, that is the creation of a political link between the conservative and radical nationalists. . . . He has many of the qualities of leadership—and time will give him more. He is cool, extremely so, and resolute. With the right kind of support behind him and a band of *real* Nationalists in the House of Commons, he would so remold Irish public opinion as to clear away many of the stumbling blocks in the way of progressive action. . . . I am not sure he knows exactly where he is going, but he is the best of the Parliamentary lot."

In March, 1878, Dr. William Carroll of Philadelphia, a leader of the Clan-na-Gael, came to London to explore the possibilities of a rapprochement between the two wings. The meeting was held at the Surrey Hotel in the Strand. Parnell was accompanied by Frank Hugh O'Donnell and James J. O'Kelly, Dr. Carroll by John O'Leary and John O'Connor Power of the Irish Republican Brotherhood. O'Leary voiced his doubt about the efficacy of "obstructionism." He said, "I might as well warn you gentlemen that I have never been able to see how Ireland is to be freed by keeping the Speaker of the English House of Commons out of bed." Carroll reiterated the position that Fenians cannot take Parliamentary oaths of allegiance. O'Donnell bore the brunt of the argument for the constitutional side. "While you are waiting to 'insurrect' the Fenians, and the last Fenian shot was fired ten years ago, if you really love Ireland should you not assist the Irish cause in every walk of life and on every occasion? Are not Fenian Irishmen bound to promote the election of honest and capable Nationalist candidates in preference to mere time-savers and place-hunters? If a hundred Fenian votes could elect an honest man, are you to wait for an insurrection and let a rotten member get the place?"

The meeting was without issue. As they left, Parnell, who had been silent during the meeting, said to O'Donnell, "The Fenians want to catch us but they are not going to. Purely physical force movements have always failed in Ireland."

In May, 1878, on a train trip to an amnesty meeting, Davitt outlined to Parnell his ideas about finding a common meeting ground of right and left wings on the land question. Parnell did not commit himself. His long-term ideas, Davitt found, were crude and somewhat naïve: If the Irish made a sufficient nuisance of themselves, the English might expel them as a body and then they would be free to set up a Parliament in Ireland. At any rate, if the Irish remained in Parliament, their demands would be the more effective if there were a strong revolutionary movement on the outside to reenforce them.

In August, Davitt departed for the United States on a lecture tour. Everywhere, Davitt preached the paramountcy of the land question. Although as a disciple of Henry George, the American economist who wrote *Progress and Poverty,* Davitt believed in land nationalization, he confined himself to the less doctrinaire approach of peasant proprietorship. He would repeat a parody of Moore's lines:

> We want the land that bore us
> We'll make that cry our chorus
> And we'll get it yet, though hard to get
> By the heavens bending o'er us.

In a speech at Cooper Union, he said, "It is our intention to convert or shoot Irish landlordism, not the landlords." Everywhere, in public and private and especially in meetings with members of the Clan-na-Gael, Davitt urged that the Irish rally behind Parnell. Thus, in New York on October 13 he said that Parnell was one of the new breed of men: "They are young and talented Irishmen, who are possessed of courage and persistency." Patrick Ford, the editor of a flaming publication catering to the lower classes, the *Irish World,* filled every issue with fulminations against the English Beelzebubs. Davitt converted Ford to the new approach, including support for Parnell. Davitt did the same missionary work with John Boyle O'Reilly of the *Boston Pilot,* which had a middle-class audience.

On October 25, Devoy sent a telegram to Charles Kickham, chairman of the Supreme Council of the Irish Republican Brotherhood, to be delivered to Parnell. In it, he offered Clan-na-Gael support to the Parliamentary party—a radical departure from Fenian philosophy—on several conditions including: The land question was to be agitated by him on the basis of peasant proprietorship; sectarian issues were to be excluded from the platform; the Irish members in Parliament were to vote together, pursue aggressive policies, resist coercive measures and advance the cause of all struggling nationalities in the British Empire.

Whether Parnell received the cable from Kickham is unknown, but it is immaterial since it was printed in the New York *Herald* and then widely reprinted and debated. Davitt thought the message was rash and premature, but it did project the issue into the public forum and put the spotlight on Parnell, who gave no direct answer, but displayed his support on the land question in a speech at Tralee in which he asked for a change in the land laws and a tribunal to fix rents. Someone shouted that it would take an "earthquake" to bring this about, and Parnell answered coolly, "Then we must have an earthquake."

There was a spirited controversy in the Irish press about the proposed new policy, which was most vigorously attacked in the papers of the champion of Fenian orthodoxy, Richard Pigott. An editorial in his paper, *The Irishman,* on November 9, stated, "We hold to the conviction which has stood the test of lengthened experience that the English Parliament is no place for an Irish patriot."

In December, Devoy sent a letter to the *Freeman's Journal* which had been cleared with Dr. Carroll, Lucy, Breslin, O'Kelly, O'Reilly and others of the Clan-na-Gael and which was tantamount to a declaration of support for Parnell and his constitutional approach. The letter stated that a policy of abstention had meant self-effacement for the nationalists at a time that its members had been enfranchised. Conspiracy was not enough, expediency must be considered.

Thus the New Departure was being forged. Joined together were Parnell's qualities as a leader, Davitt's great prestige, passionate energy and organizing ability, and the money flowing from the American cornucopia under the auspices of the Clan-na-Gael—the sinews of war without which the successful agitation to follow would not have been possible.

The vital and animating force of the Fenians in Europe also flowed into the movement, although the Irish Republican Brotherhood would not go along. In January, 1879, a three-day meeting of the Supreme Council was held in Paris. The chairman, Charles Kickham, had been sentenced to fifteen years' imprisonment in the Fenian prosecutions by Judge Keogh and had suffered years of torture. An accident which had shattered his frame had nearly blinded and deafened him. He was adamantly against the new approach, and he blocked argument with himself simply by refusing to let Davitt and Devoy have access to his ear trumpet. Although he refused the alliance, one concession was made, "The officers of the organization will be left free to take part in the open movement, such officers to be .held responsible for any words or acts injurious to the revolutionary cause."

Subsequently, even this concession was rescinded, and adherents of the New Departure abandoned the Fenians altogether. Biggar and John O'Connor Power were expelled; John Barry and Patrick Egan resigned. In November, 1880, Davitt himself was expelled after he had ceased to attend meetings of the Council.

Whether Parnell ever made a secret compact of any kind with the Fenians was a subject of dispute later when Parnell was charged with being an accomplice of assassins. Devoy claimed there was such a compact. He met Parnell and Biggar when they crossed the Channel to Boulogne to meet him in March, 1879, and in June of that year Devoy appeared in Dublin (although the terms of his release prohibited his presence in Ireland) and had a conference with Parnell in Morrison's Hotel. Parnell claimed that on that occasion he was merely a good listener, and this is borne out by the account of Davitt after Parnell's death in which he stated that Parnell had never made any agreement with the "party of violence," that he had used them without ever having been used.

XI

As it happened, this thinking along philosophical-political lines about the primacy of the agrarian problem coincided with an urgent agrarian crisis similar to that of the Famine, though less severe. A general economic recession took place in the United Kingdom from 1875 on, affecting the prices of farm commodities, which were depressed by the influx of agricultural products from abroad, particularly from the United States, where railroads were now bringing mid-west farm products readily to Atlantic ports. Farmers in Ireland could get as much as 60 per cent less for their products; families dependent on remittances from relatives in England, as so many were, received less; and there was less demand

F

for seasonal farm labor in England, which was a valuable income prop for many families.

There were at the time 600,000 tenant farmers in Ireland, about 500,000 of whom were tenants at will; the rest held leases. Most of them eked out a bare living from holdings of fifteen acres or less, with the potato, "Raleigh's fatal gift," the sole barrier between them and starvation, as it had been a generation before. Then the potato crop failed in western Ireland. From a value of £60,321,000 in 1876, it fell to £26,321,000 in 1877; it improved somewhat in 1878, but in 1879 fell again, now to £15,705,000. Suffering became rampant. A report to the Lord Lieutenant stated, "The condition of the West is daily becoming worse. The people have neither food nor clothes, no credit to buy them, no work to earn them. Pale, thin and bloodless, silent and without a smile, their condition is absolutely without hope."

The question which Ireland faced was whether it would see a repetition of 1846–1849. Would the people pay their rents "bravely" and then die? Tenants were finding it impossible to pay their rents, and evictions went up each year, from 463 in 1877, to 1238 in 1879, representing the number of families reduced to beggary. There had been a change for the better in the land laws in 1870 enacted under Gladstone, but it was not the answer to the tenants' problem. Up to 1870, when a tenant was evicted he received nothing for improvements he had made on the land, which he usually had gotten absolutely bare. Under the Land Act of 1870, the Ulster Custom was applied, and he could get, when evicted, compensation for improvements ranging up to seven years' rent. The loophole in the law, big enough to drive a coach and four through, was that the tenant got nothing when evicted for failure to pay rent; and there was nothing to prevent the landlord from raising rent to any level he pleased and then evicting the tenant for not paying it.

In the face of the spreading hardship, the English Government under the Conservatives did nothing and proposed to do nothing. The new Irish Secretary succeeding Hicks Beach was James "Jimmy" Lowther, a breezy sportsman and horse breeder who did not give a fig for Ireland's plight. Ireland was largely dependent for fuel on peat, turf cut from bogs, but excessive rainfall had transformed the bogs into mud. When Lowther was asked to establish emergency fuel depots he replied, "Nonsense, they have fuel enough to burn bonfires in honor of Mr. Davitt." When it was suggested that as a relief measure potato seed be distributed, Lowther, as a believer in depopulation and enclosures for pasture land, said that grass seed would be better. As a cure for the poor crops he suggested better instruction for farmers and prizes for good hubandry.

In March, 1879, Davitt started his program of agitation by calling a meeting for Sunday, April 19, in Irishtown in County Mayo, a county where evictions had been most severe, where cattle had been put on the evicted lands and the population had been shoved onto bog lands with grossly extortionate rents. (Conditions had always been bad there for tenant farmers, and in America, a man, asked where he was from, would reply "From Mayo, God help me.") The meeting was to protest the rents on land owned by a churchman, the Rev. Geoffrey Canon Burke, land inherited from his brother. Because he was a canon, the newspapers had not dared to criticize him.

The meeting was a success beyond all expectations. There were between 10,000 and 12,000 attending from far and wide, and there was a cavalry bodyguard of 1,000—a feature to be adopted in subsequent meetings.

The Irishtown meeting had been addressed by John O'Connor Power. Davitt, who had expounded at length on the new movement to Parnell, now wanted to bring his youth, leadership and glamour into the fray. Parnell consented to be the main speaker at a meeting to be held in Westport, County Mayo, on June 7. The Archbishop of Tuam, D∴ John McHale, one of Ireland's strongest personalities, attacked the meeting in the *Freeman's Journal*. The sponsors, he said, were a "few unknown strolling men, who, with affected grief, seek only to mount to place and preferment on the shoulders of the people."

Parnell was treading on eggs insofar as his relationships with the Catholic clergy was concerned. Would he now defy the proclamation of a powerful Catholic cleric? In answer to Davitt's worried query, Parnell replied, "Certainly, I have promised to be there, have I not?" It was a politically courageous act on his part and Davitt loved him for it.

Men and women had come from afar to the meeting, attracted by the news that Parnell would speak. Banners read "The Land for the People"—a favorite Davitt slogan—and "Down with the Land Robbers." Parnell this day made one of his most powerful speeches. Unlike those of great orators of the day, Parnell's speeches lacked flowing rhetoric; but his mind was cold, hard and almost legalistically logical, the style of his utterances was the silhouette of his thought, emerging crystal clear and sometimes epigrammatic. First he begged indulgence from the Archbishop, pointing out that to fail to appear would be a transgression of his promise, which would be morally wrong. Then he described what the conditions of the times demanded:

> We hereby declare that not only political expediency but justice and the vital interest of Ireland demand such an adjustment of the land tenure—readjustment based on the principle that the occupier of the land shall be the owner—as will prevent further confiscation of the tenant's property by unscrupulous landlords and will secure to the people of Ireland their natural right to the soil of this country.
>
> I believe that the maintenance of the class of landlords in a country is not for the greatest good of the greatest number. Ireland has perhaps suffered more than any other country in the world from the maintenance of such a class. Purchase of their holdings is the final settlement.
>
> But it is necessary to insure that as long as the tenant pays a fair rent he shall be left to enjoy the fruits of his industry. A fair rent is a rent the tenant can reasonably pay according to the times, but in bad times a tenant cannot be expected to pay as much as in good times three or four years ago. If such rents are insisted on, a repetition of the scenes of 1847 and 1848 can be expected.
>
> Now what must we do in order to induce the landlords to see the position? You must show the landlords that you intend to hold a firm grip on your homesteads. You must not allow yourself to be dispossessed as you were dispossessed in 1847. You must not allow your small holdings to be turned into larger ones. I am assuming that the landlords will remain deaf to the voice of reason, but I hope that they may not, and that on their properties on which the rents are all out of proportion to the times that a reduction may be made and that done immediately. If not, then you must help yourself and the opinion of the world will stand by you in the struggle to defend your homesteads.

Parnell, a large landowner himself, had caught the spirit of the agrarian revolt against landlords. There must be no repetition of the meek submission of the Irish farmers in the Great Famine and the consequent suffering. The tenant farmers must fight not to be evicted from their beloved land, but they must first try to get a reduction in their rents. He had summed up the new spirit in the felicitious phrase "Hold a firm grip on your homesteads," which became the battle cry of the Irish. From this point on Davitt was content to permit Parnell to appear on the stage as the protagonist of land reform while he remained in the background, supplying the organizational talent and the intellectual content of the movement. In truth, Davitt was the practical idealist, the dynamic force, while Parnell tried to apply reins to the movement, fearful that a large one might embrace unmanageable and irresponsible people.

A movement that springs spontaneously from the hearts of the people has a momentum that cannot be braked. At Claremorris in July, John Dillon, son of the famous Young Irelander, addressed a meeting which was notable in that no less than eleven priests sat on the platform, though the higher clergy, the bishops, shunned it. Parnell addressed huge meetings—at Navan, a crowd of 20,000. At the Rotunda in Dublin on August 21, Parnell again exhorted the Irish to use the power they had in their own hands, a favorite theme with him. "Show your power and make them feel it. One cannot always bite in an amiable manner. Biting is not pleasant to the person being bitten, and you cannot expect that person to be the most angelic person in the world."

On October 21, in the Imperial Hotel in Dublin, the National Land League of Ireland was created, with Parnell elected president; Patrick Egan, treasurer; and Thomas Brennan and Davitt, secretaries. The resolution forming the League put emphasis first on the immediate amelioration of the tenants' lot, and the reduction of rack rents, and secondly on the abolition of landlordism and the ownership of the soil by the occupiers of the soil. Thus the League was the culmination of the thinking of the New Departure. It was the powerful machine, oiled and driven by American money, which was to propel Parnell to Parliamentary power.

On November 2, at Gurteen in Sligo, Davitt was arrested when from the platform he urged tenants to seize enough food for themselves to feed their own. Parnell organized a protest meeting immediately, and without doubt the public clamor persuaded Dublin Castle to give Davitt a trial instead of merely revoking his ticket-of-leave. The Sligo trial was a farce which got the movement good publicity since there was a score of reporters covering it. The prisoners (there were two besides Davitt) had been admitted to bail. They were serenaded each evening after a torchlight procession and an address by Parnell, and a brass band accompanied them each morning to court. An eccentric attorney, John Rea, conducted the defense, and he turned the court into a circus. Once, when a judge mispronounced a word, he jumped up to inquire whether "it is lawful for a man in the pay of the Crown to murder the Queen's English." After a week of high jinks, the case was dropped. There were 10,000 visitors from the countryside in Sligo, and it was obvious to the Government that no jury would take the risk, even if so inclined, of convicting the patriots.

On November 22 at Balla in Mayo, the first eviction since formation of the Land League was scheduled. A tenant farmer named Dempsey was to be evicted, and a great demonstration had been called to meet on the site. Lest it get out of control, Parnell and Davitt issued a proclamation: "Men of Mayo—we counsel such of you as intend to be witnesses of the eviction scene to be dignified, peaceful and orderly in your conduct. The future of our movement depends on your attitude this day."

On the eviction day an army of 8,000 men, armed with sticks and blackthorns, marched four abreast through the village and up the hill to the hut of Dempsey's family. Banners were carried "In memoriam, Allen, Larkin and O'Brien," since the following day was the anniversary of their execution. Two columns, Parnell at the head of one, coiled around the hut, which was surrounded by constabulary. A head-on conflict seemed certain, but Dempsey stepped out of the hut and told Parnell that the eviction had been postponed. Parnell had an improvised platform constructed and held a meeting then and there. Thomas Brennan took the platform and made a fiery speech, denouncing the constabulary as destroyers of their own people, reminding them of an incident of 1847 when a member of the police fired a shot and it lodged in the breast of his own mother. Parnell then spoke and, addressing himself to Brennan's provocative speech, said, "Don't allow provocation to draw you away from your duty. I merely wished to come in your midst today for I feared a terrible event was going to happen before your eyes and I could not feel I had done my duty if I had allowed the people to go into danger and remain away myself."

The police felt that only Parnell's control of the mob had averted a bloody riot, while on the other hand, Parnell's willingness to take part in the demonstration and his courage in taking his place in the lead, further endeared him to the Irish farmers.

The land war had erupted which was to continue for years. On Parnell's advice, the farmers were taking matters in their own hands in order to keep a "firm grip on your homesteads" and get rent reductions. The Land League would let the farmers know when a process server (most hated by the Irish next to the informer) with an eviction notice was on the way. Within the legal time of three days, the process server had to serve the head of the family or nail the notice to the door. The farmers would block the road, often with boulders, cut the bridges or use other means to prevent the process server from driving up. If accompanied by a police guard, none of them would be able to get as much as a cup of coffee in the area no matter how much was offered. In one village in Mayo, in January, 1880, a crowd of several hundred people throwing stones prevented process servers from serving more than four out of a hundred warrants—even with the protection of sixty police-men. Process serving became not only dangerous but also humiliating when crowds took to stripping process servers naked.

Parnell was somewhat troubled about putting land reform before the paramount issue of Home Rule. If Home Rule were granted, land reform would be within the power of the Irish themselves and would come easily; but if the two reforms were reversed in time, there was a question as to whether a contented peasantry would be a rebellious one on the larger issue or whether it would sit on its hands. Yet, the alleviation of distress was urgent, and if a large number were to be saved from destruction, it was impossible to await the disposition of the larger issue. In later days he often said, "I would never have taken off my coat for land reform if I did not see Home Rule behind it."

In the Parliament of 1879 nothing was done for land reform. William Shaw, the new leader, believed like Butt that sweet reasonableness would carry the day, or, as someone put it, he believed in a "program of mush." He would chide the English gently for their indifference to the plight of "me onhoppy counthry."

XII

The coffers of the Land League were empty, American contributions having been spent, and so were the pockets of tenant farmers by the tens of thousands, and increasingly empty were their stomachs. So, in December, 1879, Parnell sailed to America to collect dollars, accompanied by John Dillon, M.P. Dillon, one of the remarkable group of talented young Irishmen who were to surround Parnell, was five years younger than Parnell, being only twenty-eight at this time. He was a genuine intellectual, a great reader of books and journals in French, German and Italian as well as English. He was so tall and gaunt that clothes hung on him. He had a long sensitive face set off by deep eyes. He once sat for a portrait of Christ by Henry Haliday, and the novelist George Meredith once wrote to a friend, "You are an artist. I should like you to see and study Dillon's eyes. They are the most beautiful I have ever beheld in a head—clear, deep wells with honesty at the bottom." He was to be among the most passionate fighters for Irish freedom, gaining a reputation among the English as a sanguinary rebel.

The two arrived in New York harbor on the *Scythia* on January 2. The errand of mercy had aroused American sympathies, and there was also a good deal of curiosity about the handsome, young aristocrat who was leading the army of Irish peasants. The press boarded the ship and beseiged Parnell while he was still at breakfast. A revenue cutter met the ship, bearing a delegation of distinguished citizens and also his sister Fanny, now bound to him in the cause to which she had given her heart, years before he had joined it. He was gracious to all his visitors and afterward joined his mother and two other sisters, Anna and Theodosia, at the Fifth Avenue Hotel.

In the next two months Parnell and Dillon traveled to sixty-two cities in the United States and Canada, a total of 10,000 miles crisscrossed across the continent. The trip was greatly successful in the money-raising department, the two collecting £40,000, or $200,000, but it was also a triumphal tour, for the visit gave the American Irish an opportunity for an outpouring of their sentimental pride, longing for Erin and defiance of England. Politicians, including non-Irish, joined in—governors, senators, mayors, down to chief water inspector. Everywhere, there were bands and banners and banquets, processions with armed escorts and a Niagara of oratory. The nervously impatient Parnell bore up well under it all until he reached Chicago. After having had to participate in a parade, he finally arrived at a hall filled with ten thousand people, where he expected to be able to sit down. But he then had to stand for half an hour while a white-clad Amazon recited an ode of welcome she had composed for the occasion. Afterward, in a hotel room, Parnell berated at length these Americans and their love of tedious talk and ceremony.

Parnell faced a problem in meeting with the men of the Clan-na-Gael, many of whom were unconverted to the moderateness of the New Departure. One Nationalist had predicted that it would be impossible to win them over. "He would have to talk treason in America. How then could he run the gauntlet of the House of Commons?" But Parnell was unusually successful in his efforts to win solid support. He said frankly that he did not seek armed revolt, but he was firm in his stating that he would fight for Home Rule, and he appealed to their philanthropic impulses to alleviate the present distress. Most of all, he impressed by his reserve, which somehow radiated strength and purpose. The Clan-na-Gael members contributed generously and organized the meetings everywhere, which he could not have done alone.

He spoke to an enthusiastic crowd at the New York Stock Exchange. Before an overflow crowd in Madison Square Garden he struck his main theme: "I feel confident that we shall kill the Irish landlord system and when we have given Ireland to the people of Ireland, we shall have laid the foundations on which to build the Irish nation. . . . I am bound to admit that it is the duty of every Irishman to shed the last drop of his blood in order to obtain his rights if there were a probable chance of success. Yet at the same time we all recognize the great responsibility of hurling our unarmed people on the points of British bayonets."

Many of his listeners did not agree with his pacific approach, as instanced by an old man who rushed to the platform at Troy, New York, and thrust $30 into Parnell's hand. "Here are five dollars for bread," he said, "and twenty-five dollars for lead."

At Cincinnati he made a radical statement, the "last link" speech, which no doubt pleased many extremists in the Clan-na-Gael but was to be thrown back at him in Parliament in days to come. "The feudal tenure and the rule of the minority have been the cornerstone of English misrule. Pull out the cornerstone, break it up, destroy it and you undermine English misgovernment. When we have undermined English misgovernment, we have paved the way for Ireland to take her place among the nations of the earth. And let us not forget that this is the ultimate at which all Irishmen aim. None of us, whether we are in America or Ireland, or wherever we may be, will be satisfied until we have destroyed the last link which keeps Ireland bound to England."

After a recital of the privations of the peasants, designed to rip at the heartstrings, Parnell and Dillon would pass among the audience with the collection plate. As a supplicant for funds Dillon made a greater impression, epitomizing in his appearance the curse of hunger. As someone put it, "When I saw this sleek young dude, Parnell, as well fed as anybody and a darned sight better groomed, I said to myself 'The very idea of sending a man like that to tell us that they are all starving!'—but then the other man, poor Dillon, came along with hunger written on every line of his face and I said, 'Ah, that's different, there's the Irish famine right along' and I guess my five hundred dollar bill would not wait in my pocket any longer."

Actually, since, by this time, the famine had revived memories of 1846 and thereafter, there were three other relief funds in existence: the Mansion House Fund, started by the Viceroy's wife, the Duchess of Marlborough; the New York *Herald* Fund, launched with a huge contribution by its owner, James Gordon Bennett; and the Lord Mayor's Fund, launched by Edmund Dwyer Gray, who was now Lord Mayor of Dublin and was aided enormously by his *Freeman's Journal*. Parnell argued with Gray about the administration of the fund, thus renewing the bad feeling between them.

Parnell found time to argue by cable with Lord Randolph Churchill (father of Winston), the son of the Duke of Marlborough, about Queen Victoria's contribution to the Irish relief fund in the famine year of 1847, a sore point with the Irish. Parnell insisted that, far from adding to the fund, she actually had been responsible for a net loss of £6,000. She gave £2,000, but through her ambassador in Constantinople she asked the Sultan of Turkey not to give more than she had. He therefore reneged on his previously announced contribution of £10,000 and gave only £2,000.

In Brooklyn, the famed minister, Henry Ward Beecher, sat on the platform. In Boston the equally famed Wendell Phillips sat beside Parnell. "I came here from a keen desire to see the man who has forced John Bull to listen." He addressed four state legislatures. Then came an invitation to address a joint session of Congress, an honor accorded to only a few foreigners, including the Hungarian patriot Lajos Kossuth and General Lafayette. He delivered the address on the night of February 2, at a session attended by only a few members, but the galleries were packed and the press coverage was extensive, which was most important. He concentrated on the land problem, talking of the goal of peasant proprietorship and stating that a prosperous Ireland could support a population of 30,000,000. Two days later, Parnell met President Rutherford Hayes, who was not as stuffy about protocol as President Grant had been, and visited with members of the Cabinet. On February 19, Congress passed a joint resolution that the secretary of the Navy was authorized to use any naval vessel or charter any vessel to carry relief supplies to Ireland.

Even in the early stages of the tour it became evident to Parnell that the detail and paperwork to be attended to were enormous. When the two emissaries got into a bad snarl because they failed to realize that there were three cities in the United States named Springfield, Parnell decided that they needed secretarial and administrative help. He cabled a twenty-four-year-old journalist to join them immediately. Thus one of the most important figures in the Parnell drama comes upon the stage, an insignificant scribbler at the time who was to rise to become the first Governor-General of the Irish Free State—Timothy M. Healy.

A native of County Cork, where his father was a clerk for the Poor Law Union, Healy started out as a shorthand clerk in the office of the Northeastern Railway when he was only sixteen. Then his uncle, T. D. Sullivan, owner of *The Nation,* hired him to write a weekly column for one pound a week. He came to London in 1878, and at twenty-three he already showed the acuteness and fertility of mind, the industry and the acerb wit that would later mark him for distinction. He covered Parliament and became spellbound almost at first sight of Parnell, writing rapturous columns about him as the coming savior of Ireland. In turn, Parnell did favors for him. As young Tim wrote to his brother Maurice, "Parnell in the matter of getting me admission to the House has stood by me like a brick putting down my name whenever there is an opportunity and apologizing if he missed it." Healy attached himself to Parnell, making himself useful in a variety of ways; he was Parnell's messenger boy, amanuensis, servant and even his cook. To Maurice he wrote, "He will ultimately go mad if no relief comes to him from Ireland, or break under the strain."

Healy used Parnell to climb the ladder of success. He might have reached it by another route, but he owed everything to Parnell—for which he possibly never forgave him. At any rate,

Parnell's reward was that in the end Healy turned on his master and led the fight to crush him. When Parnell had been dead twenty-five years, Healy, in his memoirs, spattered mud on the name of the departed leader.

Even in the early days, some resentment of Parnell's success seemed to obtrude. In a letter to Maurice on December 4, 1879, when Parnell was preparing to leave for America, he wrote, "I regard it as almost a calamity that our political interests compel us to idealize this man in public, so insecure do I feel as to the possible protrusion of his feet of clay at any instant before the cloud of worshippers." He hastened to add, "The tone of these remarks might be supposed to demonstrate the existence in the background of some personal griefs, but you will do me the justice to believe my assurance to the contrary."

Healy arrived in New York on February 24. He was met by the Parnell girls and was given a railway pass sent from Parnell, who met him at Davenport, Iowa. Healy smoothed out things for the emissaries from that point on. They worked their way east, and then north into Canada, where they were warned that they might expect trouble from Orangemen in view of recent assaults, but Parnell was confident that they would not attack a Protestant. When they reached Toronto, Parnell wired his mother that he was safe. He wrote the wire in French for the sake of security, he whispered to Healy, ignoring Healy's reminder that French was understood widely in Canada.

By this time Healy had become convinced that Parnell was a queer one and so was his family. In later days Healy, while ostensibly the faithful lieutenant, was to spread the charge among the English that Parnell was "half mad." After visiting with the family in New York, he wrote Maurice, "The mother, I think, is a little off her nut in some ways and for that matter so are all the rest of them." John Devoy, who worked for the *Herald,* told Healy that Fanny and Anna had asked him to steal a black cat out of the *Herald* office "to take away [James Gordon] Bennett's luck." Parnell's mother told Healy that her son was dogged by English Government spies and that his correspondence was opened by them. She said she had detectives of her own, detecting the government detectives. She advised Healy to write to her in a code arranged around the sentence "The main street must depend for support on the Irish vote which holds the balance of power. Rugose." Healy wrote his brother, "She remarked to me smilingly and in the greatest confidence that if that happened, the main street would look rather 'rugose.' About which I said there was little doubt—seeing that it might be looking all the days of my life before I should know any difference. Did you ever hear of the word 'rugose'?"

The party went from Toronto to Montreal, where there was a wonderful reception with thousands of cheering citizens. Healy said that all homes he could see were illuminated in his honor. At the end of the meeting there, Dillon not having accompanied them, Healy was asked to fill in for a few minutes. He hailed Parnell as "The Uncrowned King of Ireland"—at the time it was a bit of hyperbole since Parnell had only a handful of supporters in Parliament, but it was publicized by the New York *Herald* and was a title that stuck to Parnell for many years. It also reflected Healy's professed admiration, which bordered on sycophancy.

When Parnell reached the hotel, he found a cablegram from Biggar awaiting him. "Parliament to be dissolved. Return at once." They took a train that night. On the long trip across the bleak snow-covered wastelands to New York, Parnell relapsed from his sustained enthusiasm into a deep depression and ruminated gloomily, "I wonder if any man would pay to hear me speak a second time." When they reached New York, time was short, but Parnell organized a meeting to found the American Land League, a companion organization to that in Ireland, and sister Fanny, who attended the meeting, took prime responsibility and became the head.

"The indifference of the family toward one another," wrote Healy to his brother, "is amazing and there doesn't seem to be very much outward affection manifested." The night before they sailed, the youngest sister, Theodosia, announced to the family that she was sailing with her brother to marry her fiancé, Commander Paget. Although this was the first the family had heard of it, "Neither of the others nor the Mother seemed the least surprised or to give a damn. Parnell himself said only 'Ah.'"

On March 10 Parnell and Healy (leaving Dillon in the States to continue the work) drove to the pier in a blinding snowstorm through which the 69th Regiment, with fixed bayonets, escorted them. On the deck of the *Baltic,* Parnell stood bareheaded in the storm, "looking like a king," saluting the brave veterans of the Civil War and in turn acknowledging the cheers of the crowd amid the strains of a military band. It was the end of a successful visit which had raised the dispute from a local quarrel with Irish land-lords to a political issue of worldwide interest. In the future, American money would flow in large quantities across the sea, the New World thus redressing the grievances of the Old. In a later year, Sir William Harcourt, a Liberal minister, would complain to Prime Minister Gladstone, "In former Irish rebellions, the Irish were *in Ireland*. Now there is an Irish nation in the United States, equally hostile, with plenty of money, absolutely beyond our reach and yet within ten days of our shores."

XIII

During the ocean voyage Parnell surprised Healy. He had seemed indifferent toward his family, yet he spent a good deal of time walking with his sister Theodosia on the deck and was extremely attentive to her wishes. He was customarily abstemious and parsimonious, yet he ordered champagne on St. Patrick's Day, being in an exceptionally fine humor.

On the early morning of March 21, the ship approached the Irish shore. Parnell scanned the sea, looking for a tender to meet the ship, but none appeared. Now Parnell, whom Healy found to alternate quickly in moods, turned morose. Healy recalled, "As nothing appeared, he spoke bitterly of this neglect and asked me, did not his colleagues think it worthwhile to meet him. The morning was raw, but he grew hot with indignation. He enlarged on the work he had done in America and said it deserved a better reward than indifference."

However, his misgivings were ill-founded, and a tender appeared with the leaders Davitt, Biggar and T. D. Sullivan in it. Parnell, now cool as ice, received them unmoved. "He banished all traces of emotion and became the superman once more." No one might have guessed that he had been deeply chagrined only a short time before and was now greatly elated. The thought struck Healy then that Parnell was something of an actor, that he was not an iron man but a man with an iron mask which dropped occasionally. This feeling grew over the years into certainty, and he later gibed at him as a "splendid comedian."

Ireland was greatly excited by his return. He drove immediately to Dublin, where he was hailed as the new Perseus who had slain

Medusa and freed Andromeda from her captivity on the rock. From there he went to Cork, where the welcome was equally fervent. Bands played "Hail the Conquering Hero Comes" and a dense crowd was packed all the way from St. Patrick's Bridge to the end of Patrick Street.

XIV

Parnell immediately plunged into the election campaign. He was leader of the Irish in Britain and leader of the land agitation in Ireland; now was his opportunity to achieve the biggest prize, leadership of the Irish in Parliament.

Lord Beaconsfield, formerly Benjamin Disraeli, tried to pitch the election on the growing discontent in Ireland, which he saw as a threat of separatism from the United Kingdom. In an open letter to the Viceroy, the Duke of Marlborough, he wrote, "A danger, in its ultimate results scarcely less disastrous than the pestilence and famine which now engages your Excellency's attention, distracts Ireland. A portion of the population is attempting to sever the constitutional tie which unites it to Great Britain in that bond whch has favoured the power and prosperity of both. It is hoped that all men of light and learning will resist this destructive trend."

Gladstone, leading the Liberals in his second Midlothian campaign, refused to be detoured into a debate on a threat which seemed at the time to be a cloud no bigger than a man's hand. He waged his campaign against the foreign policy of the Conservatives. As for any aspirations Ireland might have, he would not countenance any diminution of the power of the Imperial Parliament. However, "We have got an overweighted Parliament and if Ireland or any other portion of the country is desirous and able to so arrange its affairs so that by taking some local part of its transactions off the hands of Parliament it can liberate and strengthen Parliament for imperial concerns, I say I will not only accord a reluctant consent but I will give zealous support to any such scheme." The Home Rule Confederation of Great Britain swung many Irish votes to Gladstone when it branded the Beaconsfield manifesto as a "declaration of war upon your country and your friends. The ministry is seeking to obtain a renewed term of office by sowing dissension and hatred between Englishmen and Irishmen."

In this election, Parnell put forth many candidates of his own choosing, some of whom were destined to be notables in their own right. Dillon was returned to Parliament and so was Parnell's friend, Justin McCarthy, who had been elected in 1879, a plump little man who beamed through gold spectacles and had a voice like the ripple of a pleasant stream, "the most dovelike personage outside of a cloister."

Parnell put up James J. O'Kelly against the leading Catholic layman in Parliament, the O'Connor Don, who had been in the House for twenty years, and O'Kelly won. He was a colorful person with a swashbuckling appearance and had led an adventurous life. At eighteen he had joined the French Foreign Legion and had been with the French Army supporting the ill-fated Maximilian in Mexico. He had also been with the Prussian Army when it defeated France in 1871. As a war correspondent for the New York *Herald* he had been with the insurgent Cubans and had been captured by the Spanish and condemned to death. He had long been a Fenian agent in Ireland. As we have seen, he had been one of the first to see Parnell's potential for leadership and to push him.

Thomas Sexton also entered Parliament that year. The son of a constable of the Irish militia, he had been a railway clerk and at nineteen had got a job with *The Nation* after an essay competition. He was a strange person who remained a solitary bachelor throughout his days, socializing little with his colleagues. He was much admired by them, however, for his unusual ability to master details, particularly in the financial area, and most of all for his great oratorical gift, becoming known as "silver-tongued Sexton." Like Dillon he was a prodigious scholar, and he became much admired by English members, too, for his great talents.

T. (Thomas) P. O'Connor was elected from Galway. The son of a billiard saloon keeper, he became a serious scholar of history and modern languages at Queen's College in Galway, where he met Frank Hugh O'Donnell, who was to recommend him to Parnell. After college, he became a free-lance writer. Desperately poor, he supported himself by writing for gutter publications and by translating Wagner's operas into English. He first attracted attention by a book on Lord Beaconsfield which, lacking pen and paper, he wrote with pencil on the back of advertising handbills distributed in the street. He had a job on the *Daily Telegraph* during the

Franco-Prussian War, and the vivid much-admired touches of Parisian life in the "Balloon Dispatches" were due to his active imagination and his extensive reading of French novels. When O'Donnell related this to Parnell, the latter burst out laughing as O'Donnell had never seen him laugh before. O'Connor was to become the press-relations man, or spokesman, for the party.

Healy did not run in the April elections but was elected in a by-election from Wexford in November.

Revolutions are made by youth, and to use a term that is before its time, this was a Young Turk revolution. Parnell at this time was not yet thirty-four. Davitt, Sexton and O'Kelly were the same age. O'Connor was two years younger; William O'Brien, who would join the group soon, was four years younger; Dillon, five years; and Healy, nine years.

In many districts Parnell fought candidates called Whigs, who were moderates on the land issue and Home Rule; many of them either were landlords or were backed by landlords and enjoyed strong church support. The Land League issued a manifesto: "If you vote for the landlord candidates, you are voting for famines, rack rents, evictions, workhouses and exterminations."

In County Wexford, Parnell put up John Barry, a Fenian member of the Home Rule Confederation who had powerfully promoted him for the presidency, against a Whig, Chevalier Keyes O'Clery, a prominent and devout Catholic who had served in the Papal Army and had received his title from Pope Pius IX. O'Clery therefore had the support of the local clergy, which was joined by a group of rowdy Fenians who believed that Barry, by seeking to enter Parliament, was a traitor to the cause. At Enniscorthy, Parnell mounted a platform to speak for Barry, but howls from the mob did not allow him to be heard. A rotten egg was flung at him, struck him on his beard and trickled down his face. Some rowdies tried to pull him off the platform but he clung to a railing. Another one grabbed him by the trouser leg, ripping it from top to bottom.

"I will stand here all day, I have to say a word for John Barry," Parnell yelled, but finally seeing that he had no chance to be heard, he walked off, complaining bitterly that his sympathizers in the crowd "stood around like a flock of sheep and looked on." John Redmond, in later years to be Parnell's successor, was knocked down by some Fenian ruffians. Parnell saw him bleeding and asked what had happened. As they walked together Redmond told him, and Parnell had a little laugh, saying, "Well, you have shed your blood for me at all events." Barry won.

Parnell himself was entered for two seats, in Meath and Mayo. Then he learned that he had been entered for a seat in Cork by his admirers. When he went there, however, he learned that two priests had entered his name at the instigation of the Tory candidate to split the Nationalist and thus ensure the Tory's election. Nonetheless, Parnell accepted the challenge and with the aid of Healy made a whirlwind campaign there. The local clergy were all against him, and the day before the poll the bishop, Dr. Delany, had an address read at all Masses denouncing Parnell for diverting funds from the Land League which should have gone to starving children. To this Parnell made no answer and made no outward show of resentment. (As a matter of fact, Parnell had wangled from Land League funds £1,000 for election expenses.) On the eve of the balloting he made a thrilling speech, concluding, "Citizens of Cork, this is the night before the battle, to your guns then." He won the next day.

Gladstone and the Liberals swept to victory in the nation. Parnell had won three seats, an honor that had been bestowed on no one else in the history of Ireland. He chose to sit for Cork. Of the 103 seats from Ireland, the Home Rulers had elected over 60, but the division between Parnellites and Whigs would have to await a vote between Parnell and William Shaw for the leadership.

XV

Parnell told Michael Davitt that while in America a young Irish lady had fallen in love with him and followed him across the ocean with her father. Taking up residence in Morrison's Hotel in Dublin, she conducted a siege operation against Parnell, but all her efforts were to no avail. The young lady had been misled. The Irish leader was an Englishman in all his tastes, including women.

We have had nothing to say about Parnell's social life, or, since he was a young and virile man, his love life, because there is no material about it. Dr. Sigmund Freud once wrote, "Whoever undertakes to write a biography binds himself to lying, concealment, to flummery, and even to hiding his own lack of understanding, since biographical material is not to be had, and if it were it could not be used. Truth is not accessible . . ." Freud was referring to his own specialty, the subject's love life. His statement, if it applies to no other biographical subject, certainly applies to Parnell at this time. If a man has no friends to betray his confidences, does not talk about himself and does not write letters, to construct anything vera-cious or even plausible about his love life is to try to build bricks not only without straw but without clay—that is if the information does not emanate from the woman or women involved.

There is another supposition: that Parnell had no love life. All the intense activity of Parnell in his obstruction policy and his struggle for political power between 1877 and 1880 suggests a man who has sublimated his sexual energies into another sphere. (I note that a biography by Joan Haslip refers to his affairs with barmaids and furtive railroad amours in conjunction with the well-known libertine Joseph Biggar, with whom, as a matter of fact, his relations seem to have been purely business. At the same time she refers to Parnell as being "ascetic" and "monogamous," which would seem inconsistent with indiscriminate wenching.)

Healy, in his memoirs written over forty years later, implied that Parnell dallied with women at the expense of his duties, but it must be borne in mind that Healy had an interest in denigrating the sexual morals of Parnell, since he sought in his book vindication for himself as the well-known executioner of his benefactor for flouting the moral code. He said that during the 1880 election campaign Parnell became enamoured of the "virtuous" wife of a thorough scoundrel, St. John Brenon, and tried to adopt him as a Nationalist candidate, dropping the project only because his notoriously bad reputation made this impossible.

Then he made a more serious charge. After the election, he wrote, Parnell went to Manchester to a hotel which was a hub of Irish politics. There he had a mistress, whom Healy chivalrously disguises as "Lizzie from Blankshire," a barmaid at the hotel. In her arms, Healy claims, like Mark Anthony in the arms of Cleo-patra, Parnell forgot his responsibility to the cause of his country and lingered on. In the meantime Shaw called a meeting of the Home Rule party and was reelected chairman. When Parnell shook off Lizzie's spell and returned to Dublin, he asked for a new meeting and Shaw, thinking he was absolutely safe, consented. At that meeting, on May 17, Parnell was elected over Shaw by a vote of 23 to 17.

It would be a very serious charge, indeed, if Parnell, on account of a barmaid, had been thus derelict to his mission and the ambitions to which he had dedicated himself for years. From the evidence, it seems to be a malicious invention by Healy. Other accounts state that an earlier meeting was called by Shaw, but Parnell asked his followers not to attend since it was too early to make plans until the new government had taken over, and so the election of a chairman was postponed to a later date.

The meeting in May at which Parnell ousted Shaw and acquired the last leg of the tripod of authority was notable for the appearance of a personality important in the drama of Parnell's life. T. P. O'Connor thus described him: "There was one man whom I saw there for the first time and whose demeanour particularly attracted my attention. Slightly overdressed, laughing with the indescribable air of the man whom life has made somewhat cynical, he was in sharp contrast with the rugged, plainly dressed, serious figures around him. If appearance were not deceptive, he wore the unmistakable marks of the Whig. Nobody knew him except perhaps his colleague, the O'Gorman Mahon. Mr. Parnell seemed never to have seen him before. When the time came to vote, his face grew pale and to everybody's surprise, his voice was for Parnell."

This man was Captain William Henry O'Shea, the newly elected member from County Clare.

XVI

In the House of Commons, the Government sits on the left, facing the Speaker, the Opposition on the right. The benches are separated by a gangway, and below it on the opposition side Parnell and his followers, to number about 35, took their seats, while Shaw and his followers sat on the other side with the Government. Parnell was welding his disciplined group into the smoothly functioning monolithic body that it was to be in the years to come, so tightly knit and managed that it could act and deliver its blows like a hammer. In later years Healy wrote, "We created Parnell and he created us." Certainly it was a reciprocal Pygmalion action, but without Parnell it is likely that the party would have remained amorphous and weak as it had been in the days of Butt, while if there had been no Healy, Sexton, etc. substitutes would have been found by Parnell.

The new Prime Minister was Gladstone, whom Queen Victoria had been forced to accept though she had threatened to abdicate rather than have "that half-mad firebrand who would soon ruin everything." The new Gladstone ministry seemed to open under good auspices for Ireland with the appointment of William Forster as the new Irish Secretary. As a young man, Forster had accompanied his father, a minister in the Society of Friends, on errands of mercy to Ireland to organize relief during the Great Famine. His reports have given us some of the best pictures of the scourge of the Famine. Later, Forster became an influential Liberal, and his passionate hatred of slavery led him to take a leading part in preventing aid by England to the South during the American Civil War. He also was a leader in the fight for better education for all classes. Would not this humanitarian be the best friend that Ireland ever had in Parliament?

Forster turned out to be the exact opposite, and he went down in history as the hated "Buckshot" Forster, so called because at one time, speaking in defense of his policy of repression of the Irish by arms, he said that he had ordered the police to fire buckshot instead of bullets as a humane measure. Instantly, someone on the Irish bench cried out "Buckshot Forster," and that was his name from that time on.

Why this failure? Gladstone later attributed it to the fact that Forster was hopelessly "impractical" and therefore had led England down a blind alley. There was more to it, perhaps, in the realm of psychological motivation. Justin McCarthy said of him that he was "a good man gone wrong." He had genuinely expected that his appointment because of his record in the Famine would result in a truce in the undeclared war. He had expected too that the Irish would be as meek and submissive as they had been in the Famine and was amazed to find out differently. He thus became disillusioned with the Irish long before they became disillusioned with him. It may be, too, that the charity giver is abnormally sensitive about those who "bite the hand that feeds them," and that the recoil is sharp from despised good intentions.

Gladstone was expected to be far more sympathetic to the Irish cause than Disraeli. Had he not in his previous ministry fathered two reforms, the Disestablishment Act and the Land Act of 1870? Throughout his career he had always had the Irish problem before his eyes, while in the case of Disraeli it had been, for the most part, like Nelson holding the telescope to his blind eye. In 1845, Gladstone had written to his wife, "Ireland, Ireland, that cloud in the West, that coming storm, the minister of God's retaliation upon cruel and inveterate but half-atoned injustice." In 1868, when informed that he had been called on to form a ministry, he was at his favorite exercise, cutting trees on his Hawarden estate. He rested on his axe and said, "My mission is to pacify Ireland."

Yet at this time Gladstone had no program at all for dealing with the Irish land problem, and the prevailing distress, and admitted later that it came upon him "like a flood." He said, "I did not know the severity of the crisis that was already swelling on the horizon."

At the opening of the 1880 session, the Queen's speech was read, and to the amazement of the Irish it discussed the problems of Turkey, Afghanistan, India and South Africa, but it contained not a word about Ireland, where 600,000 people were then receiving emergency relief. The Parnell party held a caucus and John O'Connor Power offered an amendment to the speech "And to humbly assure her Majesty that the important and pressing question of the occupiers and cultivators of the land deserves the most serious and immediate attention of her Majesty's Government with a view to the introduction of such legislation as will secure to these classes the legitimate fruits of their industry."

There was a debate on the amendment before it was "by leave withdrawn," in the course of which Shaw, as a true Whig, backed up Forster on delay of relief. "The rt. Hon. gentleman has given a sufficient reason why legislation should not be strongly urged at present. It is a very large question and deserves to be looked at all around." The Parnell followers now proposed a relief bill to halt evictions, with John O'Connor Power as sponsor. Finally, when the bill went to a second reading, the Government proposed to introduce a bill of its own. Gladstone, having focused his mind on the problem, now grasped the nub of it when he declared, "When the means of rent are entirely destroyed for a time by the visitation of Providence, the poor occupier under these circumstances regards a sentence of eviction as very near a sentence of death."

The Compensation for Disturbance Bill, the Government bill which was confined to tenancies under £30, mitigated the hardship of evictions by providing, out of the funds of the Disestablished Irish Church, compensation for improvements made by tenants. It was passed on July 5, after Forster pleaded for it as a law which "would put out the fire." It then went to the House of Lords, where it was debated for ten days. Lord Lansdowne, who owned 170,000 acres in Ireland while 5 million people held none, naturally fought the bill. Then Lord Beaconsfield spoke in his usual witty and cynical manner. The bill, he said, was unwise, catering to public opinion. He made an interesting statement about the will of the majority in a democracy: "What we call public opinion is generally public sentiment. We who live in this busy age and in this busy country know very well how few there are who can obtain even the knowledge necessary for the comprehension of great political subjects and how much fewer there are who having obtained this knowledge can supply the thought which can mature into opinion. No, my lords, it is public sentiment, not public opinion, and frequently it is public passion."

On August 3, the House of Lords rejected the measure by an overwhelming vote of 282 to 51. The Queen wrote in elation to Lord Beaconsfield, "Do you *ever* remember so many voting against the Government to whose party they belong? I do *not*." The vote destroyed Forster's career, though it did not appear so at the time. He was indignant, rising to say of the upper chamber that there "is no assembly in the world with so much power and so little personal labour as the House of Lords."

In the House of Commons, T. P. O'Connor moved to abolish the House of Lords. Parnell, on the other hand, felt that if the Government had had more grit, it could have forced the bill through the House of Lords. He asked the Liberals for assurances as to future legislation, but the only answer was the appointment of the Bessborough Commission, which was instructed to study the problem and to render a report to the House by the next session. The news coming now from Ireland was all violence and outrages, as the people, frustrated by the defeat of the Government bill, were taking matters in their own hands. Various Irish members aided and abetted the outbreaks by making inflammatory speeches "of a nature that would drive a nation of saints to revolution." The mood of the Irish members was not calmed when Forster, in answer to a speech of John Dillon (who had recently returned from the United States), stigmatized him with the insulting words "Its [the speech's] wickedness can only be equalled by its cowardice."

Ireland was becoming a ship aflame, and as John Morley wrote, the thoughts of responsible Englishmen were at last "violently drawn from Thessaly and Dulcino, from Batoum and Ezeroum, from the wild squalor of Macedonia and Armenia, to squalor not less wild in Connaught and Munster, in Mayo, Galway, Sligo and Kerry."

XVII

The membership of the Land League skyrocketed to the mammoth figure of 500,000 and its president, Parnell, after the Parliamentary session, swept through Ireland like an avenging angel, speaking at New Ross, Kilkenny, Cork, Langford, Galway, Tipperary, Limerick, Athlone, Ennis. Davitt, having returned from a successful trip to the United States, joined him. He had been very successful in raising funds, and Patrick Ford of the *Irish World* had made available to the League his "skirmishing fund," which had been originally designed for violent deeds. Appalled at the outrages, particularly the maiming of dumb animals, Davitt prevailed on Parnell to issue a joint circular with him condemning them.

Parnell's policy at this time was somewhat ambivalent. He was a moderate who wanted to preserve the coalition of his forces by steering a middle course between left and right, which was as perilous as sailing between Scylla and Charybdis. T. P. O'Connor told of a meeting he attended with Parnell in which a Land Leaguer said from the platform, "If you shoot down the landlords like partridges in September, I would not say a word." Parnell grabbed O'Connor and said to him using a schoolboy phrase, "Let's hook it."

Nonetheless, his words were often fire-eating enough to satisfy any radical. Thus, at one meeting he said, "Depend on it, the measure of the Land Bill in the next session will be the measure of your activity and energy this winter." Could there be a blunter exhortation and condonation to violence and lawlessness? "He talked daggers, though he used none," wrote Frank Hugh O'Donnell.

At Cork he was greeted by a crowd of 100,000, and to an onlooker viewing the wild adulation he was "like a Greek God come to take part in a festival organized by his votaries." There is no doubt that part of Parnell's appeal to the Irish and a good deal of the Parnell mystique which was now taking form rested on the distinction and even beauty of his appearance. T. P. O'Connor described him at this time, when he was thirty-four: "The beauty of his delicate features, his cheeks healthy and full, the trim beard, the whole expression pleased and yet not proud, boyish in ingenuousness and its suggestion of modest wonder and depreciation—all combined to give him a look of fresh and immortal youth." In the same vein Conor Cruise O'Brien, after discussing Parnell's qualities of leadership, states "That he should have been also—as he was—gifted with imposing stature and great physical beauty makes it easier to understand the almost superstitious veneration with which many of his followers—especially his remoter followers—regarded him. Few leaders in modern times have looked so very like a leader."

As the Irish were forming a romantic attachment for their leader, those near him were becoming aware of his idiosyncrasies. He was so superstitious that he would not sit at a table seating thirteen, and he would leave the table if someone passed him the salt, that being to him an omen of bad luck. Any untoward event, however slight, might be construed by him as a direful omen. Though detached in his human relationships, he was extraordinarily fond of animals. Once, at the crucial stage of a Land League meeting, without a word of explanation he suddenly left the dais followed by his dog. The meeting halted until he returned fifteen minutes later. Seeing the puzzled look on everybody's face, he said, "Oh, I forgot to feed the dog." That was more important than all else.

To what extent was Parnell in his career influenced by patriotism and to what extent by his own inner craving for power? To what extent was he dominated by pride as an Irishman and to what extent by his own overweening pride? These questions will always remain unanswered. There is a similar question as to whether Parnell, a large landowner, was genuinely sympathetic to the plight of the tenant farmer. It is certain that in time any armor of indifference he might have had was pierced. In the hearings of the Special Commission in 1888, when Charles Russell in his opening speech described the sufferings of the farmers, Parnell broke down and wept. To Davitt he said, "I do not recall having cried like that even in my childhood."

XVIII

On September 19 at Ennis (with no less than eight priests on the platform), Parnell made a historic declaration which ushered in a new weapon in the land war. After urging his listeners to keep a firm grip on their homesteads, not to bid for farms from which others had been evicted and to prevent "grabbers" from doing so, he said, "Now what are you going to do to a tenant who bids for a farm from which his neighbour has been evicted?" There were cries of "Kill him!" "Shoot him!"

"No," Parnell went on, "I think I heard someone say 'shoot him.' But I wish to point out to you a very much better way, a more Christian and more charitable way, which will give the lost sinner an opportunity of repenting.

"When a man takes a farm from which another has been evicted, you must shun him on the roadside when you meet him, you must shun him in the streets of the town, . . . you must shun him in the fair and in the market-place, and even in the house of worship, by leaving him severely alone, by putting him into a moral Coventry, by isolating him from . . . his kind as if he were a leper of old— you must show him your detestation of the crime he has committed; and you may depend upon it . . . that there will be no man so full of avarice, so lost to shame, as to dare the public opinion of all right-thinking men . . . and to transgress your unwritten code of laws."

At Lough Mask House, in County Mayo, there was an estate belonging to Lord Erne which had been managed for the past fifteen years by a Captain Charles Boycott, a doughty, domineering man who ran the estate with scant regard for the tenants. There was a dispute about rents in 1880. He refused any abatement and evicted the tenants, who could not pay—and then the trouble started.

All in the neighborhood applied Parnell's counsel. All his laborers left the fields at the time when the crops were ready for harvest. His servants departed, tradesmen refused to sell him anything, the postman refused to deliver his mail, the baker refused to bake his bread, the blacksmith refused to shoe his horses.

No one had threatened the least violence to him, but he was helpless. The old man wrote letters to the London *Times,* and there was a great deal of sympathy aroused for him throughout England.

He broadcast a call for help to harvest his crops and fifty Orangemen volunteered. An army service corps of 2,000 was rushed from Dublin with field pieces to guard them. They arrived by rail at Claremorris in Mayo and, convoyed by the troops, the laborers had to march the 15 miles to the estate. No food was obtainable at any price on the march, as the residents all turned their backs on the small army. Father O'Malley ordered all people off the streets and all shops closed. Seeing an old woman watching the laborers, he waved his umbrella at her and said, "Be gone. How dare you come out here to intimidate Her Majesty's troops. For shame. Be off now and if you dare to molest these 2,000 heroes after this glorious campaign, I'll make an example of you."

When the convoy arrived at the estate it was discovered that pegs for the tents had been left behind, and in a torrent of rain all—troops and laborers—were drenched to the skin. Famished, they foraged on the estate for all that was edible, eating all that Captain Boycott owned. The crops were harvested, but the cost to the Government, Forster reported to Gladstone, was astronomical. Parnell joked that each turnip harvested had cost the Government a shilling.

Soon afterward, a Land Leaguer, James Redpath, was having a talk with Father O'Malley, and Redpath said that the League was looking for a good word for this type of economic ostracism. O'Malley said, "Why not call it the 'Boycott'?" Redpath was instantly enthusiastic and said, "Between us we will make it as famous as the word 'lynching' in the United States." Thus was the word born, and it has indeed become more famous than "lynch." An international word, it is even used in Russian as "boikittirovat." Incidentally, when Captain Boycott returned to Ireland after a stay in England and found his name in common usage, he was delighted at this intimation of immortality.

Besides the case of Captain Boycott, there was the notable case of Bence Jones of Clonakilty, in County Cork, who also refused to be reasonable with his tenants. He tried to sell his cattle in the Cork market, but in the sizable crowd there was absolute silence when bids were asked—for which there was a good reason. So he sent the cattle to Dublin to be shipped to Liverpool, but the men in the service of the Dublin Steam Packet Company refused to put them on board. So he could not sell his cattle.

The boycott was the most fearsome weapon that had ever been used. If a man was declared under the ban, when his family went to church, the whole congregation would depart. At night unseen hands would dig a grave in front of his house. He would receive letters ornamented with coffins, skeletons and daggers; masked men behind hedges would suddenly leap out and scare his family out of their wits; his cattle might be found dead; even if he were bleeding to death, he would not be able to find a doctor.

The Land League held secret trials and decided against whom the boycott should be applied. The Land League was "self-elected, self-constituted, self-assembled, self-adjourned. Acknowledging no superior, tolerating no equal, interfering in all stages with the administration of justice, levying contributions and discharging all the functions of regular Government, it obtained complete mastery and control over the masses of the Irish people."

Davitt preserved a quaint letter received by the Land League, showing how it was regarded by some Irish as a quasi-official Government.

Ballyhaunta, Mayo
January 8, 1881

To the Honorable Land League

Gintlmen in a momint of wakeness i pade mi rent, i did not no there was a law aginst it or i wud not do it. The people pass mi as if the small pox was in the house, i hear ye do be givin pardons to min that do rong, and if ye will send mi a pardon to put in the windy for evryone to rede it, as God is mi judge, i will never komit the crime agin.

The Land League openly encouraged lawlessness. The 1880 harvest was actually a good one, but the League encouraged the farmers to hold onto the harvest, not deliver it to the landlords, on the theory that they were entitled to recoup for their past misery from this one good farm crop. Fanny Parnell expressed the spirit in her poem "Hold the Harvest, Boys."

Now are you men or are you kine? Ye tillers of the soil
Would you be free or evermore the rich men's cattle toil?
The shadow on the dial hangs that points the fatal hour

Now hold your corn or branded slaves forever cringe and cower.
Oh, by the God that made us all—the seignor and the serf
Rise up! and swear this day to hold your own green turf;
Rise up! and plant your feet as men where now you crawl as slaves
And make your harvest-fields your camps, or make them your graves.

XIX

There was not only the cold boycott but also hot action, since to many of the Irish "It is not enough to send them into Coventry. We must send them to hell"; and so outrages continued despite all that the police and tyrannical magistrates appointed by Forster—like Clifford Jones—could do, including petty arrests, such as those of small boys for whistling seditious songs.

The London *Times* voiced the general angry sentiment and exasperation of most of the English when it said that the only cure for Ireland was to "sink the island fifty feet below the surface of the ocean for 48 hours and then to lift it up and commence anew." Such a view outshouted more moderate voices like that of General "Chinese" Gordon, who, after a visit to Ireland, wrote to the *Times*: "I may say that from all accounts and from my own observation the state of our countrymen is worse than that of any people in the world, let alone Europe. I believe that these people are made as we are, that they are beyond belief loyal—but at the same time broken-spirited and desperate, living on the verge of starvation in places where we could not keep cattle. The Bulgarians, Anatolians, Chinese and Indians are better off."

An example of this misery was the case of a farmer in Bantry named McGrath, who had his rent raised by 80 per cent. Unable to pay, he was evicted. He and his family took refuge under an upturned boat on the seashore, where he died of exposure, receiving the last rites from a priest who held an umbrella over him. His wife, his sister and his children, after trying to retake possession of their home, were jailed. For speaking out against this barbarity, Healy was arrested, tried in the Cork Assizes under the Whiteboy Act and acquitted. He thereby won great popularity and was then elected to Parliament under Parnell's auspices. Parnell congratulated him for years as being the only one of the party "honorably acquitted in court."

To quash the semirebellion, the Government felt that it was vital to crush Parnell. As Lord Cowper, the new Viceroy appointed by Gladstone, said years later, "We considered Mr. Parnell the centre of the whole movement, the chief if not the only danger. We feared him because he had united all the elements of discontent, because we never knew what he was up to and we felt that he would stop at nothing."

So on November 2, Parnell and four other members of Parliament, Biggar, Dillon, T. D. Sullivan and Thomas Sexton, together with Patrick Egan and Thomas Brennan of the Land League, were indicted in Queen's Bench for various charges of conspiracy in preventing ejectments from land and payment of rents. Parnell said coolly, "I regret that Mr. Forster has chosen to waste his time, the Government's money and our money in these prosecutions." Biggar fumed, "Damned lawyers, wasting the public money, Whigs, rogues, Forster, damn fools." It was a reasonable prediction that no jury in Ireland would dare to convict them.

The trial was held in Dublin for a period of twenty days, during which there was intense excitement, since Parnell was the idol of the city. Cordons of police and mounted constabulary had to control the mobs which surrounded the Four Courts. Parnell sat calmly throughout the trial, clearly distinguishable since he wore a skull cap, having chosen this time to shave his head in order to stimulate the hair roots in places where it was sparse. His associates accepted it as another of his foibles. He showed little interest in the proceedings—although he had a spell of merriment when the prosecution introduced poems of Fanny Parnell as proof of sedition. On January 24 the jury reported that it was hopelessly deadlocked, one juror breaking the instructions of the Court to shout "Ten to two for acquittal." As Parnell left the courtroom he turned to Davitt and said, "Now that they have failed to get me, they will go after you."

Now the Irish Executive, convinced that regular legal process was futile, urged Gladstone to seek legislation to suspend the writ of habeas corpus so that the leaders and malefactors could be imprisoned without trial. Lord Cowper said that it would strike terror because no one would know if his turn would come next. Forster wrote to Gladstone, "When the whole population sympathizes with the man who commits an outrage he knows that hardly any witness will give evidence against him and that a jury in his own district will certainly acquit him. . . . The active perpetrators are old Fenians or old ribbonmen or *mauvais sujets*. They would shrink into a hole if a few were arrested." Gladstone in later years said that Forster induced him to believe that the whole situation could be cured by a crackdown on a few local ruffians.

XX

In the summer of 1880, Parnell had fallen in love with another man's wife, and by autumn he was engaged in an adulterous relationship with her. The lady was Mrs. Katherine O'Shea, the wife of his Parliamentary colleague Captain William Henry O'Shea, and this love affair was destined to become an affair of state with consequences of a magnitude matched in history only by the love affair of Anthony and Cleopatra. We shall discuss it fully at the point of time where Parnell's political life and love life started to intermesh at the end of 1881.

According to the account later given by Mrs. O'Shea, when she met Parnell he was suffering from nervous exhaustion and general debilitation and she became his nurse at the same time or before she became his mistress. Although he was only thirty-four, his health was already in a state of decline, and for the remainder of his life, a scant eleven years, he was not a well man.

Because of childhood diseases his constitution had never been a strong one. Undoubtedly the arduousness of his life in the preceding three years had sapped his strength. Since the start of the 1877 session, when he had embarked on his campaign of obstruction, he had been involved in a perpetual campaign, without surcease or rest, without the balm of home comforts. He had lived in dingy bachelor quarters and had eaten and slept on the run. He had no friends, no capacity for social relaxation and perhaps no balm in female companionship. He had had to commute between England and Ireland, making speeches throughout the two nations. He had made a grueling tour of America and then managed an election campaign. He had formed a new party. He had headed a revolutionary organization of the tenant farmers in Ireland—directing its operations all the while with the threat of government prosecution hanging over his head like the sword of Damocles.

Superadded to the fatigue which was the natural concomitant of this life was probably the strain of playing a role which did not come naturally to him. A retiring person by nature, he had been thrust into the back-slapping hurly-burly world of politics which, in Ireland, was often bibulous and carousing, while he was himself almost an abstainer. An aristocrat who had delayed entering politics because "I would not associate with that set," he was now a bounden brother to plebians whom he would not have touched with a twenty-foot pole in his private life. To Mrs. O'Shea in later days he referred to them as "rabble," and in the final blow-up in 1891 he erupted with what were undoubtedly his true feelings when he called them "scum" and "gutter sparrows." A person who was not born for the rostrum, he nonetheless trained himself by sheer willpower to become a public speaker, and because of his natural gifts he became a very effective one, though he never relished it. He had to expose himself to thousands of eyes, yet he hated to have people look at him, and he had the shades lowered in halls because people peering at him through the windows made him uncomfortable. Although deeply involved in Ireland's problems, he never read a book about Ireland or its history but read voluminously in technical and engineering journals, wherein he had a deep interest.

Yet, having no taste for public life, he was now up to his neck in it. To some extent, he was caught up with the cause emotionally. To a larger extent, people came to depend on him and as a man of honor and *noblesse oblige* he felt the call to duty. Most important of all was his passion for power, which he felt it rightful for him to have—he loved that power and died a premature death to preserve it. He not only loved power but, the "splendid comedian," he played the role of the man of power, the grim, tight-lipped Caesar. Most salient in his makeup was his iron will to persevere. As Thomas Sexton once said of him, "At the top there is dust which can be pushed this way or that. But underneath—all granite."

XXI

At seventy-two, William Ewart Gladstone, who had thought that he was in the process of "unwinding the coil of life," found himself, in the Parliamentary session of 1881, in a maelstrom which opened up before him the greatest work of his life, the solution of the Irish question. The question he first faced was the demand of the panicky Forster for enactment of a stiff coercion bill suspending habeas corpus. At a dinner on December 30, 1880, Gladstone revealed to the journalist John Morley that the Cabinet had agreed to it; his manner was distraught and his voice filled with anguish as if "under the painful necessity of killing his mother. It was downright piteous—the wrong features, his strained gestures, all the other signs of mental perturbation in an intense nature." The Cabinet had rejected Forster's request for the session to start in late 1880 but advanced it to January 7, 1881.

The Queen's speech proposed coercion "because of the extended system of terror." Justin McCarthy, on behalf of Parnell, introduced an amendment "Humbly to pray Her Majesty to refrain from using the naval, military and constabulary forces of the Crown in enforcing ejectment for non-payment of rent" until a land reform bill had been considered, a proposal which Gladstone termed "an insult to the crown." A debate ensued in which the amendment was defeated by 435 to 57. Parnell did not command a majority of the Irish members, with 51 for him, 22 against and 29 abstentions. Shaw voted for it, but his right-wing Whig faction had by now been practically expelled from the Nationalist Group which in December had voted that "all Home Rule members should henceforward sit in opposition."

This new rule was an important step toward party discipline and making all party members speak with one voice—that of Parnell. John O'Connor Power moved away on what he called a question of principle but was undoubtedly in most part a response to his vendetta with Parnell. Now Frank Hugh O'Donnell deserted the Parnell party, too, after writing to the *Freeman's Journal* that there is "patriotism in other halls than Avondale." (Healy wrote his brother Maurice that O'Donnell was "off his nut.") Captain O'Shea, who had voted for Parnell as leader in 1880, showed his true Whig sentiments and now sat with Shaw.

On January 24, the Government sought to introduce the coercion bill, "Protection for Person and Property Bill." An angry obstruction began. Parnell cabled Patrick Ford in New York, "We are now in the thick of the conflict. The present struggle against coercion will, please God, be such as never has been seen within the walls

of Parliament." And so it was to be. To the press Parnell announced, "The Government wants war and they shall have it."

On January 25, the Irish Nationalist party kept Parliament in
session from 4 P.M. until 2 P.M. the next day, a total of twenty-two
hours, with ceaseless obstruction during which Biggar was ejected
for transgressing the rules of the House and Healy attacked Gladstone as an "executioner." At noon there were wild cheers from the
Irish bench as Parnell coolly entered. He had been freed by the
verdict in the Dublin trial the day before.

Two days later Gladstone and Parnell met for the first time, and
Parnell, by Gladstone's account, made quite a lasting impression on
the Prime Minister. Gladstone, backing up his Irish Secretary, read
speeches of Parnell which seemed inflammatory. Parnell remained
utterly impassive in his seat. Afterward he accosted Gladstone in
the lobby. "I wonder, Sir, if I could see that portion of the speech
at Sligo, that you read aloud." Gladstone handed it to him and
after perusing it, Parnell pointed to one passage and said, "That
is inaccurate. I never said it. Thank you, Sir." He turned on his
heels and walked away, having made no request for correction or
apology, with no mention of any of the other utterances of which
the offending passage was a small part, and with no comment
whatever about them or Gladstone's use of them. Years later, in
telling of the incident to R. Barry O'Brien, Gladstone said he was
struck by "the immobility of the man, his laconic way of dealing
with the subject, his utter indifference to the power of the House."
In checking the speech for accuracy, Gladstone did find that Parnell
actually had been misquoted.

The talk from the Irish members went on, as Gladstone put it,
"sometimes rising to the level of mediocrity and more often grovel-
ling amidst mere trash in unbounded profusion." Healy alone distinguished himself by being able to make short, rapierlike speeches
which would sting an English member to answer and thus waste
more Government time. The Queen wrote to Lord Hartington,
"The Queen trusts that measures will be found to prevent the
dreadful Irish people from succeeding in the attempt to delay the
passing of the important measures of coercion."

Then came the session starting on the night of January 31, one
of the most important in English Parliamentary history. The House
was still debating the motion to take up the Coercion Bill. The

Irish members kept the debate going to midnight with endless talk; then came the first motion for adjournment. Gladstone announced, "I beg to say on the part of the Government that we propose to resist that motion." There would be no adjournment of this session.

Parnell rose to speak, and, in the words of an observer, "His mincing manners might have allured to him the most timid mouse." If the Prime Minister persisted in going on with the debate, he did not believe that time would be saved, and, moreover, he was sure that the dignity of Parliament would not be enhanced. "The House has heard a great deal about impediments placed in the way of public business. I would be very sorry to place any impediment in the way of public business." There were cries of "Oh, Oh, Oh." In his imperturbable way, Parnell continued, "Perhaps the hon. members who signified their dissent would kindly inform me when I have ever placed any impediment in the way of transaction of business by the present Government. . . . I have urged the Government not to go on with the present bill, but of course if the Government insists, then the Irish members will endeavour to fight the battle as strongly as they can, and in this course they will be supported by public opinion." The House exploded with cries of "No, No." Parnell explained that he meant the public opinion of Ireland, which he valued more "than that of the ill-informed voters who have sent the hon. members interrupting me to the House."

He then reminded Gladstone of his own conduct during the debate on the Divorce Bill when he had said "that he and 30 to 40 other members would strain every form of the House to defeat the Bill." Gladstone shouted "Give me the reference." Parnell replied, "The death of a relative of the rt. hon. gentleman and the adroitness of Lord Palmerston secured the passage of the Bill." Gladstone, aroused, called out, "Are those my words?" and Parnell glided away from the subject, saying, "I have not quoted them as the words of the rt. hon. gentleman but the substance of what he said." He sat down at 2 A.M. after branding the Coercion Bill as "cruel, wicked, wretched and degrading."

Parnell was followed by other Irish members—Justin McCarthy, Healy, A. M. Sullivan, O'Donnell, John O'Connor Power. An English member announced that he was walking out, since the air was becoming fetid and "such work is all very well for coal heavers who rely on physical strength" but not for him. At 4:50 A.M., the Speaker,

Sir Henry Brand, left the chair and the Deputy Speaker, Lyon Playfair took it. Division after division was taken on motions for adjournment, which the Irish lost by votes of about 200 to 20. Biggar roused tempers in the House by stating that the Irish were "an innocent party" who were the victims of a "violent conspiracy" of the two English parties, and in response to cries of "Withdraw, withdraw" he repeated, "I say deliberately that this is a conspiracy of Irish landlords to mislead first the rt. hon. gentleman, the Chief Secretary, then the Government and then English public opinion."

Soon after dawn, Gladstone, who had sat in the House through the night, left for some sleep and the talk went on. At 1:25 in the afternoon, the Speaker returned and resumed the chair from the Deputy Speaker. Parnell objected, saying that under the rules of the House, when the Deputy Speaker takes the chair he must retain it till the end of debate, but he was overruled.

All the while Parnell was issuing commands to his forces, cracking the whip not only on his own followers but also on the Whig members who did not sit with him but who were nonetheless intimidated by his power of command. R. Barry O'Brien gave this picture of him that day. One of his own party passes by in the lobby:

PARNELL [stopping him]: Why are you coming out of the House? You should remain at your post. It is impossible to say what may turn up at any moment.

MEMBER: I have just spoken.

PARNELL: That is no matter. A speech is not everything.

MEMBER: Here is a telegram from the Corporation of Blank protesting against the bill.

PARNELL: Then go back and read it.

MEMBER: I cannot. I have already spoken.

PARNELL: Then give it to someone else to read. Give it to me. [Another member came by, a Whig.]

PARNELL: Where are you going?

MEMBER: Just into the reading room to skim the papers.

PARNELL: Don't you think you ought to be in the House?

MEMBER: Yes, Mr. Parnell, I will return.

PARNELL:You will speak against the bill?

MEMBER: I would rather not, Mr. Parnell, I am not really able to speak.

PARNELL: You can move the adjournment of the debate. That won't take much. [Tightening his grip on the member's arm] You *must* vote against the bill. I suppose you can do that. It does not need a speech and the sooner you get back in the House, the better.

At midnight of the second day, Sir Stafford Northcote, the floor leader for the Conservatives, rose. "I think I have a right in the name of the independent members to ask for some expression of opinion on the part of the Government which may strengthen the hands, of you, Mr. Deputy Speaker, in endeavouring to put a stop to this obstruction." The Deputy Speaker said nothing, and now Irish members were repeatedly interrupted by Conservative members on "Points of order" asking for suppression of the debate. John O'Connor Power, with fine irony appealed to the chair, "Now I wish to call to your attention to the persistent obstruction to public business on the part of the rt. hon. gentlemen who have alleged points of order that are not points of order at all, and I appeal to you to exercise your authority to put down this obstruction by naming these rt. hon. gentlemen and inflicting on them the consequences."

At 1:30 A.M. a Conservative member, Milbank, complained to the Chair that Biggar had called him "a bloody fool." Biggar countered that Milbank had said to him, "Biggar, you are a mean and impudent scoundrel." Milbank explained that during a division he had seen Biggar's lips form the words "You are a bloody fool" and he had responded in kind. The Deputy Speaker declared that Milbank owed an apology to the House. Biggar muttered to his Irish colleagues that he was convinced that Milbank was a fool but that he had neither the time nor the inclination to investigate whether he was a "bloody" fool.

During this, the second night, Irish member after member took the floor in the marathon talkathon, as the Americans have been wont to call a filibuster in the United States Senate. At 4:45 A.M., on the second day, "silver-tongued" Sexton rose and made a speech lasting until 7:45 A.M., before a scattered, drowsing few which would have been considered brilliant at any time or place. Every sentence was complete, every thought finely developed. It was said by the press Sexton's speeches were the only ones in the House which could be reproduced without the need for a single amendation, and this was such a speech. When he sat down, Mr. Shaw-Lefevre rushed from the Government bench to congratulate him.

At seven in the morning, Parnell left for a few hours sleep. Biggar followed Sexton on the floor, while T. P. O'Connor was poised for a four-hour speech to follow. Biggar was still on his feet when, at 9 A.M., Speaker Brand, with a great roll of paper in his hand and a grave expression on his face, swept in. He announced that he had decided to end the debate. "A crisis has arisen which demands the prompt intervention of the Chair. I decline to call upon any more members to speak and will at once proceed to put the question from the chair."

This was a historic moment. The tradition of free and unlimited debate in the Mother of Parliaments, which had been so zealously guarded and cherished for centuries, had come to an end. The decision had been reached the previous day. Speaker Brand had notified Gladstone of his willingness to end the debate, and this had been confirmed by a meeting of the Cabinet held in the Library of the House at four in the afternoon.

The Irish were taken completely by surprise. Parnell was absent, and as Justin McCarthy wrote, "When a crisis arose, when something had to be done on the instant, we were no good. We were paralyzed. Parnell could make up his mind on the instant and do the thing without doubting or flinching." A division was taken and closure was imposed by a vote of 164 to 21. The Irish members led by John O'Connor Power left the House shouting "Liberty" or "Privilege." Thus the forty-two hour session was brought to an end.

After the adjournment, Parnell was roused and met the demoralized troop of his party in the lobby, and they then held a meeting in the library. They marched into the House for the session to start at noon in single file, with Parnell at the head. An English member, the Radical Liberal, Henry Labouchere, asked the Speaker on what authority he had taken the unprecedented action to strangle debate. Speaker Brand replied, "I acted on my own responsibility and from a sense of duty to the House." Parnell announced that he would bring forward a resolution that the Speaker had been guilty of a breach of the privileges of the House, and after a six-hour sitting the House adjourned.

On that day, February 2, Michael Davitt was picked up by the police in Dublin and brought before a magistrate who refused to

give him any information beyond confirming that he was the
Michael Davitt for whom a warrant had been issued. He was then
transported to England and was lodged in jail.

The next day the House considered a resolution to give the
Speaker power to cut off debate when the House by a 3-to-1 vote
declared the pending business urgent. The Irish members got the
news about Davitt, and Parnell rose to ask the Home Minister,
Sir William Harcourt, "I desire to ask the Secretary of State for
the Home Government whether Mr. Davitt was arrested at one
o'clock today." Harcourt replied that Davitt's conduct was "incom-
patible with the conditions of leave for a convict," and as he dwelt
on the word "convict," there were cries of "shame" from the Irish
bench. "What conditions had he violated?" Harcourt ignored Parnell's query, and his "Answer, answer."

Dillon, livid with rage, rose and started to argue, but the Speaker
reminded him that he had given the floor to the Prime Minister,
who was speaking in behalf of the change in the rules. Dillon refused to give up the floor, and he was "named," 395 being for the
motion and 33 against. When Dillon refused to leave, the sergeant
at arms cocked his head and five men walked in wearing gilt chains
with figures of Mercury around their necks. "Oh, well, if you'll use
force, I'll go," he said, and he walked out without making the customary obeisance to the chair.

Gladstone rose to speak and so did Parnell, who moved that "the
rt. hon. gentleman no longer be heard," a Parliamentary motion
that had been dead for a century until it had been revived by
Gladstone himself in the session of the year before against O'Donnell. Parnell was "named" in a division by a vote of 405 to 7, the
Irish members remaining in their seats and not voting, which was
a breach of the rules. One of the seven votes was that of Captain
O'Shea. Parnell said, "Sir, I respectfully refuse to withdraw unless
I am compelled by superior force," and when a sergeant at arms
beckoned to his men, he bowed to the Speaker and departed.

Then the other Nationalists were "named" en masse for having
refused to leave their seats during the division and were ordered
to withdraw from the hall. The doughty and picturesque the O'Gorman Mahon announced that he would not budge unless actually
lifted, but A. M. Sullivan persuaded him by stating that "The reign
of law has passed away and the reign of force has taken its place,"

and it was "to his honour and the disgrace of the House" to acquiesce.

Thus the "active" policy of obstruction had virtually come to an end, and the Parnell party had lost its most effective weapon of Parliamentary warfare, since closure could now cut off debate.

XXII

With the final passage of the Coercion Bill near, the Land League was in jeopardy, and its funds were removed to Paris, along with its treasurer, Patrick Egan. The chief organizer, Davitt, was in jail, and a successor had to be picked. A council of war was therefore summoned in Paris to readjust the organization and affairs of the League and also to consider whether drastic action should be taken at this critical juncture of affairs, such as a defiant exodus of the Nationalists from Parliament.

Biggar, Dillon, T. D. Sullivan, James J. O'Kelly and Healy left together for Paris on a Friday, with Parnell scheduled to meet them there the following day. The five waited at the Hotel Brighton in the Rue de Rivoli. Parnell did not arrive on Saturday, Sunday, Monday, Tuesday, Wednesday, Thursday, Friday or Saturday. There was not a sign of the lost leader and not a word from him. O'Kelly brooded, "Parnell is either in the Tower or at the bottom of the Thames."

O'Kelly and Egan pressed Healy as to whether, as Parnell's secretary, he had some mail which might shed light on the whereabouts of Parnell. Healy admitted that he did have some unopened letters which were in a feminine hand. He declined to open them, saying that he had no authority to do so and that he would hand them over only in response to a resolution of the executive of the Land League. At a midnight meeting such a resolution was passed, and Healy handed over one letter, which was accepted by Dillon and Egan and examined by them *in camera*. They copied an address from the letter and asked that Biggar and Healy return the next day to London and look for Parnell there.

The next morning the two set out for the Gare du Nord, but on the way there, they passed Parnell in a cab on his way to the hotel and rejoiced to see him safe. Healy rushed up to his room and knocked on his door. Parnell opened the door and snarled, "What do you want?" Healy taken aback said, "I'm glad to see you. We were very anxious about you." Parnell slammed the door in his face, the only act of rudeness of which Parnell was to be guilty in their whole relationship. It was evident that he did not want to be questioned by anyone.

Parnell slept during the day and presided over a Land League meeting that night. He tendered no explanation or apology for his absence—it was enough that he was there. Under his guidance the council chose Dillon as Davitt's successor in Land League duties and decided that the Irish membership would not secede from the House, since the dramatic gesture would be futile; that Parnell would not proceed to the United States, since it would appear that he was running away from danger; and that the party would address a manifesto to the workers of England to join them in a cause in which all lovers of liberty had a stake, a course which Davitt had advocated but Parnell, though giving consent, thought futile, since English workers were by and large anti-Irish.

His breach of faith in letting the letter be opened so upset Healy that he resigned as Parnell's secretary as soon as they returned to England. Parnell had learned of the opening of the letter but never reproached Healy for it.

Now, what were the contents of the letter? Healy stated that it was from "Lizzie from Blankshire," who was living in Holloway, having borne Parnell's child, and she was asking him for help, financial and otherwise. Healy says that Biggar, for the sake of the party's reputation, sent an emissary to her and found her in a cold, dingy garret, in bed with a baby. He gave her help and Parnell apparently did right by her, subsequently, as far as money was concerned.

This tale told by Healy has been credited, which seems strange, indeed, since it is flatly contradicted in other accounts. Davitt was not one of the group in Paris, but undoubtedly he was told fully about it, and he states in his memoirs that the letter in question was from Katherine O'Shea. There is also the account of T. P. O'Connor. "After a solemn consultation, it was decided to open some of the letters in the hope of finding some trace or clue to the vanished Chief. One of the letters was from a lady. It was scarcely glanced at but it told enough: It was the first warning the Irish party had of the opening of the tragedy that finally engulfed Parnell and went near to engulfing Ireland."

This obviously refers to Katherine O'Shea, and in her memoirs, she confirms that Parnell's associates learned early of the love affair from having opened a letter that she had written to Parnell.

This attempt to paint Parnell as unprincipled and callous, as a cad, hardly fits in with what we know of Parnell. Moreover, he was so obsessed with the fear of death that his progeny, whoever the mother might be, would have a special meaning for him. It is unlikely that he would have ignored his child, even by a barmaid. The evidence suggests that the story of "Lizzie from Blankshire" is a malicious libel by Healy to stain the name of his dead leader.

After returning to England, the jovial James J. O'Kelly, to whom Parnell became quite attached (O'Kelly was the closest resemblance to a friend that Parnell ever had), persuaded Parnell that they should return to France and try to enlist French sympathies for the Irish. Although a serious-minded expedition, it was also something of a junket to partake of the French salon atmosphere in *La Belle Époque*. Parnell wrote to Victor Hugo, "As you, honoured sir, have so well moved the sympathies of the human race for *Les Misérables*, we feel that our appeal will go straight to your heart and we are sure that you will raise your voice in favour of a brave but infortunate people." When Hugo met Parnell, he gave him the Hugo bromide, "True ideas are the sovereigns of the world. Brute force cannot persevere against them."

The two men drifted around newspaper offices and fashionable salons. Georges Clemenceau expressed his deep interest in the Irish cause. The Communard Henri Rochefort proclaimed that when he shook Parnell's hand he felt as deeply moved as when he had met Garibaldi. There were pretty sentiments expressed, but no more. The only result of the trip was that it stirred up the fears of the Catholic clergy as they saw Irish leaders mixing with the dangerous French anticlericals. Archbishop McCabe publicly deplored that "Allies for our country in her struggle for justice are sought from the ranks of impious infidels . . . sworn to destroy the foundations of all religion."

XXIII

After the Coercion Bill was passed, a companion measure, the Peace Preservation Bill, known also as the Arms Bill, was quickly passed. The Home Secretary, Sir William Harcourt, who carried this rigorous bill through the Cabinet and the House, pronounced epigrammatically, "Coercion is like caviar, unpleasant at first but becoming more agreeable with use."

On April 7, Gladstone offered his great reform measure, the Land Bill. The Irish had long said that the pattern for government action toward Ireland was coercion and then kindness, or put more colloquially, a kick and then halfpence. This bill was far more than halfpence; it was a glittering treasure, being far more pro-tenant and antilandlord than had been anticipated. Goschen called it "A Coercion Bill for Landlords." In effect, it granted to the tenants the three F's for which they had been agitating for years—fair rents, free sale and fixity of tenure. The bill would, most importantly, set up land courts to fix rents for a period of fifteen years, and a tenant could not be evicted as long as he paid the judicial rent.

Lord Hartington said later that the history of the 1881 session was "the history of a single measure carried out by a single man." This man was Gladstone, who presided over the bill from egg to earth, through thirteen drafts before it reached the House, and then sat in the House watching over it during all fifty-eight sittings. There was no collaboration with the Irish; Gladstone dismissed a proposal to talk it over with Parnell, whom he regarded as a mischief-maker or, as he put it in a letter, "a speculator in public confusion."

This landmark piece of legislation was a turning point in the relationship between England and Ireland. Up to this time, as historian J. L. Hammond put it, "Her [England's] cruelty was the steady and unconscious cruelty of egotism and arrogance. She gave Ireland, as she believed, the best she had. The calamity was that there was no nation in Europe whose best was so bad for the Irish peasant." To Gladstone, when he focused his mind on Ireland, the state of the country was "an intolerable disgrace." To his mind, the Land Bill was the last contribution he would be able to make at his advanced age. The month before, in discussing the change in House rules, he had said, "Personally my concern in the new arrangements is small—my lease is all but run out."

The bill was introduced by Solicitor General Farrer Herschell and Irish Attorney General Hugh Law. It was incredibly complicated. The Bishop of Limerick wrote to Archbishop McCabe that "since the Apocalypse nothing so abstruse had appeared." The Church, from bishops to priests, saw the benefits of the bill and were solidly for it. However, the bill, although according benefits to the tenants at will of a solid nature—and they were in the vast majority in Ireland—did nothing for the 150,000 leaseholders and nothing for the 100,000 tenants who were in arrears (some of the landlords preserved arrears on the books dating back to 1847). The bulk of the English members were as unconcerned as if the Government had asked them to enact the *Nautical Journal* into law, but there were a few landowners even on the Liberal side heavily opposed and the Duke of Argyll resigned from the Cabinet. There also were Irish Tories and Whigs representing or favorable to landlords who were opposed. The seven-foot-tall Colonel Tottenham declared that "the best manure for land is that it should be liberally salted with rents."

Parnell again having to walk a tightrope between right and left faced the dilemma of what his attitude should be toward the bill. The radicals felt that the bill did not go far enough, yet could so appease the tenant militancy that it would tear the props from under the movement. Thus, Dillon was making incendiary speeches in Ireland (for which he would be jailed) to the effect that if the Irish accepted the bill "they were going into a worse state of slavery than they ever were in before."

Parnell himself, weighing the problem with his customary cold balance, thought the bill a step forward that could not be shunted aside. He once said, "The better off the people are, the better Nationalists they will be. A starving man is not a good Nationalist." This is sound doctrine since a study of history shows that revolutions do not occur at the nadir of the people's misery. To William O'Brien, after the bill had been passed, he said, "Irishmen have a habit of talking big, but they are very much obliged to you for not taking them at their word. If we had rejected the bill, the farmers would very properly have chased us out of the country."

Yet, in view of his radical wing, he had to act on the basis of *Ne credite equo* when dealing with the perfidious Greeks bearing gifts. He had nothing to say in behalf of the bill. On June 7 Gladstone wrote, "Parnell is looking for every opportunity to impede the Land Bill without appearing to impede it." In a meeting of the party on May 5, Parnell announced his recommendation that the party abstain from voting on the second reading of the bill and said that he would resign as leader if he were not backed up. Neutrality was a brilliant tactical maneuver, but the extent of the split in opinion was shown by the divided vote, 18 to 11 to support him, and when the vote actually came, 14 voted for the Land Bill on the second reading. The clergy and the *Freeman's Journal* condemned his stand. Parnell's grip on the party at this time was obviously far from dictatorial. But by 1885, all fourteen who voted for the bill would be gone from public life, with the exception of one who was then a borderline follower, Captain O'Shea.

In the committee stage, Parnell at times used his influence to prevent the bill from being mangled—so much so that at one point Harcourt professed surprise that "Parnell seems disposed to becoming a Christian." In the debate, Healy shone for the acuity of his mind, grasping all the details and ramifications of the bill which was understood by only a very few in the House. He sprang an amendment that future rents should be not chargeable on improvements made by the tenant. It was accepted by Attorney General Hugh Law, and Healy, sitting down, said in a whisper to T. P. O'Connor, "This will save the tenants millions," and indeed the Healy amendment was important although it was to be badly weakened by judicial interpretation. (An interesting side item—during the debate electric lights were turned on for the first time in the House of Commons.)

The bill became law, receiving the royal assent on August 22. In a later year Gladstone said, "I must make one admission and that is that without the Land League, the Act of 1881 would not be on the statute books." William O'Brien gave the best summary of this momentous piece of legislation which hastened the end of feudalism in Ireland since it was the cornerstone for future legislation: "It reduced the landlords from a power as unbridled as that of a Turkish pasha over his slaves to an annuitant entitled to what was decreed by a court of equity to be a fair rent."

The final Parnell action of the 1881 session was strictly a *coup de théâtre* devised for the edification of his Irish admirers. He deliberately picked a quarrel, calling for a day for examination of the actions of Dublin Castle since coercion. After accusing the authorities of opening his mail, he said, "If I may not bring the cause of our imprisoned countrymen before the House, I may say that all liberty and regard of private right is lost to this assembly, and the ministry of the day has transformed himself from a Constitutional minister into a tyrant."

There were cries of "name him" and Gladstone rose. Not waiting for his reply, Parnell said, raising his voice, "I shall not wait the farce of a division because I shall leave you and your House and I shall call the public to witness that you have refused me freedom of discussion." With this flourish he walked out, leaving Gladstone speechless, and back he went to Dublin, where he received a tumultuous welcome, the greatest that any Irishman had received since O'Connell. The charge made by Frank Hugh O'Donnell that Parnell played to the gallery in his ascent to power seems well founded.

XXIV

Dismayed by the dissension within his party as shown in the vote on the Land Bill and by the opposition to his stand by *The Nation* and the *Freeman's Journal*, Parnell decided that he needed a newspaper entirely under his own thumb. A scabrous character, of whom we shall hear much again, Richard Pigott, owned three newspapers in Dublin which lived as much from blackmail as from circulation, *The Irishman*, *The Shamrock* and *The Flag of Ireland*. These papers were bought out by a company of which Parnell and Patrick Egan were the chief shareholders as trustees for the Land League. *The Flag of Ireland* was turned into the *United Ireland*, *The Shamrock* was dropped and *The Irishman* was discontinued in 1885.

As editor for *United Ireland*, Parnell picked a journalist who was destined to be one of the most picturesque and influential figures in the movement: William O'Brien, who was only twenty-nine at the time. Sometimes called the "Mad Mullah," he was a fanatic about the Irish cause, having been a Fenian in early youth. Words and ideas flowed from him—he had written two novels before he was twenty-one. Parnell became acquainted with him when he was a writer for the *Freeman's Journal*. He had a long face with sharp features and piercing eyes flashing out from behind spectacles, and a quick and feverish walk denoting the man of fierce and restless character.

O'Brien had been fascinated with Parnell on first sight, describing him on first impression as one with "a sweet seriousness *au fond,* any amount of nervous courage, a delicate reserve without the slightest suspicion of hauteur, strangest of all humor and above everything else, simplicity." He was to be Parnell's hero-worshiper for years.

The two discussed the job over a meal in Romano's, a restaurant in Dublin. O'Brien asked Parnell how far he could carry the fight and Parnell replied, "As far as you please, short of getting yourself hanged—or us." O'Brien said, "You know if your object is to preach moderation or to save the paper from the Castle, I am the last man to be placed at the helm." Parnell assured him that he was sure of his choice.

O'Brien was as good as his word. Every issue was an insurrection in print. When Forster read the first issue he exclaimed, "Who is this new madman?" Parnell, after reading the first issue, wired him: "Wonderful, sparkling all over." The circulation boomed to 100,-000, never equaled before by an Irish paper, and it became a strong bastion of Parnell rule.

XXV

During 1881 and 1882 Ireland acquired the same reputation for lawlessness around the world that Chicago was to have in the 1920s. The Empress of Austria used to make an annual trip to Ireland to buy horses for the Imperial Court but canceled her trip in 1881 out of fear for her safety, to the great loss of many farmers who depended on this sale. In the London Press, this item from a correspondent appeared, "The ill-fame of Ireland appears to have reached the natives of India. A lady in this station engaged a woman as an ayah, and the agreement regularly signed, sealed and delivered, is to the effect that the woman is to go with her mistress all over the world if necessary, but Ireland is especially barred at the ayah's request."

The reports of the reign of terror that reached the outside world may have been exaggerated, but lawlessness was indeed widespread and the Coercion Law, far from abating it, made it worse. Murders and sniping doubled in the year after the passage of the law. Forster's prediction to Gladstone that all that was required to deal with the unrest was to imprison a few village ruffians and ribbon-men was not borne out.

In early April, near Ballaghaderreen near Mayo, a woman begged a sergeant not to persist in the work of eviction. He ordered the troops to fire and two farmers fell dead of buckshot, whereupon the crowd stoned the seargeant to death and would have killed the others if they had not fled. A few weeks later at Granhold in Mayo armed police escorted process servers. Stones were thrown and the police started to fire. A feeble old woman was killed by gunfire, and a young girl was bayoneted. The Irish claimed that the police were drunk and produced empty whiskey bottles to prove it.

It was after this massacre that a secret organization bent on vengeance, the "Invincibles' of which we shall hear later, was formed.

The Irish Executive was becoming panicky, fearing that the problem was no longer one of individual assassination but of "a sudden overwhelming by sheer weight of members of police." Forster decided that all public assemblies, such as a crowd gathering around process servers, had to be halted and issued an order to this effect at the end of May. He wrote to Gladstone: "Insults to the police are almost past bearing—for instance, many hundreds of men and women, yelling like savages, throwing dirt, spitting in the faces of the police for hours. This of course they bear but when stones are thrown actually endangering life, it is hard to keep them quiet." Then a week later he wrote to Gladstone that he is "giving people to understand that if they drive us to it, we must fire on them."

Thus a kindly man was moved by what he considered ineluctable necessity to turn to measures which earned him the sobriquet of the "English Robespierre." He was a conscientious man who worked without rest, shuttling back and forth between Ireland and England to defend himself every few days before Parliament. He was a brave man who disregarded daily threats against his life and walked unescorted through areas where terror was rife. For all of Gladstone's later expressed distaste for Forster's methods, he backed him up over a long period, refusing his offers to resign—possibly because no alternative offered itself. He wrote Forster when the latter seemed discouraged, "It is not every man who in difficult circumstances can keep a cool head and a warm heart, and that is what you are doing."

Many arrests were made, and Forster imprisoned 1,000 without trial under the power granted him in the Coercion Law. Healy claimed publicly that one Daniel O'Sullivan, nine years old, had been arrested and prosecuted under the Whiteboy Act for carrying a torch at 2 A.M. and thus allegedly promoting an illegal meeting. The singing of "Harry Duff," a satiric poem about the police, brought about arrests. A magistrate appointed by Forster who infuriated the Irish by his harshness was Clifford Lloyd, who traveled with a retinue compared to that of the Czar traveling in Poland. Sexton found and displayed an order of a local police chief: "Men proceeding on his [Lloyd's] escort should at once use their firearms to prevent the bare possibility of an attempt on the gentleman's life. If men should accidentally commit an error in shooting any person on suspicion, I shall exonerate them."

Forster now advanced to a measure which he had disavowed some months before. On September 26, 1881, he first suggested to Gladstone the arrest of Parnell. "I do not think he is worse than the others but he is moved by his tail." (In this judgment Forster showed a good deal of insight.) A few days later, he notified Gladstone that unless the boycotting weapon were put down "they will best us." And then, "If we strike a blow, it must be a sufficiently hard blow to paralyze the action of the Land League, and for that purpose I think that we must make a simultaneous arrest of the central leaders."

I

XXVI

The touchstone would be Parnell's attitude toward the administration of the Land Act. His more radical followers wanted him
to have no traffic with it. Gladstone was relying on the Act, in
which he felt great pride, to pacify Ireland; and he was determined
that it should not be sabotaged. Dillon was arrested in May and
imprisoned until August 7 for a speech urging the tenants to
ignore the Act. Would Parnell get the same treatment?

On his return to Ireland after the Parliamentary session, Parnell
spoke disparagingly of the Act. "The bill has been brought forward
by the Government to prop up for a few years longer the expiring
system of landlordism." Parnell had cause to be skeptical about
the administration and interpretation of its provisions. The Chancellor, Lord Selbourne, had predicted that the law "will restore,
not diminish landlords' rights." The three commissioners of the
court set up to review the findings by the subcommissioners consisted of two landlords and one weak and pliant judge.

To jettison the Act, Parnell knew, would be irresponsible states-
manship. The best course would be to put pressure on the Land
Court to act with reasonable haste and to interpret the Act liberally. That would be accomplished by selecting test cases. If tenants
came forward with rents that were palpably exorbitant, relief
would be inevitable. But would such precedents aid tenants whose
rents were excessive and beyond their capacity to pay but which
might not be exorbitant? Would it not be to the interest of all
if the test cases were of the latter, more moderate category?

This thinking of Parnell was undoubtedly the soundest, and he
prevailed in carrying the party with him in a meeting at the
Rotunda on September 15. "We should be assuming an unreasonable and indefensible position in the eyes of the world," he said,
"and I venture to think in our own eyes, if we refuse to test the
Act."

To appease the radicals, however, particularly the Patrick Ford
element in America, he had to adopt the pose of an intransigent
on the issue. So Parnell cabled to Ford that he had put forward
this policy so that "surrounding districts may realize by the result
of cases decided the hollowness of the Act."

To English eyes, jaundiced with suspicion, these public statements seemed to prejudge the bias of the commissioners and
strengthen the fears of the Government. Gladstone wrote to Forster,
"It is quite clear, as you said, that Parnell means to present cases
which the Commission must refuse, and then to treat their refusal
as showing that they cannot be trusted and that the Act must fail."
Gladstone was determined that the Act should not be hamstrung
by this adventurer, this traitor to his own class who was conniving
for mean political ends. John Bright joined in pleas to Gladstone
to block any further mischief-making by Parnell. "His main object
is a break-up of the United Kingdom, for he hates us and England
even more than he loves Ireland."

Gladstone ignored the fact that Parnell, in taking his stand, was
defying irreconcilable elements of his own party who were for
the "scornful and uncompromising rejection of the Act." Dillon,
who had just been released from jail, was unwilling to treat with
the Act on any basis whatever, and he announced his retirement
from public life so that he would not have to clash with his chief.

Gladstone was scheduled to speak on October 7 at Leeds, where
he would receive the freedom of the city. Forster begged Gladstone
to use the occasion to deliver an ultimatum to Parnell, and Gladstone replied, "I mean to tell him that no force or fear of force
shall prevent the people of Ireland from having the full benefit
of the Land Act."

Gladstone received a wild greeting from the city, and in the
course of the speech said, "Mr. Parnell desires to arrest the operation of the Land Act, to stand as Moses did between the living
and the dead, to stand between them not as Moses stood to arrest
but to spread the plague." If it became necessary to enforce the
law, "Then, I say, gentlemen, without hesitation, that the resources
of civilization against its enemies are not yet exhausted."

. Gladstone emphasized that Parnell stood in a minority position.
"The people of Ireland, we believe, desire in conformity with the
advice of old patriots and their bishops and their best friends to
make a trial of the Act, and if they do make a trial of the Act,
you may rely on it, as certain as human contingencies can be, it
will give peace to the country."

XXVII

Parnell, who had no illusions about the prospect ahead, was filled with fears of prison life as it had been described to him by Davitt, most awful in his mind being the threat of solitary confinement. Yet, it was clear to him that he would have to offer himself as a sacrifice, and, in fact, to preserve his control of both his right and left wings, which were far apart on the land issue, he had been trying deliberately to draw upon himself the fire of the English. It was clear, too, that the Government, having been unable to break the back of the insurrectionary movement and fearing a boycott and breakdown of the Land Courts when they opened, would soon act against him unless he were to make a public capitulation.

Two days after the Gladstone speech he came down from Avondale, where he had been shooting grouse with O'Kelly, and met Healy, John Barry and a new member of Parliament, John Redmond, at Rathdrum station. He read in the Gladstone speech the declaration of an ultimatum and saw that *Der Tag* had come. With hundreds of patriots languishing in jail and with the radicals pressing him for a show of defiance, he could hardly try to conciliate Gladstone by asseverating his own honest desire to make a test of the Act. As Forster had put it, he was being moved by his tail. He spread the text of the speech in the *Daily Herald* over his knees and wrote out notes as the train went to Wexford.

There, bands and delegations had come from different parts of the country. He was driven through a triumphal arch. His carriage was bombarded with bouquets, women waved handkerchiefs from windows, crowds cheered from footpaths. Observing the near-hysteria, Parnell in a tense whisper said, "Healy, Healy, we have pushed this movement as far as it constitutionally can go." Healy wrote later, "I sensed his meaning for amidst bouquets and acclamations he foresaw the bolts and bars of prison."

Nonetheless Parnell delivered a fiery speech. His theme was that it was futile to expect any good from the English because all the benefits that had come to Ireland had been by her efforts alone. "The Irishman who thinks he can now throw away his arms just as Grattan disbanded the volunteers in 1783, will find to his sorrow and destruction when too late that he has placed himself in the power of the cruel and perfidious English enemy." Then he sank his shaft deep into Gladstone's good intentions. "It is a good sign that this masquerading knight errant, this pretending champion of the rights of every other nation except those of the Irish nation, should be obliged to throw off the mask today and stand revealed as the man who, by his own utterance, is prepared to carry fire and sword into your homesteads unless you humbly abase yourself before him and the landlords of the nation."

After this rabble-rousing he sat down with his supporters to a dinner which he grimly saw as a Last Supper. A colloquy took place in which he was asked, "Mr. Parnell, do you think that you are likely to be arrested after your speech today?" He answered, "I think that I am likely to be arrested at any time. So are we all. A speech is not necessary. Old Buckshot thinks that by making Ireland a jail he will settle the Irish question." Then, "If they arrest you, have you any instruction to give?" Parnell replied as he lifted the champagne glass to his lips, "Ah, if I am arrested, then Captain Moonlight will take my place." The Captain was a synonym for violence.

Across the Irish Sea, the text of the Wexford speech was widely published. To Gladstone it was the last straw. He summoned Forster for a three-hour Cabinet meeting, after which a single word was flashed across to the Dublin Police: "Proceed." Parnell's mistress, Mrs. O'Shea, from a house in which she waited near Piccadilly, wired him when the Cabinet met. Later, she advised him in a coded message that a warrant was on its way so that he might destroy or hide all papers that might be incriminating. A warrant for Parnell's arrest was signed by Forster early in the morning, when he disembarked from the mail boat.

It was the 13th, the unlucky day, of October, which Parnell always said was his "bad month." At eight in the morning, Superintendent Mallon of the Dublin police called at Morrison's Hotel; Parnell was awakened and presented with two legal documents. He dressed carefully and sat down to write a letter. Morrison, the proprietor, begged him to escape by a back way, but he refused. He was scrupulously polite to the two policemen when they returned to his room, and they were polite to him—but they asked him to hurry so that no crowd could form to impede the arrest. Downstairs, he haggled over his hotel bill, then paid it. He was bundled into a closed cab followed by two outside cars filled with constables; later, mounted policemen brought up the rear of the procession. Before they reached Kilmainham jail, he was allowed to leave the cab at a pillar-box to mail the letter he had written.

Parnell, as a folk hero, was already the subject of song, and a ballad soon was being sung in the streets of Dublin describing his arrest.

Come, all ye gallant Irishmen, and listen to my song,
Whilst I a story do relate of England's cruel wrong.
Before this wrong all other wrongs of Ireland do grow pale,
For they've clapped the pride of Erin's Isle into cold Kilmainham Jail.

It was the tyrant Gladstone, and he said unto himself,
"I nivir will be aisy till Parnell is on the shelf.
So make the warrant out in haste and take it by the mail,
And we'll clap the pride of Erin's Isle into cold Kilmainham Jail."

So Buckshot took the warrant and he buttoned up his coat,
And took the train to Holyhead to catch the Kingstown boat.
The weather it was rather rough, and he was feeling queer,
When Mallon and the polis came to meet him on the pier.

But soundly slept the patriot, for he was kilt wid work,
Haranguing of the multitudes in Limerick and Cork,
Till Mallon and the polis came and rung the front-door bell,
Disturbing of his slumbers in bould Morrison's Hotel.

Then up and spoke bould Morrison, "Get up, yer sowl, and run!"
Oh, bright shall shine in Hist'ry's page the name of Morrison!
"To see the pride of Erin jailed I never could endure!
Slip on your boots—I'll let ye out upon the kitchen door."

But proudly flashed the patriot's eye as he bouldly answered, "No,
It'll never be said that Parnell turned his back to face the foe!
Parnell aboo for liberty—sure it's all the same," says he,
"For Mallon has locked the kitchen door and taken away the key."

They took him and they bound him, them minions of the law.
'Twas Pat, the boots, was there that night and tould me all he saw.
But sorra a step the patriot bould would leave the place until
They granted him a ten per cent reduction on his bill.

Had I been there with odds at my back of two hundred men to one,
It makes my blood run cold to think of the deeds that I'd have done.
'Tisn't here that I'd be telling you this melancholy tale,
How they clapped the pride of Erin's Isle into cold Kilmainham Jail.

Parnell believed that he alone would be arrested, but he was soon joined in Kilmainham by Sexton, O'Kelly, Dillon and other leaders. *United Ireland's* headlines appeared in its boldest type: MR. PARNELL GARROTED. The text beneath read, "Saxon cowardice has done its worst. Let the cowards yell with joy as they may, the last outrage on Irish liberty has changed nothing." There was one immediate change—William O'Brien was clapped into jail to join his comrades, and *United Ireland* was suppressed.

Rioting broke out in the streets of Dublin on the night of Dillon's arrest, October 15. The scene, in a possibly colored version, was described by the weekly *Irish Times*: "Charging headlong into the crowds, the constables struck right and left, and men and women fell under the blows. No quarter was given. The roadway was strewn with the bodies of people. From the ballast office to the Bridge and from the Bridge to Sackville Street, the charge was continued with fury. Women fell shrieking and their cries rendered even more pitiful the scene of barbarity that was being enacted. All was confusion and naught could be seen but the police mercilessly batoning the people."

Forster received a deputation of the citizenry protesting police brutality. After listening to them, he dismissed the protest, saying, "It cannot be a milk-and-water business, this clearing of the streets."

A warrant had been issued for Healy, and while on his way to Ireland to surrender, a letter from Sexton intercepted him at Holyhead, urging him for the good of the movement to stay in England, where the warrant did not reach, and to fight for the cause from there. In Healy's memoirs we have this interesting sidelight: "At Holyhead a storm blew making havoc, the greatest ever witnessed in that harbour for half a century. Three ships had run ashore. The breakwater was breached for a hundred yards, and the mail-steamer had to be warped-out with ropes to prevent her from being dashed against the pier. Elsewhere a hundred vessels sank at sea. Telegraph wires were down throughout England and Ireland. . . . Humble folks said that the elements protested against the arrest of Parnell."

XXVIII

On the afternoon of the arrest, Gladstone made an address in London at the Guildhall. He too was capable of a *coup de théâtre*. At the psychological moment in his speech, a telegraph boy rushed up to him with a message. He opened the envelope and then solemnly announced, "Within these few moments I have been informed that toward the vindication of law and order, of the rights of property, of the freedom of the land, of the first elements of political life and civilization, the first step has been taken in the arrest of the man who has made himself beyond all others prominent in the attempt to destroy the authority of the law."

From the word "arrest," cheers resounded, and as the news spread, cheers reverberated in the crowds packed in front of the Royal Exchange, on the steps of Mansion House and overflowing into Threadneedle Street, King William Street and Queen Victoria Street. It was greeted as if England had just gained a military victory over a great foreign enemy. The news must have reached England before Gladstone's announcement, since soon afterward newsboys were shouting their wares: "Harrest of Parnell, Harrest of Parnell."

All over the world the news was cabled which seemed to signal the end of Parnell's political career. That night, Captain William Henry O'Shea, carrying newspapers with the sensational news, visited his wife, Katherine (they lived apart), in her home in Eltham, a suburb of London. With his habitual sneer, O'Shea gloated about the fate of Parnell, exulting that at last "He has been laid by the heels," while observing his wife carefully, since he was not sure of the true nature of her relationship to Parnell. She laughed "the laugh of tears, of jangled nerves and misery" which disarmed her suspicious husband, and said as lightly as she could, "I did not think that Parnell could keep out of prison much longer, did you?"

The next morning she received a letter.

Morrison's Hotel, Dublin
October 13, 1881

My Own Queenie,

I have just been arrested by two fine looking detectives, and write these words to wifie to tell her that she must be a brave little woman and not fret over her husband.

The only thing that makes me worried and unhappy is that it may hurt you and our child.

You know, darling, that on this account it will be wicked of you to grieve, as I can never have any other wife but you, and if anything happens to you I must die childless. Be good and brave, dear little wifie, then.

Your Own Husband

The marital relationship he adverted to was a symbolic sacrament not recognized in law, and Mrs. O'Shea was four months pregnant with his child while she was legally married to another.

Part Three

THE O'SHEAS

In this strange Irish tragedy, everything comes back in a circle to the same ultimate cause. It can safely be said that rarely in the history of the world have two commonplace persons been able to do greater public mischief than Captain O'Shea and his wife.

J. L. Hammond, *in* Gladstone and the Irish Nation

I

FROM every practical consideration, the partner of Parnell's love life was badly chosen. Not the least foreboding aspect was that she was not Irish but English. Moreover, she was a member of the English ruling class hated by the Irish for centuries. Her antecedents were not "commonplace."

Katherine Wood was born on January 30, 1846, and was therefore a few months older than Parnell. She was the thirteenth and youngest child of Sir John Page Wood, who was the eldest son of Sir Matthew Wood, Baronet of Hatherly House, of Gloucestershire. Her grandfather, Sir Matthew Wood, had been a famous lord mayor of London. Her father was in the Anglican Church. Before entering holy orders at the age of twenty-four, he had been private chaplain and secretary to Queen Caroline, the consort of George IV, and he performed the last rites at her death in 1820. Afterward he was chaplain to the Duke of Sussex. Her mother, daughter of Admiral Samson Michell of the Portuguese Navy, after her marriage had been appointed bedchamber woman to the Queen.

Among Katherine's illustrious relatives was her uncle Lord Hatherley, who was Lord Chancellor of England in the Gladstone ministry of 1866. Katherine's older brother Sir Evelyn Wood, later a field marshal, was one of Britain's most distinguished soldiers in the period closing the century.

Her father became Rector of St. Peter's, Cornhill, and then Vicar of Cressing, in Essex. Shortly after Katherine's birth the family moved to Rivenhall Place, a huge country mansion surrounded by ample grounds. Her childhood was a very happy one, and she was a normal well-adjusted child. As the youngest of the eight living brothers and sisters, she had abundant love lavished on her, being the favorite of her father, while Evelyn was the apple of his mother's eye. Evelyn was early designated for the military life, and she relates how he used to make her his willing slave during childhood by picturing to her the remorse she would feel when he was "killed in the next war"—until she realized that he was taking advantage of her credulity. The house was filled always with interesting and cultured visitors, so Katherine acquired a good deal of social confidence at an early age, as well as a proficiency in social conversation which would be a prominent talent of hers in adult life. The painter Constable was a good friend of her mother and encouraged her mother in her forte, which was the painting of miniatures. The novelist Anthony Trollope was a great friend of both of her parents and used to stay with them for the hunting season; he was a very hard rider to hounds who "stuck at nothing," which was a great cause of anxiety to her mother, because Katherine's sister, Anna, delighted to follow him. Another visitor of whom she gives an amusing account was the youth John Morley, who in later days would play a great part in the undoing of her lover, Parnell. He was so intellectual that her elders complained that they found conversing with him too much of an ordeal, so they palmed him off on the teen-age Katherine saying, "Your conversation, dear Katherine, doesn't matter as no one expects you to know anything." In their walks together she found to her surprise that he adjusted himself to the dimensions of her limited interests.

Because of her brother's army connection, house guests were often soldiers, who, of course, thrilled the young, impressionable girls. Katherine's sister, Anna, married Lieutenant Colonel Steele, of the Lancers. Katherine was attracted by a flashy and vivacious officer, Captain William Henry O'Shea, a Cornet in the 18th Hussars. He was a handsome lad, five years older than she, blond and curly headed, gay and glib, somewhat irresponsible, generous and with a ready—if barbed—sense of humor. Within a few days of their meeting they had become attached to each other and he had presented her with a poem about her "golden hair and witsome speech."

Alas, at her age, a girl's judgment is led astray by such superficials as braid and glitter. "Willie," as he was to be known to her forever after, was a crack steeplechase rider in a sporting regiment, and she watched him adoringly in the races. She was overwhelmed with grief when he suffered a grievous accident, she was overjoyed by his recovery. However, though she had known him for three years she was unwilling to become permanently attached to him. She related, "I fancy my mother understood me better than anyone," and after having an interview with Willie her mother sent him away. Willie, departing for Valencia, Spain, sent her a poem stained with heart wound: "Farewell, I know not if a merry meeting, for such a parting e'er shall make amend . . ."

Then suddenly, in February, 1866, her beloved father fell sick. For days she slept on a sofa at the foot of his great bed, in which Queen Elizabeth had slept on her way from Tilbury to London. He died and she collapsed with grief. Her mother alarmed at her state wired Willie in Madrid to come to her bedside. Thus the friendship was resumed at a time when she was in a weakened condition and experiencing the great gap of loneliness left by the loss of her father. There was a money problem too, since her father had left her mother penniless, and her mother's sister, Mrs. Benjamin Wood, had to come to her rescue. Apparently Katherine accommodated herself to convenient circumstance. "I now yielded to Willie's protest at being kept waiting longer," and they were married in January, 1867, at Brighton, when she was twenty-one. Willie was a Catholic, but religion did not interpose any obstacle, since he was a "careless Catholic."

II

When she was married the days of braid and glitter were over, since her husband, to raise money, had sold the captain's commission which his father had bought for him, commissions then being for sale in the prevailing and pernicious custom of an army dominated by an aristocratic caste concept. Willie's father, Henry O'Shea, had been a successful solicitor in Dublin and was devoted to his son and anxious to further his success in life. He first sent him to study at Oscott, where he could meet the Irish aristocracy. Then he sent him to school in France and Spain, where Willie acquired a proficiency in both languages, a Gallic wit and a cosmopolitan assurance of manner. From there he went to Trinity College, where he acquired an English accent and a lot of English friends, since Willie was an unexcelled mixer.

The next step of his thoughtful father was to buy Willie a commission in the army and give him two instructions: "First, become a smart officer; second, do what the other men do and send the bills to me." Willie fulfilled these instructions brilliantly and made his father pay for the best of clothes and housing and, no doubt, for wine, women and song. The bills soared beyond the capacity of his father to pay without doing injustice to his wife and daughter, and so, after paying Willie's last bill, for £1500, he more or less put him on his own. Having done his duty and more to his family, he died shortly before his son's wedding.

The sale of the army commission netted Willie £4,000, and he used the money to buy a partnership in his uncle John's bank in Madrid, his father's brother having settled there some years before and founded a bank. So the newly married couple were off to Madrid. In Paris, Katherine met her new relatives, who had refused to attend the mixed marriage. Her mother-in-law, a *comtesse* of Rome, was "a bundle of negations wrapped in a shawl—always in a very beautiful shawl." Her salient characteristics were her devoutness, her humorlessness and her complete conviction of the unsuitability of her new daughter-in-law. The two had a falling out over Katherine's insistence on bringing her little dog in with her when they visited Notre Dame together. Her new sister-in-law, wracked by rheumatic fever, was a carbon copy of her mother in the aforesaid traits and was also a human library of dry, solid and useless information, which she related in a thick French accent. The lack of affinity with these new relatives did not help to promote her marriage.

From Paris was a two-day journey to Madrid and a strange land and language. There she was met by a sea of faces of foreign relatives, since Uncle John had married into a Spanish family. Katherine had a difficult time making adjustments to such things as the manners of the most elegant señoras, who used their toothpicks at the table and after dinner washed their mouths publicly. She was deprived of the pleasure she took in walking freely about the streets during the day, since Willie informed her of the Spanish saying "Only the English and dogs go out in the daytime."

The qualms that had been building up in her mind about living permanently in Spain were settled when Willie quarreled with his uncle and the couple went back to England with a somewhat more attenuated capital. From this time their life began a slow but remorseless slide into penury. Having no particular training for civilian life other than a familiarity with horses gained in the army, Willie decided to start a stud farm at Bennington, Hertfordshire. He bought some good brood mares and stallions, and he had a fairly large-size operation, with a groom and twenty lads.

The bucolic life suited Katherine, since she loved the horses and the pastoral surroundings. The social life was only the round of dinners which the country gentry held for each other. Willie found the dinners highly enjoyable, but she found them wearisome, relieved only by her Puckish delight, when her turn came around, in mixing up the guests so that marriage-minded damsels found themselves next to old men and stately dowagers were flanked by raucous racing characters.

Meanwhile, the business of the stud farm was going downhill. Willie had not contemplated the risks and expenses involved in raising horses, and when his luck turned against him he turned to betting on the races, a certain step to insolvency. Eventually the bucolic idyll came to an end when Willie went into bankruptcy. Her first child had been born during this time, a son, Gerard, who was to be followed later by two daughters, Norah and Susan.

By this time Katherine had found Willie flip, impractical and without ballast, dedicated to the easy life, not only a bad provider but basically out of tune with her better mind and tastes. This incompatibility was aggravated by financial vexations and Willie's repeated long absences from home. Her family came to her aid with money. Lord Hatherley, then Lord Chancellor, sent her a check, and her aunt, Mrs. Benjamin Wood, took a cottage for her at Brighton. This aunt, Aunt Ben, as she was called, played a large part in the Parnell story merely by her existence and longevity. She was Katherine's mother's sister, having acquired the name "Wood" by marrying the uncle of Katherine's father, who now had been dead many years.

Katherine was terribly lonely, with Willie spending most of his time in London, so the family moved to Harrow Road in London to be together. By that time they were in the clutches of the moneylenders. The next stop was Beaufort Gardens. As debonair as ever, even in financial adversity, Willie continued in the social swim, attending parties at the French and Spanish Embassies and holding parties of his own. Katherine recounted, "I think Willie and I were beginning to jar upon one another a great deal now." Only replenishment of funds from time to time by Lord Hatherley

K

and Aunt Ben kept the ménage going, while Willie floated from one money-making scheme to another, none of which showed any profit.

Aunt Ben had a great fondness for her niece, Katherine, relishing her gaiety and her never-ending flow of conversation. So she proposed to buy her "swan," as she called her, a home at Eltham, at the other end of a park surrounding her own home, and to settle on her an annual income of £3,000, in return for which Katherine was to be her daily companion. The offer was eagerly accepted by the impecunious niece. This was in 1875, when Aunt Ben was eighty-three years old and could be reasonably expected to die soon and leave her fortune, which was estimated at £150,000, in most part to her favorite relative, Katherine. Certainly Katherine's proximity to her aunt until her death would enhance that prospect. From that time on, acquiring her aunt's money was a dominant thought and motivation in Katherine's life.

The personality of Aunt Ben is a highly relevant factor in the story. Since the death of her husband, she had lived in almost complete solitude in her large Georgian house, The Lodge, going out only occasionally, mostly on the grounds adjoining her house. The entire accent of her thinking was on "correct" deportment. She did not allow men to stay overnight in her house because it "perturbed" the routine of her staff. Although she had no formal religious belief, she encouraged it in others for "propriety of conduct," and every Sunday night she assembled her servants around her to recite the religious verses she had assigned. Everything was on the plane of irreproachability and orthodoxy. On a short drive, she observed that her servants tipped their hats to a passing lady. When she found out that the lady was the Empress Eugénie, she expressly forbade it in the future. She was a Legitimist.

Aunt Ben lived detached from the world of the present, with her old mode of speech and her fine mind steeped in Addison, Swift, Racine and the classical poets. She had two readers who came once a week. One was a struggling novelist who was to be the greatest of the age, George Meredith, to whom she paid £300 a year for his services. Their dialogue always began the same way: "Now, my dear lady I will read you something of my own." "Indeed, Mr. Meredith, I cannot comprehend your work." "I will explain my meaning, my dear Mrs. Wood." "You are prodigiously kind, Mr. Meredith, but I would prefer Molière today." After the reading they would have a game of badinage about his novels, he telling her of praise of their merit, like a little boy telling his mother of his prowess, while she bantered, "Oh, my dear Mr. Meredith, your conceit is as wonderful as your genius."

At Wonersh Lodge, her new home at Eltham, Katherine enjoyed peaceful security, spending mornings and afternoons reading to her aunt, writing letters for her, wheeling her back and forth on the grounds or in the great tapestry room of her home. Family morals, of course, had to be beyond reproach. To Aunt Ben the life of her niece was scrupulously "correct"—her husband was away on business in London, but every Sunday he could manage it, he was at Eltham to take his children to Mass.

Willie now turned to promoting the sale of stock in a Spanish sulphur mine. Later, he was given the job of managing the mine at La Mines, Spain, and thus he was out of the country for eighteen months. A banker, Christopher Weguelin, bought an interest in the mine, and he may have arranged to have Willie far removed since there is little doubt that he and Katherine had a love affair in her husband's absence, one of her later letters stating as much.

The sulphur extracted from the mine proved to be of low quality, so the project had to be abandoned. The investors lost all, with the possible exception of Weguelin, who may have gotten what he had bargained for. Willie was now home and broke again. Katherine gave him part of her £3,000 allowance from Aunt Ben, and soon a payment to him £600 a year became regularized, with the tacit understanding that he would not burden her overlong with his presence at Eltham.

III

In 1880 Willie decided to run for a seat in Parliament in the general election of that year. There is a certain irony that a man of forty who had failed at everything decided that he was equipped to run the country, but his case is certainly not unique either in Britain or in the United States. He ran from County Clare, where he had inherited some land. He had no political background and was typical of the candidate to whom we have referred as a Whig or Shoneen, a person—despised by ardent nationalists—with an affectation of social quality or education whose main avenue to a seat was the favor of the local clergy and whose mission when elected might be anticipated to be that of a parasitical place-hunter in the English Government.

Elected with Willie from the two-member constituency was a fabulous character, now almost eighty, the O'Gorman Mahon, who had appropriated the title without the least vestige of right. He stood 6 feet 3 inches tall, his temples festooned with snow-white curls, always wearing a red sash with his breast bedecked with medals. He had been a strong supporter of Daniel O'Connell and had first won a seat in Parliament fifty years before, in 1830, but his main occupation in life had been that of a soldier of fortune, serving under many flags all over the world—in Russia, China, India, Turkey, Uruguay, Chile, Brazil among others—not only holding all military ranks but, not to contemn the sea, being also an admiral in the Chilean Navy. In his worldwide Odyssey he had been an intimate of Czar Alexander, Louis Philippe of France and then Louis Napoleon, Bismarck and the young Crown Prince Wilhelm. He was a conqueror of hearts, too, and had fought for love as well as honor, informing Gladstone on one occasion that he had fought twenty-two serious duels in all of which he was the aggressor.

Parnell became intrigued with this romantic figure, but Mahon was disappointed in Parnell when he failed to live up to his standards. One day in the House, Sir William Harcourt accused Parnell of lying. Afterward the O'Gorman went to the table in the dining room where Parnell and T. P. O'Connor were having tea. "Of course you'll be sending that man your challenge," he said to Parnell, as if a duel were an everyday affair. Parnell smiled and shook his head. The O'Gorman departed, puzzled and chagrined at the decadent mores of the new generation.

Katherine had encouraged Willie in his political ambitions, "for I knew it would give him an occupation he liked and keep us apart." After the election, he brought the O'Gorman to Eltham to meet her, and the three went to Greenwich for a fish dinner. The hours passed in pleasant conversation as the two related how they won by kissing every girl in Clare, drinking with every man—though Willie loathed Irish whiskey—and scrambling from cabin to cabin, heaping praise on the babies and livestock.

Then the O'Gorman said, "Now, Willie, 'twill slip easier into her

THE O'SHEAS   141

ear from you," so Willie roused himself from incipient slumber to explain with some embarrassment, "You see, Katie . . ." The story came out that the O'Gorman had hardly a shilling, which he admitted with the air of a conqueror, and that Willie had guaranteed the election expenses of both, which came to £2,000. It was obvious that Willie had obtained the invaluable assistance of the O'Gorman for his election in return for this contribution. It was now up to Katherine to redeem this promise. She said she would do her best, and she did succeed in obtaining the money from the ever-generous Aunt Ben.

IV

The stage is now set for the fateful meeting of Katherine O'Shea and Charles Stewart Parnell. The account of her life up to this point is based on her autobiography, published in 1914, when she was sixty-eight and Parnell was gone twenty-three years from the earth. It was published under the name of Katherine O'Shea, which raised some eyebrows since she was then Mrs. Charles Stewart Parnell, but the name probably was adopted for commercial reasons, since she was in need of money. Thus far there are no disputes as to the facts, but as we move into her account of the meeting with Parnell, we are immediately in the thickets of doubt and the traps of uncertainty.

O'Shea, having gotten a nonpaying seat in Parliament, was eager to use it as a means of rehabilitating his fortunes. Although he seemed to be a Whig, he had voted for Parnell as leader against William Shaw, though he told Katherine that he feared that Parnell's views were "too advanced." But he apparently decided that it would be the more astute step toward his own advancement. As for Parnell, he took an immediate dislike to O'Shea when he first talked to him and said, "That is exactly the type of man we *don't* want in the party."

O'Shea's great asset was most assuredly not his intellect but his social graces and facility. Frank Hugh O'Donnell, who became acquainted with him as soon as he came to Westminster, recalled him as "likeable, gay, an amusing rattler, a bright talker, an incorrigible diner-out." Alfred Robbins, correspondent of the Birmingham *Post,* described O'Shea as "a spruce, dandified man, filled with belief in himself and disbelief in others. He was the gentleman-like adventurer, cynically contemptuous under the guise of bonhommie, never unknown in social, financial or public life, who makes the world his oyster and is never disappointed in the size of the pearls." This is not quite an accurate description. O'Shea was often disappointed in the pearls, so that, as we shall see, he was a good deal of a "whiner."

To build up his friendships in the business as well as in the political world he asked Katherine, though she was much estranged from him, to come up to London from Eltham and hold some dinner parties at Thomas's Hotel in Berkeley Square to which persons who could do O'Shea some good would be invited. Katherine, bored with her eternal waiting on her octogenarian aunt and herself eager for more social contacts, was happy to do so. Through her own family background, Katherine could reach people in high London society.

Though some leading Irish lights like Justin McCarthy attended her dinners, she was disappointed that the biggest catch, Charles Stewart Parnell, never attended though he had accepted an invitation more than once. Stories were told to her about his general inaccessibility and "how aloof and reserved" he was. She was also told that he was in deteriorating health, though no one could say what was wrong since any inquiry to Parnell about his health was met with freezing hostility. The O'Gorman Mahon said to her, "If you meet Parnell, Mrs. O'Shea, be sure to be good to him. His begging expedition to America has about finished him and I don't believe that he'll last the session out."

She was often twitted about the empty chair at dinner reserved for Parnell, and one night she sat in the chair, saying amid laughter and applause, "I assure you, the Uncrowned King of Ireland shall sit in this chair at the very next dinner that I give."

Being a woman of determination, she hunted him down at Westminster. One sunny afternoon when the House was in session in July, 1880, she drove up with her sister, Mrs. Steele, and sent to Mr. Parnell her card with her written request to see him in the Palace Yard.

He came out, a tall, gaunt figure, thin and deadly pale, looking straight at her intently with his curiously burning eyes, smiling his winsome smile. She immediately thought to herself, "This man is wonderful—and different."

Why had he not replied to her last invitation to dinner? He replied that he had not opened his mail for days (which was quite characteristic of him). But if she would give him another chance, he would undertake to appear at one of her dinners as soon as he returned from Paris, where he was to attend the wedding of his sister, Theodosia. She expressed her pleasure. As she leaned forward in the cab to say good-bye, a rose dropped from her bodice. Parnell picked it up, touched it lightly to his lips and then put it in his buttonhole. The rose, with the date and her name, was found with his private papers on his death, and the rose was put on his heart when he was put in his coffin.

He wrote her on July 17, the next day, and already he seemed infatuated. Meaningfully, he started by saying that "We have all been in such a disturbed condition lately," an obvious reference to the state of his own mind, then talked of the "powerful attractions which have been tending to seduce me from my duty to my country in the direction of Thomas's Hotel." Then confirming his intention to go to Paris the next week he wrote, "on my return [I] will write you again and ask for an opportunity of seeing you."

On his return from Paris he asked her to set the date, and again, on the morning of the dinner, he wrote her confirming that he would be there. The letters give ample testimony that whatever the mysterious chemistry at work, Parnell had fallen in love with Mrs. Katherine O'Shea on first sight.

It was a quiet dinner party attended by Justin McCarthy, her sister, Mrs. Steele, her nephew and a few others. Her husband was absent. The conversation was about small nothings, eschewing the subject of politics. She had engaged a box at the Gaiety Theatre for the party and Parnell was glad to go. There in a dark corner of the box facing the stage and screened from the audience, the two, Katherine and Charles, engaged in their first tête-à-tête. In a low monotone he told her of his American visit and his broken health. "I had a feeling of complete sympathy and companionship with him as though I had always known this strange, unusual man with the thin face and the pinched nostrils."

He poured out to her the story of the lady to whom he had been practically engaged a few years before and said it had been ruptured by her father, who threatened to cut her off if she went to Ireland to live. As for himself, he could not live in America without giving up the Irish cause. On his last trip to America he had looked her up and on the last night he had taken her to a ball. As she left him and walked up the steps she pressed a paper with a verse into his hands.

> Unless you can muse in a crowd all day
>   On the absent face that fixed you
> Unless you can dream that his faith is fast
>   Through behoving and unbehoving
> Unless you can die when the dream is past
>   Oh, never call it love.

He asked Mrs. O'Shea who had written it, and she told him Elizabeth Barrett Browning. He said, "Well, I could not do all that, and so I went home."

Such is the story Mrs. O'Shea tells of the beginning of the conjunction of their love. It is a sweet story, but she had also told in her memoirs how, as a girl, she had shown early adeptness in composing fiction plots, and this story seems to be in large part one of them. It is true that she invited him to a dinner at Thomas's Hotel; it is undoubtedly true that she was anxious to establish a friendship with him in the interest of Willie's career; his notes to her are genuine and show that he was smitten.

As for the rest, Justin McCarthy, in his *Reminiscences,* writes, "I could not help remembering that I was present on the occasion when Parnell and Mrs. O'Shea first met. It was at a luncheon party given in London by a near relative of Mrs. O'Shea and I can well recollect that even at the first meeting of them, I thought that Parnell seemed greatly attracted to her." McCarthy may have erred, but as for the theater episode, later, in 1891, Parnell consented to go to a theater in Dublin (by coincidence also the Gaiety Theatre), and on that occasion commented, "I have not been to a theatre in twenty-five years." As for the tale of the lost love (of which Mrs. O'Shea may have learned either from Parnell or from the book by his brother John), Parnell, according to the testimony of his brother, did not see Miss Woods again after 1871 and certainly had no time to be sparking her on his last trip to America when he was rushing all over the continent with no time for himself. At any rate, she had married a Boston lawyer ten years before. As for the statement he made to Mrs. O'Shea that he did not want to give up the cause of Ireland to marry her, his abortive affair with Miss Woods occurred three years before he entered politics. And as for the touching poem, there is a good deal of independent testimony that Parnell could not remember two lines of poetry.

This one remembrance of things past is not vital to the whole, but it does point up the complications we face in reconstructing the truth in this controversial love affair from conflicting report and recollection. The great contribution that Mrs. O'Shea made with her book was the documentary evidence—and the letters of Parnell that she reproduces show a man in the throes of passionate love from his first meeting with her but (although undoubtedly given encouragement) cautious in giving full rein to it. On September 9, he wrote to her from Dublin, from where he was going on to Avondale for some shooting, "I may tell you in confidence that I don't feel quite so content at the prospect of ten days' absence from London amongst the hills and valleys of Wicklow as I should have done some three months since. The cause is mysterious, but perhaps you will help me to find it or her, on my return." Two days later he wrote to her from Avondale, "I take the opportunity of letting you know that I am in the land of the living, notwithstanding the real difficulty of either living or being, which every moment becomes more evident, in the absence of a certain kind and fair face." He begs her to write to him.

On September 22 he wrote from Dublin, "I cannot keep myself away from you any longer, so shall leave tonight for London." He rushed to England but could not see her because her old nurse Lucy had just died, and she was taken up with funeral arrangements. On September 24 he wrote her, "I am very much troubled at not having seen you, especially as I must return to Ireland tonight—I came on purpose for you and had no other business." On September 29 he wrote, "I am due at Cork on Sunday after which I propose to visit London again and renew my attempt to gain a glimpse of you."

On October 17 he wrote, "My Own Love—You cannot imagine how much you have occupied my thoughts all day and how very greatly the prospect of seeing you again very soon comforts me." On October 22, he sent her from Avondale "one or two poor sprigs of heather which I plucked for you three weeks ago" and conveyed his "hope you will believe that I always think of you as the one dear object whose presence has been a great happiness to me."

By that time they were lovers in the accepted sense of the word.

V

Turning back in time, after the dinner party Mrs. O'Shea made it her business to attend the Wednesday sessions of the House, which were from 12 noon on, Parnell signing for her admission to the Gallery. He would leave when he could, and they would meet with no attempt at concealment. They would drive many miles in a hansom cab into the country, to the river at Mortlake and elsewhere, sitting there in the summer afternoon watching the gay traffic on the river, sitting there in talk or "in the silence of true friendship." She was finding out that silence was Parnell's most conspicuous attribute in social intercourse, but far from finding it a barrier between them, it was "dangerous in the complete sympathy it evoked between us." As far as Parnell was concerned (he liked convivial companions like James J. O'Kelly), her ceaseless flow of conversation undoubtedly fascinated him. (When his brother John met her soon after Charles' death, his first impression was "It must have been her brilliant conversation that first attracted poor Charlie.")

From her account, it is clear that at the start, whatever her attraction to Parnell, she pursued the materialistic aim which had motivated their meeting in the first place: the advancement of Willie's career. She made him promise that he would see to it that Willie kept his seat in County Clare—though an election was remote in time.

The first suspicion among his colleagues that there was a new factor in Parnell's life appears in a letter of Healy in early August. Healy had urged Parnell to some obstruction on a certain bill to draw public attention to the subject. To his brother Maurice, Healy wrote, "I certainly thought that he would keep on fighting a few nights, but he absolutely discouraged anything approaching obstruction. There must be a lady in the case or else he would not be in such a hurry to leave the House as he has been two or three times this week."

Healy did not know then the identity of the lady in question. According to Justin McCarthy, at the time there was a ripple of talk among Irish members about Parnell's interest in Mrs. O'Shea, but it soon died down and disappeared. They were seen coming

down from his rooms at the Cannon Street Hotel. They had had
tea in his sitting room; then he had accompanied her downstairs
to a cab, passing some members whose presence he ignored (as he
always did, she found out). In the evening they were seen dining
together at Thomas's Hotel.

An attachment to a woman on the part of the bachelor leader
might have been expected to whip up some comment, particularly
since he seemed to have been previously something of a misogynist,
but outward circumstances deceived everybody into believing that
this was no more than a transient and platonic friendship. For one
thing, the circumstances hardly augured any permanent relationship, since the lady was very much *in vinculo matrimonii*, apparently happily married to a Catholic and the mother of three young
children.

A second and stronger reason was that Mrs. O'Shea did not sug-
gest an inamorata of Parnell. The handsome, dashing leader might
well play the part of Paris, but Mrs. O'Shea did not fit well the role
of the fair Helen. At the very best, Katherine could warrant the
tepid compliment of being "handsome" or "striking." Below medium
height, she was rather plump or "fubsy." Her features were heavy,
her face was rather large and so were her mouth and nose. Her
hair, which she had always worn long, at this time was cut short
with bangs reaching almost down to her eyes. On the plus side,
photographs do not reveal that her hair was thick and chestnut-
brown, and the contrast with her snow-white skin was quite striking.

It was her bubbling personality, full of life and merriment, that
set her apart in every group. She was not to be long exposed to
public view, since she would soon slip behind a curtain for the
rest of Parnell's days. Thus, there are only a few impressions of
her. One person recalled that despite her years (she was thirty-four
at the time), she reminded him of a high-spirited, romping school-
girl. The journalist Frank Harris claimed he met them both at a
dinner given by Justin McCarthy and noted that Parnell devoured
her with his flaming eyes. "At the time she seemed to me a sonsy
[buxom] nice-looking woman with pretty face and fine eyes, very
vivacious, very talkative, full of good-humored laughter . . . evidently a lively, clever woman and excellent company."

Frank Hugh O'Donnell had more than a passing acquaintance
with her. He found her the familiar type of female whom many
males find painful. He was struck by "her clever conversation,

while a little bored by her persistent questioning. She wanted to know everything about everybody. She seemed to know everybody but there was an infinitude of things, apparently, which she wanted to know more thoroughly. Her intellectuality was slightly aggressive and I felt that I could tire of it."

We have stated two reasons why suspicions were lulled about a love affair between Mrs. Katherine O'Shea and Parnell. There was a third and most important reason: Captain O'Shea was not only fully aware of the friendship between his wife and Parnell but positively beamed on it. In fact, he often made a threesome. And now we are in the heart of the conundrum.

VI

At this point some background is necessary to illuminate the problem. When Captain O'Shea sued for a divorce on the grounds of adultery in 1889, Mrs. O'Shea entered a plea of condonation and connivance on the part of her husband. When the case came before the court in November, 1890, the defense was not pressed, and the divorce was granted on the adultery charge. Following the death of Parnell a few months after they were married in June, 1891, Mrs. Parnell spoke at some length to one Henry Harrison, a youthful member of Parliament who was a devoted follower of Parnell. He had helped her with the funeral arrangements and also with her business affairs, entangled because the will of Aunt Ben, leaving her property to her niece, was being disputed. The former Mrs. O'Shea insisted to Harrison that Captain O'Shea had been a party to her adultery with Parnell from the very beginning, abetting it for his personal advantage, and had used her as a pawn in his own game.

In 1914, Mrs. O'Shea's account of her life with Parnell was published, and the charge of connivance was absent—on the contrary, the inference was plain that she and Parnell had deceived Captain O'Shea over the course of years. In 1931, Henry Harrison published a book *Parnell Vindicated,* the thesis of which was that there *had* been actual connivance on the part of Captain O'Shea from the start and that Parnell's honor as a gentleman had not been soiled. (The adultery was, of course, conceded by Harrison, so that we have his peculiar concept of morality, on the same footing as a claim that a man is "vindicated" of murder if the victim invites him to aim at him and pull the trigger.)

How then did Harrison deal with the contradictory tenor of Mrs. O'Shea's book? He chose to put credence in what Mrs. Parnell told him in 1891 and 1892 of her love life—despite the fact that at the time she was infuriated about Captain O'Shea's part in bringing Parnell to his early death, was also embroiled in litigation with him over her inheritance and was spewing out her hatred Medea-like. As for her 1914 account, he attributes it to the malign influence of her son Gerard, who was the son of Captain O'Shea. The introduction to her book contains a letter written by Gerard to the London *Times* protesting the assertion of William O'Brien that if the truth were known "The Irish leader would have been shown to be rather the victim than a destroyer of a happy home." It was Harrison's contention that Gerard O'Shea collaborated with his mother in her book in order to redeem his father's honor and to prove that his father did not cooperate in a project to have his wife engage in harlotry for his benefit. He claimed that Mrs. Parnell was too infirm in her old age to resist her son's influence. (She was sixty-eight at the time her book was published; Harrison was sixty-six when his book was published.)

This thesis of Harrison seems to have won acceptance, largely due to the clear proof supplied by Harrison that O'Shea lied at his divorce trial when he swore that he had never been aware, until his discovery of the liaison in 1886, that Parnell was ever at his home in his absence. The Harrison thesis is not accepted by this writer. A study of the evidence and an assessment of the psychological motivations of the principals is truly labyrinthine, but to assume Captain O'Shea's knowledge of the illicit relationship is to fly in the face of clear documentary evidence, as we shall see, most especially the letters of Captain O'Shea. The analysis by Mr. Harrison seems to be a Procrustean treatment in that it trims and adjusts much of the evidence to his argument while omitting a good part of the contrary evidence. The only sound conclusion that can be drawn from the evidence is that Parnell fell so pathetically and helplessly in love with Mrs. O'Shea that he had to accept her love on whatever terms were possible—and they were on ignoble and degrading terms.

VII

In her talks with Harrison in 1891, Mrs. Parnell told him that when she met Parnell her sex life with Captain O'Shea was long since dead and that she would have regarded any attempt on her husband's part to resurrect it with the utmost repugnance. She claimed that O'Shea knew from the very start that she was having sexual relations with Parnell, though no one mentioned it explicitly. "He actually encouraged me at times. I remember especially one particular occasion very early in the affair when he wanted to get Parnell's assent to something or another, he said 'Take him back with you to Eltham and make him happy and comfortable for the night and just get him to agree.' And I knew what he wanted." (In relating this she must have been aware that if Captain O'Shea had made casually such a suggestion for prostitution, it argued badly for her past character as known to O'Shea.)

If O'Shea did so encourage it, it is strange that Parnell and Mrs. O'Shea (as it appears from Parnell's letters) did not become intimate until at least October although they had met in July and thereafter had been constantly in each other's company.

The situation described by Frank Hugh O'Donnell, who knew all three in the triangle at that time (1880–1881), sounds quite plausible. O'Donnell admitted that he was completely deceived by what he was sure was a quite innocent friendship. Parnell, he says, had no social relations with the members of the party whom he regarded with aristocratic contempt as "bootblacks" and also had no capacity for self-enjoyment, such as reading. Captain O'Shea cultivated him, and it was a relief from his loneliness to listen to Captain O'Shea's gay chatter. O'Shea professed to be sorry for "poor old Parnell" and encouraged his wife to keep Parnell company. To O'Donnell, the friendship between Mrs. O'Shea and the Irish leader appeared to be only "the noble reciprocity of souls." Moreover, O'Shea was concerned about Parnell's poor health and was glad that "Poor old Parnell can have some peace and quiet at my home in Eltham," and so it was at his invitation that the homeless Parnell stayed at his home. Confirming this, T. P. O'Connor says that at this time, although Captain O'Shea sat on the opposite side of the House with Shaw, when he and Parnell got together, they had the warm relationship of brothers.

To invite two adults of the opposite sex to closet themselves in a suburban home was opening the door to Venus. But though Captain O'Shea was fatuous and in his sleazy desire to ingratiate himself with Parnell was willfully blind, can it be said that he deliberately invited adultery? O'Donnell, certainly as cynical and worldly wise as O'Shea, was deceived. There are any number of reasons why O'Shea might have thought that his wife and Parnell would not take advantage of the convenience he offered them to make love (aside from the bare possibiilty that Parnell might be a man of honor). One reason was that Parnell was a sick man; another, Mrs. O'Shea told him that Parnell had confided to her that he was secretly married; and another, his wife might be expected to be restrained by the presence of her three children.

Parnell came to Eltham for intermittent rests during the summer of 1880, and in the autumn, for a longer period during which Katherine nursed him to health. She stated that he came at Willie's insistence. "When the visit was first proposed I said my house was too shabby, the children would worry so nervous a man, and we had better not break the routine of our life." But in the end "Parnell came, having in his gentle, insistent way urged his invitation."

It was not long before the nurse was in bed with the invalid. "I had fought against our love; but Parnell would not fight and I was alone. I had urged my children and his work, but he answered me 'For good or ill I am your husband, your lover, your children, your all. And I will give my life to Ireland, but to you I give my love, whether it be your heaven or your hell. It is destiny.' "

(This quote is hard to accept as coming from Parnell. James Joyce wrote in his notes, "He was tongue-tied and she was English." He might have added that she had read many English romances.)

A man ill and nervously exhausted, without home, starved for affection, grasped at an opportunity for love presented in the person of a woman who was by no means a beauty and was much-married though neglected by her legal spouse, a woman overflowing with life, tenderness and love. When she nursed him to health and strength, the bonds became even stronger and the dependence greater, as often happens in the patient-nurse relationship.

It was not long before she realized that her patient was a *rara avis.* Suffering from a sore throat, he conceived the idea that her indoor garden was responsible for it since "plants are such damp things." To please him she had it removed. Then he got the notion that the green in the carpet was responsible for his sore throat. So to please him she had a bit cut out and sent it to London for a chemical analysis, which reported that it was absolutely harmless. He carried a fixation for all his days that green was inimical to him, which was certainly peculiar for the leader of Ireland.

One may inquire what Parnell's attractions were to her? He was moody and his silences would disconcert many women. An inhibited personality, he lacked the conversational arts and graces to please a woman. No doubt his need and love for her brought a corresponding response, and she might have found his sweetness and gentleness of manner, as others did, irresistible. She was frank, moreover, in admitting that it pleased her to be at the center of the solar system of a man who was great and famous. She relates that during that autumn she took him for a long drive through the hop-growing district of Kent. After driving by Chislehurst common and around by the lovely Crays, they came right into a crowd of Irish "hoppers" —men, women and children, the poorest of the Irish, who had been imported for the hop picking—who were popular with the English farmers because, inured to privation, they did not grumble, as the English pickers did, about the scandalously inefficient accomodations given them. Parnell was recognized and there was a wild surge toward the carriage with cries of "The Chief, The Chief"; they crowded up, trying to kiss Parnell's hands. He lifted his cap gravely and said he was not well enough to make the smallest of speeches and would see them in Ireland, bade them to "mind the little ones" who were scrambling around the horses' legs and drove off amid cheers of "God keep your honours."

His love for her became ever stronger. On November 11 he wrote her from Dublin, "It is quite impossible to tell you just how very much you have changed my life, what a small interest I take in what is going on about me and how I detest everything which has happened during the last few days to keep me away from you—I think of you always and you must never believe that there is to be any 'fading.' "

Thus Parnell declared that he regarded his political life and mission now as secondary and even an obstacle to his passion for Katherine O'Shea.

Charles Stewart Parnell in 1881, having cut off his beard to conceal his identity in his liaison with Mrs O'Shea. Frank Harris wrote of him: "To my astonishment he was by far the handsomest man I had ever seen in the House of Commons—magnificently good-looking."

Two anti-English influences in Parnell's life: his sister Fanny,
and his American mother, the daughter of an Admiral of
the U.S. Navy. From a photograph taken in 1875.

Timothy Healy, at first a zealous supporter of Parnell, turned against him in the end. He later became first Governor-General of the Irish Free State.

Joseph Biggar, M.P., who launched the programme of "obstruction". He was only five feet tall, and was slightly hunchbacked. When he first rose to speak in the Commons, Disraeli turned to the Irish Solicitor-General and asked, "Is that what in your country is called a leprechaun?"

Joe Brady, who wielded the dagger which killed Lord Frederick Cavendish and Thomas Henry Burke in Phoenix Park. Photograph taken in Kilmainham jail in March, 1883.

James Carey, the "Informer". He bought his freedom by sending five comrades to the gallows, but was shot to death soon after by an avenger. Photograph taken in Kilmainham jail, 1883.

The only photograph of Parnell on horseback.

Charles Stewart Parnell in 1880, at the time when he fell in
love with Mrs O'Shea.

Captain O'Shea in his Hussars
uniform.

Katherine O'Shea.

Parnell photographed in 1885 in a study which Mrs. O'Shea
had built for him as an addition to her home in Eltham.

VIII

The year 1881, as we have seen, was a most hectic one in Ireland, with the activity of the Land League and the Land War, and it was equally hectic in Parliament. Parnell, who maintained his political duties at a feverish pace and at the same time was conducting a passionate if surreptitious love affair, displayed superhuman energy. He had recovered his strength and, though he was no longer in need of a nurse, was living off and on in Eltham with Mrs. O'Shea.

We have told of the meeting of the party leaders in Paris when Parnell appeared a week late and his mail was opened before his arrival. The time corresponds to an account given by Mrs. O'Shea. Parnell came down to Eltham at 3 A.M. and told her that she must hide him, since he feared arrest. She concealed him in a little boudoir dressing room off her own room, where meals were brought by the servants who thought they were for Mrs. O'Shea. While his colleagues in Paris were pacing the floors worrying that he was in the Tower or the Thames, Parnell spent his time writing speeches for future use and rereading a favorite book, *Alice's Adventures in Wonderland*, which he would read from cover to cover without a smile, always remarking that it was a "curious book."

A week later, in the terribly cold wintry weather of February, he left for Paris and asked Katherine to accompany him en route. To throw off the "pursuers" from the quarry he would take a roundabout route. In early morning they drove off unobserved to Lewisham, then went by train to New Cross, then by cab to London Bridge. From Vauxhall they went by train to Lowestoft, since Parnell planned to go to Paris via Harwich. But after a good meal at Lowestoft, Parnell was so "cheered up" that he decided to return to London, and the next day he went to Paris by the usual route, completely forgetting about his "pursuers" of the day before! Mrs. O'Shea was learning to expect the unpredictable from her lover.

This incident is even more bizarre than Mrs. O'Shea saw it. At that time there was no intimation that Parnell or his colleagues feared his arrest. Then, too, the Coercion Act did not become law until March 2, when it received the royal assent; moreover, under its provisions Parnell was safe from arrest on English soil. So, unless

L

he was suffering from a delusion (and being pursued is a familiar fantasy of madness), this was all some playacting on Parnell's part for his perverse delight. It was also an act of irresponsibility to his party and his waiting colleagues. It was no wonder that, as Healy related, Parnell did not want to be questioned when he arrived.

Soon the couple engaged in illicit romance were embroiled with the husband. Captain O'Shea had come down to Eltham suddenly with a peeve. He usually gave advance notice of his visits, but in this case he was infuriated because he thought that his wife was having him shadowed at his London apartment, where, no doubt, he had female guests. He went to a room where Parnell slept, found his portmanteau, sent it to London and in anger stalked off declaring that he would challenge Parnell to a duel and kill him. Parnell, when he heard about this, was unflustered and wrote Mrs. O'Shea, "Will you kindly ask Captain O'Shea where he left my luggage? I inquired at both parcel office, cloak room [of House of Commons], and this hotel at Charing Cross today and they were not to be found."

On July 13, O'Shea sent a note to Parnell through the O'Gorman Mahon as his second. "Sir: Will you be so kind as to be in Lille or in any other town in the north of France which may suit your convenience on Saturday next the 16th? . . ." On July 14 Parnell replied with an acceptance saying, "Your surmise that I refuse to go abroad is not a correct one." To Mrs. O'Shea he wrote, "He has just sent me a very insulting letter, and I shall be obliged to send a friend to him if I do not have a satisfactory reply to a second note I have just sent him."

Katherine's sister Mrs. Anna Steele stepped in and made peace. At the divorce trial, Captain O'Shea swore that assurances were given him that there was nothing untoward in the relationship between the couple and there would not be anything in the future reproachable in their conduct, and that Parnell would not visit Eltham in O'Shea's absence. Mrs. O'Shea claimed that O'Shea was considerably intimidated by Parnell's nonchalant acceptance of the idea of the duel and that it was O'Shea and not Parnell who backed off.

Parnell advised O'Shea through Mrs. Steele that he needed Katherine as a medium of communication with the Government, and he hoped that O'Shea would not object after the duel (when presumably O'Shea would not be around anyway to make an objection) if he continued to use her in that capacity. In one way or another, O'Shea was satisfied or put off, and as Mrs. O'Shea put it, the lovers now went on with their love affair "without further scruple, without fear and without remorse."

Now, what of Harrison's thesis that Captain O'Shea was a *mari complaisant* in view of this duel episode? Harrison accepts as true a statement made to him by Mrs. Parnell that the Captain was quite willing that she have an *amourette* with Parnell but that his vanity was outraged when he found that she had been appropriated and engrossed by Parnell. In other words, he asks us to believe that Captain O'Shea was quite willing and eager that Parnell use his wife repeatedly, but wanted to kill him when he found that Parnell was using her overlong. Is this credible?

There is another incident during 1881 which is interesting because it was the first occasion when the complication of Parnell's love life obtruded into his appearance in the political arena. In the late summer Katherine went to Brighton with her children for a vacation. While walking across the Brighton Station she was accosted by a tall man with a rough face-stubble who said to her, "Don't you know me?" She said she did not, but then recognized her lover.

Parnell explained that he had learned that she was on the way to Brighton and had slipped on the train at Clapham Junction. In order not to be recognized at Brighton, he had clipped off his beard on the train with a pocket scissors. From the Brighton station he went to a hotel. His beard looked so unkempt that he pulled a white muffler high around his chin. The manager of the hotel, when he signed in, feared that he had an infectious illness, which "Mr. Stewart," as he called himself, dispelled by complaining in a loud voice about being kept waiting in the draft with his "raging toothache."

Mrs. O'Shea persuaded him to shave his beard. Soon afterward he had himself photographed without his beard and with a ring she had given him; he presented her a photo after they had a quarrel, to remind her that he always wore her ring. (This is the photograph of the beardless Parnell which is reproduced in this book.) The consequence of this incident was that when he went to Ireland for Land League business and speaking engagements, no one recognized him. Everybody was baffled about the change. He gave no explanation, and it was marked down as another Parnell eccentricity.

IX

On October 13 of that year, as we have narrated, Parnell was lodged in Kilmainham jail, a fate for which he had prepared Katherine for some time. After his Wexford speech, Parnell showed a curious inertia, remaining in Ireland although he was fully aware of the danger of arrest. Besides the complications of his political life, it is quite possible that the inertia was due to his perplexity about the crisis in his personal life, the arrival within a few months of his child by a woman married to another.

At any rate, it is evident that Parnell's mind was now occupied with Katherine O'Shea, perhaps more than with Ireland. On the day after his imprisonment he wrote to "My Own Dearest Wifie" saying, "My only fear is about my darling Queenie. I have been racked with torture all day, last night and yesterday, lest the shock may have hurt you or our child. Oh darling, write or wire me as soon as you get this that you are well and will try not to be unhappy until you see your husband again. I have your beautiful face with me here; it is such a comfort. I kiss it every morning.— Your King"

In regard to these intimate letters it is certainly safe to say that with his towering pride Parnell would have given anything to prevent them from being published. They were a great jolt to Parnell admirers when they appeared. They do not exude the spirit of patriotism. There is no loftiness of thought, inspiration or dedication. On the contrary, his mind and heart were with his Katherine. That he managed his love life so badly and his political life so astutely is undoubtedly due to the fact that he was involved emotionally with the cause of his love, but, on the other hand, could think coldly with emotional detachment about the cause of his country. Disappointing, too, is their general intellectual content. They are full of simpering puerilities more worthy of an adolescent or an uneducated commoner than the exalted leader of the nation. However, it has been known that great minds have lapsed into baby talk when talking to women, viz. Swift's letters to Stella.

Now that he was behind bars, Parnell's disposition was to swing to the radical side. The day he entered Kilmainham a message was smuggled out from him and printed in the *Freeman's Journal*: "I will take it as evidence that the people did not do their duty if I am speedily released," which, of course, was a call to violence. In their common lodgings the leaders were able to talk freely and meet together, and they decided that they would now issue the order that had been so long discussed and urged by Davitt but for months delayed, largely by Parnell's influence: the No Rent Manifesto.

William O'Brien related that when he joined the others in jail, he was greeted by Parnell, "O'Brien, of all men in the world, you are the one we wanted most," and he was given the job of writing the Manifesto. He did this with the stump of a pencil on the back of a pink telegram, which then was smuggled out. The Manifesto was signed by Charles S. Parnell, President, Kilmainham jail; A. J. Kettle, Honorary Secretary, Kilmainham jail; Michael Davitt, Portland Prison and so on. The consensus of thought among the imprisoned leaders was that on the crest of the widespread indignation generated by the arrests it was best to launch this attempt to bring down the institution of landlordism. "Landlordism is already staggering under the blows which you have dealt it amid the applause of the world. One more crowning struggle for your land, your homes, your lives, one more heroic effort to destroy landlordism at the very source and fount of its existence and the system which was and is the curse of your race and your existence will have disappeared forever."

According to O'Brien, Parnell was definitely in favor of the issuance of the Manifesto. With his superior insight, he may have seen that it would be a failure but that this gesture to his radical supporters would strengthen his hand later, when he moved to a moderate course. The Manifesto was a complete failure. Dr. Croke, the Archbishop of Cashel, a sympathizer with the Land League, condemned it, saying that it "struck at the foundations on which society rests." The tenants ignored it in a startling rebuff to Parnell and the Land League. When Parnell was asked by a fellow inmate how the Manifesto was going, he replied wryly that it was a great success, that his tenants at Avondale were no longer paying him their rents—and, indeed, he never again collected rents of any significant amount from his tenants, and, of course, he could not evict them. This became a complicating factor in his finances.

Two days after the Manifesto was issued, Forster used it as an excuse to put down the Land League, suppressing it and all its chapters. The League died. Then the Land Courts were opened. In the opening ceremonies the Registrar announced, "The Land League is open for business," and all Ireland roared with laughter at the slip of the tongue. But the courts did open under good auspices for the success of the Land Act, since they had a full dossier of applications for rent deductions. The tenants were ignoring Parnell's advice to hang back pending decisions on test cases. When the Court granted rent reductions of 25 per cent on the first applications, the number of cases on the docket mounted. Gladstone had won in his determination that the Act was to be fairly tested.

The suppression of the Land League was not a calamity as Parnell saw it since, as he expressed it in a postscript to a letter to Mrs. O'Shea, "Politically it is a fortunate thing for me that I have been arrested as the movement is breaking up fast, and all will be quiet in a few months when I am released." A letter of February 14 to her would have been quite a disillusionment to his followers, who had faith in his fervent and idealistic leadership of the land movement. "At least I am glad that the days of platform speeches have gone by and are not likely to return. I cannot describe to you the disgust I always felt with those meetings, knowing as I did how hollow and wanting in solidity anything connected with the movement was. When I was arrested I did not think the movement would have survived a month, but this wretched Government has such a fashion of doing things by halves that it has managed to keep things going in several of the counties up till now."

The only extenuation for this truly astonishing statement was that Parnell by now had been in prison four months and was nervously exhausted. At the outset he had expected his imprisonment to be brief. In his first letter to Mrs. O'Shea he said that he expected to be home by Christmas, but as time passed his letters showed progressively more depression about his hopes for release. However, prison life was not by any means the nightmare that Parnell had expected, was nothing like the tortures Davitt had endured. The political prisoners kept their own clothes (it appears that Parnell even kept his gun on his person), ate and talked together, played handball and chess. The prison itself looked less like a prison than an apartment house; after one passed through the gloomy portals, there was a glass roof and rooms strung out along three stories. Parnell had two sunny rooms facing south. He could have gas and wood fires at night if he wanted his room warm. The prisoners wrangled with the Government about food, but after the complaints it was improved so that it was certainly adequate. The prisoners could get their fare from the outside, but as a gesture to their followers they ate only the prison food so that all their money, including the allowance given prisoners, could go to the cause. In a letter of January, Parnell wrote to Mrs. O'Shea that he had chops or grilled turkey or eggs and bacon for breakfast, soup and chops for lunch, and joint and vegetables—and sometimes oysters—for dinner.

His fellow prisoners tried to make things as pleasant as possible for Parnell. One man who had been there nine months appointed himself his butler and and served him a soda and lemon in the morning before serving him breakfast, concocted a coffee out of berries which he roasted and ground himself and brewed him a steaming tumbler of hot whiskey before the prisoners were separated at night. His companions were amused by his superstitions. A lady sent him a superb eiderdown quilt which she had made herself, a gift worthy of a king, but since it was covered with *green* satin, Parnell threw it away. One day O'Brien got a letter from one of his editors on *United Ireland* who had two children sick with scarlet fever. Parnell went into a transport of excited fear. "For God's sakes, O'Brien, quick, throw that letter into the fire. Buckshot is not going to get rid of us cheaply as that."

Whatever the comforts of this prison life, it took its toll on Parnell's delicate constitution. Frank Hugh O'Donnell visiting him in January was amazed to find him so wan and weary, leaden-eyed and hollow-cheeked. To O'Donnell he complained petulantly, "I am pestered about every fiddle-faddle and everybody who comes here must see me. Give me Piccadilly for quiet." The diet was rough for one who had been living sybaritically with Mrs. O'Shea's comforts, and he suffered from indigestion and diarrhea. What was hardest for him was the prison regime—he had been accustomed to staying up most nights and going to bed at dawn, but now he was locked up alone for the night at 6 P.M. He then had to settle himself in loneliness to read or write for hours. If the prisoners were in the infirmary they could talk together until 8 P.M., so Dr. J. E. Kenny, an ardent supporter and friend who attended Parnell, obliged him by certifying imaginary complaints, usually heart trouble, which enabled Parnell to spend a couple of hours more a day with his comrades.

Though physically separated, the leadership kept in close touch with each other. Biggar fled to Paris, where he became involved with one Fanny Hyland and was later sued by her for breach of promise. During the trial Biggar claimed that the lady's story that he proposed marriage was impossible since there was an "impediment," which on questioning from the bench he explained were two natural children whose mothers were still living. The "Biggar impediment" became a favorite joke of Parnell and his colleagues.

Healy remained in England for a time, where he was immune to the sanctions of the Coercion Law and the warrant for his arrest. He later went to America, where he had an interesting and successful money-raising expedition, dividing up the circuit with T. P. O'Connor. He relates that, at the time, Gilbert and Sullivan were so popular in the United States—even more so than in England— that signs in hotel rooms read, "Don't put out your boots and don't whistle *Pinafore*." He tells a deliciously humorous story that occurred in the South. He was crossing the Mississippi with two former Confederate brigadiers. From the poop he looked down into the hold and saw many Negroes emigrating from Louisiana huddled together with their household goods. The sight filled Healy with great sadness, since it reminded him of Irish evictions. One of his companions, removing his cigar, drawled, "Isn't that a sad spectacle, Brigadier?" The other answered, "It is indeed." Healy thought to himself, "Ah, my sadness is shared by these kind souls," but then the second one added, "Yes, to think that only twenty years ago that lot would have fetched twenty thousand dollars!"

By devious routes, those in Kilmainham heard occasionally from Davitt, who was to spend fifteen months at Portland Prison. He was treated with none of the brutality of his former imprisonment. While writing *Leaves from a Prison Diary*, he was allowed to keep a blackbird, who became a real companion, perching beside him in bed every morning to wake him up, fetching and carrying articles for him, sharing his porridge and trying with his beak to peck off the marks Davitt made on his blackboard.

With an abundance of time for contemplation and planning, the leadership discussed the subject of what new directions the movement should take. There was flaming resentment in Ireland about the imprisonments on which to build further gains. The Irish vote was potent, as shown in England in a by-election at Stafford. O'Donnell had taken up the vice-presidency of the British Home Rule Confederation and had organized a campaign to defeat the Liberal candidate, whose defeat by a small margin was attributed to the Irish vote. There was now a new doggerel for the old Irish rebel air:

> How could we leave Parnell?
> Says the Shan Van Vocht
> How could we leave Parnell?
> Says the Shan Van Vocht
> How could we leave Parnell
> Who fought for us so well
> And stayed eviction fell
> Says the Shan Van Vocht
>
> Don't lose a single vote,
> Says the Shan Van Vocht
> Don't lose a single vote,
> Says the Shan Van Vocht
> At Freedom's battle-note
> Spring at the tyrant's throat
> And smite as Stafford smote,
> Says the Shan Van Vocht

Now that the Land League was defunct by Government decree and its leaders in jail or exile, the leadership decided to finance a new organization, the Ladies' Land League, to which the League treasurer in Paris would send £3,000 a month. Unlikely as it seemed at the time, this new organization would be so effective that it would finish off "Buckshot" Forster.

The President of the Ladies' Land League was Anna Parnell. This sister of Charles, bony faced and not as comely as the other Parnell girls, had the steel-like resolve of a Lady Macbeth. As an illustration of her courage, in 1883, when Lord Spencer was Viceroy, she rushed into the street, stopped his fast-moving carriage by pulling the reins of the horses and proceeded to give him a tongue-lashing. Her corps of followers were as militant and inspired as she.

The English Government found that the Ladies' Land League carried out the League policies more ruthlessly than the men had done. They erected huts for the evicted and otherwise took care of them, as well as the dependents of any who were imprisoned. If a locality had a "grabbed" farm, it would receive no money from the ladies, the residents being held responsible collectively for letting it happen. Moreover, if a district had had no outrages, the ladies often would refuse a request for funds, since "no trace of manly opposition can be detected in your county."

Forster found himself helpless in fighting the ladies. The Government used a statute of Edward III which was aimed at prostitutes to arrest a few respectable ladies as vagrants, which raised popular feeling to a high pitch. Far from being a deterrent, the threat of arrest produced a flood of ladies eager to be martyrs. A rumor that the headquarters of the League was to be raided brought forty ladies running there. An example of the women's spirit was related by T. P. O'Connor. While in America, he heard that his sister had been imprisoned, and he was much upset. When he returned he rushed to visit her. "I found her quite collected and not in the least miserable; her main theme was the almost cowardly grief, as it appeared to her, with which her townspeople had followed her arrest and progress to gaol."

X

It is evident from his letters to her that Parnell's thoughts were not on the Ladies' Land League or the great cause as much as on his Katherine. Corresponding with her was a difficult project since his letters had to evade two sets of eyes. First, he could not let the correspondence be known to his warders, of course, since that would give the English a powerful club over him; and second, it had to escape the eyes of Captain O'Shea, who might be at Eltham when the mail came. One device was to send out by a friend who visited him letters addressed to a "Mrs. Carpenter" at a London address, where Mrs. O'Shea could pick them up. A more frequently used subterfuge was to mail her a formal letter addressed to "Mrs. O'Shea," asking her to mail an enclosed letter to an important personage. The letter inside would always be for her, addressing her as "Darling Queenie" or "Darling Wifie." Later, they used a formula for invisible ink, so that their communications could be written without detection between the lines of an ordinary letter.

Parnell chafed and writhed at his imprisonment while his mistress was carrying his child, a separation not made easier by the querulous complaints of his beloved that "You are surely killing me and my child." He tried to arrange a visit by her as "Mrs. Bligh," a friend, but then abandoned it fearing that she might be

recognized. On December 14 he wrote to calm her "Rather than
that my beautiful Queenie should run any risk, I will resign my
seat, leave politics and go away somewhere with my own Queenie,
as soon as she wishes." Considered apart from the emotional pressure he felt, it puts his concern for Katherine O'Shea above the
holy cause of his country. On December 16, apparently in answer
to her plea that he make a deal with the Government and be released, he wrote, "I could not very well make any arrangement or
enter into any undertaking with the Government unless I retired
altogether from politics."

The torment of Mrs. O'Shea during her pregnancy and after the
birth of the child was increased by the fact that her husband, Captain O'Shea, was hovering over her with all kinds of attentions as
the proud and thoughtful father-to-be. The amazing deception she
had perpetrated is described in her memoirs: "Willie became more
solicitous for my health and wished to come to Eltham more frequently than I would allow. He thought February [the month of
the birth] would seal our reconciliation, whereas I knew it would
cement the cold hatred I felt toward him and consummate the love
I bore my child's father."

Apparently, when she learned that she was pregnant, she arranged
to have intercourse with her husband, a device that has been used
by wives from time immemorial. She and Parnell could not have
been sure that Parnell was the real father unless she had been sure
of her pregnancy before she had given herself to her husband. By
the same token, if Willie were sure that he was the father, he must
have felt assured that Parnell had not touched her. Parnell was
obviously cognizant of the situation, since on January 7 he wrote
her, "London would be best if you could get him away on any
pretext; but if you could not, Brighton would leave you most free
from him." On January 11, he wrote her, "I do trust you have
been now relieved for a time by his departure and that you are
getting a little sleep. It is enough to have killed you several times
over, my own Queenie."

Henry Harrison, maintaining his thesis that Captain O'Shea was
the accommodating husband, has no choice but to call her statement
a lie, since it is so gross, "so flagrant a defilement of Parnell's love-
story, so odious a dishonour of her own womanhood"—this description applying to relations with her own legal husband. In whatever
way Harrison chooses to characterize it, the tenor of the letters

between the guilty pair and their secrecy in correspondence demonstrate that Mrs. O'Shea "pulled it off," though she found the maintenance of the deception in Willie's presence an unbearable agony.

Parnell himself considered their love so sacred that their "marriage" was real (she was always "wifie" and he was her "husband"). What could have been his reaction when he learned of the deception of Willie—or did he plan it with her? In her book she refers to a patched-up quarrel late that summer, after which he presented her with the photograph we have referred to. Could that quarrel have occurred after the revelation? One can imagine her explanation to him. "What else could I do? If it were known that I bore a child to you, it would be all over with us. Your public career would be smashed, and my hopes of inheriting Aunt Ben's fortune would be over. She would never leave her fortune to an adulteress. What I did was only an emergency expedient and will not have to happen again. Is our love profaned by something that was purely a mechanical, physical act without love, etc., etc."

The child was born on February 16, 1882, and the next day Parnell received the news and wrote her, ". . . your poor husband burst into tears and could not hold up his head or think of anything until my darling's note arrived that everything was bright." The little girl was strong and healthy for the first few weeks but then started to fade away. In her memoirs she wrote, "Willie was very good; I told him my baby was dying and I must be left alone. He had no suspicion of the truth and only stipulated that the child should be baptized at once—urged thereto, I think by his mother and sister. I had no objection to this. Parnell and I had long before agreed that it would be safer to have the child christened as a Catholic. . . . [Thus she implicates Parnell in the deception.] I made an altar of flowers in my drawing room, as the child was much too ill to be taken to church, and there the priest, Father Hart, came and baptized Sophie Claude."

XI

By the spring of 1882, the English Government had come to the conviction that the hard-fisted policy of coercion toward Ireland was a failure, insofar as obtaining internal peace there. The London *Times* said editorially on March 25, "The Irishman has played his

cards well and is making a golden harvest. He has beaten a legion
of landlords and outflanked the largest of British armies in getting
what he thinks his due. As the sufferers in a material sense are
chiefly of British extraction, we cannot help a little soreness. Yet
reason compels us to admit that the Irish have dared and done
as they have never done before."

Gladstone had progressively become more distrustful of the judgment of Forster, and this feeling was widely shared by the Cabinet.
On one occasion in the Commons the Irish members brought up
the case of Dr. Kenny, whom Forster had removed from the Dublin
Medical Board. Gladstone turned to Forster in surprise on the
Government bench and asked, "Is that really so?" Forster had
interpreted the suspension of habeas corpus to mean that he had a
free hand in any kind of punitive action.

During Parnell's imprisonment, when the Irish members who
had previously spurned the Land Act introduced amendments to
it at the opening of Parliament, the possibility appeared to Gladstone that Parnell might be in the mood for an accommodation, a
modus vivendi. In a later account, Maurice Healy told how he had
conferred about the bill with Parnell in Kilmainham. They had
been working over the bill together for an hour when suddenly
Parnell dropped the paper on the floor as if he had been stung.
"What's wrong?" asked Healy. Parnell replied in a hushed voice.
"It has thirteen clauses. It will never do." Then there was a gleam
in Parnell's eye. "Add that silly clause you were talking about a
while ago." And so an amendment was added which later proved
to be of great value.

The Land Court, contrary to pessimistic predictions, was making
sharp reductions in rents. With the load of cases before it, no careful investigations were made, but, as it was put, decisions were made
by the "rule of funk." As one subcommissioner said, "I go out and
smell the land after breakfast and sneeze out my decision after
lunch." As the landlords saw that they were going to realize less
in rents, they put more pressure on their tenants to collect arrears,
and this was becoming the primary cause for evictions. Frank Hugh
O'Donnell wrote a series of letters to the *Times* about the problem
and the *Times* agreed editorially, "The arrears question is in reality
the core of the Irish question." O'Donnell then proposed to Herbert
Gladstone, the son of the prime minister, that Parnell be released
as an act of pacification and that his release be linked to new legis-

lation to help tenants who were in rent arrears; and Parnell, in turn, would work for peace.

Conciliation was in the wind when Parnell was released on parole on April 10 after six months of imprisonment to attend the funeral in Paris of his nephew Henry, the only child of his sister, Delia, who had died suddenly at the age of twenty-one. Parnell, on arrival in England, went immediately to Eltham, where Katherine put his dying child in his arms. She overwhelmed him with her tears and her entreaties to somehow end his imprisonment and return to her.

Back in London Parnell saw O'Shea and asked him to play the role of go-between with the British Government. Mrs. O'Shea wrote, "He wished to conciliate Willie as much as possible and believed that his politics might now prove useful." No doubt, at Eltham, Mrs. O'Shea pointed out to Parnell that the only way to keep her husband manageable in their open friendship was to cater to his vanity and give him an important responsibility. After the duel episode, Parnell continued to occupy an ambiguous position in the household, as far as Captain O'Shea was concerned. He was "the man who came to dinner," one whom O'Shea had invited to his home to regain his health but who had now dug out a niche for himself. The only pretext he had given was that he needed Mrs. O'Shea as an intermediary. During his imprisonment he had used her to mail letters to important personages, which were of course letters to herself. Now Parnell saw an opportunity to put this pretext on a solid footing by giving the Captain a chance to be an intermediary. O'Shea might play the part very effectively, too. He was an Irish member who was not a Nationalist, and he had good social ties with the Liberals. As one with a curvilinear view of the world, he was a master at intrigue and back-stairs dealing and thus might well perform the responsibility, perhaps better than anyone else.

On April 13, O'Shea wrote to Gladstone, implying that he had been deputized to work out an accord. One passage in the letter shows O'Shea, building up his self-importance, to be an egregious fool: "The person to whom Parnell addresses himself in many cases (much as I differ with him in serious matters of politics and policy) is myself. Eighteen months ago Mr. Parnell used every effort to induce me to take over the leadership of the Party." O'Shea was a fool to express as a fact what was obviously absurd. To anyone believing that Parnell had ever said anything of the kind to O'Shea, it would be proof that Parnell took him for a perfect dunce.

On April 15, O'Shea wrote to Joseph Chamberlain, the president of the Board of Trade, enclosing a copy of his letter to Gladstone and stating, "As you appear to be a minister without political pedantry, I enclose a copy of my letter to Gladstone. I ask you how the Liberal party is to get in at the next election and the one after that and so on, without the Irish vote."

When Gladstone received O'Shea's letter, he sent it on to Forster with a note saying that "very much depends on the personality of the correspondent." Forster replied that O'Shea was "a clever fellow but vain and untrustworthy." There were two avenues now open for negotiation with Parnell, through O'Donnell or through O'Shea. The Cabinet decided that negotiations should be pursued by Chamberlain through O'Shea but if Chamberlain were unsuccessful, his efforts would be officially disavowed as those of an individual not acting in behalf of the Government. And thus was born the link between Chamberlain and O'Shea which was to be a fateful one for both of them and for Parnell.

Joseph Chamberlain was to leave his mark on this period and on a later generation, since he was the father of Sir Austen Chamberlain and of "Peace in our time" Neville Chamberlain. He was not born into the aristocracy but was of the middle class. After a university education, he went into the screw-manufacturing business and was such an astute businessman that he retired before he was forty with a fortune of £100,000. He became a reform mayor of Birmingham in 1873 and proclaimed, "By God's help, the town will not know itself"—and he was true to his word. He municipalized the gas and water systems and saw to it that the water was pure; he conducted a vast program of slum clearance and a fight for better sanitation which resulted in cutting the death rate in some areas by half.

In 1876, he entered Parliament at the comparatively mature age of forty, but despite his age and the fact that he did not belong socially to the Establishment, recognition was rapid. He was a Radical Liberal, his program being "Free church, free land, free schools, free labour." He allied himself with Sir Charles Dilke, an aristocrat who was also radically inclined to the point that he publicly attacked the subsidies to the Crown, particularly the dowries lavished on the Queen's daughters. He became also a close friend of John Morley, editor of the *Pall Mall Gazette,* a rising intellectual. By 1880, the Radical Liberal faction was so strong that Gladstone had to put Chamberlain in the Cabinet, much as he disliked him personally, and Dilke had a place as undersecretary for foreign affairs, for which Dilke was well prepared, since he had been previously an ardent globe-trotter.

Obviously, Chamberlain had great gifts. He was extremely ambitious—"Pushful Joe" he was called. He was sharp, thorough and tenacious in argument, and also deadly in riposte. He once set Disraeli back on his heels when he said in the House that Disraeli never told the truth except by accident. T. P. O'Connor wrote of him, "He has a violent temper, a masterful will, a shallow judgment, a changeful purpose. Believing himself always right, he forces men to adopt his opinion or quarrels with them."

Chamberlain and Dilke were both friends of the Irish Nationalist movement. As early as 1874, when he ran unsuccessfully from Sheffield, Chamberlain had advocated Home Rule for Ireland. He had been opposed to coercion but had gone along with the Coercion Law in 1881 because he thought that Irish outrages were alienating the English workman. Now Chamberlain believed that Forster had made a mess of things and that it was imperative that a fresh course be adopted.

In answer now to the letter from O'Shea, Chamberlain answered guardedly, with a threat of pogroms unless the Irish modified their policy, ". . . the leaders of the Irish party must pay more attention to public opinion in England and Scotland. Since the present Government has been in office they have not had the slightest assistance in that direction. On the contrary, some of the Irish members have acted as if their object was to embitter and prejudice the British nation. The result is that nothing would be easier at the moment than to get up in every large town an anti-Irish agitation almost as formidable as the anti-Jewish agitation in Russia."

The problem, as Chamberlain described it, was to work out a suitable *quid pro quo* for Parnell's release. On April 19, Parnell returned from Paris, and on the night of the 21st, he and Captain O'Shea sat together in the dining room at Wornersh Lodge, working out the treaty. Mrs. O'Shea wrote, "Willie wanted me to join them but I would not leave my baby, and when the daylight came and they went to lie down for a few hours' rest before Parnell left for Ireland, my little one died as my lover stole in to kiss us both and say good-bye."

It would take a masterful dramatist to depict this bizarre scene of mixed tragedy and satire. Two men worked together through the night but both with their mind on the little life being extinguished, the one grieving under the delusion that he was the father, the other grieving over his first-born, knowing that he was in fact the father, but being forced to conceal his grief and indeed to pay condolences to the other. "Oh, what a tangled web we weave, when first we practice to deceive."

The treaty they drafted provided that the Government do something to make a satisfactory settlement on the arrears question and that leaseholders be permitted to share in the benefits of the Land Act. In return, the Irish leaders would withdraw the No Rent Manifesto and "we should also then be in a better position than we ever occupied before to make our exertions effective in putting a stop to the outrages which are unhappily of late so prevalent."

O'Shea left Eltham early the next day, summoned by a wire from Sir William Harcourt, who wanted to discuss the pact. Apparently, Parnell had become suspicious or unhappy about O'Shea as an intermediary, because he wired to Justin McCarthy that morning from Eltham that he would like to see him in London in the afternoon. When Parnell came up, he gave McCarthy a copy of the agreement to give to Chamberlain. Refusing the proffered *douceur* of an extension of the parole, Parnell was back in Kilmainham jail by April 24, and from there he wrote a letter to McCarthy to go to Chamberlain with the agreement. McCarthy did the errand and Chamberlain accepted it from him without comment.

O'Shea felt that he had to have more to show to the Cabinet than the terms of the agreement. He told his wife that Parnell was too "shifty" to carry out any agreement unless his signature was attached to it, so he would go to Kilmainham and get a letter from him covering the terms. Parnell tried to stop him, writing him that "If you come to Ireland, I think you had best not see me," but O'Shea came over on April 28 and Parnell wrote Katherine, "He came over to see me and so I thought it best to give him a letter as he would have been dreadfully mortified if he had nothing to show."

M

The letter from Parnell to O'Shea started out by saying, "I was very sorry that you had left Albert Mansions before I reached London from Eltham," since he wished to tell O'Shea that he had decided to give McCarthy a copy of the agreement. The letter hit the highspots of the agreement and concluded that a settlement of the Irish problem "would I feel sure enable us to cooperate cordially for the future with the Liberal party in forwarding Liberal principles"—a most indiscreet statement, since it might be construed as an agreement on Parnell's part that as part of the price for his release he had agreed that his Irish Nationalists would be the tail on the Liberal Party kite for the future, while the independence of the party in the past, as he had often said, had been its main strength and hope.

XII

Parnell's fears about O'Shea's capacity as an intermediary were fully justified. When O'Shea returned to London, he did not deliver the agreement and the letter to Chamberlain, who had deputized him to act on the Government's behalf, but delivered them instead to Chamberlain's enemy, Forster. He also reported to Forster the conversation he had had with Parnell and quoted Parnell as saying that "the conspiracy which has been used to get up boycotting and outrages will be used now to put them down." This damning admission by Parnell that he had been guilty of organizing crimes in the past was one which he was too astute to have made.

Forster passed the documents on to Gladstone with a disparaging, even scoffing, remark. On the other hand, Gladstone was pleased. To Forster he wrote that he was "at a loss to gather your meaning when you say 'The result of the meeting is less than I expected.'" As for the last paragraph, he said with delight over this apparent offer of support for the Liberals, "This is a hors d'oeuvre which we had no right to expect and I rather think have at present no right to accept. I cannot help feeling indebted to O'Shea."

The next decision was that of the Cabinet as to accepting the terms. Gladstone prepared the Queen for the shock by telling her that there was a shift of sentiment in the country against arbitrary imprisonment and then pointing out that the Government had won against the No Rent Manifesto. Her only reaction was to send a wire to Harcourt which said, "Is it possible that Mr. Davitt, known as one of the most treasonable agitators, is to be released? I cannot believe it."

In the Cabinet discussions, Lord Cowper, making the strongest case against acceptance, said, "We, apparently despairing of restoring order ourselves, let them out on condition that they will help us and that they will refrain in the future, not from the conduct for which they were imprisoned, but only from the more outrageous policy to which they afterward committed themselves, and even then they are willing to do so only in return for fresh legislation in favor of the tenants." Forster said that Parnell should be released only if he made a public declaration of penitence. This was obviously impractical, since such an abject declaration would cost Parnell his standing among his countrymen and would make it impossible for him to use his prestige to promote peace in Ireland. Forster could not obtain the support of a single member of the Cabinet. This large Yorkshireman, with his tousled red hair and the forelock reaching down to his eyes, the extravagant dress with pockets in his suit large enough to hold a baby, seemed wilder than ever to his colleagues, who were convinced that the ordeal he had endured had broken his nerve and now his judgment.

Accepting Forster's resignation, which accompanied that of Lord Cowper, Gladstone wrote to him, "I have received your letter with much grief, but in this it would be useless to expatiate. I have no choice. Followed or not followed, I must go on."

On May 2, Gladstone announced in the House that Lord Cowper and Forster had resigned and that the main figures in Kilmainham —Parnell, Dillon, O'Kelly and O'Brien—would be released. (Sexton had been released after a few weeks of imprisonment because of his health.) He said that the House would consider the Arrears Bill and that there was no present intention to renew the Coercion Law. Then, in a triumph of casuistry or hypocrisy, he announced, "It is an act done without any negotiation, promise or engagement whatever."

When Parnell was released, he caught a cattle train to Rathdrum. A follower of his who accompanied him on the trip home to Avondale told how, when he came to his home, all the servants were lined up, weeping copiously while they greeted him. Parnell acted as casually as if he had been away for only a day or so. The reunion with his sister Emily was equally emotional. She was seated in the drawing room and did not even rise to greet him.

EMILY: Ah, Charlie, is that you?
CHARLES: Yes, Emily.
EMILY: I thought they would never let you out.
CHARLES: Why, what did you think they would do to me?
EMILY: I thought they would hang you.
CHARLES [with a smile]: Well, it may come to that yet.

Two days later, on the 4th, the deposed Foster was defending his conduct in office and attacking Parnell, "The real reason why these gentlemen were arrested was that they were trying to carry out their will, their 'unwritten law,' by working the ruin and injury of the Queen's subjects by intimidation of one kind or another. A surrender is bad enough, but a compromise or arrangement is worse. I think that we may remember what a Tudor King said to a great Irishman in former times, 'If all Ireland cannot govern the Earl of Kildare, then let the Earl of Kildare govern Ireland.' . . . in like manner if all England cannot govern the honourable member from Cork, then let us acknowledge that he is the greatest power in Ireland today."

At that moment cheers rang from the Irish benches as Parnell, cool and debonair as always, entered the House and walked toward his seat. It was his supreme moment of triumph as he gazed frigidly at the man who had imprisoned him for six months and who had paid the price for it by being removed from office and utterly discredited.

Gladstone, answering Forster, said that he, Gladstone, had no right to extract from Parnell a penitential confession of guilt and denied that there had been a deal. Parnell buttressed this argument when he said that in no communication had there been any mention of any kind of his release. Technically that was correct.

Listening to the debate was the new Irish Secretary succeeding Forster. Chamberlain had expected to be offered the post but instead, to his chagrin, Gladstone had given the post to another. The new Secretary was Lord Frederick Cavendish, a brother of the leading Whig in the Liberal Party, Lord Hartington. But there were more than political reasons for the appointment. He was the husband of the favorite niece of Mrs. Gladstone. He had served as private secretary to Gladstone in former years and the Prime Minister loved him as a son. Cavendish would serve under the new Viceroy, Lord Spencer, who unlike Lord Cowper would have Cabinet rank. Cavendish was held in high esteem, and there were eulogies for him on all sides. Thus Harcourt said, "All that I can say of him is that I think he is too good for the job."

XIII

On May 5, Michael Davitt, in Portland Prison, received a letter from Parnell written in an unusually formal manner. Addressing him as "Dear Sir," it said, "Dillon and I propose to meet you at Portland Prison tomorrow on your liberation and to accompany you back to London."

The following day the gates swung open. On the train back to London Parnell was in a black mood, cursing the lawless state of Ireland, and his true bent to moderation—if not conservatism— was displayed without any attempt at concealment. Davitt recalled, "He spoke of anarchy as if he were a British minister bringing in a coercion bill." He directed his invective against the Ladies' Land League, particularly criticizing it for its extravagance, although Davitt suspected that this was merely a pretense. Trying to calm him, Davitt said that his sister, Anna, had at least kept the ball rolling, to which Parnell replied, "I don't want to keep the ball rolling anymore."

Changing the subject, Parnell said that the Government might bring in a land purchase scheme and even a plan for Home Rule, and then, in a characteristic sudden switch in mood, he became jocular. He started to allot posts in the Irish Government among the four of them (O'Kelly was in the party) and declared that Davitt was best qualified by experience for the post of minister of prisons.

Parnell was probably gruff to Davitt because in framing the Kilmainham Treaty he was leading the party to a new course of moderation and the relinquishment of violence in favor of constitutional action, and he was not certain that all would follow him, or what resistance he might encounter. Aside from conferring with Justin McCarthy, he had acted alone. William O'Brien said that the only intimation he had had while in Kilmainham about the Treaty was that one day, in reference to the well-known story of a peasant who had obtained release from jail on conditions of good behavior, Parnell joked to him, "Don't pitch into me too hard, O'Brien, if like Mickey Calligy, I sign conditions and go out."

Parnell sincerely believed that in the settlement he had done well for the country and for the cause. Was it a defeat to win the promise of relief to those in arrears, more inclusive land legislation and the end of coercion? While the Radicals had misgivings, probably the majority in Ireland agreed. Michael O'Hara, in his book about the period, wrote, "He secured concessions of the greatest value which had all the appearances and much of the substance of a complete and sweeping victory. The Nationalists of the country were thrown into a state of exultant jubilation." T. P. O'Connor wrote that Parnell had "beaten all the mighty resources from soldiers to gaol of the Government and he stood supreme, more unchallenged than ever in his control of the Irish people."

Mrs. O'Shea stated frankly that her importunities were the most important factor in bringing about the accord. She says that he was uneasy about the reaction of the radical faction, especially in America, from whence the money flowed. After all, he told her, the Coercion Act would have expired in a few months and it would be said that if he had waited, no pledges at all would have been necessary, since renewal of coercion was improbable. Yes, he feared the Radicals. "I hold them now with my back to the wall, but if I turn to the Government, I turn my back to them, and then what?"

While Parnell, on the ride to London with Davitt and Dillon, was pondering the implications of the new state of affairs on his future, at the same hour in the late afternoon of this day, May 6, a deed of dreadful note was taking place in Dublin which would throw all previous calculations out of joint.

XIV

Lord Frederick Cavendish, on the night of May 5, rushed to catch the mail train for Ireland from Euston Station. He was late by a few minutes, but so was the train, and he congratulated him-

self on his success in catching the train which would enable him
to attend, on the morrow, the investiture ceremonies of Lord
Spencer as Lord Lieutenant at Dublin Castle. Little did he know
that he had been successful in establishing his rendezvous with
Death.

In Dublin, a secret group of terrorists, the Invincibles, had been
formed committed to the belief that only the extinction of the
prominent enemies of Ireland in the English Government would
solve the woes of their country. One of its members bore a name
which was destined to live forever in infamy in Ireland. He was
James Carey, a bricklayer turned building contractor, who was
known in Dublin for his piety and good works. He was a town
councillor and had been mentioned for lord mayor. James Carey
had been a Fenian since his teens and had been treasurer of the
Irish Republican Brotherhood. Now he was a leading member of
the Invincibles.

The Invincibles had marked Forster for liquidation but, although there were nineteen tentative sallies against him, he survived. Once, two assassins had tracked him in Phoenix Park, but when
they saw him walking with his lovely daughter they lost heart. Forster himself was aware of the plots against his life but shrugged
them off. "I am convinced that I am not destined to die that way."
The day before Forster left Ireland for good, the assassins decided
to kill him on the train leaving Westland Row at 6:45 P.M., which
they had learned he was scheduled to board. However, during the
late afternoon Forster accepted an invitation to dine at the Royal
St. George Yacht Club at Kingstown and so left instead on the 5:45
P.M. train. An hour later the assassins ransacked the train in vain.

Now "Number One" gave the order for the murder of Thomas
Henry Burke, the permanent Under Secretary, who was so important in the administration that he was considered the "real" Dublin Castle. In the eyes of the Irish, since he was one of them, he
was a traitor. On May 5 the assassins searched the streets vainly
for him.

The people of Dublin were in a gay, relaxed mood, celebrating
the new turn of events. On the night of the 5th a torchlight procession hailed the release of Parnell and Davitt and the ouster of
the hated Forster. The following day, there was a cordial greeting
to the procession and cavalcade honoring the new Viceroy and the

new Irish Secretary. An English paper received a dispatch from its Dublin correspondent saying, "No Viceroy in recent years has been received with greater cordiality."

In the afternoon of the 6th, nine of the Invincibles assembled in Phoenix Park, having been informed that Burke would walk through the park late in the afternoon. High on a footpath near the main road and directly opposite the Viceregal Lodge, the main body of murderers assembled. Two men, Carey and Smith, a gardener employed in the Lodge who knew Burke by sight, sat in a jaunting car as lookouts.

Lord Spencer left Dublin Castle first and asked Lord Cavendish to join him, but the latter said that he would join him in the Viceregal Lodge later. Lord Spencer drove through the Park, stopping for a time to look at a polo match in progress. Cavendish followed later in a hackney outside car. He dismissed it at the gates of the Park, preferring to walk, tempted by the sylvan beauty of the Park. It was a fine spring afternoon, a Saturday, and in the fading sunlight the Park was filled with ballplayers, bicyclists, picknickers and spectators for the polo match. Burke drove up to the gates and proposed to dismiss the two armed detectives who usually guarded him and walk through the Park. But on being told that Lord Cavendish was walking ahead, he drove up to meet him, then dismissed the car and the detectives, and commenced walking through the Park arm in arm with Lord Cavendish.

Burke was spotted by Smith and Carey, and they drove up to the main gang, composed of Brady, Kelly, Fagan, Caffrey and Curley. "Mind, the man in the grey suit," said Carey. Burke's companion was unknown to them. Then Carey and Smith walked to the Island Street Bridge. It was 7:17 P.M.

The band of men approached the two unsuspecting men walking casually along, engaged in pleasant conversation. There were three men in the first row, then two rows of two men each. An outside car came along and the group opened ranks to allow it to pass through, and Cavendish and Burke passed by them too. Then the band swiftly wheeled around. The men were equipped with surgical knives used for amputations which a woman, Mrs. Frank Byrne, is believed to have bought in London and carried to Dublin in her petticoats. Joe Brady, a young stonemason of herculean build, stooped down as if to tie a shoelace and then leaped up at Burke, grasping him around the body with his right arm (he

was left-handed) and, after turning him around, stabbed him again
and again in the neck. Lord Cavendish started to beat Brady with
an umbrella he was carrying. After he had dispatched Burke,
Brady turned on Cavendish with the cry "Ah, you villain" and
felled him with a terrific stab in the breast. While the two men
lay dying, the youngest member of the gang, twenty-one-year-old
Tim Kelly, cut their throats. The men then mounted a sidecar
and drove from the park, not knowing the identity of the second
man they had killed.

The total time consumed was three minutes, but it was to set
the cause of Ireland back many years. While the assassins were
engaged in their bloody work, two cyclists drove through them
but were so absorbed with the many stones on the road that they
ignored the melee, though one recalled the cry "Ah, you villain."
To distant onlookers it looked like one of the many scuffles,
friendly and unfriendly, that took place with the release of animal
spirits after a week's work. A hundred and fifty yards away a
police officer was exercising his horse but noted nothing.

Then someone stopped and screamed.

A few minutes later, Lord Spencer, reading his paper at the
Viceregal Lodge, heard the shriek from a man who had jumped
over the palings and run up to the Lodge, "Mr. Burke and Lord
Cavendish are killed." The news reached officialdom in London
that night at a reception at the Austrian Embassy. Gladstone and
his wife heard the news as the they were returning to Downing
Street from the reception, and they went immediately to the side
of their niece, Lady Cavendish. "Uncle William, his face like a
prophet's in its look of faith and strength, came up and almost
took me in his arms and his first words were 'Father, forgive them
for they know not what they do.' Then he said to me, 'Be assured
it will not be in vain.' "

XV

Davitt was awakened at 5 A.M. in his room at the Westminster
Palace Hotel by his friend Henry George, who was in England
to see about the publication there of an edition of his book
Progress and Poverty. George gave him a message about the ghastly
deed. A short time later Parnell who had stayed overnight at the

hotel, entered his room badly shaken and in a state of deep shock, saying over and over again, "How can I go on if I am stabbed in the back this way?" Healy, Biggar, John Barry and Arthur O'Connor joined them. Even the cocky Healy had lost his equilibrium; feeling that the cause of Irish freedom was now lost for at least a generation, he proposed that all Irish M.P.'s resign en masse.

The group decided that a manifesto should be drawn up disavowing and condemning the murders. Parnell edited Healy's rough copy, according to the latter doing a fine job. "Without training, Parnell had a severe and just literary taste," and he eliminated some of the more purple emotional passages. In part the manifesto read, "We feel that no act that has been perpetrated in our country in the exciting struggle of the last fifty years has so stained Ireland as the cowardly and unprovoked assassination of a friendly stranger, and that until the murderers of Cavendish and Burke are brought to justice that stain will sully our country's name."

Feeling that the policy of pacification which he had pledged had been stultified by the act, Parnell went to O'Shea's home and asked him to convey to Gladstone a message that he, Parnell, was willing to resign—an offer that Gladstone appreciated as a gesture of *bona fides* but declined. Joined by Justin McCarthy, Parnell called on Sir Charles Dilke and then on Joseph Chamberlain, who were friends of the Irish cause, to see how much could be salvaged from the wreckage. Dilke said that in spite of the murders he was determined to continue to be a Home Ruler *quand même*. Dilke was surprised to see that Parnell was far from the man of steel of their past acquaintance. "I never saw a man so cut up in my life. He was pale, careworn, utterly unstrung."

Chamberlain, like Dilke, was reassuring that in time the Irish cause would not be unduly prejudiced. While they were in Chamberlain's home, O'Shea joined them. Chamberlain took McCarthy aside and suggested to him that in view of the ugly public mood that it might be unwise to let Parnell walk the streets. McCarthy said that he suggested this to Parnell when they went outside and Parnell brushed it aside. "He said rather sharply that he had done no wrong to anyone and that he intended to walk in the open streets like anyone else." While walking along, a man on top of a bus shouted, "There's Parnell," but aside from that there was no notice given to him.

Parnell's decision to call in O'Shea that day was to cause him some grief in a later year. Captain O'Shea did something unusual that afternoon. He went to the Home Minister, Sir William Harcourt, and applied for police protection for himself and for Parnell, for himself at his flat and for Parnell at Eltham. O'Shea had the idea that he was in danger (a belief probably shared by no one else) since it was known that he had been instrumental in Parnell's release. Granting the request, Harcourt said that "he was glad that Parnell was now suffering himself some of the tortures he had inflicted on others during the past two years."

This application for police protection became a controversial point some years later, as we shall see, when the crucial question arose as to whether Parnell was terrified that day about the danger to himself, not from the English but from the Irish irreconcilables who regarded the Kilmainham Treaty as an act of treachery, and who might therefore take Parnell's life as they had taken Cavendish's and Burke's. Parnell denied that this application for protection had been made with his knowledge, much less at his request. O'Shea's story that the request had been made by Parnell when they were together in a cab conflicts with McCarthy's account that Parnell, leaving Chamberlain's home, insisted on walking. Of course, the fears for Parnell's safety that were expressed by Chamberlain were fears about retaliation from the London population, not from the Irish terrorists.

There is another controversial aspect to the day's events. Henry Harrison, as a major point in his brief that Captain O'Shea was aware that his wife was living in sin with Parnell, cites this application for protection for Parnell at Eltham while O'Shea himself was to be protected in London. He adds this to what he regards as the incriminating opening of Parnell's letter to O'Shea written April 28 in Kilmainham jail—"I was very sorry that you had left Albert Mansions before I reached London from Eltham"—which proves that O'Shea knew Parnell was with his wife in his absence.

It is indisputable that O'Shea knew that Parnell was with his wife when he was not there, but knowledge of illicit love is another matter. The request to Harcourt and the opening sentence of the Parnell letter, on the contrary, tend to disprove guilty knowledge and condonation. Does a cuckolded husband want to advertise his cuckoldry? If cuckolded, would he not want to keep it from public notice rather than flaunt it? If willing to have it exposed to others, was it not because he felt it harmless and thought others would feel the same way?

To cap the events of May 7, Mrs. O'Shea recounts that she wired Willie to bring Parnell to dinner at Eltham that night. So Willie came with the invited guest, her lover, who had spent previous nights with her, but who greeted her now as if it was the first time he had seen her since he had gotten out of prison.

XVI

In Dublin an intensive police manhunt for the murderers began immediately. The only clue at the start was black-edged cards found in the boxes of Dublin newspapers the next day saying, "The deed was done by the Irish Invincibles." The following day, in answer to the Parnell manifesto, a manifesto of the Invincibles was delivered to the newspapers. "As to the monster Burke he has preyed upon the liberties and lives of his countrymen for many years and has deserved death a thousand times at our hands. And as to Lord Cavendish—his very name stinks in the nostrils of the Irish people by the inquisitions of his brother, Lord Hartington, and the wholesale evictions of his father the Duke of Devonshire, driving thousands of the rightful owners of the soil to the poorhouse, exile and death."

The Government offered a reward of £10,000 for the murderers and even a £1,000 reward for helpful hearsay information. Although there were very many in on the secret (Carey had even spoken to several people in the Park while waiting for Burke), there were no takers. Since a cab had been used by the assassins, jarveys by the hundreds were questioned without success.

In Parliament on May 8 all members wore black and many wore crepe in their hats. Gladstone announced sadly, "I find it difficult to say the word, yet Sir, I must say that one of the very noblest hearts has ceased to beat." Then he added that "as to the future Government of the country [Ireland] all previous arrangements must be reconsidered and to some extent recast." This foreshadowed that, far from being abandoned, coercion would now be stiffer than ever. Parnell spoke briefly of his grief and that of his party, "I want to state my conviction that this crime has been committed by men who absolutely detest the cause with which I have been arrested and who have devised this crime and carried it out as the deadliest blow" to the cause. This evoked groans from many Liberal and Tory members.

Contrary to dire predictions, the English people behaved with great forbearance to the Irish people in their midst. Lady Cavendish set an example of high-mindedness when she wrote to Lord Spencer that she was ready to give up her husband "if his death were to work good to his fellowman which indeed was the whole object of his life." Some of the newspapers were a bit nasty, the *Evening Standard* publishing an editorial demanding that Davitt give up the murderers. Davitt himself was most perplexed about the identity of the culprits. Knives hitherto had never been used by the Irish, and Davitt speculated to friends that the deed might have been done by anarchists from the Continent who were trying to get into the Irish struggle.

XVII

The issue of the negotiations leading to Parnell's release did not die. At the opening of the May 15 session, Gladstone was asked if he would produce the letter which led to the release of the Irish prisoners, and Parnell volunteered to read it. He then read the text of the April 28 Kilmainham letter, handed to him by Captain O'Shea, to whom it had been addressed.

The letter he read omitted the compromising last paragraph which expressed the hope that the program "would I feel sure enable us to cooperate cordially for the future with the Liberal Party in forwarding Liberal principles." Immediately, Forster, aching for revenge, leaped at Parnell. "May I be allowed to ask the hon. member for the City of Cork, did he read the whole of the letter?" Parnell replied, "I did not keep a copy of the letter. My hon. friend the member for Clare [O'Shea] has furnished me with a copy of it. It may be possible that one paragraph has been omitted." O'Shea said he would explain later, since he had no further copy. Forster, gloating, thrust a copy he held into O'Shea's hands. Amid cries of "Read, Read," O'Shea was forced to read the whole of the letter.

"That fool will make a mess of everything," Parnell muttered to his colleagues on the bench. He had put Parnell in a most suspicious light, that of a trickster, by giving him a truncated copy of the letter. In addition, Parnell discovered for the first time that his letter designed for only Chamberlain to see had been put by O'Shea into the hands of his enemy Forster.

Worse was to follow. At 12:45 A.M., O'Shea rose to explain his part in the negotiations. With his usual pompous vanity he started by saying that until Parnell was released on parole he had had no communication with him since he saw him in Dublin three days before his arrest, when "I gave him admirable advice to which I must do him the justice to say the hon. member did not pay the slightest attention," and thus he landed in prison.

O'Shea's explanation made it clear that a bargain had been struck. A young Conservative member, the future Prime Minister Arthur Balfour, made a slashing attack on the Liberal Government for making this pact with terrorists. "I do not believe that any such transaction can be quoted from the annals of our political or Parliamentary history. It stands alone. I do not wish to use strong language but I am going to say it stands alone in its infamy." Gladstone replied to Balfour that no bargain had been made. It was said of Gladstone that he could always find two meanings in a simple statement while the rest of the world could find only one. In this case, by the most abstruse reasoning, Gladstone found that no treaty had been made. His main point was that Parnell had not been told he would be released, *ergo,* there was no bargain. Besides, he had been imprisoned under the Coercion Act on suspicion, and since his new attitude of cooperation had lifted the cloud of suspicion, there were no longer any grounds for holding him.

The long debate that night was resumed as soon as the next session started with an official Conservative assault on the Government led by Sir Stafford Northcote. Irish members Healy, John O'Connor Power and O'Donnell tried vainly to deflect the attention of the House to the pending business, the Arrears Act. Then Forster launched another telling attack on Parnell, made possible by O'Shea's bungling of his mission. He read from a memorandum he had written immediately after O'Shea had returned from Kilmainham with Parnell's letter and related his conversation with Parnell, quoting Parnell as saying that "the conspiracy that has been used to get up the outrages and boycotting will be used to put them down." He also read another amazing quote that O'Shea attributed to Parnell, "There will be a union with the Liberal Party."

Joseph Chamberlain then rose to defend Parnell, at the same time taking a jab at O'Shea, who had by-passed him in favor of Forster when he had returned from Kilmainham with the Parnell letter. As for the missing paragraph, he had heard O'Shea, "when he was giving me a copy of the letter, say that there had been one sentence which might give rise to misapprehension and which he would wish to withdraw." Chamberlain said that he had paid no attention to it at the time. Regarding the statement that the force that raised the conspiracy would be used to put it down, Chamberlain said, "That any man in his senses, let alone a clever man like the hon. member of the city of Cork [Parnell], should make an incriminating confession like that seems so absurd that I confess that even when it came as a report of a conversation with the hon. member from Cork, I arrived at the conclusion that these might have been the words of the hon. member for Clare himself, in which case it would have been a matter of small importance." Here there was a burst of laughter at O'Shea's expense. Chamberlain went on, "The hon. member for Clare although a personal friend of the hon. member for the city of Cork is no follower of his. He is, on the contrary, his political opponent."

The results of O'Shea's mishandling were most damaging not only to Gladstone but to Parnell personally. To many English members, and even to some Irish, it appeared that in reading a clipped copy of the letter, Parnell had been a party to an attempted deception of the House and perhaps of the Irish themselves. To advanced Nationalists it appeared that Parnell had paid a high price for his release, and in New York soon afterward, Patrick Ford was calling for Parnell's resignation and for replacing him with Davitt as leader. To those in the Irish party hierarchy who knew of the affair with Katherine O'Shea, it appeared that in these all-important negotiations Parnell had used a thoroughly unreliable person as a favor to his mistress.

XVIII

The new coercion bill, introduced May 11, was more severe than Parnell had expected. The harshest provision allowed the right of trial by jury to be suspended in grave cases of agrarian crimes at the discretion of the Government; trial by three judges would be substituted, and even in cases of jury trial the venue could be shifted to England. Magistrates could convict summarily on charges of boycotting, incitement and membership in secret societies. The police could search private homes and establish night curfews. Ratepayers of a district had to pay for injuries to a person occurring in their district and also for the cost of the extra police sent into their district.

Parnell conducted a remorseless fight against the bill, using the weapons of obstruction to the fullest extent possible. Twenty-four sessions of the House were taken up in the committee stage, the Irish members fighting the bill sentence by sentence and sometimes word by word. On the single clause putting a levy on the taxpayers of a district for outrages committed there, Parnell kept the House in continuous session for thirty hours. On July 1 the Deputy Speaker, Mr. Playfair, suspended eighteen Irish Nationalists, including Parnell, and most of the leaders, though some had been absent from the House for days. It was an unreasonable measure, put down to the desire of an old, weak man wanting to appear strong. The House then adopted a Closure Bill to block further discussion, and the bill was passed by the House on July 11, becoming law within a week. It would be administered by the new Irish Secretary, Sir George Trevelyan, son of the Charles Trevelyan who had administered relief to Ireland during the Great Famine.

While the bill was being debated and Parnell was using every device at his command to soften it, he tried to establish a private link of communication with Gladstone. He could not hope to be able to communicate directly with Gladstone, since in the eyes of the English he was "steeped to the lips in treason." He could not let the Irish know he was in communication, because he was under considerable suspicion for what was alleged to be his capitulation in the Kilmainham Treaty.

Parnell hit on the idea of using Mrs. O'Shea as an intermediary. At the time he was challenged to the duel by Captain O'Shea he had made this suggestion flippantly. He had used the Captain in the Kilmainham negotiations. Now, in spite of the disastrous experience, he would use the wife. She was an intelligent woman of the highest social standing as an Englishwoman, and his "Queenie" was a most imperious person who would have no difficulty talking on equal terms to the prime minister of the greatest empire the world had ever seen. At the same time, he would be able to rationalize his relationship with her by formalizing further the excuse he gave the Captain for seeing his wife. It all fitted admirably together, and thus Parnell's Aspasia became now his Egeria.

On May 23, Gladstone replied to a letter from Mrs. O'Shea introducing herself as a niece of Lord Hatherley and suggesting that he see Parnell. Gladstone's declination was couched in most diplomatic terms, that he wanted "carefully to avoid any act or word that could injure his [Parnell's] position or weaken his hand for doing good." However, in reply to her next letter, he agreed to meet Mrs. O'Shea on June 2 at Thomas's Hotel at 3 P.M. He was there on time and was agreeable and courteous while he discussed Parnell and the Irish problem. On June 17, she sent him a memorandum written by Parnell, who indicated that he was putting a leash on violence in Ireland and that he had arranged that no part of the invested funds of the Land League could be drawn without his signature. In return, he suggested that treason-felony provisions be excised from the Coercion Bill and that the duration be limited to three months from the assembly of a new Parliament if the present government were dissolved within three years.

Mrs. O'Shea wrote again, in reply to a Gladstone suggestion that the correspondence cease, pleading that she not be "boycotted." On June 29, Gladstone returned the memorandum of June 17 with a note referring to two murders in Galway. "I do not doubt that your friend [Parnell] does all he can but these savage murders exhibit an unstaunched source of mischief that goes far to destroy all confidence." The communications continued by letter. Parnell's efforts to mitigate the severity of the coercion bill by this *sub rosa* method were futile, and it is doubtful, in the prevailing mood of the country, that Gladstone could have relaxed the harsh features of the bill.

In her memoirs, Mrs. O'Shea wrote, "After the first interview with Mr. Gladstone, I had frequently to see him in Downing Street, taking him drafts, clauses and various proposed amendments of bills affecting Ireland that Parnell proposed, altered and suggested privately to Gladstone before putting them before the House." On these occasions she would meet Gladstone in his office, he would offer her his arm and they would walk up and down

N

the room ("I talk better so" he would say), and he would refer to Parnell as "Your friend"—thus, "Your friend should do so and so" or "I am prepared to concede to your friend . . ."

From Gladstone's papers it appears that Mrs. O'Shea's account is somewhat misleading. She was not a constant visitor, but saw him personally only three times, since Gladstone discouraged personal interviews. Then too, Parnell was less a collaborator in legislation, as she implies, than an unsuccessful petitioner.

Mrs. O'Shea's correspondence with Gladstone lasted for five more years. In view of Gladstone's angry reaction when Mrs. O'Shea's relationship to Parnell erupted into scandal in 1890, eight years later, it is relevant to inquire as to whether Gladstone was aware of it at an earlier time. It is a hard question to answer definitively since, in the absence of ocular proof, a deduction as to a guilty relationship depends largely on attitudes, and Gladstone's attitudes were those of a Christian; he preferred to believe the best of his fellowman.

Mrs. O'Shea stated that, as a man of the world, he knew the truth from the very beginning. ". . . he knew before the conclusion of our [first] interview and allowed me to know that he knew, what I desired that he should know, that my personal interest in Parnell was my only interest in Irish politics."

What Mrs. O'Shea did not know was that the relationship was known to and discussed by the British Cabinet. Parnell had been shadowed by Government detectives for over a year. In Dilke's diary, for May 18, there is an entry about a statement made by Sir William Harcourt when he opposed a suggestion that O'Shea be employed as an intermediary to sound out Parnell about an acceptable coercion bill. "At the Cabinet meeting Harcourt told the Cabinet that the Kilmainham Treaty would not be popular when the public discovers that it had been negotiated by Captain O'Shea, the husband of Parnell's mistress. He informed the Cabinet that . . . after this it would hardly do for the public for us to use O'Shea as a negotiator." Since Dilke was not a member of the Cabinet, it is assumed that this choice morsel was relayed by his friend, Chamberlain. It is not certain that Gladstone had attended what was not a meeting of the full Cabinet, but Harcourt would have been remiss in his duty if he had not conveyed this information to the Prime Minister.

Gladstone sent a copy of Mrs. O'Shea's first letter to him together with his reply to Lord Granville, who sent to him this comment, "Your decision appears to me to be quite right and your letter excellent. She is said to be his mistress." Gladstone was therefore fully informed.

On the other hand, as an indication of Gladstone's skepticism, we have the statement of one of Gladstone's secretaries, Sir Leveson-Gower, that Gladstone rebuked him when he mentioned the rumor of the liaison, saying that he did not believe that Parnell would "imperil the future of Ireland for an adulterous intrigue." Gladstone might have believed that it was quite natural for Parnell to use Mrs. O'Shea as an intermediary, as his letter of September 26, 1882, to Lord Spencer states, "Her letters I cannot control but do not encourage. I think she has been of some use in keeping Parnell in the lines of moderation and I imagine he prefers the wife to her husband as an organ."

A factor that would tend to dissipate suspicion was that Mrs. O'Shea not only was relaying the messages of Parnell but was employing the opportunity to get an undersecretaryship of some kind for Willie, which would seem to Gladstone to be the act of a devoted wife. In reference to this suit, O'Shea wrote her on August 26, "I see G.O.M. got back to town yesterday but I dare say he smells a rat and will not see you yet awhile." G.O.M. stood for Grand Old Man (but to one wag, it was "God's Only Mistake").

Mrs. O'Shea was not able to secure a sinecure for her husband, and the idea took root in Willie's mind that he had played the part of savior in the Kilmainham negotiations; he had saved Parnell, the Nationalist Party and the Irish cause, but Parnell, the ingrate, refused to pay him off. On August 31, he wrote his wife from Dublin, where he had been forced to remain because he had broken his arm in an accident, "Great number of inquiries but Mr. Parnell, although in next street, never sent [inquiry]. P. for Pig . . ."

Part Four

THE DICTATORSHIP

I

ARNELL'S STAR was climbing to its zenith. The Kilmainham Treaty and its aftermath had put him firmly in the saddle as leader of the party. He had acted dictatorially in making commitments for the party in exchange for his release, and no one in the party had challenged him. He had thereby consigned "Buckshot" Forster and his minions to political oblivion and, in the absence of the terrible event in Phoenix Park, he would have been able to secure the end of coercion. The radicals who might have pounced on him for his pledges of moderation had lost influence, since they were linked to the "lunatic fringe" responsible for the Phoenix Park atrocity.

Parnell added to his prestige when he was successful in obtaining, after the passage of the new coercion law, a law to help those in arrears in rent. The law, applying to tenancies under £30, provided that if a tenant satisfied the court that he could not pay the rent in arrears and if he payed the rent for 1881, he could then be liable for only one year's rent of that due in 1879 and 1880, with the state paying the rest. The House of Lords first rejected the bill, but then approved it when Irish landlords saw that they would salvage at least two years rent out of what seemed a hopeless debt.

During the debate there was an unusual magnanimity on the part of the English in seeing the Irish point of view. In asking for approval of the bill, the Irish Secretary, Trevelyan, said, "Men are being turned out of their houses actually by battalions who are no more able to pay the arrears of those bad years than they are to pay the National debt." Gladstone said, "There may be outrages—which all things considered—the persons and the facts— may be less guilty in the sight of God than evictions," a startling admission since in the past, the English looking solely at outrages and the Irish looking solely at evictions, had each pointed the finger of guilt at the other, saying, "It's you who are guilty."

The Arrears Act turned out to be a far-reaching boon. Of 135,-997 claims no less than 129,952 were granted. Parnell could say that as a result of his negotiation he had been able to get, in addition to Forster's ouster, a total of £1,534,000 from the English treasury to help the Irish farmers.

Parnell, turning the party toward constitutionalism and parliamentary objectives, frowned on extremist organizations. In August, at Morrison's Hotel, Dillon asked Parnell for £500 for the Ladies' Land League. "No," answered Parnell sharply, "they have squandered the money given them and I will take care that they get no more." The League had spent £70,000 while he was in Kilmainham. Davitt reminded him that their debts had to be paid, so Parnell gave them a check but ordered the League disbanded. Dillon asked, "Do you mean to carry on the war or slow down the agitation?" Parnell answered bluntly, "The latter." When Davitt asked him if land nationalization, his pet project, would be made part of the platform, Parnell answered simply, "No." Then he asked Davitt to cease urging the plan in Ireland, though he was at liberty to sponsor it in England, and Davitt loyally acquiesced.

On August 20, Parnell wrote to Mrs. O'Shea indicating some uncertainty about his grip on the party machinery which he did not reveal to others. "The two D's have quarrelled with me because I won't allow any further expenditure by the ladies and because I have made arrangements to make the payments myself for the future. . . . They are in hopes of creating a party against me in the country by distributing the funds amongst their own creatures and are proportionately disappointed."

The suppression of the Ladies' Land League cost Parnell the friendship of his sister Anna, who refused for the rest of her life to talk to her brother, even to greet him on the street when they met by chance, or to acknowledge the letters he wrote to her. The rupture of this family tie caused Parnell great pain, particularly since in the same year he lost his favorite sister, Fanny.

William Redmond and Davitt had been on a money-raising expedition to New York, and at a farewell reception for Davitt a poem composed in his honor by Fanny was read. Redmond went out to Bordentown to see Fanny, who was not at home. He recalled, "She returned in a great state of excitement with a copy of the New York *Herald* in her hand. It was at the time of the Egyptian War and there was a rumor of an English defeat. I remember well seeing Fanny burst into the drawing room and saying, 'Oh, Mother, an Egyptian victory. Arabi has whipped the Britishers. It is grand!' That was the last time I ever saw Fanny Parnell alive."

The next day she was found dead in bed. Mrs. O'Shea relates that she saw the news in the paper while Parnell lay sleeping, exhausted after an all-night session. She woke him to tell him. "He was terribly shocked and I could not leave him all that day. For a time he utterly broke down."

Fanny Parnell, who had feared an early death, left an enduring monument behind in the form of a poem entitled "After Death." It has been hailed as one of the finest patriotic poems in any language. Healy, many years later, wrote, "It will live forever." We have called Fanny Parnell the Julia Ward Howe of the Irish revolutionary movement, and it is interesting that the first few words of her poem almost match those of "The Battle Hymn of the Republic."

Shall mine eyes behold thy glory, O my country? Shall mine eyes behold
    thy glory?
Or shall the darkness close around them, ere the sun-blaze break at
    last upon thy story?

When the nations ope for thee their queenly circle, as a sweet new
    sister hail thee,
Shall these lips be sealed in callous death and silence, that have known
    but to bewail thee?

Shall the ear be deaf that only loved thy praises, when all men their
    tribute bring thee?
Shall the mouth be clay that sang thee in thy squalor, when all poets'
    mouths shall sing thee?

Ah! the harpings and the salvos and the shoutings of thy exiled sons
    returning!
I should hear, though dead and mouldered, and the grave-damps should
    not chill my bosom's burning.

Ah, the tramp of feet victorious! I should hear them 'mid the shamrocks
    and the mosses,
And my heart should toss within the shroud and quiver as a captive
    dreamer tosses.

I should turn and rend the cere-clothes round me, giant sinews I should
    borrow—

Crying, "O, my brothers, I have also loved her in her loneliness and sorrow."

"Let me join with you the jubilant procession; let me chant with you
her story;
Then contented I shall go back to the shamrocks, now mine eyes have
seen her glory!"

Parnell had not contemplated the establishment of a new land association, but he yielded to arguments as to the usefulness of such an organization, and the Irish National League was formed in October, 1882. Healy recalled how he brought the constitution to Parnell before the meeting in Morrison's Hotel. Parnell was in bed, and when asked what was wrong, he answered in deep melancholy, "Oh, something always happens to me in October." Beside his bed Healy worked on the draft at a table with four candles. One went out, and Parnell sat up and blew out another. "Why have you given us less light?" asked Healy of Parnell, who answered, "Don't you know that nothing is more unlucky than three candles?" Then he added scornfully, "Your constitution for a new league would not have had much chance for succeeding if I had allowed you to work with three candles."

Healy was impressed in a gruesome kind of way by Parnell's somber manner. "Yet I marvelled that anyone could believe that the Almighty would allow his decrees in the government of human affairs to be affected by a candle more or less."

This league in the path of moderation was, unlike the Land League, not an independent organization but firmly under the thumb of the Parliamentary party—which meant Parnell. The chief plank was not land reform but Home Rule. The new league, being his own creation, was a much more effective instrument for control by Parnell, so much so that Frank Hugh O'Donnell attributed to him the Machiavellian plan of wrecking the Land League when he was in Kilmainham in order to supplant it later with one of his own design. At any rate, things had worked out admirably for Parnell.

The destiny of the Nationalist cause was now firmly in the hands of one man. He was the head of the Parliamentary party, in controy of its funds, the owner of its official newspaper and the head of the Irish National League, which became a political arm to strengthen and augment the party.

Parnell was now a virtual dictator. The movement became

known as Parnellism or the Parnell Movement, and its adherents were named Parnellites. Later, in his book *The Fall of Feudalism in Ireland,* Davitt wrote, "It was not Parnell who built up the name and legend of Parnellism or claimed or disclaimed his dictatorship but Timothy Healy, T. P. O'Connor, James J. O'Kelly, William O'Brien of *United Ireland* and Thomas Sexton. In fact, I found Parnell himself far less Parnellite in its extreme sense and infinitely less intolerant in matters of principle and policy than his brilliant young lieutenants. Unlike them he was fair and considerate in his dealings, seldom if ever personally dictatorial in the use of his power or the assertion of his authority. In fact it was a curious instance of the irony of fate that those who had preached Parnell's autocracy as a dogma of absolute political faith for nearly ten years, were the chief opponents of the same leader in the crisis of 1890."

Davitt refers to Healy and Sexton as opportunists who clothed Parnell with absolutism and then wielded that power as regents while the leader was absent because he was sick or absorbed with Mrs. O'Shea. Davitt further indicates that Parnell gave full leeway to these self-appointed deputies: "He never ruled with an iron hand. No leader was ever more indulgent or interfered less with his followers or gave wider field for discussion or criticism within the ambit of the national movement. His rule was loyally acknowledged by the party because it was enormously sagacious and also no man could without exciting ridicule make himself a rival."

Another source of Parnell's strength is adverted to in a letter from Biggar to Frank Hugh O'Donnell in 1886: "We have plenty of personal jealousy between the different members of the party. I mean the prominent members. No one would like to see any other of their number leader, and this assists Parnell to hold his place."

The selection of Parliamentary candidates was claimed for Parnell, but actually it was to be exercised by his lieutenants, who thus built up power for themselves while proclaiming the august supremacy of Parnell, as did Healy when, in Liverpool, he orated, "What we have wanted for two hundred years in Ireland was an honest dictator and we have at last got one in the person of Mr. Parnell. Men with only tin-pot intelligence should not be allowed to strike a discordant note against the great national tocsin which Mr. Parnell is clanging to the national ear."

Davitt himself was not a member of the Parliamentary party and therefore could hew a path of relative independence. He never gave blind worship to the Parnell icon. Once, in a speech, he said frankly, "Mr. Parnell is broad-minded and sagacious enough to know that leaders are accidents to the cause with which they are identified and that no movement dependent entirely upon personal capacity or individual distinction can be a strong and aggressive political weapon." When Davitt opposed Parnell in the final crisis, there was no question that his personal integrity was intact—the others had certainly compromised themselves by the lavish encomiums they had poured on their incomparable and infallible leader.

II

Throughout 1882 the police in Dublin had put all their resources behind the task of solving the Phoenix Park murders, but to no avail. By the end of the year, the police felt that they were closing in on the murderers. There was an attack on a shopkeeper who had sat on a special jury in a Lough Mask trial, then there was an attack on a judge. The police rounded up suspects, and under the Secret Inquiry Clause of the Crimes Act an investigation was kept going. Suspects were remanded by magistrates from week to week while scraps of evidence were laboriously put together. Among the prisoners were Carey and the other assassins, who scoffed at the inquiry. Carey was the most derisive, threatening to sue the Government for libel and false arrest. One afternoon a government prosecutor, adjourning the proceedings before the magistrate, announced, "Next week we shall connect the accused with the Phoenix Park murders." A chorus of laughter came from the dock.

The police were convinced that they had the culprits in their hands, and as they saw it, their job was to wear down the nerves and play upon the fears of only one man, the weakest link. They decided that that man was James Carey. One day the shutters of the warder's peephole in his cell were purposely left open, and Carey could see Superintendent Mallon going in and out of the adjoining cell with a pad of foolscap paper. Carey was seized with the agony of doubt. The next morning Carey, affecting an air of insouciance, asked the warder, "Who is in the next cell?" The warder answered, "Hush, there's black business going on there." That evening Carey saw through the shutters the Crown's prosecutor, George Bolton, go in and later come out wearing the smile of the cat which has swallowed the canary. The next morning Carey, terrified that he had been betrayed, said to the warder, "For God's sake, man, tell me who is in that next cell?" The warder replied in a whisper, "Dan Curley."

Carey then asked to see Mallon. When the Superintendent came into the cell Carey became hesitant, and Mallon affected a lack of eagerness, as if Carey were too late. This had the effect of making Carey unburden himself to the heart's content of the Government. It had, of course, all been a trick, since there had been no one in the cell next to Carey.

Fortified by brandy, Carey went into court that afternoon to betray his associates, who sat dumfounded. As Carey passed Dan Curley in the dock he said, "Ah, Dan, I was too quick for you." During the trial which followed, the flippancy and hypocrisy of Carey in the box disgusted even the Queen's Counsel, as when he said that he had informed to "save innocent lives." As a result of his testimony Joe Brady, Dan Curley (the godfather of Carey's youngest child, then two months old), Timothy Kelly, Michael Fagan and Tom Caffrey were convicted and hung.

There were heartrending stories about the deaths of the misguided patriots. Joe Brady was the first to be hung, and there was a nun who visited him daily, attending to his wants and conveying messages to his family. Unknown to him, she was the sister of the murdered man Thomas Burke, for whose life he was to pay. On the scaffold the last words of Brady were "Poor Ireland, poor old Ireland"—there were no words of pity for himself, but only for the fate of hapless Ireland which caused such an awful deed to be done.

The Government had the considerable problem of spiriting Carey to a place beyond the reach of vengeance. On the way from the prison the cab passed the house where Curley's widow lived, and Carey said, "God rest your soul, poor Dan Curley." The detective with him exclaimed in disgust, "What, after you sending him to his death!" Carey, beard shaven off and under the name of Power, was smuggled aboard the *Kinfaus Castle* off the coast of England and joined his wife and six children. At Cape Town, the family transferred to another ship, the *Melrose*, bound for

Port Elizabeth, where they were to be settled. Twelve miles off Cape Vacca, Carey was shot to death by a bricklayer, Patrick O'Donnell, who had been on board the *Kinfaus Castle*. When Carey's wife rushed to the saloon she was greeted by O'Donnell, "Shake hands, I was sent to do it." Some believed that O'Donnell, as an Irish Republican Brotherhood agent, had tracked Carey onto the ship, but as he had bought his ticket weeks before the Government had decided to put Carey on the *Kinfaus Castle*, it is probable that O'Donnell learned the identity of Carey on board from something said to him by Carey's young son.

O'Donnell was brought back to England, tried for murder and convicted, the Government making no attempt to elicit the tie with the I.R.B. There were many pleas for a commutation of his death sentence, but they were refused, Sir William Harcourt pointing out that O'Donnell showed not the least sign of remorse. A monument to his memory was raised in Glasnevin cemetery in Dublin, the money having been raised by a ladies' committee in New York headed by Mrs. Frank Byrne.

The name of Carey became an epithet of stark and incomparable infamy in Ireland. An Irish newspaper once reported that in a suit for separation a wife was asked on the stand, "Did you not call your husband's uncle 'Carey, the informer'?" She replied, "No, I did not go as far as that. I called him the anti-Christ."

III

The anti-Irish in and out of the English Government were convinced that Parnell had instigated or at least was implicated in the Phoenix Park murders. As we shall see, they persisted in that belief for years. When it was learned that Carey had confessed, Harcourt jubilantly went about saying, "The starch will soon be out of the boys," which was interpreted as a reference to Parnell and his cohorts. The failure to implicate Parnell was a great disappointment, so much so that it was said that Superintendent Mallon lost prestige with the Government instead of gaining it by winning the confession.

Nonetheless, his inveterate enemy Forster attacked Parnell in the House on February 22, 1883, in stinging terms such as seldom had been heard in that chamber. As the *Times* said, "Mr. Forster's stern interrogatories fell on Mr. Parnell's face like the lash of a whip." Forster tried to inculpate Parnell in the murders. "It is hard for me to understand how he did not know it and why he did not separate himself from it altogether and disavow and denounce it." Then he said, "I will repeat again what the charge is which I make against him. Probably a more serious charge has never been made by any member of the House against another. It is not that he himself directly planned or perpetrated outrages or murders, but he either connived at them or, warned by facts and statements, he determined to remain in ignorance." On these words Parnell hissed, "It's a lie." All eyes turned to him and there arose cries of "Answer, answer." Parnell asked T. P. O'Connor to reply and "the Irish cockney" did do so with great verve. Later, when it was thought that he intended to ignore the matter, Parnell rose to move the adjournment of debate, thereby giving notice that he would answer the charge at the opening of the next session.

The following day all the benches and the galleries were packed, peers and high churchmen crowding into the chamber expecting to hear a defense by Parnell to the charges of countenancing and abetting the murders. The actual speech stunned the English hearers and made the Irish exultant. Far from trying to exculpate himself, Parnell merely thumbed his nose at the English accusers, denied their right to judge him and, more than that, said that he was not concerned with what they thought about him. "I have been accustomed during my political life to rely upon the public opinion of those whom I desired to help and with whose aid I have worked for the cause of prosperity and freedom in Ireland and the utmost I desire . . . is to make my point clear to the Irish people at home and abroad."

As for the charges, "A gentleman has asked me to defend myself. I have nothing to defend myself from." As for Forster, he could go to Hell, which was synonymous with the present coercive administration of Ireland. The present Secretary, Trevelyan, was merely an apprentice boy. "Call him [Forster] back to his post. Send him to help Lord Spencer in the congenial work of the gallows in Ireland. Send him back to look after the secret inquisitions in Dublin Castle. Send him back to distribute the taxes which an unfortunate and starving peasantry have to pay for crimes not committed by themselves. All this must be congenial work for the right hon. gentleman." He concluded, "Although the horizon may

be clouded I believe our people will survive the present oppression as they have survived many and worse misfortunes and although our progress may be slow it will be sure."

This was truly a tour de force, the elixir of true patriotism and
proud defiance. In Ireland it aroused exultation and national
pride at a time when Ireland was under the yoke. Of the speech,
Sir William Harcourt said grudgingly, "Parnell's words, though
detestable, were well conceived from his point of view. Posing as
a man who would admit to nothing, apologize for nothing and
give in to nothing—this is just what the Irish admire."

IV

At this time Parnell was in an uncomfortable financial position.
His tenants had taken advantage of his political eminence to forego
the payment of more than a dribble of rent, and he had spent
heavily trying to develop stone quarries and other natural resources
of Avondale without success. He had been forced to put a mortgage of £12,000 on Avondale, and at the end of 1882 he had to
advertise it for sale. Thus, his financial difficulty came to Ireland's
attention.

In the enthusiasm that swept Ireland after the answer to Forster,
T. D. Sullivan in *The Nation* suggested that the Irish people, as a
manifestation of their gratitude to Parnell, raise enough money
to pay off the mortgage and more. The goal was £17,000, which
would be called the Parnell Tribute. By the middle of May, the
testimonial lagged, with only £7,688 subscribed, a large sum, but
not adequate for the purpose.

One of the keys to Parnell's unusual ascendancy over the Irish
for a decade is expressed in words once applied to President Grover
Cleveland, "We love him for the enemies he has made." Time and
again when Parnell's appeal seemed to be fading or when the gulf
between the disparate wings of his party seemed to be yawning
too wide to close, someone would attack him and then the people
would unite behind him. Before, it had been Gladstone and
Forster. Now, the source of attack was the unlikeliest for Catholic
Ireland to spurn, the Pope.

There was a peculiar rapport between Anglican England and
Catholic Rome—strange indeed, since English rulers in the corona-

tion ceremony had to denounce Catholicism as a superstitious faith. During the Napoleonic Wars, England and Rome had been allied against the scourge of Jacobinism, and victory had been followed by the restoration of the Roman states. The Church had helped England by excommunicating those who took part in the 1798 rebellion and later had refused sacraments to Fenians. Although the Parnell movement had attracted the support of many priests, the top hierarchy, with a few exceptions like Archbishop Croke, were opposed. When Parnell and his colleagues were tried for conspiracy in December, 1880, the prosecution read a letter from Archbishop McCabe decrying "doctrines which pushed to their logical conclusion will strike at the good faith and mutual confidence which are the foundations of social life." At the same time, the *Osservatore Romano* in the Vatican attacked Biggar as a *pizzicagnolo* (a bacon seller) and wrote of Parnell, "Instead of demanding better legislation he urges his auditors to confiscation and allows them in his presence to utter prayers for assassination and armed revolt."

Gladstone, an amateur theologian, was by conviction very much anti-Catholic, having written a tract on "Vaticanism" which had taken the Vatican to task for the doctrine of papal infallibility. Yet he had no hesitancy about asking the Holy See, as a good friend, to do what it could to make the Irish behave. In December, 1881, he wrote to the English Cardinal Newman that Irish priests should "fulfil the elementary duties of citizenship. Of Christianity, of priesthood, it is not for me to speak." Cardinal Newman replied that Gladstone was overestimating the power of the Pope in political matters. The next month, however, Pope Leo XIII addressed a letter to Irish bishops advising that the people be admonished "not to cast aside obedience due to lawful rulers." A Radical Liberal, Joseph Cowen, protested in the House, "If we want to hold Ireland by force, let us do it. Let us not call on the Pope, who we are always attacking, to help us."

When Gladstone heard of the projected Parnell Tribute he thought that surely this was a case where the Pope could effectively intervene to prevent good Catholics from giving their money to a benighted Protestant. An Irish Whig M.P. and good Catholic, George Errington, was going to Rome, so Foreign Minister Lord Granville gave him a letter to the Pope and some verbal instructions about the Parnell matter. Errington talked with the Pope.

And then on May 11 came a rescript from Cardinal Simeoni, the prefect of the Propaganda Fidei, to the Irish bishops stating that as to Mr. Parnell "and his objects . . . it is therefore the duty of all the clergy and especially the Bishops to curb the excited feelings of the multitude."

When the Irish people learned that this condemnation of the Parnell Tribute had come about through English pressure, indignation mounted to a high pitch. An old woman stopped Archbishop Croke on the street and asked, "Arrah, Your Grace, is it true that the English are trying to make a Protestant of the Pope?" Bishop Butler of Limerick immediately sent a subscription to the testimonial, and four Maynooth professors (who later became bishops) followed suit. The cry went round "Make Peter's Pence into Parnell pounds," and it became a point of honor to contribute to the fund. While Peter's Pence fell that year to the lowest in thirty years, the Parnell Tribute soared to the sky. From £7,688 at the time of the Papal rescript, it rose to £15,302 three months later and six months later to £37,000, to which £3,000 from abroad would be added by the end of the year. Gladstone had second thoughts about his appeal. "It is absurd to think that the Pope exercises any influence in Irish politics," he concluded ruefully.

On December 11, a deputation headed by the Lord Mayor of Dublin called on Parnell at Morrison's Hotel to give him a check for £37,000 and invite him to a banquet in his honor. It was expected to be a wordy, fulsomely emotional affair, but they did not take into account the personality of Parnell. The Lord Mayor began a speech, but after two sentences Parnell interrupted him. "I believe you have got a cheque for me?" The Lord Mayor said yes, then launched again into the panegyric. Parnell again interrupted him. "Is it payable to order and crossed?" The Lord Mayor nodded. Parnell then took the check from his hand and indicated that the ceremony was over.

At the banquet the next night there was a great crush of people. The police made no attempt at all to provide an avenue for the guests, and women in high slippers and long evening gowns had to fight their way for a block through high snow. For the stupendous sum given to him, paid by the sweat of thousands of poor peasants in defiance of their supreme spiritual leader, Parnell had the most perfunctory thanks in a political speech of an hour. All he said was, "I don't know how adequately to express my feelings with regard to not only to Your Lordship's address, to the Parnell National Tribute but also with regard to the magnificent demonstration. I prefer to leave with historians the description of tonight and the expression of an opinion as regards the result which tonight must produce." Thomas Sexton turned to Tim Healy, seated next to him, and said, "A labourer would acknowledge the gift of a penknife more gratefully."

The hostility of the Church to Parnell was turned back here, and it should be noted that in this case the hierarchy in Ireland was unsympathetic to the position of Rome became of pressure which had been put on it from England. But the Irish Church, no matter how much Parnell tried to woo it, would always look on him with a jaundiced eye and in the end would pull him down. The radicalism of the Land League certainly did not appeal to it, and the Church in Ireland opposed Home Rule struggle on the grounds that the presence in Parliament of a hundred Irish who were mostly Catholic was a salutary influence for the protection of Catholic interests in the British Empire at large.

As a Protestant, Parnell was automatically suspect by the Catholic Church, but there were more grounds for uneasiness. He attended no church at all. In France he had associated with prominent anti-clericals, and when Georges Clemenceau had visited the House of Commons, Parnell was unusually attentive to him. Parnell never said anything publicly offensive to the Catholic establishment, though Frank Hugh O'Donnell related that on one occasion in days when they were close, Parnell said to him, "I believe the Church to have been the constant enemy of human progress in every country and in every age."

O'Donnell, who was a close friend of the Church hierarchy, claimed that Parnell hurt himself irretrievably with the Church by a position he took in 1880 in the Bradlaugh case, a case which threw the House into a tumult, "an ecstatic transport of excitement," as Gladstone described it to the Queen, such as he could not remember. Charles Bradlaugh, a notorious atheist as well as a believer in such offensive ideas as the open distribution of contraceptives, was elected to a seat from Northampton. He announced that if he took an oath "in the name of God" it would mean nothing to him, as "an unmeaning sound." He was therefore barred from taking the oath. A Select Committee recommended that he be allowed to "affirm" and Gladstone endorsed this, but the House rejected the proposal by a close vote. Bradlaugh, a man of bull-like stature, rushed to the bar and demanded to be given the oath; after refusing to leave the members' bench, he was dragged off to the bell tower and confined there for a day.

Bradlaugh in subsequent years was repeatedly reelected from Northampton and repeatedly refused a seat. The case kept the House in an uproar, and there were a series of weird scenes, such as Bradlaugh's trying to enter the House when he had been ordered excluded and being dragged step by step down the stairs by six policemen, his clothes being almost torn from his body, or Bradlaugh's rushing one day up to the bar, kissing a book he pulled out of his pocket, signing some paper and holding it aloft, declaring himself sworn in.

In the session of 1880, there were twelve Nationalists who voted in favor of the admission of Bradlaugh on affirmation, and one of the twelve was Parnell. The Church never forgot that the Irish leader had favored the admission into Parliament of an atheist.

V

The years 1883 and 1884 were tranquil years for the Parnellites in Parliament. While Ireland was held in a tight clamp by the Coercion Law passed in 1882 there was little that the Irish could do but wait till it expired before pushing for meliorative legislation. Parnell himself was absent from the House most of the time. Dillon was away for a good deal of time in America and Australia. Justin McCarthy and T. P. O'Connor were busy with literary endeavors. William O'Brien was elected from Mallow in 1883 but devoted himself to *United Ireland,* which kept Irish hearts palpitating with its lurid and martial prose. Healy spent four months in early 1883 in Richmond prison with Davitt and J. P. Quinn for making subversive speeches. While there, he worked hard on legislation, and when released, he and Sexton kept the party going in Parliament during the period of the lull.

Fissiparous tendencies within the party were kept in check by the desire of dissidents like Dillon to maintain the facade of unity, and also by the adroitness of Parnell and his commanding personality. He was eager to solidify the Church behind the party.

In 1884, he took an important step by making the clergy *ex officio* delegates to all county party conventions in which Parliamentary candidates were chosen. He liked to josh Davitt and once said to him, "You know the clergy are very useful against extremists like you when we are away in London."

Davitt's obsession about land nationalization (which he had absorbed through the single-tax ideas of Henry George) was a problem for Parnell. When he received the freedom of the city of Drogheda in April, 1884, Parnell attacked the idea frontally. "Ownership by anybody we are told is theft. The desire to acquire land is everywhere one of the strongest instincts of human nature. It was the very basis and foundation of the Land League."

Davitt asked him how he could defend private ownership of land in view of the tenor of the speeches he had made in the early days of the land agitation. What would he do if he were the head of an Irish Parliament? Parnell laughed and answered, "The first thing I would do would be to lock you up."

Parnell's position as a constitutionalist, which he had adopted since the Kilmainham Treaty for himself and for the party, was endangered in 1883 and 1884 by radical elements who were using the most violent of destructive weapons—dynamite. This had the blessing of Patrick Ford, who had repudiated Parnell's moderate policy. "The Creator called nothing into existence in vain. Dynamite is a blessed agent." There were attempts to blow up the Tower, Westminster Hall, the House of Commons, London Bridge, and Victoria, Paddington and Charing Cross stations. The Irish revolutionaries were never successful dynamiters, attributed by some to the fact that as Catholics they were too much worried with thoughts of the hereafter.

"Big fools," Parnell said of the dynamiters, "If Charing Cross had been blown up, twenty Irish members would have been killed in a nearby hotel." Yet, while Parnell did not talk daggers now as he done a few years before when he sounded like a crypto-Fenian, he would not speak out openly against them. "No, I dislike outrages as much as any man but I am not going to act police for the English people. They murder and plunder all over the earth and then they howl when somebody is killed in Ireland because the killings are of no use for them."

William O'Brien related that in 1885, when Russia threatened in Afghanistan, Parnell considered a project for a raid on Ireland by 500 Fenians to be carried in Russian ships and commanded by General Phil Sheridan of Civil War fame, but rejected it as impracticable. Parnell talked to O'Brien at some length about the futility of thinking in terms of military insurrection in Ireland. He said that the Wexford pike had been a useful weapon in 1798, when the redcoat's rifle could fire only three bullets, but today the British soldier had a repeating rifle. Geographically, Ireland was in an impossible position, being too close to England, and was too small. George Washington, he said, succeeded because of the vastness of the land in which to run and hide. Guerrilla warfare was out of the question in Ireland because there were mountains only on the rim and the flat lands in between could be cleared in a few days by an army carried by the railroad. Obviously Parnell had given a good deal of thought to the problem.

Parnell took active part in only one by-election. After Healy's release from prison in June, 1883, Parnell asked him if he would resign his seat from Wexford and stand for Monaghan because Parnell was anxious to make an inroad for the party in the northern counties of Ireland. Healy consented and his candidacy was confirmed by a county convention in Castleblaney. Parnell promised to appear at the meeting the next Sunday to make an address. Inexplicably he did not show up, but the large crowd was treated to one of Sexton's spellbinding orations. Before the contest ended, however, Parnell appeared, with no apology or explanation for his absence, and threw himself into the campaign. His presence, said Healy, was "electrical." Healy won the election, and Parnell was delighted.

Healy recalled that after the poll, "We toured the county that evening and from our brake Parnell shouted to every group at a cross-roads, 'Healy! Healy! Healy!'" The evocation of that joyous memory obviously stirred Healy's old affection for Parnell, since, with a nostalgic pang of emotion, he added in his memoirs, "For me to part with such a leader seven years later was a cruel wrench Without 'side' or snobbery, Parnell was a *grand seigneur*."

VI

In this review of 1883–1884 the next political event of note is the visit of the Prince of Wales and his wife to Ireland in 1884. Gladstone was hoping that Parnell would show magnanimity and be a warm host, but he was disappointed. Parnell declared that the Constitution was applied unfairly to Ireland and that the visit insulted the Nationalist party. "I fail to see upon what ground it can be claimed from any lover of Constitutional government under limited monarchy that the Prince is entitled to a reception from the independent and patriotic people of Ireland or to any recognition save from the garrison of officials and landowners and place-hunters who fatten upon the poverty and misfortunes of the country."

The coldness and hostility which was displayed dismayed and shocked the Princess. In some towns all the houses were shuttered and no one was on the street. In Cork, cabbages and rotten eggs were thrown at the procession. In some places the royal couple could see black flags hung and signs reading "We will have no prince but our Prince Charlie."

The quiet years of 1883 and 1884 were succeeded by the hectic years of 1885 and 1886. By 1884 Parnell, only thirty-eight, was a worldwide figure, one of the best-known men in Parliament outside of Gladstone, the leader of the Nationalist movement in Ireland of five million and the spiritual leader of another fifteen million Irish all over the world.

Great strides had been made in land reform. Land proprietorship had not been achieved, but the liberation of the tenants from landlord oppression had been won. The great work of achieving Home Rule lay ahead.

Amid the optimism that was felt in high party circles, there was recognition of one threat: At any time the covert love affair, by now well-known to the party hierarchy, could explode into public notoriety. During the Monaghan election campaign, Healy related, a telegram for Parnell had been opened by mistake by the election chairman, an M.P., J. F. Small. It read, "The captain is away. Please come. Don't fail. Kate." Since the envelope was torn up, no one had the courage to tell Parnell about it. Healy said that Small not only kept the wire but gave it to M.P. Phil Callan, who was an enemy of Parnell. Parnell learned of this and succeeded in getting rid of both Small and Callan at the next elections.

The complications of his love life were reaching into his political life, but Parnell fondly imagined that he was keeping it a secret while it was increasingly becoming public property.

VII

The enormous idolatry of Parnell could be appreciated by Mrs. O'Shea when her lover returned "home" from his visits to Ireland. It was a point of honor that he would not feel or look into his pockets until she had the opportunity to explore them. She would find astounding congeries of gifts—little medals with images of saints, scapulars and badges, many of them deposited in his pocket by sweet-faced nuns; brand-new handkerchiefs of vivid-green embroidered with four-leaf clovers, a gift of the "colleens"; a "quare bit ave a stone" or "a farden me mither give me," a fragment of what might have been a bird's egg, from the little boys, and from the hardy fellows, some gruesome scrap of rope that had been used to hang some scoundrel, or a flattened bullet that had gained some fancied power by going through someone's heart.

The adoration was present in her own home. Her new cook, Eileen, was so excited when she learned that the resident house guest was Parnell that she could not attend to her cooking, so he had to see her for a moment. She fell to her knees and kissed his hands, a homage widely accorded in Ireland. Eileen and the parlor maid, Mary, vied with each other in attentions to him, to his embarrassment. They bought lockets and put his picture inside. When he told them that they must wear them inside their dresses since he did not want his presence known, they promised faithfully to keep the secret and swore vengeance on the other if absolute silence were not preserved.

This heroic figure for Ireland was to Katherine a child at some times, an unfathomable adult at others. Like a highly strung child he was subject to "night terrors," during which she had to hold him until he was fully conscious for fear that he might hurt himself; when they were over, they were followed by profuse perspiration and deep sleep. Even when he was in deep sleep his thoughts were troubled, and she would often hear him mutter something like "Steer carefully out of the harbour—there are breakers ahead." He had been a sleepwalker since childhood, and when he traveled he always put the hotel door key in a box with a spring lock, for fear of walking out of the room.

There were, too, his childlike superstitions. Once, he cut his finger and asked for cobwebs to wrap around it; her children, fascinated, brought him cobwebs—and also spiders. Mrs. O'Shea was struck with horror when she saw what he was about to do. He explained to her that he had once hurt his fingers in some machinery at Arklow and his servant had dressed the wound with cobwebs.

She once bought a diary bound in green. When he saw it on the mantelpiece he threw it into the fire and held her back from rescuing it. He said he would buy her another. At that time diaries were bound in only three colors—green, purple and red. Purple, he said, was offensive to him because it was the color of sorrow, red was offensive because it was the color of blood. Since the other choice was to give her no book at all, he settled on a red one as least offensive. She asked him how he had acquired his superstitions. He attributed them to Irish nurses, but his mother must have had some part. There were stories about her examining the numbers on horsecars in New York to be sure that she was not boarding one with a 13 or a multiple of that number.

He was not a conversationalist or an outgoing companion, being interested in his own hobbies. His reading consisted of magazines on mechancs and engineering, which was the natural bent of his mind rather than politics. He spent countless hours assaying small pieces of quartz from a stream at Avondale and trying to extract gold from them. In the end his efforts resulted in extracting only enough gold to line Katherine's wedding ring, but the hope of getting rich from gold was a lifelong obsession for him. An amateur architect, he made sketches of the new railroad station being built at Brighton and had a cattle shed built along the same lines at Avondale. His mother, returning from America, was so pleased with the building that she chased out the cattle, put in a floor and used it for social entertainment. Parnell was greatly riled but, being ever courteous to his mother, let her know in a gentle but firm way that he wanted it to be reconverted for the original tenants.

He and Katherine spent many hours watching the stars together. He became very much interested in astronomy while reading the books of Sir Robert Ball and Sir William Herschel. He had a magnificent telescope he owned sent to him from Avondale and mounted it on a pedestal in her Eltham garden, where they would watch the stars and the courses of the planets till dawn. During daytime hours they would go to the Greenwich Observatory, for which Parnell had an entrance permit.

The ties between the couple became ever closer. He was the model of monogamous devotion. When he was away he would send one telegram in the morning and another before retiring at night. If he were away more than two days she could expect a daily letter in addition to the wires. His letters from Ireland showed his yearning for her. "I often wish that I had wings and an invisible suit so that I could fly across every evening after the day's work is done."

In its furtiveness, it was a sad back-street romance. She often went to the House to take him to dinner, meeting him a few blocks away and driving him back to within a few blocks. He hated to come back alone to Eltham, so she·would wait for him at different stations, he would alight from the train and they would drive home together. She would pace up and down a station such as Waterloo Junction, choosing it because, due to the early morning trains, it was never completely shut down, and she would comfort herself in the endless wait by saying over and over again, "He always comes, he always comes."

She told how loath he was to leave her to fill his political engagements in Ireland. Sometimes when he was scheduled to leave at a certain hour, he would putter around endlessly with one thing and another and then be elated to find that it was too late to go, not the least discomfitted by the knowledge that thousands would wait in vain for him. No doubt that was why he failed to show up for the election meeting at Monaghan when he had promised Healy that he would appear.

VIII

Always over their head hung the sword of Damocles in the person of Captain O'Shea. Until Aunt Ben died and left her fortune to Mrs. O'Shea there must be no scandal, and, of course, Parnell's political life must not be destroyed.

In March, 1883, Katherine O'Shea gave birth to a girl, named Clare, and in November, 1884, she gave birth to a second girl, Frances. These were claimed as his children by Captain O'Shea at the time of the divorce trial in November, 1890, but were conceded afterward by him to be Parnell's children—a fact which could hardly be denied since the children unmistakably resembled Parnell. The arrival of these children begotten by Parnell but bearing the name of O'Shea and under O'Shea's control while a charge to him is the ugliest situation that can arise in our society from an illicit sexual relationship.

The fact that these children were born by her in 1883 and 1884 are omitted entirely in the memoirs of Mrs. O'Shea. It is certainly remarkable that there should be such a gaping cavity in the post-1882 narrative. Henry Harrison finds in this a confirmation of his theory that O'Shea must have winked at the whole extramarital affair, that he must have been a *mari complaisant* knowing that Parnell and his wife were together while he was estranged from her. He could not have ignored the birth of two children, a fact which could hardly be concealed from the world.

If he were a deceived husband, as it appears that he really was, how then does one fit this new development into the framework? The answer is obvious: Mrs. O'Shea deceived her husband by the same means by which she admitted she had deceived him in the case of Parnell's first child, Sophie Claude, born in 1881. She had relations with him at the appropriate time and then told him that he was the father. She probably found it too embarrassing to state this in her story. O'Shea claimed that they did have marital relations. After the divorce trial, for example, we have a letter from Healy written on December 3, 1890, to his wife. It says, "It seems that O'Shea maintains that Clare is his own child and he told

[Henry] Labouchere that whenever Kitty came up to his flat in Victoria Street she insisted on renewing their old relations, and he swears he will keep Clare on this account."

O'Shea must have been aware of the truth in the back of his mind. But the human mind has a strange capacity for adjustment and self-deception when confronted with an unpleasant truth—it merely draws the blinds, particularly when every practical motive compels one not to see.

> I swear 'tis better to be much abused,
> Than but to know't a little. . . .
> He that is robb'd, not wanting what is stol'n,
> Let him not know't, and he is not robb'd at all.

So lamented Othello in his grief. To O'Shea the certain revelation of his wife's adultery would have the most grievous consequences for him—it would drive him into the divorce courts; it would deprive him of any hope of sharing in Aunt Ben's huge fortune; it would deprive him of £600 a year, which was about a fourth of his income; it would have grievous consequences for the three children who were his own, it would deprive him of the connection with Parnell which was a vehicle for influence. It would be a nasty situation. And so the self-delusion which was the better part of prudence continued. (Meanwhile he sported with many other women. At the time of the divorce suit, Katherine claimed that she could prove seventeen adulteries on his part.) Moreover, in assessing this curious relationship one must take account of the relative strength of the personalities involved—O'Shea was something of a fatuous fool, while his wife was a strong-minded woman with an agile tongue, quite capable of pulling the wool over his eyes.

As for Parnell, the enforced sharing of his beloved with the man he despised and whom Katherine claimed to despise was indeed to taste the dregs. It speaks loudly for his emotional dependence on Katherine O'Shea that he had to enjoy her love at the price of sordidness and the cheapest of trickery, to fondle his children while knowing that they belonged legally to a man he despised.

From the correspondence that is available, it appears that the relationship continued to be the same masquerade, conducted on the same devices, pretenses and pretexts as in 1880 to 1882. Parnell, when in Ireland, would write a formal letter addressed to Mrs. O'Shea enclosing a letter to be mailed to some person. Apparently he had cooked up some pretext that it was desirable that the letter should have an English postmark. The enclosed letter was for Katherine, and the rigmarole was necessitated by the fear of an unexpected visit by the Captain to Eltham, and the chance that he might inspect incoming letters.

On May 30, 1884, a letter from Parnell indicates that he had taken O'Shea with him for a few days' shooting at Avondale, so they were apparently on good terms. Then trouble erupted. On August 4 O'Shea wrote to Parnell, "You have behaved very badly. While I have often told you that you were welcome to stay at Eltham whenever I was there, I begged you not to do so during my absence since it would be sure at the least sooner or later to cause public scandal." Then he spoke of his intention to resign his seat. On August 7 the unflappable Parnell replied, "In reply to your letter, I do not know of any scandal or any grounds for one and can only suppose you have misunderstood the drift of some statements that have been made to you." He then concluded the cool and cynical letter by asking O'Shea to please set the date for the resignation and let him know as soon as he could.

On August 7 Katherine, obviously alarmed, also wrote to calm her husband, adroitly bringing into focus the matter of Aunt Ben's money. ". . . and for the children's sake, I would not like to die yet as they would lose all chance of Aunt's money . . . and certainly we have a better right to all she has than anybody else."

The communications between Parnell and his mistress indicate how their meetings had to be set to avoid Captain O'Shea's attention. Thus, a letter by Parnell from Eltham to Katherine while she was in London said, "Do you think I had best wait here or go up to London and wait for you? We finished our committee yesterday so if he [Captain O'Shea] goes early, I could return perhaps early enough to see you for a few minutes." Another example of subterfuge happened early in 1885, when Parnell wanted to bring some of his horses to England. Lest O'Shea learn that he had his horses at Eltham, Parnell wrote a formal letter to Mrs. O'Shea to use as a "blind" in case the Captain should raise a fuss. It read "My dear Mrs. O'Shea—I have sent two horses to London today (Euston) and should feel very much obliged if you would allow them to stand in your stables for a few days until I can make other arrangements."

Later he put them in a stable nearby but away from Eltham. And so the curious relationship continued, while all waited for Aunt Ben to die.

IX

In early 1885 there were negotiations between Joseph Chamberlain and Parnell relating to the Home Rule problem, negotiations which proved abortive. However, they were to have the gravest implications for the climactic Parliamentary battle over Home Rule and, in addition, for Parnell's personal life, due to the ever-present nexus of his political life and Mrs. O'Shea.

Joseph Chamberlain, leader of the Radical Liberals, was looking forward to the coming elections and the retirement of the aging Gladstone; he looked on himself as the successor to Gladstone. There was a strong conservative Whig faction in the Liberal party with which he would have to contend for leadership. Chamberlain was looking for some coup to cover himself with distinction, and it occurred to him that it might be found if he solved the vexing Irish problem on his own. After all, was he not regarded as the patron saint of the Irish Nationalists, an anti-coercionist who had gotten Parnell out of Kilmainham? William O'Brien told how Chamberlain, the constant friend of the Irish, had wrapped his arm around him when he had entered Parliament in 1883 and had said to him, "Ireland will have to send a good many men like you if you are going to kick John Bull out of his easy chair."

In these negotiations Chamberlain used as an intermediary with Parnell the same one he had used in the Kilmainham negotiations in 1882, Captain William Henry O'Shea, who, Chamberlain undoubtedly knew, was the husband of Parnell's mistress, who had ready access to Parnell and who, Chamberlain possibly believed, could wield a club over Parnell.

On November 27, 1884, O'Shea brought a memorandum to Chamberlain containing Parnell's purported views on the Irish Government issue, but in O'Shea's handwriting. Thus encouraged, Chamberlain sent on December 17 a letter to an Irish friend, W. H.

Duignan, with an outline of his scheme. It would not provide for an Irish Parliament since the scheme was a local-government plan. County boards would elect a central board to sit in Dublin which would take over education, land administration, railways, sanitation, public works, communications and internal taxation. Police and justice would not be included for the time being.

When one examines this plan and the Home Rule Bill of 1886 there is not much substantive difference, the main difference being that the Home Rule Bill of Gladstone provided for an elected Parliament which was important not only symbolically but because it would be the embryo from which fuller powers and complete self-government could develop.

On January 5, Parnell wrote a warning to Captain O'Shea, "You must give him [Chamberlain] to understand that we do not propose the local self-government plan as a substitute for the restitution of the Irish Parliament but solely as an improvement of the present system of local self-government in Ireland." On January 13, Parnell wrote in the same vein again to O'Shea. Parnell had therefore made his position clear enough but according to Chamberlain's biographer, J. L. Garvin, O'Shea suppressed these letters and Chamberlain did not become aware of them till later.

What stake did O'Shea have in the success of these negotiations? A considerable one besides ingratiating himself with Chamberlain. On March 2, he wrote to Mrs. O'Shea, "Today C. promised me the chief Secretaryship [of Ireland] on the formation of the Government after election. This is an enormous thing, giving you and the chicks a very great position." On May 4, he cautioned her that "Gladstone ought not to know this."

Parnell, however, would not be obliging and come through, although no doubt O'Shea expected his wife to put pressure on her friend. On March 17, O'Shea wrote her lugubriously, "I have just seen P. but he appears to funk making a treaty. It is too bad as it is a great chance especially as it would probably allow of my being Chief Secretary in the next Parliament."

Chamberlain tried to build a fire under Parnell by getting support from other elements in the Irish picture. The previous December, the increasingly important Healy, presumably Parnell's faithful lieutenant, was sounded out, and Healy said he personally was in favor of the Chamberlain plan. Labouchere, who had a long talk with Healy, quoted him as saying, "Parnell is half-mad. We always act without him. He accepts this position. If he does not, we should overlook him. Do not trouble yourself about him. Dillon, McCarthy, O'Brien, Harrington and I settle everything." But in a subsequent talk Healy conceded Parnell's primacy. "Anyone going against Parnell would be nowhere just now because the Irish have got it into their heads that union is strength."

Chamberlain also solicited the aid of the Catholic clergy (though he would seem to have little claim on their friendship since the Radical Liberals and the clergy were at dagger points on many issues such as the radical opposition to denominational schools). Cardinal Manning spoke to the two Irish cardinals and five Irish bishops who were in London on the way to Rome, and on April 20 he reported to Chamberlain's friend Dilke, "The Cardinal [Croke] declared that the Roman Catholic clergy were ready to pacify Ireland if we should pass Chamberlain's local government scheme. The bishops would be ready to denounce not only separation but an Irish Parliament." On April 30, Cardinal Manning saw Parnell and advised him of the bishops' attitude. Chamberlain seems to have been misinformed then that Parnell expressed his approval of the Chamberlain plan. A year later, in June, 1886, when Chamberlain was seeking to establish that Parnell had deceived him, he inquired of Cardinal Manning as to the conversation a year before, and Manning replied as to his recollection, "He was less satisfied and I understood him to accept the scheme but not as sufficient or final. I did not take it as more than not opposing it."

The Cabinet itself had not voted on the Chamberlain plan and did not do so until May 9, 1885, when it was rejected. All the peers except Lord Granville were against it, all the commoners except Lord Hartington were for it. Gladstone deplored the decision, "Ah, they will rue this. Within six years, if it please God to spare their lives, they will be repenting in sackcloth and ashes."

Parnell, like any cagy politician, was shopping around for the best offer and thought he might get it from the Conservatives. Playing one party against another, he believed that a carrot of Irish votes dangled before the Liberals might be less effective than the stick, the fear that the Conservatives might get them. Parnell had become on increasingly good terms with the Conservative, Lord Randolph Churchill, a restless, eccentric character, who stood out

in the House with his goggle eyes, his ferocious upturned mous-
tache and the somewhat impudent and irreverent way he addressed
the House, with one hand akimbo on his hip. Parnell grew to like
him personally for his wit and joyousness, his originality and resourcefulness. Then, besides these personal qualities, Churchill professed to be a stalwart friend of the Irish.

X

In 1885 the three-year term of the Coercion Law was drawing to
its expiration, and the vital question was whether it should be
renewed. The Liberals were chagrined that Ireland held no gratitude
to them for the pains they had taken in the last few years to teach
them the road to virtue. Dilke relates that in Dublin in a walk he
took with the Viceroy, Lord Spencer, in May, 1885, only one man
lifted his hat, while a number of men called out to Spencer,
"Murderer." At the insistence of Lord Spencer, the Cabinet decided
to ask for a renewal of coercion. Lord Randolph Churchill said
openly in a speech at St. Stephens Club and gave private assurances
to Parnell that the Tories, if they took over the Government, would
not renew the Act.

Parnell decided that the time was ripe for the Irish Nationalists,
augmented by by-election additions to almost 40 in number, to try
to overthrow Gladstone's Liberal Government. He sent wires to all
missing members to drop everything and rush to Westminster. On
June 8, there was a division on a budget request for an added tax
on wine and spirits. As the members trooped through the lobby,
it was apparent that the vote would be close. Each successive Tory,
as he left the lobby, was almost torn to pieces as he was asked what
his number was. The Nationalists under Parnell cast 39 votes
against the Government. The vote was announced and the scene
became bedlam. The Gladstone Government had lost by 263 to
252, and was out of power. The Irish benches rang with cries "Remember Coercion." On the Tory benches "a collection of bores and
the bored became a mass of screaming, waving, gesticulating luna-
tics," while Churchill, standing on the bench, waved a green handkerchief and emitted wild yells "like a wild animal fastening its

P

teeth on the prey." Sitting imperturbably, Gladstone wrote over a dispatch case on his knees a report to his Queen, of whom he had written the year before to Lord Rosebery, "The Queen alone is enough to kill any man." He would not have to contend with her for a short time.

"Congratulations," said T. P. O'Connor to Parnell, who had supplied the votes for the overturn, and Parnell, with a quiet smile said, "We shall see, we shall see." Holding the balance of power, he was the master of the situation.

Even with the Liberals out of power, Chamberlain retained hopes that Parnell might ally himself with him on the basis of his local-government scheme, and on June 10 he asked O'Shea to quiz Parnell about it, indicating strongly that he would pledge to oppose the resumption of coercion. Parnell was noncommittal. Then Chamberlain got the idea that the way to put the plan over would be to go to Ireland and make some speeches on the subject.

Chamberlain believed that he had Parnell's promise to use his good offices in his behalf to pave the way with introductions, arrangements, etc. But to Chamberlain's dismay, *United Ireland* came out with a bitter editorial on June 26. A few months before, in a gesture of snobbery, it had tagged Chamberlain as a "shop-keeping Danton," a reference to his background in trade. Now William O'Brien's pen was dipped in vitriol. He editorialized, "Base as we consider the conduct of radical ministers to have been in abetting the horrors which the Gladstone government have carried out in Ireland, we never could have supposed they would have stooped to the arts which they are now attempting to practice in order to curry favor once more with the Irish people. We plainly tell Messrs. Chamberlain and Dilke that if they are wise they will keep out of Ireland altogether. We do not want them here. Let them stop at home and look after their own affairs. In plain English, this proposed tour of theirs is simply adding insult to injury."

The tone of this editorial was, of course, adding Parnell's insult to Chamberlain's injury, since it emanated from Parnell's newspaper (though Parnell probably was not advised of this blast, since he had given O'Brien free rein). Chamberlain sent the editorial to O'Shea, with the inscription "Dear O'Shea" and exclamation points. It was an implied reproach to O'Shea that he had fallen down on the job as an intermediary. O'Shea poured out his venom of hate to his wife in a letter to her the next day: "My Dick—We are of opinion that the formula holds good. No rational beings who have had dealings with Mr. Parnell would believe him on oath. We know that he has recently said that he is under no obligation or promise to me!!! The marks are of admiration, not of surprise. He has not told the lie to my face, but the man, who after promising to assist in every way Mr. Chamberlain's journey to Ireland, can let his paper the same week abuse him like a pickpocket, is not to be respected by Mr. C. and I have already told the *scoundrel* what I think of him." The letter concludes, with mixed humor and self-pity, "I am worried if not out of my wits, out of my hair. The little left came out this morning after a sleepless night and I am balder than a coot is. Such fun. I wonder whether I shall die soon or if the day will come. Would I understood it had come when I was asked to come to Kilmainham."

The very next day O'Shea wrote Katherine that he had castigated Parnell before a distinguished group of House members saying, "Poor devil, he is obliged to allow himself to be kicked to the right or left and look pleasant. But he has the consolation of having been well paid for his trouble—£40,000, the tribute of the priests and people of Ireland."

Seething with frustration as he saw his hopes for the Irish secretaryship go up in smoke and mortified at the failure of his mission, O'Shea wrote to Chamberlain on June 28, indicating quite clearly that (contrary to Parnell's specific injunction to the contrary in writing to him) Parnell had conveyed oral assurances through him to Chamberlain that he would support his plan. Of a talk he just had with Parnell, he said, "I laid particular stress on the many assurances of (in my opinion) a most binding nature which I had taken to you from him regarding the present business. He did not appear disposed to go any further. I cannot however doubt that on reflection he will see the necessity of altering a position of political and personal cruelty to you and myself."

On July 11, Chamberlain offered Parnell a formal alliance on the basis of his plan, and now he made it clear it would not be a substitute for a separate Parliament under a Home Rule plan, but Parnell had lost all interest. He replied that the more favorable Tory attitude on abandonment of coercion might foreshadow a proposal for an acceptance of a plan for legislative independence of Ireland and therefore it would be best "not to encumber the Irish question" with the Chamberlain plan. And thus the whole project ended with a refusal on Parnell's part to engage in any further *pourparlers*.

The humiliated Chamberlain, a friend of Parnell previously, as time went on became more and more convinced that he had been hoodwinked by Parnell. Labouchere told him that he had been duped. "My own experience of Parnell is that he never makes a bargain without intending to get rid of it and that he has either a natural love of treachery or considers that promises are not binding when made to a Saxon." As for O'Shea, the Figaro who nurtured in his mind the paranoid obsession that he was a neglected states-man who had been ill-treated, he became more vindictive than ever in his hatred of Parnell. O'Shea had misrepresented Parnell's attitude to his plan to Chamberlain throughout the negotiations, and he now poured salt on the wound and continually sought to convince Chamberlain that Parnell had imposed a fraud on his guileless nature. Chamberlain, who had been the friend of Home Rule, would be the most important agent in destroying it.

XI

In examining the correspondence of Captain O'Shea in 1884 and 1885, one can deduce certain facts about the baffling *ménage à trois* relationship.

O'Shea writes his wife addressing her by her affectionate nickname "Dick" and signs himself with the nickname she gave him, "Boysie." It seems that he regarded Katherine with affection and believed the feeling was reciprocated. When he is ill, he asks her to come to London and take care of him. There is in the letters no hint of reproach or suspicion regarding the ambiguous role of the intruder, Parnell. On the contrary, O'Shea writes as if there were a community of interest between him and his wife in advancing his career. He writes of his hopes of the Irish secretaryship, "This is an enormous thing giving you and the chicks a very great position." Clare and Frances were born at the time, and he considers them as among his "chicks" with no suspicion that they might be progeny of friend Parnell.

In these letters, which denote a harmony of interest which he thought existed between himself and his wife, a striking feature is the continual derision and diatribe against Parnell. Since he engages in this screed without restraint or apology, the conclusion is inescapable *that he thought that Katherine felt the same way*. The relationship becomes more explicable—his shrewd wife had sold him on the idea that her motivations are purely opportunistic, that she scorns Parnell but is cooperating with him in a platonic friendship and coddling him for the purely selfish purpose of advancing the interests of Willie and herself, and for no other reason. Thus, when the occasion arose when he needed her help, as it was to arise soon, she had to deliver or else impair the image of the role she had described for herself.

This charade had commenced in 1880 when Aunt Ben was eighty-eight and expected to depart this life at any moment, leaving Katherine her money, which she might expect to use to persuade Willie to any course she wished in solving her personal life. But Aunt Ben continued to live on, and now, in 1884, she was ninety-three and the charade had to continue, in the same hope that existed at the beginning, that she would depart this life at any moment.

XII

In the new Conservative government which took the place of Gladstone's government, the Prime Minister was Lord Salisbury. He was of the Cecil family, descended from Lord Burghley, Queen Elizabeth's great councillor. Of him the inimitable T. P. O'Connor wrote, "He is not a very attractive personality, for he is lumbering, uncouth, ponderous beyond the ordinary, black in visage, pale in cheek, heavy and awkward in frame—he strikes one as a very rough piece of nature's carving, not in the least like the delicate and more refined material out of which we suppose aristocrats to be composed. And yet he cannot help being interesting for he is an intellectual man and he has about him the unmistakable atmosphere which great birth and the great privilege it commands gives to most aristocrats."

In the new government Lord Carnarvon was the Irish Viceroy and Sir William Hart Dyke the Irish Secretary. In accordance with the tacit pledge to Parnell, coercion was abandoned. A notable piece of legislation pushed through by the Conservatives was Lord Ashbourne's Act which provided Government money to the amount of £5,000,000 so that tenants in Ireland could buy their land if they reached an agreement with the landlords on the price. The state would put up half the purchase price and the tenant would make repayment over a term of forty-nine years at an interest of 4 per cent. This was another step accomplished by Parnell's influence in the overthrow of feudalism in Ireland.

Parnell was exploring the means of fulfilling what he conceived as his life's work, the achievement of Home Rule for Ireland. Negotiations started to roll when Sir Charles Gavan Duffy, the Young Irelander who had emigrated to Australia and had become Prime Minister of New South Wales, suggested a plan for Ireland to Lord Carnarvon and also suggested that Justin McCarthy might act as a go-between with Parnell. McCarthy told Lord Carnarvon that Parnell was the dictator of the party, that "He really stands in front of the Irish people and wields them," and warned him that Parnell was "cold, narrow and unimaginative." On July 26, Carnarvon wrote Lord Salisbury of his intention to meet with Parnell. "I do not believe that Parnell is disposed to be immoderate. On the contrary as the final struggle draws near, he seems to me to grow more moderate in his objects than perhaps could be expected."

The meeting took place on August 1 in Lord Carnarvon's sister's house at 15 Hill Street, with the blinds drawn and all the carpets drawn up since the family was away. Carnarvon started the conversation by saying that he sought information only and that he must warn that as the Queen's representative he would not hear anything of separation. Parnell agreed and spoke of the need for protection of property and land rights in Ireland and his desire to advance the country economically. As for tariff protection, Carnarvon agreed on its desirability but added, "what a row there will be in England!"

As to the sum and substance of the talk, in which Parnell felt that there was a meeting of minds, Parnell later summarized, "The Conservative Party if they should be successful at the polls would offer Ireland a statutory legislature with a right to protect her own industries and this would be coupled with a settlement of the Irish land question on the basis of purchase and on a larger scale than that proposed by the Prime Minister."

Parnell was now sanguine about the chances for Home Rule from the Conservatives, since Carnarvon must have had clearance from Lord Salisbury. The Tories, with their control of the House of Lords, could bring about revolutionary reforms easier than the Liberals could enact moderate ones. But that bright hope was to come to naught since, as Salisbury was finding out, there was a difference between what was desirable and what was politically feasible with the squirearchy and the Court putting pressure on Salisbury. At the time, the influence of the Queen on many Conservative members was considerable, and Lord Salisbury had to assure her that "He entirely agrees with your Majesty in thinking that the Irish Nationalists cannot be trusted and that any bargain with them would be full of danger." Parnell was misled into putting reliance on Lord Randolph Churchill, who wrote to a friend, "Let us only (if returned to office with Irish aid) be enabled to occupy a year with the Irish question. By that time I am certain Parnell's party will have become seriously disintegrated. Personal jealousies, government influences, Davitt, Fenian intrigues, will all be at work . . . and the bishops who in their hearts hate Parnell and don't care a scrap for Home Rule will complete the rout."

After the 1885 session the Queen dissolved Parliament and an election was set for December. In opening the campaign, Parnell showed his high confidence by declaring, "If they have not succeeded in squelching us during the last five years they are not likely to do during the next five. . . . They will either have to grant to Ireland the complete right to rule herself or they will have to take away from us the sham share in the English constitutional system which they extended to us at the Union and govern us as a Crown colony."

Parnell's strategy was to get the highest price for his support and to let the Liberals as in a horse race set the pace. Chamberlain, smarting from the rebuff by Parnell on his local-government plan, was against any offer or even encouragement to the Nationalists and wrote to Gladstone, "Parnell is not to be depended on. On the whole I think the only choice is to let the Irishmen stew in their own juice." From time to time in the past Gladstone had uttered words encouraging to Irish hopes of self-rule. As early as February, 1881, he had upset the Queen quite badly when he stated in Commons that he favored Irish control of Irish affairs if the question "What provisions do you propose to make for the supremacy of

Parliament?" were answered. Now Gladstone spoke kindly if vaguely of Irish aspirations in the Hawarden Manifesto, which Parnell told the New York *Herald,* was "the most remarkable declaration on the subject ever uttered by an English statesman." Parnell tried to coax Gladstone further to outline his ideas, but Gladstone demurred, stating that it was "premature to usurp the functions of a Government."

Then Parnell made the fateful decision which may have changed the course of history. *Iacta alea est.* He threw the support of the Irish Nationalists in English contests to the Tories. T. P. O'Connor, who drew up the manifesto, related that though Parnell "made few changes, there was a hesitancy about him, an appearance of internal struggle which was somewhat surprising and disquieting." The manifesto denounced the Liberals as "men who coerced Ireland, deluged Egypt with blood, menace religious liberty in the schools, the freedom of speech in Parliament and promise to the country generally a repetition of the follies and failure of the Liberal administration."

The result of the election was Liberals in the lead with 335, Tories 249 and Parnellites 86. With so many contests almost evenly balanced it was believed that the Parnell manifesto backing the Tories had cost the Liberals an irreducible minimum of 30 seats. Gladstone himself spoke of the election as having been "pronounced with an Irish brogue."

The loss of these Liberal seats to the Tories was greater than the margin by which the Gladstone Home Rule Bill was to be defeated a few months later. Was the Parnell decision therefore a piece of folly? It is a nice question. In Parnell's behalf it must be pointed out that Gladstone had specifically asked the electorate to give him a majority in Parliament independent of Irish Nationalists. If Gladstone had obtained such a majority he need not have introduced a bill for Home Rule at all. Future history demonstrated that the Liberals introduced Home Rule bills only when they depended on Irish votes to stay in power. On the other hand, it can be said that Parnell was swayed by his own prejudice against Gladstone, having hated him from the time he had been shut up in prison. According to many accounts, he gibed many times at Gladstone in frank displays of his hatred, believing him to be a pretentious hypocrite (a belief which was not unique by any means). Mrs. O'Shea told how he derided the "Grand Old Spider" to her and said that his hatred for Gladstone never wavered.

In Ireland the personal triumph of Parnell was phenomenal. With the great extension of the franchise that was enacted by Parliament in 1884, Parnell had been expected to increase his strength from about 40 to 65 seats. Instead he had won 86 out of 102 seats in Ireland and had won 85 out of the 86 contested seats. The Liberals were snuffed out of existence in Ireland. Parnell swept even Ulster, which returned 18 Nationalists to 17 Tories. Ireland had spoken with one voice for Parnell. Gladstone said years later to R. Barry O'Brien, "That settled the question. When the people express their determination that way, you must give them what they want."

In England there was stunned disbelief in the results. The Queen told Lord Salisbury, according to her journal, that the elected Irish members were "mostly low, disreputable men who were elected by order of Parnell and did not genuinely represent the whole country."

On this day, the greatest day of triumph of his life, was Parnell in Ireland supervising and pulling the wires for the Nationalists to be elected? No, indeed, on this day of days he was in Liverpool, England, toiling and sweating, performing all kinds of chores in order to win a seat for the man who was no friend of Ireland and whom Parnell despised above all others—Captain William Henry O'Shea. Such was the incubus cast on him by his fatal love for Katherine O'Shea.

XIII

Captain O'Shea was a thorn in the side of the Irish members. He refused to sit with the Parnellites and from the Government side kept up a sibilant flow of sneering and supercilious comment and, what was even more galling, an appearance of deprecating amusement at the plebian mannerisms, accent or mode of dress of his Irish colleagues. When reminded by Mrs. O'Shea of the intellectual attainments of many of them, he retorted, "I can rejoice in but cannot sit with unvarnished genius." Once, Parnell told Katherine that a member had waited in the lobby to kill him. When she expressed alarm, he said, "Oh, he was too drunk to kill anybody. But I wish Willie would not annoy the members so. From what I could make out, Willie smiled at his pronunciation of 'Mr. Spaker, Sorr' and Willie's smile is a bit of a twister sometimes."

Another annoyance was that O'Shea forever paraded his intimacy with Chamberlain and forever echoed anything Chamberlain had to say. One member grumbled, "Listen to him, then, with his 'Chamberlain and I.' Will ye tell me how much is 'Chamberlain' and how much is 'I' in that cabal?"

As the general election of 1885 loomed, Captain O'Shea now confronted not the loose, informal operation of 1880, when he had been elected, but a well-oiled party machine designed to enforce strict party discipline. Candidates were selected at county conventions which seemingly operated autonomously but were actually controlled by a party caucus which had already picked the candidates at a Dublin meeting and steam-rollered its own candidate in. If an undesirable candidate had backing in the local area, some stratagem would be used to sidetrack him, such as getting some well-respected cleric to sponsor him—then at the convention the cleric (working with the Parnellites) would listen gravely to the arguments against his candidate and reluctantly withdraw him in favor of the Parnellite candidate.

The candidate, when picked, moreover, had to take this pledge, "I . . . pledge that in the event of my election to Parliament I will sit, act and vote with the Irish Parliamentary party . . ." A candidate who had not fulfilled the pledge was honor-bound to resign.

O'Shea refused to take the pledge. In a meeting with the Irish leadership, including Parnell, in the latter part of October, 1885, James J. O'Kelly told him, "it was not in the power of mortal man to get him in for any National constituency without the pledge and even [Parnell] could not do it." He was advised to try for a constituency in Ulster, where he might run as a Liberal.

Mrs. O'Shea was determined to get Willie a seat. She wrote that her motive was to keep him away from Eltham, which hardly seems plausible. Possibly she was motivated by some affection. But more probably the need to demonstrate that her relationship with Parnell had value for O'Shea when in need and possibly a guilty conscience at the long deception drove her to make amends. O'Shea had asked that Parnell go to Lord Richard Grosvenor, the Liberal whip, and ask that he provide a Liberal seat for O'Shea, but Parnell told Mrs. O'Shea he could not take the risk, since it would leak out.

So Mrs. O'Shea went to see Lord Richard herself and asked him point-blank for a seat in Liverpool for Willie. After an hour of arguing the difficulties, Lord Richard said he would consider it. This dauntless woman then wrote directly to Gladstone, who replied that he would tell Lord Richard how sorry he would be if O'Shea were not returned. It is obvious that the leadership of the Liberal party in the United Kingdom was not taking time out to be deferential to one Katherine O'Shea, but to one whom they knew to be the close friend or the mistress of Charles Stewart Parnell.

Captain O'Shea, as might be expected, was pouring out to Katherine his bitterness toward the treacherous Parnell, who was ungrateful for the many services he had rendered him, "He [Chamberlain] and all my life friends say that if he [Parnell] had any feeling, any spark of honor, he would have told his party that he was under such a promise and such an obligation that my seat must be secured or he would resign his leadership." That blast on October 25 was followed a week later by "I have been treated in blackguard fashion and I mean to hit back a stunner. I have everything ready; no drugs could make me sleep last night and I packed my shell with dynamite. I cannot hurt my friend's reputation [i.e., Chamberlain's] and it will send a blackguard's reputation with his deluded countrymen into smithereens."

From a dramatic point of view, it would be desirable that O'Shea was brandishing a threat to uncover the scandal by a divorce suit, but all the circumstances show that O'Shea had in mind evidence he was trying to find that Parnell was intimately involved in terrorist activities including the Phoenix Park murders.

Katherine O'Shea had a whim of iron. "I grimly determined that I would make Lord Richard Grosvenor's life a burden until I had landed Willie safely on the Liberal benches." To her, Lord Richard said on one of her visits, "I am not at all sure that I approve of you in your political capacity; you are so terribly strenuous and determined."

Her domination of Parnell seems to have been complete. She sent Parnell to Liverpool to see what he could do to ensure O'Shea's candidacy—he could put pressure on the Liberals by threatening to stand for a seat in Liverpool himself. She also conveyed to Grosvenor the terms of a deal she had wangled out of Parnell, "If Liberal party adopt O'Shea as candidate for Exchange Division of Liverpool and withdraw their candidate from either Kirkdale Division of Lancashire, whichever of these two it might be arranged that Parnell should stand for; the latter would secure the Liberal candidates, the Irish votes in the other six Divisions of Liverpool and the Bottle Division of Lancashire, . . ."

The command faculties of Mrs. O'Shea were such that while she was managing her husband's bid for a seat she took time out to help one Samuel Montagu who was running in the Whitechapel division of London. Montagu was a business associate of Willie, engaged in trying to get a loan for the Spanish Government. "I . . . wired to a London agent of Parnell's (under such name as he would know the message emanated from him) to beat up the Irishmen for Montagu, told Parnell I had done so and then set myself again to attend to Willie's candidature."

Parnell, instead of concentrating on the greatest election contest and the greatest opportunity in Irish history, was in Liverpool pulling the strings for O'Shea. His plan was to be nominated and then withdraw in favor of O'Shea if the Liberal candidate, Stephens, were withdrawn. He sent Katherine a wire "Send W. [Willie] a tip to be civil" since he was irritating the Irish in Liverpool by braying about Parnell's perfidy. Meanwhile whines came from O'Shea, "I wonder the little girls have not written me; no one cares a bit about me except my poor old mother."

On another visit by Mrs. O'Shea to Grosvenor, he yielded to her pleas that he go to Liverpool himself to put pressure on the local boys to supplant Stephens with O'Shea, but he asked her to accompany him. She looked at him quietly and kept a grip on her self-control with all the force she possessed. What! Was he mad? Go to Liverpool to help her husband by the side of her lover! "Was this man a monk, a priest, an absolute child to think these things could be?"

Then, as she watched Grosvenor doodling on the blotting pad, she realized the truth, that he was afraid of antagonizing Parnell by helping her husband. So she reassured him that "Parnell is in Liverpool working quietly for Willie," and she explained that

Parnell was playing a game in behalf of O'Shea, not against him, by announcing his candidacy.

Such were the infernal complications of this love affair.

O'Shea became pessimistic about his chances for the Exchange division of Liverpool and made another demand of his wife, that Parnell withdraw his candidate, T. P. O'Connor, from the Scotland Division of Liverpool in favor of him. "He [Parnell] will not like doing it yet [it is the] only way to redeem his character." But things worked out when the Liberal candidate, Stephens, retired in favor of O'Shea under the pressure of Grosvenor, who told Stephens that Gladstone wished it. Parnell stepped out of the race and spoke everywhere in the district in favor of O'Shea, working even on election day to get the Irish voters to the polls.

All this went for naught when Willie was defeated by a handful of votes. Then came the demand that Parnell dreaded most, that he get O'Shea a Nationalist seat in Ireland at a by-election "to redeem his honor," as the Captain put it.

XIV

Parnell said that it was completely impossible. There was only one vacancy. T. P. O'Connor had been elected from both Galway and from the Scotland Division of Liverpool and would elect to sit for the latter, but Parnell could not put O'Shea over in Galway. "I am popular with the rank and file voters," said O'Shea, "and I would be sorry to be on good terms with the rapscallion crew of the party." Parnell, busy thinking, said, "Well then you need not be sorry, since you are unpopular with them." Parnell asked, would he take the pledge? O'Shea said "No." "Well, then," replied Parnell, "there is no more to be said."

O'Shea would not take the "no" of Parnell as final. He nagged his wife—she must see Gladstone, she must see Grosvenor, she must keep after Parnell.

In January, 1886, the first allusion to the love affair appeared in print, in the *Irish Times,* in something said by Phil Callan, who had been turned out of his seat by Parnell and who knew about Mrs. O'Shea from the telegram which had been opened by Small in the Monaghan election campaign and then handed to him by

Small. In a letter of January 15, Parnell wrote from Ireland to Katherine that Callan intended mischief, that one Blake "asked me whether I had ever spoken to a lady in London about C. [Callan] and turning him out and that C. had told him that he had evidence I had and that is why I would not agree to his candidature. The 'Lady in London' is, of course, Mrs. O'Shea and that is how her name is going to be introduced into the matter. . . ."

With this threat of further publicity, Parnell was nervous now about intervention for O'Shea, which would have to be more than intervention—it would have to be the strong-arm pressure. He told Katherine of his fears of "these English hypocrites." He spoke of the party resistance and the blow to their faith in him, "I can force Willie upon Galway but it will be such a shock to my own men that they'll not be the same again." It tore him apart to have to do it. No one knows how many tears were shed by Katherine, what entreaties she made. Mrs. O'Shea brought in, no doubt, an argument with clear logic: that Willie in his frantic, vindictive mood would be dangerous if disappointed.

Parnell finally consented. "I'll run him from Galway, I'll get him returned, I'll force him down their throats and I'll be through with his talk of pledges."

XV

The Nationalist party leaders had looked on with dismay as Parnell fought for O'Shea in Liverpool, one of the few exceptions made to the party's blanket indictment of Liberals. It was a thunderbolt when they learned that Parnell proposed to ram down their throats in Galway as a Nationalist candidate, O'Shea, a man who was not only personally obnoxious to them but one who was no friend of Irish Home Rule or the tenant farmer, a man who refused to take the party pledge which had been established as the *sine qua non* for office.

The first to hear about it was T. P. O'Connor, who heard it from Parnell in the Palace Yard at Westminster. O'Connor recalled, "My blood ran cold. I saw clearly the disastrous consequences that must follow." He immediately wired Healy in Dublin suggesting that they both resign in protest. He went to the Metropole Hotel in

London to see Biggar and found him in bed with a cold, under a huge bearskin. When T. P. told him the news, Biggar sat bolt up-right. "O'Shea! Damned Whig! He won't sit for Galway, sorr. Damned nonsense, sorr. I'll go to Ireland at once. I'll stop it. Damned Whig." And he jumped out of bed and started dressing, forgetting about his cold. The two set out for Dublin.

When he got O'Connor's wire, Healy composed a letter of protest for the *Freeman's Journal,* pointing out that O'Shea had just been defeated as a Liberal, that he always sat on the Government side and that he nearly always voted against Irish measures or abstained. This made him an impossible candidate for the Nationalists. The *Freeman* was by now a Parnellite paper, and the publisher, Edmund Dwyer Gray, refused to accept Healy's letter for publication when he received that same night an election address from O'Shea stating that he had Parnell's support for the seat, which Parnell confirmed by wire.

Biggar and T. P. O'Connor read the O'Shea address when they reached Dublin in the early morning. They came to Healy's home when he was about to retire after an all-night wrangle with Gray, and he greeted them in his nightshirt. O'Connor said that in view of the fact that Parnell had taken a public position, he could not oppose him though O'Shea's candidacy was nothing short of a dis-grace. Biggar and Healy felt otherwise and immediately left for Galway.

The two insurgents started to mobilize opposition in Galway. O'Shea had arrived on an earlier train. Public sentiment was in favor of a Nationalist named Michael Lynch, and Biggar and Healy set out to organize a convention to nominate him. The perplexed Lynch asked what it was all about, and Healy, drawing him to a corner of a room, confided to him, "It has its entire origin in a woman of evil character and is an abominable scandal."

Healy and Biggar were receiving a stream of wires begging them to desist from their contumacy. From O'Brien, "Is it possible you do not see how you are being victimized? It is a question of life and death. Your dearest friends will be against you." From Dr. Kenny, "I would prefer to see you dead than pursuing your present course." O'Brien wrote to Dillon, "Parnell is plainly bound by some influence he cannot resist," that the rebels had used all means short of openly breaking with Parnell but since Parnell remained adamant, the issue at stake was whether the Parnell leadership could be maintained if it were flouted in Galway.

Biggar and Healy fought on. Biggar was anything but a Puritan in his private life; on the contrary, he was a first-class wencher, but he felt that private vices must be kept private and in this case a seat in Parliament must not be bartered for a woman's favors. He composed a wire to Parnell saying, "Mrs. O'Shea will be your ruin" (how prophetic he was) but on Healy's entreaty he changed it to "The O'Sheas will be your ruin." As whispers spread about in Galway about the connection, O'Shea got down on his knees before the bishop, the Rev. Dr. Carr, and swore to him that the rumor about his wife and Parnell was utterly untrue.

O'Shea saw the tide of public feeling running against him and wired Parnell, "All hope gone unless you can come at once." To which Parnell replied, "Will arrive Tuesday morning. Believe can overcome difficulty."

O'Brien, Sexton, T. P. O'Connor and Tim Harrington drew up a manifesto of support and sent to each Parliamentary member a wire, "Parnell has intimated to us his leadership is at stake. Healy's speech has created the impression that the party generally is against Parnell. Will you authorize us to attach your name to our public declaration of support?" Fifty names were subscribed, a quite impressive number to be rounded up on short notice.

Copies of the *Freeman* containing the manifesto with the signatures arrived on the same train with Parnell, accompanied by an entourage of T. P. O'Connor, Sexton, J. J. O'Kelly, the party whip, John Deasy, and Parnell's secretary Henry Campbell (O'Brien having arrived the previous day). O'Connor related that on the train Parnell was in a good mood, saying that he would in Galway "use all the resources of civilization," the phrase Gladstone had used in reference to his intent to imprison Parnell when speaking in Leeds in 1881. O'Connor related that Parnell to while away the time suggested a conversation about religion to him, but not being a theoretical or speculative thinker, Parnell could only contribute to the subject the statement "I was born a Protestant and will die a Protestant."

They arrived at the Galway station, which was connected by a subway to a gigantic hotel at one end, a very spacious station resembling a monument or a tomb—and indeed it was a monument in the midst of a town of fallen fortunes to a dead dream, that of making Galway a great international gateway to the United States. Biggar had suggested when he learned of Parnell's coming to "Mob him," and there was a mob at the station, but they gathered not around Parnell but in a menacing way around T. P. O'Connor, one man trying to knock his hat off with a stick. Parnell came to his side and escorted him to the Railway Hotel.

Later, in the hotel dining room, Parnell sat around a table with Healy, Biggar and a few others, discussing the situation. Almost at the start, Parnell held forth his hand in an eloquent gesture. "I hold an Irish Parliament in the hollow of this hand. The man who strikes at this hand strikes at the hopes of the Irish nation." In the face of this argument and under what O'Connor called "the frozen glare of Parnell's brilliant and mysterious eyes," Healy seemed to quail visibly, and soon tears ran down his cheeks as he strove to make amends, denying that he had acted under the influence of any personal feelings. Biggar made no apology and speaking coolly seemed about to bring the subject of Mrs. O'Shea into the conversation when Healy jumped up and grabbed him by the collar.

There was a meeting of the town citizenry in a converted chapel called Young Ireland Hall. Parnell, who was chairman, said in a stirring peroration to his speech, "If my candidate is defeated, the news will spread around the universe that a disaster has overwhelmed Ireland. The world will say, 'Parnell is beaten. Ireland no longer has a leader.' " Parnell was calm and collected during the speech. As Healy wrote, "If his heartstrings writhed, his stoicism did not fail." Then William O'Brien carried the day in a dazzling speech in which he recounted the achievements of Parnell and indicated that a glowing future for the nation might be lost.

And so, in a wave of emotion, Lynch came forward and for the good of the country withdrew in favor of O'Shea. Biggar would not recant, but said only, "Mr. Chairman, all I have to say is that I don't agree with you." Then Captain O'Shea was nominated as the candidate for Galway. He did not take the pledge and was to be the only Irish Nationalist member who did not vote for Home Rule when the vote came.

It must have been a bitter and humiliating experience for Parnell, and the fact that he bore up so well during it may be a testimony to increasing callousness as the years went by. He had thought that his word would be sufficient, but he had been compelled to go to Galway and beg for support, knowing fully that his followers by now suspected, quite strongly, that he was forcing a candidate down their throats because he valued his relations with his mistress above the interests of his country.

Parnell did try to adopt another reason for pushing O'Shea's candidacy. In December, 1890, at the time of the party crisis, Tim Harrington wrote to the *Freeman's Journal,* "Mr. Parnell during the Galway election explained to his followers that he had only adopted Captain O'Shea as a candidate at the special request of Mr. Chamberlain, stating that under the circumstances he did not feel justified in stating so publicly." Harrington stated that this explanation was "received with incredulity"—understandably so, since it is not customary to reward mediocrities used as messenger-boys with seats in Parliament, especially if their political philosophy is an antagonistic one.

Many years later letters came to light between Parnell and Edmund Dwyer Gray of the *Freeman's Journal.* They indicate the agony of indecision in Parnell's mind and also the agony of doubt as to how much the party members knew of his love affair. On December 24, which was some weeks before the events at Galway, which occurred between February 4 and 7, Parnell wrote Gray that he owed nothing to O'Shea, having discharged his debt fully in trying to get O'Shea a seat from Liverpool. However Chamberlain was very much interested in getting him a seat. Therefore, "do you think I would be justified in saying to you that if you can induce the leading members of the party to tolerate O'Shea's unpledged candidature for Galway, neither would I oppose it?" Thus he tried to get Gray to act as a buffer, but Gray, on December 26, refused the role. "There is only one way of doing it in my opinion —for you openly to take the responsibility."

It has been argued that O'Shea, the recipient of the gift of a seat at such a risk to Parnell's leadership, could hardly have been unaware that his wife was Parnell's mistress, and therefore he had engaged in blackmail. But that assumption ignores O'Shea's colossal vanity and his purblindness in evaluating his worth in the world. He genuinely felt that Parnell owed to him his political life since he had arranged the Kilmainham Treaty and that his services, though they did not bear fruit in the local-government negotiations with Chamberlain, might be more successful in the coming Home Rule struggle. This is borne out by a letter of January 26 which Chamberlain wrote to O'Shea, the contents of which were undoubtedly suggested by O'Shea. "Surely it must be to the interest of the Irish party to keep open channels of communication with the Liberal leaders. If any possible cooperation is expected, it is clear that a great deal of preliminary talks must be held. Can you get Mr. Parnell's exequatur for one of the vacant seats? It is really the least he can do for you after all you have done for him."

Parnell in this instance had won; he had bulled through his choice, only because of the obssesive fear of his followers of the chaos that might follow the loss of solidarity that had been achieved around the personality of Parnell. There was inevitably some disenchantment with the leader. Biggar had resisted him to the end. Parnell had now clear notice that Healy could be counted on to fight him again on a question of principle. Healy wrote that he later regretted his desertion of Biggar in the Galway crisis. "No gain came by propping up Parnell's worm-eaten pedestal and within four years O'Shea had remorselessly overthrown it."

XVI

After the general election in 1885, Parnell had announced, "Ireland has been knocking long enough on the English door with kid gloves . . . now it will knock with the mailed fist."

With Parnell support the Salisbury regime had a majority of only two votes. Before the Galway by-election, the Conservative government of Lord Salisbury had fallen, overthrown by Parnell, who held the balance of power and was now the arbiter of the life or death of any government.

Parnell played his cards warily. Doubtful now that the Conservatives would grant Home Rule, he had to wait and see, while he said frankly in an interview with the Boston *Herald*, "I expect the settlement to come from the Liberals."

On December 16, 1885, the National Press Agency published what were purported to be the authoritative views of Gladstone but were actually obtained in an interview with his son, Herbert

Gladstone, who was more advanced on the Home Rule question than his father. It was futile for Gladstone to protest that this was merely speculation on his views. The statement, which was thereafter labeled the Hawarden Kite, said in part, "Mr. Gladstone has definitely adopted the policy of Home Rule for Ireland and there are well founded hopes that he will win over the chief representatives of the moderate section of the party to his views. . . . There are only two alternatives—coercion and conciliation. Coercion has been made well nigh impossible by the action of the Tories, its chief champions; and in no circumstances will the Liberal party ever consent to exceptional repressive legislation for Ireland again. Conciliation can be effectual on one condition—the support of Mr. Parnell and this would be granted only to a measure for the establishment of a Parliament in Dublin."

The publication of the Hawarden Kite was embarrassing to Gladstone because he was in the course of conveying a proposal to the Salisbury government through Salisbury's nephew, Arthur Balfour, that if Salisbury brought before the House a plan for settling the question of Irish self-government, he, Gladstone, would not oppose it as a party matter. Mrs. O'Shea was writing to Gladstone, transmitting urgent requests from Parnell that he sketch his plans for Irish autonomy, since his election speeches seemed to say that he would back it if the Irish electorate did. Gladstone repelled these advances, telling Mrs. O'Shea that Parnell should make his overtures to the Conservatives. "Let me refer to facts public and patent. Up to this moment the Nationalists are the ostensible allies of the Government and opponents of the Liberals. By their means the Government have gained and we have lost a majority in the towns," and in a letter three days afterward he said, "The Nationalists are in the face of the world in practical alliance with the Tories. Any communication of views from me to them would be certainly regarded as the offer of bribe from me to them to detach them from the Tories. It is therefore impossible."

However, the Conservatives were swinging away from the alliance with Parnell to an anti-Irish position. There was constant pressure from the Queen. There was anti-Irish prejudice whipped up by the London *Times*. Thus, Bismarck's action in expelling 37,000 Poles from West Prussia was hailed as "Home Rule for Prussia" not "Home Rule for Poland," and "It is time to recognize the truth written large in history that there are certain antipathies which have to be accepted as ultimate facts."

Then, too, there was the keen disappointment among the Conservatives that the Irish had not been able to deliver more votes and seats to them. "I did my best for you," said Lord Randolph Churchill to Justin McCarthy, "and now I will do my best against you." He, as well as other Conservatives, felt that there were more votes in taking up the cause of Protestant Ulster, which would be oppressed by Dublin rule. Then there was the disgruntlement felt by Salisbury and Balfour that they had been forced to eat dirt in discarding coercion. So the Conservatives turned down emphatically Gladstone's offer to help them find an Irish solution. As Winston Churchill put it in his life of his father, "His [Gladstone's] letter was treated with contempt. No other word will suffice. A public calamity forsooth. 'His hypocrisy' wrote a minister, to whom the letter was shown, 'makes me sick.' "

On January 26, 1886, the Conservatives announced that they would introduce a new coercion bill and would seek to suppress the Irish National League. Parnell immediately denounced it. "History will not record a more disgraceful, unscrupulous *volte-face* than that executed by the Conservative Party when they found out that our vote was not numerically enough to keep them in office."

The Conservative Government survived this turnabout by only a few hours, then was overthrown on an amendment to the Queen's address moved by Jesse Collings, a follower of Chamberlain. The new Irish Secretary, W. H. Smith, had no sooner reached Dublin to accept his new office when he received a wire that he was out. The Collings amendment dealt with farm policy, the so-called "three acres and a cow" amendment, but it sufficed for Parnell to boot out the Conservatives. The margin of defeat almost exactly corresponded to the Irish vote in Parliament, so Gladstone, taking office, could be under no illusions as to what was expected of him.

Thus, the great statesman Gladstone "kissed hands" for the third time, although the Queen had expressed her disinclination to "take this half-crazy and in many ways ridiculous old man for the sake of the country." In the new Liberal government five who had been in the previous Cabinet refused to accept posts because they were unalterably opposed to Home Rule—Lords Hartington, Derby, Northbrook, Selbourne and Carlington. Chamberlain and Trevelyan agreed to join the Cabinet provisionally to explore the issue.

One of the newcomers in the Cabinet was the new Irish Secretary, John Morley, a foremost figure among English writers on political and philosophic problems. He had been editor of the *Morning Star* and the *Fortnightly Review,* and then, as editor, had transformed the *Pall Mall Gazette* from an organ of jingo Toryism into a leading organ of liberal radicalism. He was an agnostic, and Healy said he had solved the problem of God by spelling the word with a small G. Intellectually, he was a close counterpart of Gladstone, with whom he loved to dissect Homer. As a champion of Home Rule, his view was based less on moral grounds (as were Gladstone's) than on the practical view that the Irish were a divisive factor in the English scene and were better removed. Morley had made the classic statement "Ireland would be easy to govern were not its people intractable and all of its problems insoluble."

Gladstone's relations with Chamberlain, which should have been an effort of conciliation, were completely flubbed. Chamberlain had a large following of Radicals, and it was known that he was estranged from Parnell on account of the fiasco of his plan for Ireland. Yet, it is probable that Gladstone, at seventy-six, viewed "Pushful Joe" with a jaundiced eye, not relishing the presence of such an abrasive personality in the Cabinet. He offered the Admirality to Chamberlain, which he declined on the ground that he had no training for the post. Perhaps he had in mind W. S. Gilbert's caricature of Sir Joseph Porter. Chamberlain countered with a request for the Colonial Office, and Gladstone exclaimed deprecatingly, "Oh, a Secretary of State" and said that he had already offered the post to Lord Granville. Gladstone made no effort to soften the refusal, so Chamberlain had to be content with the Local Government Board. Perhaps a catering to Chamberlain's vanity might have avoided the ultimate catastrophic outcome.

Chamberlain's exasperation was increased when Gladstone decided to cut the salary of Jesse Collings, Chamberlain's follower, who was secretary of the Local Government Board, from £1500 to £1200 a year. "Damn, Damn, Damn," wrote Chamberlain to Harcourt, "Collings has more votes than all his peers put together. And this is his reward."

The main problem for Gladstone was what kind and how much

Home Rule would satisfy the Home Rulers. In January, 1885, at Cork, Parnell had made one of his most famous declarations, "No man has a right to fix the boundary to the march of a nation. No man has the right to say to his country 'Thus far shalt thou go and no further.' We have never attempted to fix the *ne plus ultra* to the progress of Ireland's nationhood and we never shall." * This was fine campaign oratory, but pragmatically concessions would have to be made to imperial bonds if some of the shackles were to be cut off. The content of a possible bill had been the subject of letters forwarded by Mrs. O'Shea to Gladstone since 1884, but Gladstone had made no commitments.

The circumstances under which Parnell in his matter-of-fact way revealed the epoch-making news to his colleagues that Gladstone had decided to bring forward a Home Rule bill has been described by William O'Brien. It was on a cold winter's night in January at Morrison's Hotel, and Parnell had just arrived from England. "With his characteristic indifference to personal comfort, Parnell had neglected to order a fire and his mutton cutlet was growing cold and his pint of Rhine wine unopened, while he doggedly made his way through bundle after bundle of letters awaiting his arrival. All of a sudden the very room lighted up for some of us like a bit of heaven, when raising his head from some dull document concerning God knows what, he remarked casually and without comment 'We are to have a Home Rule Bill. Will you gentlemen kindly turn it over and let me have your suggestions as to what we want—I mean what we can get.' "

Then, of the effect on his hearers, O'Brien reported, "The youth of a more fortunate time will never understand the glow of incredulous rapture the words sent through the fibre of one like myself who had entered upon the Via Dolorosa of the Nationalist struggle with an all but fatalist persuasion that it was bound to end in failure, penal servitude or the gallows."

There was general agreement among the Irish members that Parnell should handle all the negotiations as a plenipotentiary.

* These words are inscribed in letters of gold on the magnificent Parnell monument in Dublin. The statue and column, the work of the great American sculptor Augustus Saint-Gaudens, was dedicated in 1910, the funds having been raised by a subscription among Irish-Americans. The monument stands on Dublin's main street, O'Connell Street, and is located across from the historic Rotunda, which is now a moving picture theater.

Dillon said that Parnell should speak "as the accredited leader and ambassador of the Irish people." Parnell accepted the responsibility of acting alone. As he said to O'Brien, "One has got to take the risk. If you succeed, everybody will feel it was he who won, and if you fail they will be obliged to you for having saved them from the responsibility."

Parnell and Morley conferred closely about the bill. Meanwhile a tremendous opposition was building up against the measure. Lord Randolph Churchill, the erstwhile friend of the Irish Nationalists, was now fanning the fires of civil strife in Ulster. Visiting there, he compared Gladstone to Macbeth before the murder of Duncan and declaimed, "For two hundred years your motto, your password, your watchward, your cry, has been 'No surrender.' " Writing back to Belfast from England, he said, "Ulster will fight and Ulster will be right." The Queen prodded Lord Hartington and Forster to form a party within the party to fight Home Rule—in her private conversations she spoke of the Irish much as George III had spoken of the American colonists. More serious was the increasing disaffection of Chamberlain, whose vanity was again trampled on; he complained that he was kept in protective detention in not being consulted about the bill and on March 15 threatened resignation in a letter to Gladstone. "It appears to me a proposal of this kind must be regarded as tantamount to a proposal for separation. I think it even worse because it would set up an unstable and temporary form of government which would be a source of perpetual irritation and agitation until the full demands of the Irish Nationalist party were conceded." On March 26, he resigned from the Cabinet with George Trevelyan and took a seat below the gangway, though on the side of the Government.

The press of the nation was overwhelmingly against the proposal —in London all papers were opposed except one. All intellectuals were solidly opposed—Huxley, Tyndall, Tennyson, Browning, Froude, Herbert Spencer. The General Assembly of Presbyterians in Ulster passed resolutions against the bill. Churchill in England declaimed that it would be a betrayal of the Protestants of Ireland. "They are essentially like the English people, a dominant, imperial caste and it is only Mr. Gladstone who could imagine for a moment that the Protestants of Ireland could recognize the power or would satisfy the demands of a Parliament in Dublin."

The feeling in the upper social circles was most intense. The Duke of Westminster tore down from a wall in his house a painting of Gladstone by Millais, and Morley related, "At some of the political clubs it rained blackballs." At one time it posed an awkward situation for Gladstone. It was customary on the Royal birthday for the Prince of Wales to dine with the Prime Minister. Gladstone wrote to Morley, "I am becoming seriously perplexed about the birthday dinner. Hardly any peers of the higher ranks will be available and not many of the lower. His [the Prince's] position will be very awkward if he comes and witnesses a great nakedness in the land." Enough seceders finally did consent to come, but it was said that if, after dinner, Lord Hartington had proposed a lack of confidence vote in Gladstone, it would have carried overwhelmingly.

As for the Irish, there was at best sober exuberance about a bill which, as it shaped up, offered only a halfway house to freedom. Foreign relations, the armed forces and the questions of war and peace were to be reserved to the Imperial Parliament, but the Irish were to be totally excluded from the Parliament, so Ireland could be involved in a war in which it had no voice. Contrary to Parnell's desire for tariff protection, the Irish Parliament would have no power to levy excise duties. The Irish constabulary would remain for the time being outside of Irish control, though it eventually would be turned over. And Ireland was to pay one-fifteenth of the cost of the Government as its Imperial contribution. Parnell haggled hard on this point with Morley, contending that it should be at most one-twentieth.

On April 5, close to midnight, Morley brought Parnell in to talk with Gladstone and they discussed the issue of the contribution. Parnell, in Morley's words, showed himself to be "extraordinarily close, tenacious and sharp." His main argument was that the lack of power on the part of Ireland to collect customs duties should lessen the Imperial contribution. At midnight Gladstone excused himself, saying that he regretted that he could not stay up as late as he had in former days. At the door he whispered to Morley, "Very clever, very clever."

Parnell went from Gladstone's office to the Library, where he met O'Brien and said of the man who was to outlive him by eight years, "I never saw him closely before. He is such an old, old man. His face is a bunch of wrinkles. Once he yawned and I really thought that he was dying. He will never live to see this through."

Two nights later Parnell gave a full report of the state of the bill to a group at the Westminster Palace Hotel, including McCarthy, Sexton, O'Kelly, Dillon, E. D. Gray and Healy. The niggardliness of the bill's provisions for self-government was a disappointment. Parnell said, "Gentlemen, I share your regrets. I took up my hat at one point today to leave and break off negotiations. If any of you wishes to resume them in my place, and think you can do better, then take my place." The members expressed their confidence in Parnell.

XVII

On April 8, 1886, Gladstone delivered a memorable speech as he introduced the Home Rule Bill. The journalist Frank Harris in his memoirs recalled the scene.

The House was so thronged that members sat about on the steps leading from the floor and even on the arms of the benches and on each other's knees . . . the visitors that night were so world famous that these men [Herbert Bismarck and the Marquis of Breteuil seated next to him] were not even mentioned in next day's papers. Not a seat was vacant in any of the galleries; even that of the peers was crammed; every diplomat in London seemed to be present; and cheek by jowl with the black uniforms of bishops, Indian princes by the dozen blazing with diamonds lent a rich Oriental flavor to the scene.

I had heard Mr. Gladstone often before and especially on the war in the Sudan a few years earlier when he had risen I thought to great heights, but this performance of the Old Man was none the less remarkable. His head was like that of an old eagle—luminous eyes, rapacious beak and bony jaws; his high white collar seemed to cut off the head of a bird of prey from the thin, small figure in conventional, black evening dress. His voice was a high, clear tenor; his gestures rare but well chosen; his utterance as fluid as water; but now and then he became strangely impressive through some dramatic pause and slower enunciation which emphasized, so to say, the choice and music of the rhythmic words.

Though I did not believe in him at all and was indeed repelled by the conventional Christian sentimentality he poured out on us when deeply moved, I could not but admit that the old man was singularly eloquent and the best specimen of the Greek rhetor of modern times.

Everyone knew that the proposals were the mere resultant of a dozen opposing forces, yet he seemed so passionately sincere and earnest that time and again you might have thought he was expounding God's law conveyed to him on Sinai. He was a great actor and as Mr. Foster once said, could persuade himself of anything and the House of Commons of tragic absurdities.

. . . the effect [after the two-and-a-half-hour speech] was prodigious; for five minutes the whole House cheered and the people in the galleries sat spellbound.

A few nights later Parnell spoke. The House nothing like as full; the galleries more than half empty; the Indian dignitaries conspicuous by their absence; not a bishop or archbishop to be seen. Yet the scene to me was more impressive. There he stood, a tall, thin, erect figure; no reporter had ever said that he was handsome, yet to my astonishment he was by far the handsomest man I had ever seen in the House of Commons—magnificently good-looking. Just forty years of age, his beard was beginning to grey, but what drew one was the noble profile, the great height and the strange blazing eyes in the thin, white face. . . .

He began amid Irish cheers but very quietly in his ordinary voice. I soon noticed that the hands holding his coat were so tense that the knuckles went white; he hadn't a single oratorical trick; he spoke quite naturally but slowly as if seeking his words and soon I began to feel that words to this man stood for deeds . . . I felt very much as I had felt when drinking in Bismarck's great speech in the Reichstag five years before, that a great man was talking and the words were prophetic and the place sacred.

After their initial disappointment, a wave of enthusiasm swept the Irish ranks about the bill. At last, Ireland would be rid of Dublin Castle with its horde of hacks, informers and renegades. Coercion would be a thing of the past, a bitter memory. Ireland would be able to hold its head high, with its own Parliament and, of course, this would be the advance base from which to advance to full independence. Healy declared that with this bill he could "go to the most extreme organization of extreme Irishmen here or abroad," and, indeed, there were few dissenters anywhere. One of those few was John Boyle O'Reilly of the Boston *Pilot*, who wrote, "It leaves Ireland with a chain around her neck like a wild beast."

The debate on the bill was spirited. Opponents were throwing into Parnell's teeth his statement made years before in the American tour of 1880 that Ireland would "sever the last link that binds Ireland to England." They were throwing into Gladstone's teeth his stricture on Parnell in 1881 that he was "marching through rapine to dismemberment."

In a speech at St. James's Hall, Lord Salisbury discussed the capacity of peoples for self-government. "You would not confide free representative institutions to the Hottentots, for example." He went on to say that the democratic institution "works admirably when it is confided to people who are of Teutonic race," but not to others. Forever after, the Irish believed that Lord Salisbury had classed them as Hottentots.

Chamberlain's oratorial prowess in his assault on the bill awed Gladstone—"He never spoke so well for us." Chamberlain pitched his main argument on the exclusion of Irish members from Parliament, which he described as the first step to total separation. To Parnell this was not a vital point, though on the whole he preferred to keep his members away from England, believing that the best brains were needed in Ireland and that Irish interference in English affairs would serve as the pretext for English intereference in Ireland. To Chamberlain the argument was only a convenient weapon of attack, as he admitted to Dilke, "The retention of Irish members is to me only the flag that covers other objections," the main objection to the bill being that the glory was not to be his. His eye was on the premiership and soon after the bill had been defeated he said to Jesse Collings, "If Gladstone retires, all would come pretty quickly."

Objections mounted and resistance stiffened. Gladstone wavered and told Parnell that there would have to be concessions on some points, such as Irish representation in Westminster. Parnell reserved the right to try to amend the bill in the committee stage. Gladstone advised Parnell that after the second reading the bill might have to be suspended or hung up until the autumn session. On May 27, Parnell saw Gladstone for the second time, and Morley recorded, "Parnell courteous enough but depressed and gloomy. Mr. Gladstone worn and fagged."

A conference of fifty-five Chamberlain followers on May 31 sealed the fate of the bill. A letter from the venerated John Bright swung the meeting to a decision to vote against the bill in its present form. Bright was said to have believed that at best his advice would merely result in a decision to abstain. Years later he told R. Barry O'Brien that he was sure that his position was right at the time.

The bill would have resulted in enacting "nagging friction. Give no Irish party leader an opportunity of raising an anti-English cry —that is what a good Home Rule bill ought to do."

On June 6, the eve of the vote, Parnell delivered a speech which was so masterful that Morley said its effect was to "make even able disputants on either side look little better than amateurs." In closing he said, "I say with just as much sincerity of belief and just as much experience as the right hon. gentleman [Trevelyan] that in my judgment there is no half-way house between the concession of legislative autonomy to Ireland and the disenfranchisement of the country and her government as a Crown Colony. But I refuse to believe these evil days must come. I am convinced there are a sufficient number of wise and just members in this House to cause it to disregard appeals made to passion and to choose the better way of founding peace and good-will among nations; and when the numbers in the division lobbies come to be told, it will also be told for the admiration of all future generations that England and her Parliament in this nineteenth century were wise enough, brave enough and generous enough to close the strife of centuries and to give peace and prosperity to suffering Ireland."

Gladstone closed the debate in an impassioned utterance. He attacked Chamberlain for having "boxed the compass" with his various positions. "He has trimmed his vessel and has touched his rudder in such a masterly way that whatever direction the winds of heaven may blow they must fill his sails." At the end he implored the House "Think, I beseech you, think well, think wisely, think not for the moment but for the years that are to come before you reject this bill."

The vote on the second reading was 343 against, 313 for and was immediately followed by the dissolution of Parliament.

Chamberlain was the villain in the eyes of the Irish. As he passed Parnell in the lobby, Parnell said bitterly to his colleagues, "There goes the man who killed Home Rule." He might have included Captain O'Shea, the poisoner of Chamberlain's mind, in the indictment. To his colleagues, Gladstone said prophetically, "Those of you who will be in public life during the next twenty years will have experience of the mischief he can do."

In another general election in July, seven months from the preceding one, and this time on the issue of Home Rule, the Irish switched from an alliance with the Tories to an alliance with the Liberals. Gladstone was now hailed by the Irish members in the most ecstatic terms, and Parnell praised him as "the illustrious Englishman for whose equal as a statesman we have to search the pages of history in vain." In the words of William O'Brien he was "an old man with a face like a benediction and a voice like an archangel's." Gladstone waged a most vigorous campaign, and when he appeared in Manchester he got "a reception that an Emperor might envy." At the same time, Chamberlain was leading the faction that was to be known as Liberal Unionists. In a speech at Cardiff, amid cries of "Traitor," he accused Gladstone of having consulted with and having been guided by Irish revolutionaries. Lord Randolph Churchill was particularly effective in the attack, labeling the Home Rule Bill as "this monstrous mixture of imbecility, extravagance and political hysteria . . . this farrago of superlative nonsense."

The Conservatives waged a clever propaganda campaign. English workers were made to believe that Home Rule would mean that the Irish would cross over in droves to lower their wages, though the logical connection was never spelled out. To accompany the Home Rule Bill, Gladstone had introduced a land purchase bill (to settle the land problem under English auspices before it came before an Irish Parliament); the Conservatives claimed that the bill would cost the British treasury £150,000,000, and even Irish voters in England could not see why the land tyrants of Ireland should receive such a bounty.

The Conservatives founded the Primrose League as an electioneering device (in honor of Disraeli, who was said to be fond of primroses though he never said a word about them except that in one of his novels the hero said he would like a salad of primroses). The Primrose Dames under the Duchess of Marlborough organized branches known as habitations all over England, and wives and daughters of dukes and earls invaded the humble abodes of artisans or laborers or were their hostesses at picnics; they intimidated shopkeepers and instructed farmers to keep their laborers in the field on election day if they were not sure of their vote.

The result on election day was a stunning triumph for the Conservatives and an indefinite shelving for Home Rule. On August 2, Gladstone visited the Queen to submit his resignation and told

Morley that the conversation was made up of nothings "in the scrupulous avoidance of anything which would have seemed a desire on her part to claim anything in common to me."

XVIII

Until Home Rule was granted, as Parnell told his Katherine quite often, he feared the consequences of the revelation of his personal life, since he was not unaware of the reaction that could be expected from "English hypocrites." The defeat of Home Rule made it mandatory that his underground family life remain underground. But in 1886 the personal tragedy that would overtake Parnell came closer as the hoodwinked Captain O'Shea finally became convinced of the truth about his wife and Parnell.

After being elected a member from Galway, O'Shea's position in Parliament was not as comfortable as it had been before. Completely beholden to Parnell for his election, he nonetheless shunned his leadership, and this smacked of ingratitude even in the eyes of the English members. The tale being choice gossip, there was wide feeling that O'Shea had paid a price for his seat that was too high for a gentleman to pay. O'Shea felt himself slighted by many who had been his boon companions and hosts. By now the thought had finally penetrated his mind that the opinion was widespread, if not universal, that his wife was the well-established mistress of Parnell.

Again he queried his wife about the relationship and again she told him the bland lie that the man who was the father of her last three children was merely a platonic friend. On April 26, 1886, he wrote her "With regard to Mr. Parnell I believed your assurances, but I have scores of times pointed out to you that however innocent in themselves the frequent visits of a man to a woman during the absence of her husband is an offence against proprieties."

In the last weeks of May, Captain O'Shea was on the Continent at Carlsbad. One day he was sitting under a tree with a friend, Mrs. Pell, who was reading the English papers which had just arrived. "Oh, Captain O'Shea," she said, "here's your name in the *Pall Mall Gazette*." She started to read the item, but then suddenly realizing the truth, she turned red, stopped and stammered, "Oh, I can't go on."

The item was captioned "Mr. Parnell's Suburban Retreat." It related that on May 21, while Parnell was in a brougham on the way from the railroad station to Eltham after midnight, he had collided with the truck of a market gardener, which led to the disclosure that he was the guest of Captain and Mrs. O'Shea at Eltham. It was an elementary deduction that since Captain O'Shea had been sojourning on the Continent, Mr. Parnell must have been the guest of Mrs. O'Shea after midnight, a rather unusual time for a platonic friend to pay a social call.

Captain O'Shea immediately wired Katherine demanding an explanation, and she was ready with a wire reiterating her usual smooth, brazen denial. She followed the wire with a letter to "My Boysie, I have not the slightest idea of what it means, unless indeed it is meant to get a rise out of you . . . I do not see that it has anything to do with us and I am inclined to agree with Charles, from whom I heard this morning, who says in respect to Healy that it is better to put up with a great deal of abuse rather than retaliate, for it is ill fighting with a chimney-sweep, for right or wrong you'd only get soiled." As an explanation she enclosed a letter she had received from Parnell saying, "I had a couple of horses at a place in the neighborhood of Bexley heath but as I am now unable to be much away from London have turned them to grass for the summer. I am very sorry that you should have had any annoyance about the matter. . . ."

They hoped that Captain O'Shea would swallow that.

Now the couple began a flight from home to home to evade the eyes of any detector and the knowledge of Captain O'Shea. In June, Parnell took a house in Eastbourne, and then another one on July 31. Then the Sussex *Daily News* carried an item that Parnell was staying at Eastbourne. In answer to O'Shea's inquiry, Katherine replied that all she knew was that Parnell's brother and family had a house there. She said, "I am disgusted at your desire and evident attempt to drag my name into a newspaper again when it has not been even mentioned." Then striking a note which had not failed in the past to give Willie a practical slant on matters, she added, "I am writing in haste as I have to go to Aunt about money-matters."

By the end of the year the relation between the O'Sheas was one of complete estrangement. In early December she wrote Willie, "I am perfectly disgusted with your letter. It is really too sickening after all I have done. The only person who has ever tarnished your honour has been yourself." He replied in a letter addressing her no longer by the affectionate nickname "Dick" but "Dear Kate" and signed not "Boysie" but "W. H. O'Shea." Advising her to consult a solicitor, he wrote of his unwillingness to see her. "I shrink from the possible eventualities of discussion with you, especially before our daughters."

Captain O'Shea resigned from Parliament. While the division was taken on the Home Rule Bill he sat in the gallery in abstention. Two days later he applied for the Chiltern Hundreds (the ceremonial form of resignation). No longer could he be kept in line by any hope of using Parnell's influence for his advancement. No longer would he listen to false assurances from his clever and nimble-tongued wife.

On December 30, 1890, after the divorce trial, Parnell, in a statement to the *Freeman,* made it clear that from 1886 O'Shea's eyes were completely open as to what had transpired since 1880. "Captain O'Shea was always aware that he [Parnell] was constantly there [at Eltham] in his absence from 1880 to 1886 and since 1886 he has known that Mr. Parnell constantly resided there from 1880 to 1886," an admission that O'Shea knew after 1886—but not before —that his wife had been Parnell's mistress for those years.

Yet O'Shea was not yet willing to act—the silent restraining hand in the drama was Aunt Ben, who defied longevity tables and continued to live on. She was ninety-four in 1886 and O'Shea was willing to bide his time until her death, which he thought was momentary.

XIX

There was a certain rhythm in Parnell's political life of tumultuous climaxes followed by protracted lulls. After the climactic battle over Home Rule in 1886, there was a lull of two years during which all the Nationalists could do was maintain a holding operation until the Liberals under Gladstone had a chance to regain power in the next elections. For Parnell the period of quiescence was Heaven-sent since he was ill for most of the period and therefore unavoidably *hors de combat*.

The exact nature of the illness has never been brought to light. William O'Brien has said that he had Bright's disease, but there is no confirmation of this. Mrs. O'Shea wrote, "He was suffering from nervous breakdown chiefly brought on by gastric trouble which in turn was produced by overwork and the strain of political life." Speaking in May, 1888, before the Eighty Club on the agrarian movement known as the Plan of Campaign, which we shall later discuss, Parnell said of his condition in late 1886 and in 1887, "I was ill, dangerously ill. It was an illness from which I have not entirely recovered up to this day. I was so ill that I could not put pen to paper or even read the newspaper."

Mrs. O'Shea wrote that she took him to see a noted specialist, Sir Henry Thompson, because "His nerves had completely broken down and I felt terribly worried about him." Sir Henry related later that a man calling himself Mr. Charles Stewart visited him for advice. "I should have taken him and did take him for a quiet, modest, dignified country gentleman." When the doctor started to discuss a recommended diet, Mr. Stewart asked if he could bring into the consulting room a woman friend whose relationship to him he did not illuminate. This was Mrs. O'Shea. After outlining diet and prescribing medicines, Sir Henry told them that Parnell's circulation was bad and therefore it was imperative that he should always carry with him a change of shoes and socks lest his feet get wet and cold. Sir Henry guessed the identity of "Mr. Stewart" on the next visit, but did not disclose the fact to Mrs. O'Shea until after Parnell's death.

To Parnell's illness was added the ordeal imposed by the marital complication. The switch of habitat from one place to another certainly told on his nerves and gave him little peace of mind. After Eastbourne the next home for the couple was Tressilian Road in Brockley. The renting agent testified in the divorce trial that at the time of the lease, in January, 1887, Parnell introduced himself as Mr. Fox, but later said his name was Clement Preston. When he was reminded that his name a few minutes before had been Fox, he said to the bewildered agent that Fox was the name of the gentleman he was staying with. Items were now appearing with some regularity in the press, which thwarted his desire for anonymity. On February 26, in the *St. Stephen's Review*, it was mentioned that at Brockley he never went twice successively to the same station, followed by a tongue-in-cheek comment, "His complications have told considerably on his nerves and he has a constant fear of being waylaid." The *Times* of November 26 revealed the Brockley address and the assumed name of Clement Preston, "With response to the mystery which has attached to Mr. Parnell's recent movements, we are enabled to inform the public . . ."

Mrs. O'Shea continued to maintain with bravado the fiction that Captain O'Shea's suspicions were some spectral fantasy that he had better dismiss. When he brought the item in *St. Stephen's Review* to her attention, she replied, "No one thinks anything of *St. Stephen's* and it is so evidently the old rumor again that I think you will be very unwise if you take any notice of it." On April 22, Mr. Pym, her solicitor, addressed a letter to O'Shea in which he said, "Mrs. O'Shea most emphatically denies that you have or ever had the least ground for the unworthy suspicions you have chosen to affix to her credit. The particular friend you alluded to has been a rare visitor to her house and he only became a friend of the family upon your introduction and by your wish."

In their increasingly futile attempts to live and love in privacy, Parnell took a house in London at York Terrace in Regent's Park, and she would meet him there. However, when separated from her, he could not stand the loneliness and would come "home" to Eltham despite the risk, sometimes in the middle of the night after a late session of the House.

They communicated in code, using words from his assaying operations, "tailings" for O'Shea, and other code words like "middlings," "deposit," "slag," etc. There was the need for shabby ruses and often quick thinking. For example, one afternoon when they were together at Eastbourne they drove to Pevensey, where a crowd pouring out of a train recognized Parnell and forced him to make a speech. Thereupon Mrs. O'Shea quickly composed an item that "Mr. Parnell had been visiting his sister at Hastings and on visiting Pevensey with her . . ." and he gave it to the Press Association, thereby hoping that this would avert any further prying by a curious scribe.

XX

There was increasing talk now about his personal idiosyncrasies, his aberrant appearances in public, his peculiar dress, his eccentricities of manner. In December, 1886, he asked William O'Brien to meet him for a conversation about the disputed tenant league program called the Plan of Campaign. Parnell was in a nursing home at the time, and they arranged to meet behind the Greenwich Observatory. Parnell suddenly emerged from the fog. As O'Brien described it, "After groping around helplessly . . . I suddenly came upon Parnell's figure emerging from the gloom in a guise so strange and with a face so ghastly that the effect could scarcely have been more startling if it was his ghost I met wandering in the eternal shades. He wore a gigantic fur cap, a shooting-jacket of rough tweed, a knitted woollen vest of bright scarlet and a pair of shooting or wading boots reaching to the thighs—a costume that could not well have looked more bizarre in a dreary London park if the object had been to attract and not to escape attention. But the overpowering fascination lay in the unearthly half-extinguished eyes flickering mournfully out of their deep caverns, the complexion of dead clay, the overgrown fair beard and the locks rolling down behind almost to his shoulders. It was the apparition of a poet plunged in some divine anguish or a mad scientist mourning over the fate of some forlorn invention."

O'Brien had assumed that they had met in this deserted spot for secrecy, but to his astonishment after they had discussed their business Parnell suggested that they go to London together for dinner at a gay and most public place, the Criterion. There, over their food, Parnell talked continuously, convivially and, what was unusual for him, in a semiphilosophical vein. "Life is not supportable," he said, "without the friendship of a woman, be she good or bad. You would never have got young men to sacrifice themselves for so unlucky a country as Ireland only that they pictured her as a woman." O'Brien, feigning ignorance of Mrs. O'Shea, asked if he couldn't get one of his sisters to care for him. Parnell continued, "Science will never do anything worth talking about until it gets outside the little world. I don't see why it should not some day.

Once innoculate a man with a virus that will enable him to support life in the atmosphere and a journey to the planets and even to the stars won't be much more difficult than that of Columbus when he set out to discover America."

Later Parnell told Mrs. O'Shea of the meeting and said ruefully, "All I got for getting up to see O'Brien was that he went about telling people that I am insane."

As for his appearances in the House of Commons, as Sir Henry Lucy wrote, "Banquo's ghost was not more fitful in its comings and goings." Word that Parnell was on the floor would empty the lobby, restaurant and library, such was the fascination of the man for the members. His dress was often bizarre, a yellow-ocher rough suit with a pot hat of rich brown—as Lucy put it, "the dress a triumph of laborious art, giving Mr. Parnell an appearance which is a cross between Mr. Oscar Wilde and a scarecrow." Lord Randolph Churchill once asked Frank Harris, since he knew Parnell better, whether he disguised himself for the purpose of visits to Mrs. O'Shea. He pointed out that his appearance was always changing, once his beard was full, then it was close cropped, now his hair was down over his collar, then cropped close and again the top of his head might be clean-shaven as if he had been playing priest. "What does it all mean?" asked Churchill of Harris. "I told him the truth as I saw it," wrote Harris, "that Parnell was one of the strangest human beings I had ever met."

Sometimes his pale and haggard face would be seen as he walked to the post office of the House and then to the library with his mail. These visits might be weeks apart. (He once commented to someone that it was amazing how many letters answer themselves in a fortnight.) He would then leave by the winding back stairs used by messengers and policemen without having talked to anyone.

Dining was considered as much a part of the business of being a member as being in attendance at the House, but Parnell was not invited to these dinners, and for a very excellent reason—no one knew his address. To consult the Irish members was futile since they could give no help. Parnell would say to his colleagues, "Write to me at Avondale. It may take a few days but the letter will eventually reach me." (Complaining of his being harassed at the time of the Hawarden Kite, Gladstone said that he envied "Parnell's method for self-effacement.")

The lieutenants did their best to cover up for the leader. As Sir Charles Gavan Duffy said, "If he was dumb, it was not that he was barren, but that he was supremely prudent. If he was idle and inactive, it was because he preferred to work through agents, and he became inaccessible and invisible not to drink the cup, of course, but to keep his mind fixed on profound strategy. Never had a man colleagues who lent themselves more cheerfully to these assumptions."

But among themselves the lieutenants of the evanescent leader were exasperated. Tim Harrington wrote to Dillon in 1888, "I am dreadfully afraid that this condition of things will end in something unpleasant," and Davitt, who openly grumbled about Parnell's lingering in Mrs. O'Shea's arms, said when Parnell failed to show up for a meeting with him, "We are all getting very tired. How long can this sort of thing be tolerated?" After his split with Parnell, Justin McCarthy declared in his indictment, "The English Liberals would never have endured even Mr. Gladstone as a leader for a single year under such conditions. We were willing to endure anything rather than find public fault in the face of the enemy."

As time went on and Parnell was increasingly absent, the faces of newly elected members became less familiar and even unknown to him. Once, as he was walking along the street, he was greeted by someone. "Who was that?" he asked his companion and, on being told, replied, "Ah, I did not know we had such an ugly man in the party."

XXI

Despite grumblings there was no move for mutiny or even an expression of overt opposition. Like the Church, the party was built upon a rock, the rock of Parnell, in whom there was union and there was an omnipresent fear that without him union would be gone. At Christmas time of 1886, O'Brien wrote to Healy, who was suspect of disaffection, "The only possible ground of estrangement between us is as to Parnell, as to whom there is nothing more unalterably fixed in my mind than that he is the cornerstone of our Cause and that the moment I would feel bound to renounce a frank allegiance to him would be the last of my public life."

Despite the fact that his vigor was diminished and sometimes he was out of the arena altogether, Parnell was by no means a *roi fainéant,* and no one was under any illusions that he had abdicated even temporarily. Everything was done and hallowed in his name. Just as his reserve and silences awed when he was present, *a fortiori* now his total absence seemed to add to the mystery and power of the Parnell name. Moreover, his looser hand on the tiller seemed to make it easier for him to navigate safely between the Scylla and Charybdis, the left wing which was pushing the agrarian movement and the right wing represented mainly by the Church, which stood for law and order.

The agrarian problem in Ireland was renewed by the steep drop of almost 30 per cent in agricultural prices in 1885, in which imports from the United States played a large part. Tenants were unable to pay their rents, even the judicially fixed rents under the Land Act of 1881. When Parliament reassembled in August, 1886, after the elections, Parnell drew the attention of the House to the distressed conditions in Ireland, and though disavowing any intent to lead an agitation as he had done five years before, he asked for quick relief. If a tenant were unable to pay his rent for the year he should be allowed an abatement of 50 per cent. The alliance with the Liberals was now functioning, and Gladstone hurried home from Germany to support the bill—which the Conservative government rejected.

With Home Rule as his target, Parnell was disturbed that the lawlessness of a new land agitation might rile English sensibilities and alienate goodwill, particularly among the Liberals, sorely needed by the Irish. He was not passive. Aside from the bill he had introduced in Parliament, he asked contributions from the Irish National League of America to an antieviction fund, in view "of the imminence of trouble and peril which has seldom been equalled, even in the troubled history of Ireland."

That Parnell gave further encouragement to the agrarian agitation that shaped up is debatable. O'Brien claimed that, while Parnell felt it impolitic to take a public stand, he was "in absolute agreement with the men who might be prepared to suffer the penalties." At any rate, his paper *United Ireland,* on October 25,

1886, published an article entitled "A Plan of Campaign," which though unsigned was known to have been written by Tim Harrington, Secretary of the National League. It outlined a plan under which tenants on an estate were to offer the fixed rent to the landlord less a reasonable abatement in view of the agricultural stringency. If the landlord refused to accept the reduced amount, it would be handed over to a managing committee made up of the tenants. Thereafter the individual tenant would not speak or deal with the landlord except through the committee, which would negotiate with the landlord and if necessary defend any action taken in the courts.

The Plan won immediate acceptance, particularly in the south and west of Ireland. Mass meetings were most successful, not only in spreading the gospel but in intimidating would-be land grabbers and persuading landlords to be reasonable before tenant pressure was applied. Parnell was able to say afterward that "no agrarian movement in Ireland was ever so unstained by crime." The Plan was put into effect on eighty-four estates, mostly large ones, on sixty of which there were abatements made voluntarily by the landlords. On the remaining ones there was trouble of some degree.

The most famous of the cases involved the estate of Lord Clanricarde in Galway, which had 1900 tenants and a rent roll of £25,000 a year. The old marquis had died fourteen years before and of the new marquis there had been no physical or ocular evidence in Galway since—he had not even returned for his mother's funeral. Despite his riches, he lived very meanly in London. Henry Labouchere, who knew him well, used to tell how the marquis had once addressed an indignant letter to his landlord about the grossly unsanitary condition of the house he lived in—not to get the conditions improved but to get his rent reduced. He was the patron of the notorious courtesan Skittles (who gave the title to a book a few years ago by Cyril Pearl *The Girl with the Swansdown Seat*). In December, 1882, the new marquis had written a letter to the *Freeman's Journal* saying that his father had devoted his life to the welfare of his tenants but that he had been "wounded by their ingratitude and had asked his son to remember it." The marquis raised the rents of the tenants constantly in the years after 1882.

When the tenants refused to pay the higher rents, eviction notices rained down on them and five hundred constables were mobilized to be sent to the estate to carry them out. The current Irish Secretary, Hicks Beach, came to Ireland and, after some weighing of the equities, applied what he called "pressure within the law"—that is, a refusal on his part to furnish the soldiers and police needed to enforce the marquis' rights. A more enlightened policy was in the course of being established when Hicks Beach resigned and was succeeded by Arthur Balfour, Lord Salisbury's nephew. His new post was to be the first significant step in Balfour's meteoric career.

The Irish were due for a shock in the new Secretary. As T. P. O'Connor put it, "The impression he would give to a stranger who saw him for the first time would be that he was a more than unusually mild member of the race of curates . . . he might be described as almost ladylike in his manners and appearance." An aristocratic intellectual, a student of philosophy who habitually slouched languidly on the bench, hands in pockets, a scented handkerchief in his coat pocket, he had such feminine qualities that he had been called in his university life "Clara." However epicene in appearance, Balfour was to prove the most masculinely aggressive administrator of English law that Ireland had seen in the century. As Gladstone said once in debate, the "supposed lisping hawthorn bud" had turned out to be a "tiger lily."

Under Balfour's guidance, a new and harsh coercion bill, the Crimes Bill, was introduced on March 28, 1887, which empowered the Lord Lieutenant to suppress associations and combinations "illegal in their intent and operation," enabled trial to be removed to venues most promising for the prosecution and enabled two magistrates to imprison in certain cases without trial. As this bill was being rushed through Parliament, and it was expedited by the use of closure, the *Times* was whipping up favorable sentiment for it by publishing a series of articles on the Irish conspiracy called "Parnellism and Crime." On April 18 it published a facsimile letter implicating Parnell which was to be a *cause célèbre* later. On June 10, when the House leader, W. H. Smith, brought in the closure motion, the Nationalists and Liberals withdrew from the debate. In the year of Queen Victoria's Jubilee, the bill was called "an unconscious testimony to the triumphant failure of the Act of Union."

Parnell urged the Irish people to make the best of a bad situation and to exhibit restraint in the face of the new Act, so as not "to retard the progress of the great Liberal Party in their path of justice to Ireland." Time and again now he showed his dread that something violent or bloody might happen to estrange Gladstone from the Irish cause he had lately embraced. To Davitt he pointed out the danger and opportunity—only 100,000 out of an electorate of 4,000,000 in England had to be converted to the Liberal cause for Home Rule to triumph. "I don't care who leads the struggle after I've gone but I am anxious the old country should get some kind of Parliament, and unless Gladstone can do this no other Englishman can."

Balfour administered the Crimes Act with a ruthlessness and lack of compunction that infuriated the Irish and led T. P. O'Connor to make the observation, "The most dangerous are not the robust and bold tyrants but the men of effeminate minds and temper. Their vanity leads them to do things that look strong and their effeminacy induces a certain tendency to political hysteria that has very crude and callous elements."

In contrast to the handful of M.P.'s imprisoned by Forster, Balfour arrested no less than twenty-four and in the case of some, including William O'Brien, kept them in jail for more than a year. A notable departure from Forster's policy was Balfour's insistence that political prisoners be given the same treatment as ordinary criminals. In Parliament Lord Salisbury defended this policy against strong protests from the Liberals, saying that lenient treatment was a "strange, maudlin and effeminate doctrine." Political prisoners were thus forced to wear prison dress, sleep on a plank bed, have their heads shaved and take their exercise with burglars and sex criminals.

O'Brien did not object to the prison fare or the plank bed, but he refused to do menial tasks, give servile salutes and, most important, he would not wear prison garb. Because of the last objection, he had to lie in bed all day for lack of trousers and underwear, and Balfour made "William O'Brien's breeches" a stock weapon of ridicule. One morning, however, when the turnkey opened his cell door he found O'Brien immaculately dressed in a well-cut suit of the best blarney tweeds, shirt, collar, green silk necktie, boots and soft hat. A warden had smuggled the clothes in. O'Brien's sartorial triumph, the epic of Tullamore jail, was recited everywhere.

Released from prison O'Brien reentered the House on February

16, 1888, and, clad in that prison suit, exultantly taunted Balfour in a great speech beginning "Here we are face to face," in the course of which he said, "We are for peace and the brotherhood and happiness of the two nations. If you are for eternal repression and eternal discord, we are for appeasing the dark passions of the past."

John Dillon, during this period, spent six months in jail for advising tenants to pay no rent, but because of the state of his health he yielded to prison rules requiring wearing of prison garb. Afterward, he went to Australia for a year where he was extraordinarily successful in raising funds for the cause.

While Parnell was sitting on the sidelines, the prestige of Dillon and O'Brien soared with the Irish public, a fact which would be ultimately of great importance for Parnell, since they would have the decisive voice in the leadership crisis two years later. A popular ballad exalted both of them:

> 'Tis hard to be choosing when no man is hollow
>   Where all are reliable, changeless as fate,
> But 'tis a certain and safe rule to follow
>   Honor those whom our foes the most hate.
> And keeping that rule in view
>   Where is most credit due,
> Whose are the names that so brilliantly shine,
>   Whom do the robber crew
>   Hate as we know they do?
> Honest John Dillon, staunch William O'Brien.

XXII

Until the alliance with the Liberals could bear fruit in Home Rule, Parnell had to carry water on both shoulders lest the delicate balance of his forces in England and Ireland be disturbed. This explains, as much as his ill health and his absorption in Mrs. O'Shea and his two children, his policy of relative desuetude on the political front.

In December, 1886, he discussed the Plan of Campaign with John Morley. When Morley told him that the reaction in England was unfavorable to it, he said that he would try to moderate the agitation. According to Morley, "He was anxious to have it fully understood that the fixed point in his tactics was to maintain the alliance with the English Liberals." Then followed the confrontation with O'Brien behind the Greenwich Observatory, which we have described, and O'Brien's pledge to him that the Plan would be limited to the estates where it was already in operation.

Although Parnell kept the Plan of Campaign within bounds, it was a considerable success, being responsible for a reduction in the number of evictions by 40 per cent and in a large number of voluntary rent reductions by landlords. Boycotting was a prime weapon used under the Plan, and sometimes priests themselves found it best to attend National League meetings. There were complaints to the Holy See, followed by a visit from Rome by Msgr. Persico in July, 1887. This was followed by a circular of the Congregation of the Holy Office in Rome condemning the Plan in April, 1888. It caused consternation in Irish ranks and widespread doubt as to whether the Plan of Campaign could be sustained in the face of the displeasure of the Church. Dillon, however, struck out boldly, declaring that "That document is not binding on the conscience of any Irishman at all" since it "was advice on a temporal matter from a quarter whose advice has not always been wise advice."

As we have noted, on May 8, 1888, Parnell in a speech at the Eighty Club in London explained that he had not known about the Plan of Campaign when it was launched because of the incapacitating illness which prevented him from even reading a newspaper. In effect, he washed his hands of the Plan of Campaign but did not condemn it, saying merely that it would have to be replaced. Of the Church circular, he said it was bound to be "a disastrous failure," but left what he called the "document from a faraway place" to the judgment of the Catholics in the party.

Thus Parnell, with an equivocal position again, walked skillfully through a narrow defile, covering himself so that he was safe from attack by rabid agrarian zealots on the one hand and by conservatives and churchmen on the other. But his failure to give strong endorsement to the Plan wounded some of the activists, particularly O'Brien, who was ready to bleed for the cause. There was some caustic comment. When Parnell became ill in the autumn of 1886, he had notified the press that he was suffering from a gastric attack and was under his mother's care. Parnell's using his illness as an excuse for disassociating himself from the Plan of Campaign prompted Frank Hugh O'Donnell, in Germany to write:

The Leader's Mamma

Who is being sent to guard
My freedom from a prison ward
Perhaps my pate from truncheon hard?
My Mother.

Who kept newspapers far away
That might have forced me plain to say
My mind upon the coming fray
My Mother.

I rest my head upon her knees
And thank my stars—oh, gratefully
That heaven still preserves to me
My Mother.

The Papal prescript died an inglorious death as the party "sat on the Pope." A meeting at the Mansion House passed a resolution endorsed by fifty-nine members of Parliament which branded the "allegations of fact" in the circular as unfounded and attacked the Church for being a silent partner to the subversion of justice taking place in Ireland. Subsequently, a mass meeting in Phoenix Park endorsed a resolution which, in effect, declared that the people's representatives had a mandate from a higher source than the bishops. It was a stunning blow to the Church in Catholic Ireland, and by the end of 1888 the Pope said that the pronouncement of the Church had been "widely misunderstood."

In his eagerness to keep the Liberals on his side, Parnell failed to sense an unprecedented shift of sentiment—the Liberals were now aching to make a "cause" of the oppressed and persecuted Irish. The day after Parnell had spoken deprecatingly of the Plan of Campaign, Gladstone said in a speech, "I say boldly that the real authors of the Plan of Campaign are the present Government," and two weeks later, he was saying that although the Plan of Campaign might let loose base passions, "I say that there are many circumstances in which it is an infinitely smaller evil to use the machinery than to have the people perish." Soon Gladstone was defending boycotting as "the only weapon of defence belonging to a poor and disheartened people." Such are the vicissitudes of politics.

The passionate embrace by the Liberals of the Irish Nationalists astounded the Irish themselves. Liberals crossed over to Ireland to attend National League meetings, and no Liberal meeting in England was complete without Irish visitors, preferably a brace of Irish martyrs to weep over who had spent time in prison under "Bloody Balfour." English visitors trooped over Ireland to bring back stories of persecution and oppression, and the recital of these wrongs became as popular for English lecture audiences as narratives of returning African explorers. It was said that at long last the English had discovered Ireland. The "Union of Hearts" became increasingly bathetic. Pictures of Gladstone were now seen everywhere in Ireland's homes, restaurants and theaters. A deputation of English Liberals was cheered in the Rotunda, a delegation of Irish mayors visited Gladstone at Hawarden, and in the vows of mutual love English nonconformist ministers clasped hands with Irish Catholic clerics.

The coldly realistic Parnell looked cynically on the kissing bee. He kept his association with the English at a minimum, consistently refusing all blandishments from English hostesses aimed at having his presence grace the great houses. After a conversation he had just had with John Morley, he laughingly said to Mrs. O'Shea, "Morley said to me, 'The people must be made to wake up a bit.' They imprisoned me for causing agitation in Ireland and now they *want* agitation if not outrage." To his friend M. J. Horgan of Cork, who expressed enthusiasm about Gladstone, he replied coldly, "I think of Mr. Gladstone and the English people what I have always thought of them. They will do what we can make them do."

During this honeymoon period politically, there were forces quietly building up against Parnell beneath the surface. The Church smarted with resentment from the slap in the face it had received concerning the Plan of Campaign and believed that it must have had Parnell's tacit approval. The party appeared monolithic in its support behind Parnell, but there were murmurs of dissension. In 1888 Davitt wrote, "Most of the evils inflicted upon

us by Tory rule are on account of the Liberal alliance." Dillon
and O'Brien objected to Parnell's moderation. Also, the carping,
disenchanted Healy, apparently was watching for the flaws in the
once-adored leader to crop up. To his brother Maurice, he wrote,
"Parnell has got a fixed idea that Gladstone is so certain to live
long enough to secure himself a majority that he himself need
make no further fight. He must be more or less enervated by ill-
health," and again, objecting to one-man rule, "Any step would
be justifiable to compel Parnell to take action in consultation with
the party, as his unaided evolutions are now generally hurtful."

XXIII

At this time, before the climactic events in the life of Parnell,
let us pause to examine the character and personality of this
uncommon man. Despite the conflicting impressions of him reported by those close to him—who, with the exception of Mrs.
O'Shea, were not really close to him at all—there is a sufficient
consensus of views as to his salient traits.

What was most remarkable at the time and what remains remarkable to historians in retrospect was that a man so unlike the
great mass of Irish should have assumed over the Irish a command
more absolute than anyone before or since. Sir Charles Gavan
Duffy, returning after his long stay in Australia, marveled to find
in command, a proud, silent, isolated man who had none of the
eloquence of Grattan, who was not a joyous companion like O'Connell and had none of O'Connell's passion and humor, and was
completely unlike Isaac Butt, who had the aforesaid qualities of
Grattan and O'Connell to which were added an exact knowledge
of Irish history and interests. Davitt, while acknowledging his greatness, wrote, "He had neither wit nor humor, eloquence or the
passion of conviction, academic distinction of any kind, scholar-
ship or profession, Irish accent, appearance or mannerism. [As a
leader] he was a paradox."

For a statesman, he was remarkable for his ignorance. Davitt
gave him credit for some knowledge, saying that his "ignorance"
was one of the legends that grew up about him—Davitt is alone

in that judgment since all others attest to his intellectual barren-
ness. A hostile critic like O'Donnell and a warm friend like M. J.
Horgan agree that he had no knowledge of Irish history. We have
the testimony of Mrs. O'Shea, "Parnell was not a well-read man
. . . he was a maker of history, not a reader of it. He took no
interest in reading as such, but for works on subjects interesting
to him—mining, engineering and later astronomy, he had an in-
satiable appetite." His naïvete at times amused and amazed his
colleagues. Justin McCarthy, a classical scholar, once told him that
he was realizing the dream of a lifetime in going to Athens, and
Parnell asked him whether Athens was really a nice spot for a
vacation, apparently thinking it a resort. T. P. O'Connor said, "I
never saw a sign that he had ever read a single novel or drama."
He constantly mangled quotations, as Mrs. O'Shea herself related.
Healy told how Parnell once wanted to quote Thomas Moore's
lines about Ireland, "First flower of the earth and first gem of the
sea," and rendered it, "First flower of the earth and first jewel
of the ocean." When the misquote was called to his attention,
Parnell shrugged and said he felt that he had improved on the
poet.

The English leaders in Parliament made the same observation.
Joseph Chamberlain recalled, "He often dined with me. I should
not say he was socially interesting. I thought him indeed rather
dull. He did not seem to have any conversational powers." John
Morley said of him, "Apart from the business of the moment, he
contributed little to ordinary conversation because among other
reasons he had no knowledge, not even the regular knowledge of
common education and the man of the world."

"Apart from the business of the moment"—that is the nub of
the matter. In the business of the moment, as a field commander
in the battle, he dominated and won admiration from friend and
foe. His vision was clear, he had an instinct for the jugular and
his mind was incisive; as a political animal he was a master in
grasping the art of the possible and acting accordingly. He commanded the admiration of an intellectual like Gladstone. "He took
such a thorough grasp of the subject at hand, he was so quick and
treated the matter with such clearness and brevity." Morley said
that in clearness of perception of facts he surpassed anyone with
whom he had been brought into contact in literature and politics.

"He measured the ground with a slow and careful eye and fixed tenaciously on the thing that was essential at the moment. . . . Napoleon said he liked generals who saw things as they were as through a military field-glass and did not compose them as imaginary pictures. That was undoubtedly a quality of Parnell." Cecil Rhodes, who conferred with Parnell about his idea that the Imperial Parliament might become truly Imperial if colonies which made contributions to the Empire might send representatives to Westminster, said of him, "Parnell is the most sensible man I have ever met." In Parnell's later Parliamentary days, when his appearance grew more and more eccentric, an English M.P. said to McCarthy, "There is only one sensible man among you, and he is mad."

The Irish members included many of great intellectual attainments, yet Parnell dominated them all by the force of his mind. Davitt said that he had a "hard, strong comprehensive mind. Once he had grasped a problem, the power of concentration made him a match for superior minds." This is illustrated by his speech on Home Rule which Morley said made others look like amateurs. Justin McCarthy stated that one had merely to talk to Parnell briefly to realize that he was a man of commanding intelligence. "He never talked in commonplaces. He took in new ideas slowly but when they got in they germinated and became fertile again." As a Parliamentary strategist he was without a peer. No lieutenant ever came to him with a suggestion of a tactic of which he had not already pondered the pros and cons. Healy wrote, "Parnell was simply superb. No one was like him for seeing the difficulties of a situation and for getting out of them."

Parnell was never a smooth speaker. His delivery was jerky and he often paused as he groped for the right word. Contrary to the mode of the time, his speeches were not florid or rhetorical or filled with vaulting thought and classical allusions. Lord Bryce said that his speeches reflected a mind which was "directed to immediate aims and wanted the originality which is fertile in ideas and analogies. The impression one gains might be compared to that which one receives from a gray, sunless day with an east wind in which everything shows clear but hard and cold." Yet it was this lucidity and compression of thought which were praised by Gladstone, whose own speeches were at the opposite extreme, Dis-

s

raeli once having accused him of being "inebriated with the exuberance of his own verbosity." Parnell, said Gladstone, had "the rarest of all qualities in a speaker, measure." And on another occasion he said, "I have always envied the member from Cork his gift for saying precisely what he wants to say—neither a word more or less."

It was not qualities of intellect, however, which set Parnell apart. The journalist Frank Harris, who knew him, said that although he was an ignoramus, "Parnell was of the stuff of great men through greatness of character." After his death, the *Times* said that his "ruinous force of will" was as great as that of Bismarck, and Morley said that his instinct for *"Realpolitik"* was like that of Cromwell. Chamberlain, like Gladstone, called him "remarkable" and compared him in nonscrupulous conduct and masterful will to Napoleon.

Command came as easily to Parnell as if he had been born to it. That he reveled in it is evident from the extraordinary way in which he and Mrs. O'Shea addressed each other—he called her Queenie and she called him King. Was this only banter? Their favorite horses were President and Dictator. Frank Hugh O'Donnell claimed that power was his only goal. "He never meant Ireland more harm than absolutely necessary to put himself on top—and he did not think that any harm at all." Mrs. O'Shea tells that she was appalled that he viewed his followers impersonally, as a general views his pawns in battle. Once he said to her, "While I am leader, they are my tools or they go." When she protested, "But they are human beings," he replied, "In politics as in war there are no men, only weapons." An acute observer, Sir Charles Dilke, had the impression that Parnell regarded himself as engaged in a cold war. "He acted like a foreigner. We could not get at him as we could at any other man in public life. Dealing with him was like dealing with a foreign power."

Early in his leadership, as we have commented, his mien of coldness and aloofness were part of the role he liked to play of the grim-visaged Caesar. Occasionally in the early days the poker face would break down—once, he saw a woman in a crowd searching for something to wave and when she finally waved her baby at him, Parnell burst into laughter. His brother John was aware of the playacting. He relates that he passed Charles walking on the street with followers when he was at the height of his fame. There was no sign of recognition but a wink. "Charles simply wished to show that he had seen and recognized me but did not want to disturb his demeanour of perfect composure and aloofness." Like other dictators before and since, he had adopted the principle *major e longinquo reverentia.*

As time passed, his coldness and remoteness from his followers became less assumed and more genuine; he seemed to repel human contact. Sir Henry Lucy wrote, as an observer, that in the late 1880s an Irish member "would no more think of invading the sacred precincts of the Grand Lama as to approach Parnell without an invitation." His outer coldness became so formidable that Charles De Key, an American journalist, wrote, "To meet him was like being introduced to a tortoise which can remain for hours in the same position and seem absolutely uninterested not only in the person who approaches but in the world in general."

The reflection of his aristocratic contempt for his followers may be found in his remark to Mrs. O'Shea about his unexplained absences from meetings he had promised to attend: "Never make any apologies to the rabble, that is one of the secrets of power." Yet in the spirit of patrician superiority, of the *grand seigneur,* he never showed anything but graciousness in his conduct to the members and utmost respect for their sensibilities. In the *New Review* soon after his death, Healy wrote, "The stories of his hauteur and insolence to his followers are simply lies. In ten years, perhaps not more than once have we seen him other than affable and courteous." Justin McCarthy was equally emphatic on this point. Alfred Robbins, Parliamentary correspondent for the Birmingham *Post,* wrote in a memoir that a member who had addressed him as "Parnell" was reproved "*Mister* Parnell, please." T. P. O'Connor branded this story as a fabrication, since it was completely out of character for Parnell.

There are, on the contrary, many stories of his indulgence in order to avoid wounding anyone's feelings. When Davitt complained to him of the amount of oratory that members were lavishing on an unimportant measure, he said, "Oh, you must let them show themselves off now and then a little. Otherwise they might inflict the same speech on you in Ireland." Once, O'Brien, in the House, wrote hastily a statement for him in which the composition was poor and the handwriting worse. Parnell stumbled through it painfully. When O'Brien apologized to him for it, Parnell waved the apology aside. "It was a very fine statement and had a great effect."

Another misconception which his colleagues refute was that he was a rabid hater of England. I have read an article which stated that when anyone talked about erasing all the differences between the two races and making them one "he ground his teeth and his pale cheeks grew white with rage." Davitt, however, wrote that he never heard a bitter anti-English utterance from him. McCarthy stated that Parnell was "equally beyond the contagion of enthusiasm or the provocaton of hate." The incarnation of the Carlylean man, he was intent about reaching the goal but was unemotional about obstacles, including the human ones, in his path. His natural method of thinking was that of an engineer who sets out to cut a channel and, encountering an obstacle, figures out a way to circumvent it, but would regard it as foolish to waste any emotion on it. It should be noted also that a man who was deeply in love with an English woman and who had the deep feeling that the English sense of justice would prevail to win the Irish cause can hardly be described as anti-English.

This unemotionalism set him apart from the Irish members. As one put it, "Abandoned to itself, Celtic emotionalism alternates between internecine anarchy and moody quietism. Only under disciplined leadership does it become formidable." The Irish, moreover, have an instinct for retaliation—if someone offends, you don't try to conciliate him but reply in such terms as to make him an enemy for life. A freedom from imagined grievances as well as freedom from gratitude enabled Parnell to lead most effectively. It was not only in these inner traits but in outward characteristics that Parnell differed from his colleagues. While they drank heavily, he was almost abstemious. While they all swore like troopers, he never used a term stronger than "my goodness." He once was asked by Mrs. O'Shea whether he had an aversion to the word "damn" and he replied that it had never occurred to him to use it.

There is general agreement that Parnell's personality had an hypnotic effect on members of the party that clothed him in a nimbus of awe. The Parnell mystique had built up long before his death. It was hard to explain even by those who knew him best. T. P. O'Connor said it was the strange glare from his eyes that made men quail. Sir Charles Gavan Duffy felt that his charismatic appeal to his party members and the Irish people rested fundamentally on the psychological domination that the English garrison had always exercised in Ireland and the habit of submission by the Irish to the English overlord.

Davitt said, "Magnanimity or gratitude he had none. His mind had few if any generous impulses." Lord Bryce agreed that "he never showed much magnanimity or said a generous word." His graciousness in not hurting the feelings of others was probably good breeding, but on the other hand, he never shared the glory with others, never gave credit to his comrades or showed any solicitude for their welfare. The benign Justin McCarthy once told T. P. O'Connor that he never knew Parnell to have a good word about a colleague, that there was always a hidden sneer. Thus, talking of James J. O'Kelly's fabulous adventures, Parnell, who was on closer social terms with him than he was with anyone else in the party, sneered that O'Kelly might be trusted to take the best care of his own life. Instances cited by his brother John of his generosity show that at best he gave with ill humor. He tells how after Parnell had made a speech at Wicklow a man followed his carriage mile after mile, enthusiastically cheering and waving his hat. His companion said to the expressionless Parnell, "You might just say a word of encouragement to that fellow. He has followed you for miles and he hasn't gotten as much as a smile out of you," to which Parnell replied, "Let him run awhile longer, seeing that I have let his rent run for seven years."

He could forgive anything but a slight to himself. He hounded figures like John O'Connor Power and Phil Callan out of the party for what he regarded as personal insults. Again, on the negative side, while he was regarded as infallibly trustworthy in his earlier public life, it was believed that in later years a certain corrosion developed in his character. The correspondence between Biggar and Healy shows that when Parnell installed Captain O'Shea as the candidate for Galway he made a promise to the prospective candidate, Michael Lynch, that he would take care of him in another constituency if he withdrew. But this was a pledge he refused to honor.

As if to prove our generalization true by exception, we have the testimony of one who found Parnell always warm and generous. M. J. Horgan, a solicitor of Cork who was his election agent, tells how he asked Parnell in the summer of 1881 (when Parnell was starting his own love affair) if he would attend his wedding in England. Parnell said, "To be sure. It is good that you are getting someone to take care of you." Thus encouraged, he asked Parnell if he would be his best man, and he smilingly assented, saying, "That is the least I can do for you." That Sunday, Parnell drove up to the church immaculately dressed, his appearance making a great stir, insisted on taking the groom out for a drink to brace him up, kneeled in the ceremony, stayed for the reception and behaved perfectly. Thereafter he was a great friend of the family, and when he stayed with them at Cork he was almost boyish in his efforts to please them.

That Parnell was as glacially cold and emotionless as contemporaries tended to view him was refuted in retrospect, first by his love affair with Mrs. O'Shea, which he pursued with an all-consuming passion, and second, by the events in his fall from power, when he fought with fury and passion for his right to rule. His granite-like exterior up to the last phase of his career was due in great measure less to a lack of inner passion than an iron will. As Alfred Robbins wrote, "He could fall into a cold and deadly rage when provoked, he could sink almost into hysteria when roused to sudden passion, but he could restrain himself with a rigidity I have never seen in any other public man."

Certainly one of the most compelling of his traits was his morbid, overweening pride, the pride which so extinguished vanity that Healy commented that it was useless to try to flatter him, the pride which prevented him from taking anyone into confidence about his ill health, the pride which restrained him from taking counsel with any of his comrades or asking for understanding when he became enmeshed in the divorce suit, or agreeing to any compromise regarding his leadership. It was a pride which may have made him feel that he was free to flout or to be above ordinary conventions and rules of morality governing the sanctity of the marriage bond.

"What I am, I am—what I am not, I cannot be." These were his words to Katherine O'Shea which expressed his philosophy. He could not and would not bend his life to suit others. Morbid and superstitious, he explained to Mrs. O'Shea that he was a fatalist, that his life was written in the stars. Believing in himself, he did not see how he could ever fail, and certainly the fates had been kind to him up to this point. So with confident heart he plunged ahead to another overwhelming success—and then down the abyss of final disaster.

Part Five

THE FORGERY

I

FOR A NATION bursting with nationalist pride and revolutionary ardor, Ireland had more than a fair quota of renegades, informers and place seekers who made English rule easier—perhaps made it possible. The scabrous character Richard Pigott was one of the ubiquitous pseudopatriots who were for hire to the highest bidder and used Ireland's agony to line their own pockets. He started in journalism as an errand boy for *The Nation*. Even in his youngest days Pigott had the problem of expenditures exceeding income and made up the deficit by the sale of indecent photographs. He drifted around newspaper offices until the proprietor of a paper which had lost its circulation donated the paper to him. When the paper was suppressed by the Government in 1865, it thereby won public esteem and circulation shot up after the ban was lifted. Pigott was now launched and became the owner of three newspapers, *The Irishman, The Flag of Ireland* and *The Shamrock*.

In his papers Pigott posed as an ultra-Nationalist, and in 1867 he was sentenced to twelve months' imprisonment for attacking the Manchester executions. He swore in court that he was a Fenian, but it is well-agreed that he never joined the Fenians. His jail companion was A. M. Sullivan of *The Nation*, who had given him his start. He professed a great friendship with Sullivan and shared gifts received by Sullivan, but he was no sooner released than he started a libelous campaign against him. Pigott soon hit on the money-making tactic of selling his editorial policy to one side or the other, and from this it was a short step to blackmail. Thus he put the screws on Isaac Butt by threatening to publish Fenian attacks on him and once extorted £1000 from him. Pigott was chronically in need of money. He had a pretentious home in Kingstown, had many women friends and was an avid collector of pornography. He was a jaunty, bouncy man, a great swimmer who

frequented seaside resorts, where he insisted on being called
"Major."

When the New Departure was being discussed, Pigott's papers
were the most vocal opponents, labeling it as treason to the militant spirit of Fenianism. Then, swinging to the other extreme,
when the Land League was established he tried to extract money
from Parnell and Patrick Egan by threatening to attack it for its
radicalism. When Forster became Irish secretary, Pigott tried to
ingratiate himself with him and extract money by defending the
English administration. By 1881 Pigott had become so disreputable
that the circulation of his papers had fallen disastrously and he
was glad to sell them to Parnell. He tried to persuade Parnell to
retain him in some capacity, but Parnell would have none of him.

Pigott promptly squandered the funds he had received from the
Land League and was soon in want again. The former self-styled
Fenian now became an outright renegade—having squeezed all he
could from Irish patriots he now turned to the more abundant
English purse. He contributed articles to the *St. James Gazette*
entitled "By an Old Fenian," then wrote a series of articles com-
piled into a pamphlet, "Parnellism Unmasked." He became acquainted with another scurrilous character, twenty-seven-year-old
Edward Caulfield Houston, son of a prison warden, former reporter
for the Dublin *Daily Express* who was now secretary for the Irish
Loyal and Patriotic Union, an organization subsidized by British
funds to fight Irish nationalism.

Houston was convinced that Parnell was personally behind murders and crimes such as the Phoenix Park murders and that it was
only necessary to find the evidence. He found others of the same
persuasion who backed him with money, including Lord Richard
Grosvenor, whom we have met before as Liberal whip, who put up
£450. Houston proposed to Pigott that he try to unearth this evidence. Pigott at first declined, saying that it was impossible since he
knew that it was a rule in Fenian organizations to destroy all documents. But when Houston said that he would pay Pigott a guinea a
day plus his hotel and travel expenses if he would undertake the
job, Pigott saw the situation in a different light and consented.

For many months Pigott's pockets jingled with gold coins while
he traveled about Europe in style. Meanwhile he filled Houston's
ears with nonsense of his own invention. He traveled repeatedly

from Paris to Lausanne, saying that he had found one Eugene Davis in Lausanne an invaluable informant. For the most part, Pigott's letters did not mention names. A typical letter might read "Dear Sir: I am following up the search and I have come across X and I have seen Y and I hope to see Z." Although Pigott occasionally dropped a name, Houston later admitted, "I have purposely kept myself in ignorance of the persons with whom Pigott was in treaty."

In time Houston became impatient and indicated to Pigott that unless results were forthcoming the stream of guineas might dry up. Then Pigott said that he definitely was on the track of evidence that he was sure would finish off Mr. Parnell for good. There were six letters written by Parnell and five by Patrick Egan which had been left in a black bag (how often the little black bag appears in swindles) by Frank Byrne of the Land League when he fled Paris for America to escape extradition after it had been charged that his wife had brought the surgical knives used for the Phoenix Park murders to Ireland. In March, 1886, Pigott produced copies of these letters. They were shown to various persons in London by Houston, but little interest was shown. Lord Hartington said that he had no advice to give on their use, W. T. Stead, publisher of the *Pall Mall Gazette,* refused an offer of them for £1000 and G. E. Buckle, editor of the *Times,* also turned them down.

Nonetheless, Houston told Pigott to purchase the letters. Pigott said that he had to go to America to get permission from a Fenian, Breslin, which was only an excuse for another junket. In July, Pigott said he had arranged to purchase the originals in Paris if Houston met him there with enough money. Houston, accompanied by a Dr. Maguire of Trinity College (a Professor of Moral Philosophy, no less), took rooms at the Hôtel Des Deux-Mondes. In the conspiratorial gloom of night Pigott came to them and showed them the letters. He said that two men, Tom Brown and Maurice Murphy, were waiting downstairs for payment. From £850 advanced him by Dr. Maguire, Houston gave Pigott £500, which was the agreed purchase price, plus £105 more as a bonus for his good work, and kept the rest as a bonus for himself for his good work. Houston and Dr. Maguire were so overjoyed with the find that they did not ask to see the two men or ask anything about them.

With his booty, Houston rushed back to London. He returned to the *Times,* now with better luck. Buckle sent him to the manager of the paper, John Cameron Macdonald, a Scotsman whose lack of canniness in this case casts discredit on the reputation of the race. Although his acquaintance with Houston was of the thinnest sort, Macdonald was so elated that he asked no questions. He showed the letters to the solicitor for the *Times*, Mr. Soames, and a handwriting expert who apparently encouraged the step. He then paid Houston £1780.

The following spring, the *Times* began a series of articles entitled "Parnellism and Crime." Though unsigned, they were written by Wolfe Flanagan, son of an Irish judge (information relayed by an Irish maid in the home of one of the *Times* owners). The tone of the articles can be appreciated from this excerpt from the first one: "Be the ultimate goal of these men what it will, they are content to march toward it in company with murderers. Murderers provide their funds, murderers share their inmost counsels, murderers have gone forth from the [Land] League offices to set their bloody work afoot and have presently returned to consult the constitutional leaders on the advancement of the cause."

II

When the readers of the *Times* opened their papers on April 18, 1887, they were startled. The sedate and conservative *Times*, in keeping with its dignity as the most respected newspaper in the world, always used only a single headline in small type for the most earthshaking news, and each page was an unbroken succession of printed lines. Now, in shocking contrast, the readers saw staring at them the reproduction of a letter by a new process called facsimile. The letter, dated May 15, 1882, a little more than a week after the murders in Phoenix Park was as follows:

Dear Sir:

I am not surprised at your friend's anger, but he and you should know that to denounce the murders was the only course open to us. To do that promptly was plainly our best policy.

But you can tell him and all others concerned that, though I regret the accident of Lord F. Cavendish's death, I cannot refuse to admit that Burke got no more than his deserts.

You are at liberty to show him this, and others whom you can trust also, but let not my address be known. He can write to the House of Commons.

Yours very truly,
Chas. S. Parnell

The body of the letter did not purport to be in Parnell's handwriting, only the signature.

The *Times*, in introducing this letter on the day of the second reading of the coercion bill, said it was "documentary evidence which has a most serious bearing on the Parnellite conspiracy and which after a most careful and minute scrutiny is, we are quite satisfied, authentic." The scrutiny had actually been of the most cursory sort.

Mrs. O'Shea told how Parnell received the publication at Eltham. Wornersh Lodge was surrounded by curious neighbors who were aware of Parnell's presence; so to keep them away she had put a seven-foot-high paling around the garden and had made a thick rose hedge on one side. Nonetheless, to make their consciousness of Parnell's presence felt, the neighbors used to cut out excerpts from the *Times* and paste them on the gate. In this way she became aware early in the morning of the facsimile letter. For his peace of mind, she tried to keep the *Times* away from Parnell at breakfast (which was after noon), but he insisted. So she propped it up against the teapot as usual and he read it meditatively, buttering and eating his toast all the while. He made no remark until he had finished breakfast, then while clipping his cigar he tossed the paper to her, saying, "Now for that assaying I didn't finish! Wouldn't you hide your head with shame if your King were as stupid as that, my Queen?" He then unconcernedly turned to his assaying of gold, working with a new machine which had a balance that gave the weight of infinitesimal parts of a grain. After two hours he covered it with a glass case, then lovingly padded it with a cloth lest a rough movement in the room disturb it, and set out for the House.

When Parnell entered the lobby of the House he found it agog with excitement, and a crowd immediately formed around him. He professed complete ignorance of the letter, saying that he had not seen the *Times* that morning since he rarely looked at newspapers. The pose of insouciance adopted by the "comedian" gave him an opportunity to demonstrate his superiority over petty events that disturbed others. Tim Harrington took him to the library to examine the letter, which Parnell surveyed with icy calm. Pointing to the first letter, the capital "G" of the signature, Parnell said only, "I did not make a 'G' that way in 1882." Harrington, who had expected him to tear a passion to tatters, was astonished and dismayed, and said to a member, "My God, if that is the way he is going to deal with the letter in the House, there is not an Englishman who will not believe that he wrote it." (This illustrates the difference between Parnell, guided by cold, analytical reason, and his followers, who were ruled by emotions. To them the letter should have been an occasion for a torrent of emotional indignation, to him the marrow of the case was the signature, and if a letter was formed incorrectly then the whole case against him fell, and that was all there was to it.)

The Irish, knowing well that Parnell was a person very cautious and circumspect in action, were convinced from the start that the letter was a forgery. The English, on the other hand, even the Liberal allies of Parnell, found it hard not to accept it, since it had been printed in the *Times,* which, as Morley wrote, was "the most powerful, the most responsible newspaper in the world, greatest in resources, authority and in universal reknown." Parnell entered the House as Sexton was denouncing the letter as a fabrication, and he gave Sexton's speech many. "Hear, Hear's." Although urged to speak, he did not do so until 1 A.M. "Sir, when I first heard of the precious concoction, and I heard of it before I saw it because I do not take in or even read the *Times* usually, when I saw what purported to be my signature, I saw plainly that it was an audacious and unblushing fabrication. . . . I certainly never heard of the letter. I never directed such a letter to be written. I never saw such a letter before I saw it in the *Times.*" He was surprised that the *Times* had permitted itself to be "hoodwinked, hoaxed and bamboozled. . . . I unfortunately write a very cramped hand, my letters huddle into each other, but the signature in question is written by a ready penman who has evidently covered as many leagues in letter paper in his life as I have yards."

Parnell then walked out into the lobby and engaged a Mr. Henniker Heaton in conversation. While everybody assumed he was talking to him about the awful event, Mr. Heaton later related that what Parnell said to him was, "I have just read in the after-noon papers that a mountain of gold has been discovered in West-ern Australia and that some tons of the specimens have been sent home to you. May I see some of the crushed specimens?" Heaton said that he would give him some that he had in his locker. (A week later Parnell told him that he had been assaying it since that time in his workshop and gave him an analysis that coincided exactly with that given by a famous metallurgical concern.)

The letter was the topic of discussion everywhere. The Prime Minister, Lord Salisbury, taunted Gladstone that he associated with an "ally tainted with the strong presumption of conniving at assas-sination." Gladstone presumably was a moral leper since he em-braced in friendship a man who condoned a crime which had resulted in his nephew's death. The forged letter put Parnell in a far worse light than that because it showed him cravenly begging indulgence for himself from murderers, presumably to save his own skin. The Irish members asked for the appointment of a select committee of the House of Commons to look into the letter, but after three days' debate the House voted by a majority of 84 that the publication was not a breach of its privileges.

The Government advised Parnell that his recourse, if the letter was a forgery, was to sue the *Times* for libel and the Government would pay the expenses. Morley advised him against it, saying that the best that could be expected from a jury of English shopkeepers was a hung jury and if he sued in Dublin the verdict "would not be worth a guinea insofar as affecting English public opinion." Parnell told W. S. Stead of the *Pall Mall Gazette* that he feared that in a libel suit "They will rake up every outrage that has taken place in Ireland in the last ten years in order to cover the floor with a bloody puddle in which they can besmirch the Home Rule cause."

Over a year passed, and this seemed the end of the matter, leav-ing the reputation of Parnell irremediably blemished in the minds of many. And then a bizarre stream of events occurred.

Frank Hugh O'Donnell had retired from English politics in 1885 and was living in Germany, forgotten by everybody—including the London *Times*. He had not been included in the indictment of Parnellism made by the *Times*, having been mentioned only tan-gentially as among the followers of Parnell. He wrote to the *Times*,

T

asking why Frank Byrne of the Land League had been erroneously described as a secretary of Parnell. The *Times,* in answer, referred to an effort on the part of O'Donnell to "vindicate" himself. On this basis O'Donnell sued the *Times* for libel. No one could figure this out, except that with his irrepressible vanity, O'Donnell wanted to share the limelight with Parnell. As Healy put it, "The intrusion of the 'Derby Dog' in the great race at Epsom [Downs] would have been more appropriate."

The next unusual event was that the attorney chosen to defend the *Times* was none other than the Attorney General of the Government, Sir Richard Webster. At that time the leading law officer for the Government could accept a private brief, but it seemed grossly inappropriate that the man who in his public capacity was entrusted with deciding whether Parnell was or was not correctly charged by the *Times* with an alliance with murderers should be appearing here for the *Times* in a cognate case. Worse was to follow. The case of *O'Donnell v. Walter* (John Walter was the principal owner of the *Times*) was tried before Lord Chief Justice Coleridge on July 3, 1888. Counsel for O'Donnell was hard put to make any kind of a case of libel and had to fall back on the thesis, which was far from true, that O'Donnell was such a prominent member of the Nationalist party that the allegations made as to Parnell and Dillon necessarily included him. Then came the next extraordinary event. O'Donnell, who was suing the *Times* for libel, did not take the stand in his own behalf. He might do so after the *Times* made its defense. The astonished Lord Chief Justice warned that the *Times* by its defense might preclude this.

Ordinarily, the *Times*' logical defense would be to move that the plaintiff be nonsuited since he had failed to make a prima facie case. However, the enemies of the Irish cause saw an opportunity to use this case as a forum to air the charges. Sir Richard spent three days in a long-winded speech. As for O'Donnell, Sir Richard said that the *Times* had not aimed a shaft or even a pebble at him since it was hardly aware of his existence. He then launched into a discourse on the *Times*' charges against Parnell, repeating and reaffirming them. Then he read some new letters written by Parnell and Patrick Egan to buttress the imputation of murder.

The Parnell letter published on April 18 of the year before did not fully prove the *Times'* case against Parnell, since it purported only to show that Parnell had merely ratified post-factum the Phoenix Park murders. The *Times* claimed that Parnell had set in motion the machinery of assassination and was thus responsible for the heinous deeds that followed. To close the ring some proof was needed of Parnell's prior instigation of murder. Pigott, who was now virtually on the *Times'* payroll, was always willing to oblige with a letter, so Sir Richard read now a very damning letter from Parnell. It was dated January 9, 1882, when Parnell was in Kilmainham jail, and read as follows:

> Dear E.
>
> What are these fellows waiting for? This inaction is inexcuseable; our best men are in prison and nothing is being done.
> Let there be an end to this hesitency. Prompt action is called for.
> You undertook to make it hot for old Forster and Co. Let us have some evidence of your power to do so.
> My health is good, thanks.
>
> > Yours very truly,
> > Charles S. Parnell

Obviously this letter called for Irish violence. But Pigott stepped over the line of credulity here. To many fair-minded English who were bitterly anti-Parnell, it was inconceivable that Parnell could have been so stupid as to smuggle this letter out of Kilmainham, which could get him hanged, when he could have readily conveyed the same message orally to one of his many visitors. In another way the letter was to be Pigott's undoing. Parnell happened to be a stickler for correct spelling, and the forger, who had a weakness for using the letter "e," had misspelled both "inexcusable" and "hesitancy." As soon as Parnell saw this letter, he immediately noted the misspelled words and suggested that the forger might be trapped through these misspellings.

The Attorney General read aloud this new batch of letters, constituting a fresh assault on Parnell, on the pretext that he was endeavoring to show that O'Donnell was not mentioned in any of them. He then said that of course the defense would not prove them or force them to be disproved since they concerned persons who were not defendants in this case. In this disingenuous manner he had managed with impunity to defame Parnell.

The Lord Chief Justice delivered a withering summing-up. "Who asked him [O'Donnell] to intervene? Why he intervened and what his object was, he alone knows. It has been suggested that vanity has prompted him to stand before the public in a conspicuous position, that he has been actuated by what I may call an advertising desire. But there may have been other motives in the heart of a man who has been separated from companions who have not placed their confidence in him." The jury without leaving the box gave a verdict in favor of the *Times*.

Parnell was boiling with anger. The Attorney General had made a mockery of the revered system of English justice in order to pillory him and the Nationalist cause in a court of law without giving him the right to defend himself. He made a personal statement to the House repudiating the letters imputed to him and then demanded again that a select committee of the House be set up to investigate the letters. Morley warned him against this course, saying that he would get no justice from the Conservative majority, but as Morley wrote Harcourt, "I told Mr. Parnell our views yesterday afternoon with the usual effect that we might as well have saved our breath to cool our porridge." As it had the year before, the Government refused the demand for a select committee of Parliament.

III

The Government made a counterproposal: it would appoint a special judicial commission to look into the changes. As originally framed, its proposal was to appoint a commission "to consist wholly or mainly of judges with statutory power to enquire into the allegations and charges made against the members of Parliament by the defendants in the recent action." But when the motion was introduced formally, to the astonishment of Parnell, the Irish members and the members as a whole, it had been broadened to include "the allegations and charges made against members of Parliament *and other persons*." The "other persons" were obviously not only members of the Nationalist movement but also the Land League and the Irish people as a whole.

Parnell was taken aback when he was asked by the Government

leader in the House, W. H. Smith, after a half-minute statement, if he chose to accept it, even before the Special Commission Bill had been printed. In great disgust and anger Parnell asked why he was given an option at all. The Attorney General had said that if the charge were not true, it was the worst libel ever launched on a public man. If that were so, said Parnell, the Government should be determined on an inquiry "whether the honorable member, this alleged criminal, likes it or not."

There was no illusion about how the cards were being stacked against the Irish. It was not the forgery that was to be investigated, but the Tories would now try the whole Nationalist movement on all the charges made by its enemies—in effect, as Burke said, a whole nation was to be indicted. The inquiry would trace all kinds of crime to the Land League and the Irish National League and then make all members, including members of Parliament, constructively guilty. Harcourt protested against a procedure in which the Irish members would be forced to answer "a sort of hotch potch, miscellaneous slander." Morley wrote, "It was one of the ugliest things done in the name and under the forms of law in this island during the century."

Was this Commission the idea and handiwork of Joseph Chamberlain? Parnell believed so, as did others. The Press Association attributed it to "the artful Mr. Chamberlain." Later, Attorney General Webster, when the inquiry had turned sour, wrote to Solicitor General Clarke, "Every day I curse Chamberlain and the Unionists for their obstinacy."

Chamberlain, having deserted with his Unionists the banner of Gladstone in 1886 on Home Rule, was now something of a political Ishmael. He had a haven with neither the Liberals nor the Conservatives and faced the necessity of making humiliating concessions to enter either camp. In February, 1887, he had said to Lady Stanley, according to her diary, "Of course I shall be prime minister. Of that there is nothing more certain," but now he saw the prospect fading fast. Gladstone had formulated the choice in policy toward Ireland "Conciliation or coercion." Chamberlain had started on a remarkable turnabout in political philosophy which would ultimately make him a jingoist Conservative, and his first step had been to swing from his former anticoercionist policy to becoming an advocate of coercion. But he could see that public sentiment was rolling against him. Yet, having broken with Gladstone, he had no choice but to become more intensely coercionist. As his biographer J. L. Garvin put it, "Denouncing dynamiters, assassins, separatists, agrarians, outrages, Parliamentary intimidation, he employed a new and sulphurous power of incitement." Formerly Parnell's political friend, he was now his bitter enemy and made no bones about it.

Chamberlain was given a mission by Lord Salisbury to serve as a negotiator on fishery arrangements with the Canadian Government and the United States and left for America in October, 1887, not returning until March, 1888. While in America, he met the twenty-four-year-old daughter of the Secretary of War, Mary Endicott, and though the widowed, twice-married Chamberlain was more than twice her age, he proposed to her and was accepted. Letters written to his fiancée, published after his death, give some illuminating glimpses into his mind. When the Special Commission was being discussed before being formally proposed, he wrote to her exultantly, "I am convinced that this Commission will elicit some astounding facts and if the result is to show that more than one member of the Nationalist party has been dabbling in assassination the effect would be prodigious."

Parnell had planned to introduce amendments to the Special Commission Bill in the committee stage, but to his consternation the Government made a motion for closure which foreclosed any action by him on this line. Parnell attributed this maneuver again to his enemy Chamberlain. Now the venomous hatred between the two broke out into the open. On July 24, Chamberlain declared in a speech in the House that his confidence in Parnell had been shaken by "his apparent reluctance to face a full enquiry."

Infuriated, Parnell made a frontal attack on Chamberlain a week later, saying, "I have never put forward men to do dangerous things which I shrank from doing myself nor have I betrayed the secrets of my colleagues in council. My principal recollection of the rt. hon. gentleman, the member from West Birmingham, before he became a minister is that he was always most anxious to put me forward and my friends forward to do work which he was afraid to do himself; and after he became a minister my principal recollection of him is that he was always most anxious to betray to us the secrets and counsels of his colleagues in the Cabinet, and to endeavour while sitting besides those colleagues and while in consultation with them to undermine their counsels and plans in our favour. If this enquiry is extended into these matters and I see no reason why it should not, I shall be able to make good my words by documentary evidence which is not forged."

In a scene of excitement, T. P. O'Connor shouted loud and clear at Chamberlain, "Judas," and Biggar shouted, "Judas Chamberlain." In a letter that day to Miss Endicott, Chamberlain wrote, "The scene was pretty hot and shows how excited these Celtic gentlemen are getting now that there is a chance of their being found out."

The next day, Parnell renewed the personal assault. "It is not the first time that you have poisoned the bowl and used the dagger against your political opponents when you could not overcome them in fair fight." Chamberlain retorted that he had not done anything behind Gladstone's back and that the latter had been aware of the Kilmainham negotiations and those about the local-government scheme and that Parnell had deliberately misled him on the local-government issue. Parnell said that that "was erroneous and unfounded" and that Chamberlain had been misled by a "third person," who was clearly Captain O'Shea.

The war of words now spilled over into the columns of the *Times*. On August 2, Captain O'Shea in a letter to the *Times* continued his role of the loyal henchman of Chamberlain, and he was eager now, if he could, to have revenge on Parnell. On the local-government scheme, O'Shea corroborated Chamberlain—and a good deal more. He said that he had presented it to Chamberlain at Parnell's request. "The scheme was altogether Mr. Parnell's and Mr. Chamberlain adopted it with considerable hesitation because of its not being in accord with Radical principles." This remarkable and mendacious letter went a good deal further. O'Shea cast scorn on Parnell by saying that he had stood over him at Kilmainham while he signed the "letter of surrender." He then referred to the day after the Phoenix Park murders and, accusing Parnell of a faulty memory of events, he said, "Full of horror as Mr. Parnell was that day, not only that two lives had been sacrificed but that a third was in danger . . ."

The "third" was obviously the life of Parnell himself, and O'Shea's testimony would confirm the accuracy of the forged letter published in the *Times* since it would tend to show that Parnell feared that the Invincibles would take his life too unless he made peace with them, as the letter showed him doing. It is no wonder that the *Times* hailed O'Shea's letter as an "important historical document." The *Times* editor, Buckle, immediately contacted Chamberlain to ask him whether his friend O'Shea would be a witness before the Special Commission, and it was arranged.

On August 7, Chamberlain wrote the *Times* that he would produce proof of Parnell's perfidy on the local-government scheme, but in a letter of August 13, to everybody's surprise, he openly admitted that he had no such proof and that Parnell had not treated his scheme as a substitute for an Irish Parliament. What had happened to alter Chamberlain's plan to discredit Parnell? The correspondence with Miss Endicott makes this clear. He had previously acquainted her with the fact that Captain O'Shea was amusing but "cynical and unscrupulous, like all Irish politicians." He had intended to base his case largely on oral evidence by O'Shea. But in talking with him, he recalled that O'Shea had written a letter to Parnell in the early stages of the negotiations that put Chamberlain's position in a bad light. It was certain that Parnell had kept the letter. On August 8, Chamberlain wrote to Miss Endicott of the blundering intriguer: "Unfortunately O'Shea put his thoughts and interpretations into my words and in writing to Parnell credited me with his own political morality. What will happen if this letter is produced? In my own defence I must throw over O'Shea and say what is the truth, that he grossly misrepresented me. But then if he misrepresented me, may he not also have misrepresented Parnell? And he is my chief witness against Parnell. Altogether it is a nice dilemma."

The sortie against Parnell had not been fully successful. Chamberlain wrote to Miss Endicott that he had concluded that O'Shea was "indiscreet and therefore a dangerous person," but they remained close friends since they had a common interest, the destruction of Parnell, and the Special Commission, they hoped, would discredit him, demolish him and remove him from the scene in disgrace.

IV

The Special Commission consisting of three anti-Home Ruler judges, Mr. Justice Hannen, Mr. Justice Smith and Mr. Justice Day, started its sittings on September 17, 1888. The Commission was to examine 445 witnesses, ask 150,000 questions and have 128 sittings. Attorney General Webster appeared for the prosecution, which was, in effect, the *Times.* The *Times* obtained an order for discovery of documents against forty-six Irish members, State archives were placed at the disposal of the *Times* and officials of the Irish executive in Ireland aided them. All the apparatus of the State on the side of the London *Times* was geared to try a political and social revolution. For his pains in asking for an inquiry into what he claimed to be a forged letter, Parnell was on trial with sixty-four other members of Parliament and Michael Davitt on various allegations—that they were members of a conspiracy seeking absolute independence of Ireland from England, that they had promoted an agrarian agitation against the payment of rent with a view to expelling from Ireland the "English garrison" and, most important, that by their speeches and money payments they incited persons to sedition and the commission of crimes, including murder.

The management of the defense was entirely in the hands of Parnell, who was given a fund of £30,000 by the Irish National League to defray defense costs. Sir Charles Russell, who was later to be Lord Chief Justice of England, was in charge of the defense, and he was assisted by a young man looking like an undergraduate who later was to be a wartime prime minister, Herbert Asquith. Davitt and Biggar defended themselves. In the award of briefs, Tim Healy, who was by now a well-known and highly regarded lawyer, received a sharp slap in the face from Parnell, which exacerbated the hostility that Healy felt for him. On September 6, Healy was offered a brief by Parnell's personal counsel, Sir George Lewis, but on October 2, he received a letter from him rescinding it, saying, "I have had a long talk with Mr. Parnell today and he considers that the case insofar as it affects him has taken such a turn that it is desirable that you should appear as counsel only for yourself." Healy, seething with anger, wrote to brother Maurice that he had found out "that the letter was written and the words practically

suggested by Parnell himself who gave no explanation to Lewis."
Davitt, in 1903, wrote, "I strongly pressed for the employment of
T. M. Healy but Mr. Parnell's recollection of the Galway incident
intervened." Parnell never forgot a slight, and Healy was not to
forget this public humiliation.

On October 31, Captain O'Shea appeared as a witness before the
Special Commission against Parnell. He was genuinely convinced
that Parnell was implicated in murders and outrages, that as a
result of the investigation Parnell would be disgraced and perhaps
sent into penal servitude. He was ready to do his part in accomplishing Parnell's ruin. The once trim and dapper O'Shea was
now worn and seedy in appearance, looking older than his forty-
eight years. He clasped and unclasped his hands nervously, sometimes cupping his hands over his head, his eyes seldom raised from
the floor and seldom meeting the hate-filled stare of Parnell.

The first point made by O'Shea was that Parnell, as a condition
of the Kilmainham pact, insisted that a fugitive terrorist, P. J.
Sheridan, should have the warrant against him canceled and that
Parnell continued to insist on this although O'Shea told him that
Sheridan was a "murderer and concocter of murder." Then the
testimony shifted to Parnell's conduct on the day after the Phoenix
Park murders.

Q. [ATTORNEY-GENERAL] Do you recollect on one of the occasions
of that day Mr. Parnell saying anything about himself?
A. Yes, he spoke of the danger in which he was.
Q. When was that?
A. That was in a cab on the way back from Mr. Chamberlain's
house.
Q. Do you remember what he said?
A. Yes, he said he was in personal danger and asked me to get
police protection for him.

The focus then turned to the facsimile letter.

Q. Now will you look at the signature on the letter dated May
15, 1882. In whose handwriting do you say that signature is?
A. I know nothing about signatures.
Q. I know that you are not an expert. But as far as you can say,
in whose handwriting do you believe that signature to be?
A. It appears to be Mr. Parnell's signature.

On cross-examination by Russell, O'Shea admitted that he had dined with Mr. Buckle of the *Times* before agreeing to give testimony. He could not remember ever having said that he would have revenge on Mr. Parnell or that he had a "shell packed with dynamite" for him, though Russell was holding in his hand the letter to Mrs. O'Shea with those words of his.

Healy rose to cross-examine. Parnell said to him nervously, "What are you going to ask him?" He was afraid of a line of questions which might bring Mrs. O'Shea into the case. "I shall ask nothing sensational," said Healy, knowing what was troubling him, "but will confine myself to showing that Biggar opposed him at Galway." "But you will confine yourself to that?" Healy reassured him and then with two questions wound up the examination. O'Shea left the stand, not glancing at Parnell, whose stare followed him out of the courtroom.

O'Shea was the first witness who had anything to offer that was relevant to the heart of the case, Parnell's complicity in crime. A mass of turgid testimony on crime in Ireland preceded and followed O'Shea. The judges had stated, "We have no commission to consider whether the conduct of which they are accused can be palliated by the circumstances of the time or whether it should be condoned in consideration of benefits alleged to have resulted from their action." So alleged facts, unweighed and unevaluated, piled up. Sir Richard Webster droned on and on, reading testimony from previous cases, ignoring the suggestion of the judges that they were well able to read it themselves. Delaney, implicated in the Phoenix Park murders, whose life had been spared, gave testimony that was relevant. But on the other hand, "There was the peasant from Kerry in his frieze swallow-tail and knee-breeches and the woman in her scarlet petticoat who runs barefoot over the bog in Galway. Witnesses were produced in a series that seemed interminable to tell the story of the five and twenty outrages in Mayo, of forty-two in Galway, of sixty-five in Kerry, one after another, and all in immeasurable detail. Some of the witnesses spoke no English and the English of others was hardly more intelligible than Erse. The three judges groaned." Thus Morley described the proceedings.

The apparatus of the English Government and the apparatus of the Irish Nationalist movement were pitted against each other. The Irish National League in the United Kingdom and in the United

States became a vast intelligence and counterintelligence organization. Agents were planted and opposing agents were bought. Irish men and women working in telegraph offices intercepted and relayed the British messages which went over the wires. Thus, in one instance, it was learned that a Government witness was on his way from Canada to London. He was met at Queenstown by "detectives," escorted to London by them, plied with liquor on the way, thus giving up all his secrets to the Irish. Most of the messages were in code which the Irish had to decipher. On one occasion Archbishop Walsh tried his hand after all others had failed and solved it using Poe's "Gold Bug" formula of building from the assumption that "E" is the most common letter in the alphabet.

There was the case of P. J. Sheridan, a former Land Leaguer with a reputation for inciting outrages who now lived in the United States, running two sheep ranches in Montana. The *Times* learned his whereabouts and contacted him. To its agent Kirby, Sheridan said that he had evidence so incriminating that Parnell would have to leave the British Isles, that the Clan-na-Gael, knowing of his disaffection, had sentenced him, Sheridan, to death, but he was determined to be revenged on the revolutionary movement, etc., etc. He asked £10,000 immediately and another £10,000 later, the payment to be made ostensibly for purchase of his sheep. The messages were intercepted by the Irish, and surprised and baffled about one considered a loyal comrade, they contacted Sheridan. What he told them gave all a good laugh. "If I could get hold of the money, the *Times* could whistle for its money. I have nothing to say and nothing to give." The decoded intercepted messages from the *Times'* agent were published in the *Freeman's Journal,* and the decipherment led to a change in the telegraphic messages used by the British armed services. Commented Healy, "This was the sole good to the State from the Forgery Commission."

As the Commission waded through the welter of testimony, Parnell was bored and was increasingly absent. Russell expressed his irritation to R. Barry O'Brien. "Your friend Parnell is a selfish fellow. He thinks only of himself. He takes no trouble about any part of the case except the forged letter. There are specific charges against others and against the movement generally and Parnell ought to trouble himself about these charges and help us to meet them, but he will not come to consultations except to discuss what directly concerns himself." Parnell's irregular attendance at the hearings grieved Russell, who continued, "It is studied disrespect and it is bad policy to say the least. It is sure to prejudice his case." Parnell's reply to O'Brien was, "Oh, Russell is something of a bully and you must tame him a little." His mind was on his mechanical experiments. Once, he came to the hearings with a big parcel. When Davitt asked what it was, he answered that it was a soldering iron and six pounds of lead.

As the advocate representing sixty-five clients, Russell was aware of the breadth of the case and was gravely concerned about it. Parnell, with his scalpel-like mind which cut to the heart of the case, could see that if the forged documents fell, then the main prop for the whole case of the prosecution would be gone.

V

"When will we get to the forged letters?" Parnell asked impatiently as the weeks went by.

Parnell and the defense knew that Pigott was the forger, and, in fact, he had privately confessed. As soon as the facsimile letter appeared, Patrick Egan, who was then living in Lincoln, Nebraska, said, "That's Pigott." Parnell originally thought that Captain O'Shea had been the author of the scheme, but by the summer of 1887 Egan had convinced Parnell that it was Pigott.

The Liberal member Henry Labouchere, an erstwhile Chamberlain follower who remained a stout friend of Home Rule and Parnell, tried various means of enticing Pigott to a private meeting and was finally successful. On October 28, 1888, soon after the Special Commission started hearing witnesses, Pigott met in Labouchere's home with Parnell and Sir George Lewis, Parnell's counsel, as well as with Labouchere. Pigott freely admitted that he had forged the letters. "How did you take Houston in so easily? Is Houston a complete idiot?" Labouchere asked. "No," replied Pigott, "he is clever up to a certain point but he thinks he is twice as clever as he really is, and that kind of person is readily hoodwinked." Labouchere heartily agreed. Why had he taken so long to concoct the letters? "Well, I like traveling about," Pigott answered. Pigott expressed his fear that he might be prosecuted for perjury and asked Sir George's advice as to what to do. Sir George replied that since he had not forged a negotiable instrument the situation was not beyond repair. If he confessed to the *Times* and stayed out of the witness box, he could not be prosecuted. Pigott said that the *Times* would give him £5000 for his testimony, adding, "I want to know what you are willing to give." That ended the conference.

Testimony by Labouchere, Lewis and Parnell would carry little weight in court. Passions ran so high at the time and the cleavage in English society was so great that the testimony of those in the Parnell camp would be dismissed as self-serving. Pigott was well aware of that. He could be discredited only if he were broken down in court, and Pigott warned the *Times*, to the dismay of that Parthenon of purity, that he had best not take the stand since he would rather not be cross-examined.

It was not until February 15, almost five months after the start of the proceedings, that the Commission approached the question of the letters. The *Times* now evidenced some desire for further delay. John Cameron Macdonald, the noncanny Scot who managed the *Times,* under cross-examination by Asquith began to show the extraordinary fallibility of the world's most respected newspaper. Macdonald had assumed that the writing of the body of the fac-simile letter was done by Parnell's secretary, Henry Campbell. Had he not noticed that the handwriting was almost the same as that of letters purportedly written by Egan? How was it that there were no envelopes for the letters and why had he not inquired about them? Then this confession of ignorance:

Q. Did he [Houston] tell you how he had gotten them from Mr. Pigott?
A. No.
Q. Did you ever ask him?
A. I never asked him. I particularly avoided the subject.
Q. Why did you avoid the subject with such care, Mr. Macdonald?
A. I understood he did not want to be asked.
Q. Did he tell you so?
A. No, but he said he was bound to secrecy and asked me to respect that secrecy.

The *Times* now wanted to introduce a handwriting expert, but the judges wanted to pursue further the source of the letters and Houston was called. He recited the history of his relations with

Pigott and the discovery and purchase of the letters. Houston admitted that he did not know the source from whom Pigott had obtained the letters. "I have purposely kept myself in ignorance of the persons with whom Pigott was in treaty." He did not know Parnell's handwriting and had no samples of it. "I accepted them on Pigott's faith because of the intrinsic probability of the letters themselves."

The judges now wanted to hear from Pigott. The man who took the stand was a frock-coated, stoutish-built man who gave his age as fifty-four but looked sixty, white-bearded, bland, smiling, "having the general appearance of a coarsely composed and rather cheapened Father Christmas."

Parnell muttered almost audibly, "The rat caught in the trap at last."

VI

The direct examination by Sir Richard Webster was brief, but the court was stirred with anticipation when Pigott was asked, "Had you anything to do directly or indirectly wth the writing of the letters?" and he replied, "Nothing whatever. It is quite untrue that I forged them."

Pigott was questioned about his alleged confession to Labouchere. He denied that he had made one, saying that Labouchere had told him that if he could show that he had swindled the *Times* he would be received with a torchlight procession in the United States and would get a seat in Parliament. Laughter broke out in the courtroom. Pigott mopped his brow as Sir Charles rose for the cross-examination.

Sir Charles started by asking if Pigott would be good enough to seat himself at a table and write a few words for him. "Livelihood" —leave a space please—"likelihood," "your own name," "proselytism," "Patrick Egan," "P. Egan," "hesitancy with a small h." Webster jumped up and demanded that the page be photographed. Russell said with some asperity, "Don't interrupt my cross-examination," as he handed the page to the secretary for the Commission.

Pigott testified that he was not aware of the forthcoming publication in the *Times* of the series of articles "Parnellism and Crime." He was then shown a letter from him to Archbishop Walsh dated

March 4, 1887, three days before the series started. Had he written it? Yes, but he understood that it was under the seal of the con-fessional. Justice Day, who was an ardent Catholic, exploded with laughter. Pigott, obviously in great consternation insisted, "I think it established a state of confidence which should not be broken." Sir Charles replied, "Really, Mr. Pigott, I am afraid that I cannot oblige you."

The letter to Dr. Walsh began, "Briefly I wish to say that I have been made aware of the details of certain proceedings that are in preparation with the object of destroying the Parnellite party in Parliament."

Q. Did that passage refer to these letters among other things?
A. No, I rather fancy it had reference to the forthcoming articles.
Q. I thought you told us that you did not know anything about the forthcoming articles.
A. Yes, I did. I find now I am mistaken. I must have heard some-thing about them.

"Try and not make the same mistake again, if you please," said Russell drily.

He continued to read from the letter. "Your Grace may be assured that I speak to you with full knowledge and am in a posi-tion to prove beyond all doubt or question the truth of what I say."

Q. Do you believe the letters to be genuine.
A. I do.

Russell continued to read, "And I may further assure Your Grace that I am also able to point out how the design may be successfully combatted or finally defeated."

Q. Now, if those documents were genuine documents and you be-lieved them to be such, how were you able to assure His Grace that you were able to point out how the design might be suc-cessfully combatted and finally defeated?
A. Well, as I say, I had not the letters actually in my mind at that time so far as I can remember. I do not recollect the letters at all.
Q. You told me a moment ago without hesitation that you had them in your mind.

A. But as I say it had completely faded out of my memory.

Q. That I can understand.

A. I have not the slightest idea of what I referred to.

Q. Assuming the letters to be genuine, what were the means by which you were able to assure His Grace you could point out how the designs might be successfully combatted and finally defeated?

A. I do not know.

Q. Oh, you must think, Mr. Pigott, please. It is not two years ago, you know. Mr. Pigott, had you qualms of conscience at that time and were you afraid of the consequence of what you had done?

A. None at all.

Q. Then what did you mean?

A. I cannot tell you at all.

Q. Try.

A. I cannot.

Q. Try.

A. I really cannot.

Q. Try.

A. It is no use.

Q. Am I to take it then that the answer to my Lordships is that you cannot give any explanation?

A. I really cannot.

Russell then read the letter of Dr. Walsh in reply to Pigott, saying that he could not interfere and that if Pigott had anything to contribute it "should be brought out in the light of day." Pigott claimed that the Archbishop could not have written the letter because "I think he is too much of a gentleman to part with private letters." But then Pigott's letter of reply to Dr. Walsh's declination was read, in which Pigott wrote, "I can assure you I had no other motive in writing save to avert if possible a greater damage to people with whom Your Grace is known to be in strong sympathy." He, Pigott, had acquitted himself "of what I conceive to be my duty in the circumstances."

Q. Assuming the charges to be true and the letters genuine, why was it your duty?

A. I cannot tell you. I do not believe that correspondence refers

U

in any way to the letters. It must have referred to something else.

Q. What else?

A. I cannot tell.

Q. Do you mean a new story that has not yet been published.

A. Yes.

Q. Which you have not even confided to Mr. Houston?

A. Yes.

Q. Nor to Mr. Soames?

A. Nor to Mr. Soames.

Q. But kept locked up in your bosom?

A. I suppose so. I do not know.

Q. It must have been something far more serious. What was it?

A. I have no idea.

Q. Can you give the Lordships any clue of the most indirect kind as to what it was?

A. I cannot.

Q. Or from whom you heard it.

A. No.

Q. Or when?

A. Or when.

Q. Or where?

A. Or where.

Q. Have you ever mentioned this fearful matter whatever it was to anybody?

A. No.

Q. Is it still locked up hermetically sealed in your bosom?

A. No, because it has gone away out of my bosom.

As the courtroom rocked with mirth, the profusely perspiring Pigott left the witness stand for the day.

The cross-examination of the following day, February 22, was to demolish Pigott completely.

Russell started out by reading another letter by Pigott to Dr. Walsh, in which he wrote that the forthcoming publications "would produce a bad effect if published, seeing that it is an artful admixture of what I believe to be true and what I suspect to be false." Now Pigott shifted his ground completely.

Q. Which of the Parnell letters did you think were not genuine?

A. All of them because I could not recognize the handwriting in the body of them.

He said that he had written a letter to Houston remonstrating when they were published, but Houston, in the courtroom, said he had received no such letter. At this point the management of the *Times* must have felt like sinking through the floor.

Now Russell produced other letters to show how Pigott had tried to extract money from others by playing both sides against the middle. On June 2, 1881, he had written to the Irish secretary, Forster, that in his newspapers he had opposed the Land League. "It is my firm conviction that the present Government of Ireland is doing just as much or perhaps more in the way of reform as a native government would or could do. I have besides come to regard a self-ruled Ireland and still more an independent Ireland as simply an impossibility." But as a result, "I have been boycotted, the circulation of my papers has fallen off." And, "inasmuch as I have suffered in my attempts to aid them [the English] in the great work they have undertaken for reconciling Ireland to English rule," he deserved a reward. "To come to particulars a sum of 1500 pounds will get me out of debt."

Forster replied that he deeply appreciated Pigott's patriotism and selflessness, but that it was a policy of the English Government not to subsidize any newspapers.

Leaving Forster temporarily while his recent biographer, Wemyss Reid, sifted the correspondence, Russell showed how Pigott had tried to blackmail Patrick Egan. In a letter of February 27, 1881, concerning some material he had been asked to print, Pigott had written him, "My own opinion is that the whole affair is a tissue of falsehoods but it is so artfully done and so apparently truthful that if published it would, I think, be likely to do much harm. . . . But I consider myself bound to you, and bad as I am I can truthfully say that I have been always true to those who trust me." At this the whole decorum of the courtroom dissolved into an uproar, and the laughter of Justice Day, known as a dour, gloomy Catholic, exceeded all others. From that time on, "Laughter literally shook his [Day's] side and was sort of an obligato to the evidence of the miserable wretch in the rack. His whole frame shook, his eyebrows shook, his long whiskers shook, he could not contain himself."

In a letter to Egan two weeks later Pigott had written, "To come to the point, therefore, I am in desperate straits. I must have money somehow or throw up the sponge at once." Egan, in effect, answered him, "Publish and be damned."

At this point Russell showed that the letters of Parnell produced by Pigott were actually, though they sounded cryptic, merely notes that Parnell had written during the negotiations for the sale of the Pigott newspapers in 1881, notes such as "Send full particulars. What amount does he want? Other letters to hand." Pigott had merely changed the date, of, say, June 16, 1881, to June 16, 1882. Pigott admitted that "the coincidence is curious."

Now more letters to Forster were read, begging letters in which Pigott said, "I feel that this is my last chance and if that fails only the workhouse or the grave remains." He said he had a claim on the English Government. Forster, although he could not see it, advanced money out of his own funds to enable Pigott to move to Cincinnati, where his sister lived, and make a fresh start. Pigott merely pocketed the money, but in 1883 he wrote to Forster again, saying that his sister had just died (she had died the year before) and now he needed money to move to New South Wales. Unable to play further on Forster's sympathies, Pigott now resorted to blackmail—he threatened to state publicly that Forster had hired him to write against the Land League, thus rehabilitating his reputation as a true "patriot who had fallen victim to British wiles." Temporarily he had shelved the idea. "The temptation to fall into the plans of the people who made the proposal can hardly be regarded as otherwise than almost irresistible. Therefore I may be excused for considering the rejection of the proposal entitles me to some consideration at your hands."

Wringing his hands amid the continuous laughter, Pigott said, "This is very amusing to you but it certainly is not to me." The laughter rose to a new crescendo. Mrs. Sidney Buxton wrote that day in her diary, "It was all very funny but I could not help recalling Becky Sharp's 'It is easy to be virtuous on 5000 pounds a year.'" As Russell continued to read the letters, Justice Hannen asked if there was any further point to it, and Russell replied that he wanted to get to the bottom of the affair. "So do we," said Hannen, "but you needn't use such a long rope."

As a clincher, Russell showed Pigott that he had the previous day misspelled "hesitancy" in the same way as it was misspelled in the alleged Parnell letter which was introduced in the O'Donnell trial. Pigott had a fantastic explanation. "I heard that remark [about the misspelling] made long since, and my explanation of my misspelling is that having that in my mind I got into the habit of spelling it wrong." Russell showed him letters of his in which the misspellings appeared. "How do you account for that? Your brain was not injuriously affected at that time." Pigott figuratively surrendered. "I cannot account for that."

Among Pigott's last words—in a wan voice—as he left the stand for the day were, "I don't pretend to be very virtuous."

VII

That night, which was Thursday, Pigott relaxed at the Alhambra Music Hall, where an acquaintance asked him if he did not think that Russell's cross-examination was superb. "Ah, yes,"—Pigott sighed—"but then he had such excellent material to work with, did he not?"

Pigott knew that the game was up and that a prison sentence for perjury loomed, and his thoughts were all on his four small boys. He was a widower. On Friday, he addressed a letter to Houston asking him for £33. "I am told I am to be prosecuted for perjury and I therefore require the money to send home to my poor children." On Saturday morning, he suddenly appeared, like an apparition, before Labouchere at his home while Labouchere was at his desk writing. "I suppose you are surprised at seeing me here," said Pigott. Labouchere, who could not have been more surprised, replied, "Not at all, not at all, pray take a seat." Pigott said that he wanted to confess to him and another witness. "I shall go to prison and perhaps I am better off there than anywhere else. The only thing I regret is the position of my children who will starve." Labouchere sent a message to the journalist George Augustus Sala, who lived nearby. "Can you leave and come here at once? Most important business." When Sala arrived, he found Pigott reading the *Times*, his hands shaking badly. Pigott proceeded to tell the story of the forgery, saying that he had traced Parnell's signature by holding it over a windowpane.

On Monday, Pigott wrote to his housekeeper in Dublin enclosing a blank check for his bank balance. "It will only be, I fear, five pounds. I fear you may look out for the worst." Later in the day he sent her a telegram instructing her to destroy his papers, which she did. He spent some time with his Dublin solicitor, a Mr. Shannon, and undoubtedly obtained some money from him, since he sent another letter with money for his boys. Then, in spite of the fact that the hotel, Anderton's, in Fleet Street, was under police guard, he paid his hotel bill and disappeared into the night.

The next day, Tuesday, February 26, was the day he was supposed to resume the stand. Seats were at a premium as the throng anticipated the fun of again baiting the caged animal. The usher in the crowded courtroom called out, "Richard Pigott," but there was no answer, and he was not in the passage where witnesses sat. Finally, to the question of Russell, Webster had to answer, "We don't know where he is." He had bolted—that was certain. Parnell went to Bow Street to swear out a warrant for Pigott's arrest, and he was followed by a loud, cheering English crowd, surely a novel experience for him.

On that day Pigott was in Paris at the Hôtel Des Deux-Mondes. Two days later he arrived in Madrid and checked into the Hotel Embajadores. He sent a wire to Shannon to send some money to him under the name of Ronald Posonby. That night, by peculiar coincidence, Captain O'Shea, in Madrid on business, saw Pigott in a cafe reading a paper over a bottle of beer and noticed how his hands were trembling.

Pigott's wire to Shannon was delivered to the police in London, and a wire was sent the next day to the Madrid police to arrest him. At four-thirty in the afternoon the police came to the door of his hotel room and demanded to see him. After some hesitation he admitted them. Then, leaning over his luggage, he took a revolver out of a handbag, put it into his mouth and fired.

Labouchere raised a fund for Pigott's boys in his magazine *Truth*, and Dr. Walsh saw to their education. They were given a new surname so that their parentage could not be traced.

VIII

The blackguard Parnell now became a public idol. When he first entered the House of Commons after the Pigott suicide on March 1, not only the Irish members but the whole Liberal party membership, with a few exceptions like Lord Hartington, rose in homage to him. Gladstone turned and bowed to him. Sir Edward Clarke, the Solicitor General, later described the scene. "I saw Mr. Parnell standing erect among the whole standing crowd. He took no notice of it whatever. He had not asked them to get up. When they had finished standing up, they sat down and he took no notice of their rising or their sitting down, and when they had resumed their places he proceeded to make a perfectly calm and quiet speech in which he made not the smallest reference direct or indirect to the incident, extraordinary as it was, which had just happened. I thought as I looked at him that night that the man was a born leader of men—calm, self-confident and powerful."

Not since Warren Hastings had been acclaimed in 1813 had there been a scene like this in the House of Commons. That night was the apogee of his remarkable career. He was forty-two and had less than three years to live. "If 'twere now to die, 'twere now to be most happy."

He was not moved by the demonstration because he was cynically aware of the fickleness of the English public. When Tim Harrington asked, after the acclaim in the House, "Isn't it wonderful?" he replied with a laugh, "Yes, wonderful. But how much more pleased they would have been if the forgery had proved genuine." That night, when Mrs. O'Shea asked if he was not proud and happy, he said, "They would all be at my throat in a week if they could!"

He was immediately elected a life member of the Liberal Club. On March 8, he was entertained for a second time at the Eighty Club, and there shook hands with Lord Spencer to cheers and the waving of handkerchiefs. The *Pall Mall Gazette* commented, "It was the shaking of hands between two nations, the burying of the historical animosities, the last consecrating touch to those life-long efforts [of Gladstone]." An onlooker wrote, "What struck me most was Parnell's indifference to all that went on around him. He could

not have had a more sympathetic audience, but he seemed not to
care whether he was in touch with them or not. The man has no
heart, I think."

A few days later, he appeared as guest of honor at a meeting in
St. James's Hall to protest the treatment of Irish prisoners. Morley,
who was to preside, met him in a carriage to take him to the meeting. Parnell carried a small package, and as he opened it, Morley,
knowing of his superstitions, expected to see some talisman. But
it was a rose, a white rose from Mrs. O'Shea that he always wore
in his buttonhole. When he arrived, "In a moment everyone was
up and for the next five minutes St. James's Hall was even as
Exeter Hall when the Salvation Army has a field day. Cheer followed cheer in endless succession. The whole hall was white with
handkerchiefs. Ladies waved their scarves and handkerchiefs and
cheered as if they never would stop."

At a reception given by Mrs. Sidney Buxton, Parnell had a
cordial meeting with Mr. and Mrs. Gladstone. Gladstone, talking
of the Irish problem, made some allusion to an event of the 1840s
and for confirmation turned to Parnell, who gave him a blank
stare of ignorance. "Thank goodness, that's over. The old man talks
too much" was all Parnell had to say to his Katherine when he got
home. Soon afterward he attended a soiree of the Women's Liberal
Association, and the women went wild over him. "There he is,"
"There he goes," "I *must* shake hands with you," "*I* managed to
shake his hand.". . .

How different things would be in less than eighteen months!
Parnell himself found amusement in all these ovations. "You see,
my dear," he said to his love, "these people are not really pleased
with me. They thought I had written those letters and now they
are extolling their own sense of justice in cheering me because I
did not write them. I might as wisely shout myself hoarse if a
court of law decided that Gladstone had not told somebody to rob
a bank."

"But don't you feel a little excited and proud when they all cheer
you?" Katherine asked, and he replied, "Don't be too pleased with
the clapping of these law-lovers, Queenie. I have a presentiment that
you will hear them another way before long."

All of this was gall and wormwood for Captain William Henry
O'Shea. This man whom he had expected to be branded a criminal
—this man who had ruined his public career, who had appropriated

his wife and had cuckolded him before the world—this man was riding the crest of the waves in triumph, while he was out in the cold. The feckless, frustrated place hunter blamed all his failures on Parnell. Then there was a worse blow. On May 19, 1889, Aunt Ben finally died at the age of ninety-seven, and her will was filed for probate. She had left £144,000 to her niece and companion, Katherine. It had been left to her outside of the marriage settlement, and nothing had been left to his children. So, after waiting all of these years, he now found that he had been tricked. Katherine and her lover Parnell would enjoy the money while he would be dependent on her bounty for crumbs.

This was too much for him to bear.

Part Six

THE DISINTEGRATION

I

FOLLOWING the Pigott exposure there was a third interlude of tranquillity in Parnell's public life lasting for eighteen months, during which his command of the party was seemingly stronger than ever after the utter rout of the attack against him. The voices of the enemies of the Nationalist cause were muted, though Lord Salisbury commented acidly that all the Pigott episode proved was that one Irish Nationalist could forge the signature of another.

The cornerstone of Parnell's policy was alliance with and reliance on Gladstone. Every effort on his part was directed to implementing the alliance, little realizing that he was thereby constructing the scaffold for his own execution. Thus:

In July, 1889, Parnell, at Gladstone's request, voted his party against a motion made by the Radicals to defeat an added grant to the Prince of Wales.

In a conversation with Morley, Gladstone inquired about the O'Gorman Mahon and was told that Parnell had retired him in 1885. "Ah, it would comfort me to have someone older than I beside me in the fight for Home Rule," Gladstone said. When this was related to Parnell, he resurrected the old warrior, then in his late eighties, and gave him a seat from Carlow.

When Parnell accepted the unusual honor of the freedom of the city of Edinburgh, he said that if there were an armed rebellion in Ireland after the grant of Home Rule "You could stamp out that rebellion as remorselessly with your power as you would a rebellion in the heart of Edinburgh." That was designed to calm British fears and make Gladstone's task easier.

Gladstone had proclaimed, "The flowing tide is with us," and so it seemed. Many Liberal Unionists now deserted Chamberlain and returned to Gladstone's side, and by-elections, watched eagerly by the Irish Nationalists, recorded victory after victory for the

Liberals. Gladstone could say to his friend Dr. Dollinger, as 1889 drew to its close, that unless he were removed or, "which would be more serious, Parnell may die," the success of Home Rule after the next general election was assured.

The hearings of the Special Commission continued, but the drama and suspense were over, and, as Parnell had predicted, the whole case collapsed in the public view when the letters were discredited. Healy withdrew and advised Parnell to do the same, saying that the whole miserable proceeding had been foisted on the Irish, but Parnell, mindful again of Liberal sensibilities and British respect for law, declined to do so. He appeared as the first witness for the defense on April 30 and was subjected to two days of cross-examination.

He scored often with his nonchalant rejoinders. At one stage there was a £5 check payment he could not account for. The Attorney General eagerly pursued the matter. Then Parnell recalled it: "My subscription to the Wicklow Harriers." At another point he was asked bluntly if he had ever joined a secret society. "Yes," he replied. Expectantly, he was pressed for the name. "The Foresters," he answered to Webster's chagrin. Parnell must have savored his performance. He made one damaging and even cynical admission. He was asked, in regard to the undoubted fact that there had been secret societies in Ireland, "Why did you tell the House on January 7, 1881, that secret societies had ceased to exist in Ireland?" He replied, "It is possible that I was trying to mislead the House of Commons on that occasion."

One of the spectators was the daughter of the former Prime Minister, Mary Gladstone (Mrs. Drew), and her diary notations are interesting from the standpoint of what she was to record at a later day. "May 2. Parnell before Commission. Attorney-General's manner odious in cross-examination. Insolent, ungentlemanlike, treating Parnell like dirt. He [Parnell] really exhibited all the fruits of the Spirit, love, patience, gentleness, forbearance, long-suffering meekness. His personality takes hold of one, the refined delicate face, illuminating smile, fire-darting eyes, slightly tall figure." On May 8, she wrote, "Loved Parnell's spiritual face, only one's heart ached over his awfully delicate frame and look."

In December, 1889, Parnell accepted an invitation by Gladstone to visit him at his Hawarden home. They discussed the future of Home Rule legislation when the Liberals came to power after the next elections. The content of that conversation was to be a critical matter in the great crisis which was to occur a little more than a year after. Mary Gladstone continued to be fascinated by Parnell. "He looks more ill than anyone I ever saw off a death-bed. A most mysterious man of compelling power and difficult to define quite where this latter lies. Voice low and weak. Good nose—he is forty-three."

At dinner she was delighted when, in reply to her question "Mr. Parnell, who do you think is the best actor?" he replied, "Your father, of course." Parnell was amused too by an incident which took place when they were walking about the grounds and Gladstone was showing the ruins of previous buildings. Mary said, "Papa, you have omitted all reference to the most interesting part of the ruins, the dungeons," and the former jailer showed great discomfiture in the presence of his former prisoner.

The Nationalist party withdrew from the hearings of the Special Commission in July when the tribunal refused to give them access to the records of the Irish Loyal and Patriotic Union (which would have shown many Tory contributors), but their case had been made. Parnell instituted a suit for libel against the *Times,* and the paper paid him £5,000 in settlement on February 13, 1890, a sum which came in quite handy for Parnell, who was then low in funds.

On February 13, 1890, the report of the Special Commission was published. Its findings acquitted Parnell of the heinous charges but, on the other hand, stated that he and his movement "did not denounce the system of intimidation which led to crime and outrages but persisted in it with knowledge of its effects." There were enough dicta and *obiter* dicta of this type to which the Salisbury Government could point as justification for its repressive rule in Ireland. When the Government sought to enter the report in the journal, an angry debate erupted. Parnell denounced the Government. "You wanted to use this question of forged letters as a political engine. You did not care whether they were forged or not. It was a very good question to win elections with." Lord Randolph Churchill joined in the condemnation, saying, "A nemesis awaits a Government that adopts unconstitutional methods. What has been the result?" Then, Churchill continued in a fierce whisper, "Pigott, a man, a thing, a reptile, a monster. Pigott, Pigott, Pigott." In his frenzied attack Churchill seemed to lose all self-control, a manifestation of an affliction which would become more acute.

Gladstone felt that the House, which had voted the inquisition, should now express "its reprobation of the false charges of the gravest and most odious description, based upon calumny and forgery," and though his speech won cheers from both sides, the House defeated the resolution by a vote of 339 to 268 on March 10.

Parnell's prestige could hardly have been higher. That month, amid great cheering, the party passed unanimously a resolution containing these words, "Congratulating our leader Mr. Parnell upon the providential exposure of the plot for his destruction, a plot the most cowardly and nefarious ever formed against a political leader in the history of British political life . . . we once more reiterate in the name of our party and the united Irish race our ever increasing confidence in the wisdom, honour and integrity of our great leader and our lasting gratitude for his priceless services to the Irish race . . ."

II

After the death of Aunt Ben, Mrs. O'Shea abandoned Eltham completely and moved to No. 10 Walsingham Terrace in Brighton, living more or less openly with Parnell there, though for appearance's sake he took the adjoining house. These homes were in a lonely row of houses by the sea, two miles west of the town. Of their life together there, she related, "If it was not glaringly inconvenient, I was always rather proud and interested in the popular interest Parnell attracted wherever he went." Apparently, after having been successful in inheriting her aunt's money, Katherine had no further fear of scandal, and the dodges and devices adopted since 1886 were now abandoned.

This was a happy household, including Mrs. O'Shea's two daughters by the Captain, Norah and Susan (the son Gerard lived with his father), the two daughters by Parnell, Clare and Frances, who were six and five years old respectively in 1889, and two dogs on whom Parnell doted, his setter Grouse and a mongrel terrier, Pincher, whom he had found half starved, wandering on the streets of Killaloe. Except for a few days of shooting now and then at Avondale, Parnell spent all his time here, since he appeared rarely in the House of Commons in 1889 and 1890.

In the basement of the home, there was a room in which a fur-

nace was fitted up where Parnell used to burn crushed ore before
assaying it, and he spent hours there oblivious to the passage of
time. Mrs. O'Shea related that the only way she could get him to
go out for a healthful gallop on his horse President across the
Downs was to get his cap and whip and show them to his dogs,
whereupon they would raise such a racket that he had to get out
of doors. There is something grotesque, almost absurd, in the
image of the Irish leader as the "mad scientist" in quest of gold
and so little interested in his political responsibilities that he ab-
sented himself from Irish affairs for months at a time. Truly he
could say, as did Francis Bacon near his life's close, "My soul hath
been a stranger to me in my pilgrimage." Although he never read
a book about Irish history, he frequented Smith's secondhand book-
shop in North Street, where he would pore by the hour over old
books on mechanics and mining. Another haunt was a little shop
in Pool Valley, where he would watch intently the process of cutting pebbles and polishing crystals which were sold there. Although
he had the sketchiest knowledge of mechanics and engineering, he
conceived the idea that he could invent a roll-proof ship and
thereby make his fortune, and for months he launched model floats
from the under-deck of a Brighton pier.

The couple had lived a life of lies for years awaiting the death
of Aunt Ben, and Parnell had endured ignominy and humiliation
in permitting his two children to masquerade as the children of
Captain O'Shea. Now that the money was hers, Katherine thought
that at last she could buy out her husband; for an adequate sum
he should permit himself to be sued for divorce for one of his
many adulteries and thus the mess could be cleared up. But then
a complication developed which she should have foreseen. Human
greed generally overreaches itself and it did in this case. By corner-
ing this huge fortune all for herself, she laid herself open to a
probate suit by all the other Woods, including her brother, the
distinguished soldier, that the will made by a woman in her
nineties to her close companion be set aside on the ground of
undue influence, so now the estate was tied up in litigation and
Mrs. O'Shea's plan to bribe her husband had gone agley.

x

III

On Christmas Eve, 1889, Parnell was served with papers naming him as corespondent in a suit for divorce filed by Captain O'Shea. The wronged husband had waited more than three years in his certain knowledge of the love affair. Even now there were good grounds for hesitation. Almost fifty years old, he had no desire to be free for a second marriage. He was loathe to brand the mother of his three children as an adulteress in public, and the scandal would hurt him professionally in the banking circles where he eked out a living as an agent of a Madrid bank.

There were monetary considerations, too, which argued against a divorce action. By refraining from bringing a divorce suit he could extract money from his wife, a form of blackmail. The amount of money Katherine would have in her possession depended on how she made out in the probate suit. By bringing a suit for divorce O'Shea was hurting her chances in that suit, since adultery was regarded as a kind of moral turpitude which might carry over to the circumstances under which Aunt Ben made her will. Thus Katherine might be left with little or no money for another form of blackmail he probably had in mind, arising from the fact that he was legally the father of two girls whom he must have known by now by their facial resemblance to be the children of Parnell.

Though his financial interest pointed in the opposite direction, Captain O'Shea chose to bring the divorce suit, and he joined the rest of the Woods as a contestant of the will against his wife, which would give him small share in the end, if any. Why did he adopt his course? He was motivated, of course, by his bitter hatred of Parnell and his lust for revenge. But there is more to the motivation than that. It is very probable that O'Shea was used as a pawn by Parnell's political enemies to accomplish his ruin.

Alfred Robbins, Parliamentary correspondent of the Birmingham *Post,* who was on intimate terms with Joseph Chamberlain's political faction, related later in a book about the period, "In August 1889, I was asked by one on the inside of the Liberal Unionist machine whether Parnell would be politically ruined by a divorce suit, the recent Dilke instance being given as a promising precedent. . . ." This was only four months before O'Shea brought his suit.

The evidence that Chamberlain encouraged and abetted the suit is circumstantial. As we have seen, he had written Miss Endicott in July, 1888, that O'Shea "is an indiscreet and therefore a dangerous person." Certainly he would be on his guard not to put anything in writing to incriminate him in this shoddy maneuver to destroy Parnell. What went on in private between the two we do not know, but a hint, a wink or a nod might have been sufficient to propel the pliant henchman in the desired direction.

Yet despite Chamberlain's need for caution, the correspondence is most illuminating. The letters of Captain O'Shea make it evident that Chamberlain was made acquainted by him with the vicissitudes of his personal life. On November 3, 1888, O'Shea wrote to him, "I daresay that a great many people have some notion of the state of affairs but I am most anxious for my children's sake that nothing about it shall be actually published because a very large fortune for them may depend on it not coming to print." From Paris, on his way to the Riviera with his new bride, Chamberlain wrote in reply only, "I sympathize with you in your domestic anxiety which must have added to the wear and tear of the last few months."

In October, 1889, O'Shea wrote to Chamberlain of his intent to institute the suit for divorce and Chamberlain replied, "I am sincerely sorry that you should have such cause of anxiety and trouble. I have heard nothing and know nothing beyond what you have told me. I am not sure that the boldest course is not always the wisest." Chamberlain's disclaimer of any knowledge of the marital problem was patently disingenuous—if he did not know, he was the only one in high politics who did not know of it, and Dilke's diary indicates that Chamberlain was at the Cabinet meeting in 1882 when Sir William Harcourt told them that Mrs. O'Shea was Parnell's mistress. The seeming aloofness that Chamberlain assumes in this letter is surely attributable to the caution of a wily politician that he should not expose himself to any damaging charge afterward. The last sentence of the letter is surely a pat of approval, and after the suit was launched Chamberlain patted O'Shea approvingly again when he wrote him, "Now that you have taken the decisive step I may be allowed to say that it seems to have been forced on you."

In August, three months before the trial, O'Shea wrote exultantly to Chamberlain, "He who smashes Parnell, smashes Parnellism." Ten days after the divorce was granted. O'Shea wrote to

Chamberlain about a reward for himself—a seat in Parliament. "You are quite right, a borough would suit me better than a county . . . If you want to back me in the House, this is the moment to strike and exact a promise." The idea that Chamberlain would incriminate himself by getting O'Shea a seat in Parliament at this time is a silly one—but it seems unreasonable that even a person as airy minded as O'Shea could have harbored the idea that Chamberlain was now obligated to him unless some baited words had been used by Chamberlain in the past, encouraging him in his course of action.

IV

A remarkable feature in the remarkable tale of Parnell's downfall was that even though all the lieutenants had known for years of the love affair and, therefore, should have had no doubt as to what lay ahead, for a period of eleven months after the suit was filed all remained in a state of blissful contentment, with not even a quiver of anxiety displayed as to the future of the leader and hence of the party. Of course, Parnell had just emerged unscathed from the forgery commission, and more than ever he appeared to be the romantic hero cloaked in invincibility. This new assault was regarded as another foul tactic of "Pigottism," or, as the *Freeman's Journal* put it, "another weak and puny resort" of his enemies.

Also, was there something in the temperament of the Irish politician that preferred the bliss of ignorance to the folly of being wise? Did the congenital optimism of the race infect the politician? Davitt later commented that it is a marked trait of the Irish politician to imitate the ostrich whenever anything disagreeable appears on the horizon or to "apply to politics the methods of Christian Science."

"Oh, he's like a cat, he will always land on his feet" was the reaction of Biggar to the new hazard, and his breezy confidence was shared by his colleagues. Biggar died in London soon afterward, at the end of January, 1890; characteristically, Parnell did not attend the funeral or even pay his respects at the funeral home. Biggar's death would be a grave loss for the movement that could not be foreseen at the time. In the great leadership crisis ahead, he alone, as the initiator of the obstruction policy and Parnell's old comrade in arms, could have talked to him hardheadedly as an equal; all others in the Parliamentary party were regarded by Parnell as his creatures.

An important factor in dispelling any nervousness was the absolute assurance that Parnell radiated. On January 9, 1890, Justin McCarthy wrote to Mrs. Campbell Praed, who was collaborating with him on a novel, "He proposes to lead the party just the same until the trial commences which is surely the right course to take as he does not admit that there is any ground for the action." To William O'Brien, Parnell wrote, "If this matter is ever fully gone into, a matter which is exceedingly doubtful, you may rest assured that it will be shown that the dishonour and the discredit have not been on my side."

This seemed to convey the thought that he had something up his sleeve which would repel the charge, though it was hard to conjecture what it could be. This was strengthened by the report of his interview with Michael Davitt, who alone had the courage to beard the lion in his den, to confront him and to ask him to throw light on the case as he felt Parnell was under an obligation to do. No sooner had Davitt given an indication of the reason for his call than Parnell launched into a tirade about labor organizations that Davitt had sponsored in Ireland. "I thought you were opposed to class movements. What is trade unionism but land-lordism of labour? I would not tolerate them as head of a Government. They are opposed to individual liberty and I would keep them down as Bismarck does in Germany." This bluster was designed to deter Davitt from further questioning on this delicate matter, but Davitt persisted. Parnell then told him that he "would emerge from the whole trouble without a stain on his reputation" and that Davitt could convey that advice to the comrades, which he proceeded to do.

It was this misleading statement which later infuriated Davitt and made him attack Parnell without quarter as a "cold-blooded sensualist." While Davitt assumed that Parnell meant that he was not guilty of adultery, Parnell may have meant only that, in his view, he had behaved honorably.

Parnell continued to rule the party as before, which, among other things, meant that he visited the House of Commons as rarely as he had before. His colleagues gave him a banquet of tribute in July on his forty-fourth birthday, of which O'Brien wrote that the atmosphere "was not free of a foreboding note of forced gaiety not far removed from tears," but this is the account of the emotional O'Brien in retrospect. Later, Parnell attended O'Brien's wedding. It had been planned as a private ceremony, but when Parnell expressed a desire to attend, it was made a public affair and Parnell's presence drew the attendance of seventy Irish members of Parliament. During the ceremony Parnell bore a wistful look and afterward said to Archbishop Croke, "How happy I should be to be married like that."

The Liberal leadership was more realistically aware of the impending crisis poised by the revelation of Parnell's personal life and was surprised by the attitude of the Irish members. Soon after the suit was filed, Morley consulted with Dillon, who dismissed the suit as of little consequence unless squalid details emerged, which he did not anticipate. Morley disagreed. On February 3, after a talk with George Lewis, Parnell's counsel, Morley wrote Harcourt, "I can only say that when the time comes, Walter [owner of the *Times*] will have five thousand pounds worth of revenge. It will be a horrid exposure and must, I think, lead to the disappearance of our friend."

On November 4, as the trial drew near, Gladstone wrote forebodingly to his chief whip, Arnold Morley, "I fear that a thundercloud is about to burst over Parnell's head and I suppose it will end the career of a man in many respects invaluable." John Morley decided to find out directly from Parnell how things stood, since the Irish and the Liberals were allies whose cause rested on each other. At dinner with Parnell at Brighton soon before the trial, Morley asked him point-blank whether the divorce suit would lead to his disappearance from public life, to which Parnell replied, "Oh, not in the least. The other side don't know what a brokenkneed horse they are riding," obviously referring to O'Shea. He added, "The Irish people are very slow to give a man their confidence and they are still more slow to withdraw it."

Morley relayed this to Gladstone and wrote to Harcourt. "The Irish will not throw him over in any case and if the Irish don't, no one else will." It is significant that at this early stage the Liberal leaders were thinking of the possibility of ditching Parnell. The second in command, Harcourt, frankly detested him. The interesting question relates to Gladstone and his lieutenant, John Morley.

V

Was Parnell's unconcern merely a pose? Probably not. Up to the day of the trial, he had hoped that he might extricate himself and emerge unscathed.

Mrs. O'Shea told Henry Harrison after Parnell's death that if she had been able to pay O'Shea £25,000, O'Shea would have consented to let her divorce him instead of vice versa. But this expectation came to grief because the will contestation tied up her aunt's estate and she was unable to borrow on her expectancy, though she tried till the end. O'Shea himself told his counsel at one point that he could have £20,000 as the price of dropping the suit.

Parnell had no money and his hopes, too, centered on Katherine's winning in the estate dispute. He had run through the money he had received in the Parnell Tribute. According to his brother John, he spent £90,000 between 1881 and 1891 and was £50,000 in debt at the time of his death. As to his personal expenditures, he was most parsimonious, what the Irish call a near man, buying the smallest cigars and the least expensive dinner when dining at the House of Commons, but he ran up huge dining bills at outside restaurants which he never paid. He spent lavishly on exploiting the mineral potential of Avondale, and nothing came of it. John said that in 1888 his brother expected a second Tribute, saying to him, "Well, John, politics is the only thing I ever got money from and I am looking for another subscription."

There was another hope, a slim one, besides buying O'Shea off. Mrs. O'Shea entered a defense of connivance on the part of O'Shea, thus admitting her adultery but interposing a bar of condonation; she also entered a counterclaim, a startling one, that her husband had committed adultery with her sister Mrs. Steele. By brandishing these defenses she hoped to deter O'Shea from going through with the suit.

These defenses, which were pure bluff, turned out to be very ill advised. O'Shea did not give ground at all, and Mrs. O'Shea had to give ground and abandon them. Parnell was most anxious to marry her and give her his name, and she was most anxious to get rid of Willie once and for all. When her counsel, Frank Lockwood, spoke of the chance of blocking the divorce, she shouted,

"Remain married to him! Then may my death be not long!" But entering the defenses initially, which she did in a tantrum, proved to be disastrous, since it enabled O'Shea to testify at the trial and give evidence to refute the claim of connivance; it was this evidence which proved most damaging and degrading to Parnell's reputation.

The case came up for trial on November 15 and 17. Parnell was not represented, and Mrs. O'Shea had only a watching brief. O'Shea had an opportunity to present all the evidence he wanted without fear of cross-examination. There was testimony offered about the false names of Mr. Fox and Mr. Clement Preston, which smacked of cheap methods of disguise. There was testimony about the numerous changes of domicile and the subterfuges and evasions to conceal the liaison. The correspondence since the awakening of O'Shea in 1886 showed conclusively that he was a gullible but deceived husband.

The most damaging testimony was the "fire escape" testimony of Caroline Peters, a maid at the Brighton home in Medina Terrace in 1884. She testified that Parnell, using the name of Stewart, came in secrecy to visit Mrs. O'Shea, that they drove together only at night, that the couple were generally in a locked room together and when the maid wanted to deliver a message she had to knock and wait five or ten minutes until the door was opened a crack wide. When Captain O'Shea came, she said, Parnell would rush up to the second floor, lower himself from the "fire escape," meaning a balcony, and present himself ten minutes later at the front door. She claimed that this had happened at least three times.

Parnell was in the office of the *Freeman's Journal* that day reading the press copy as it came in, and when he saw Caroline Peters' testimony he exclaimed, "What blackguard testimony is this!" Indeed, the testimony has all the earmarks of a fakery that would have been destroyed on cross-examination if a defense had been offered. If Parnell presented himself at the door ten minutes later, what was incriminating about being there in the first place? If he appeared before Captain O'Shea under his right name and identity, why bother with an assumed name? The home was surrounded by others, and was it not ridiculous to visualize a bearded Romeo sliding down a rope from the balcony in full daylight under the full gaze of others?

The verdict of Judge Butt was all that might have been expected under the uncontradicted testimony. Summing up the evidence he stigmatized Parnell as a man "who takes advantage of the hospitality offered him by the husband to debauch the wife" and said, "If the husband were a conniving and consenting party, why should there have been all the disguises, why should there have been the assumption by Mr. Parnell of names which do not belong to him, such as Fox and Preston?" He granted the decree nisi (it would become final in six months) and gave O'Shea the custody of all the children below the age of sixteen, a most serious blow to Parnell since two of them were his children. Before the trial Parnell had considered spiriting them out of the country and had consulted a solicitor about countries on the Continent where they might be safe from legal process.

The impact of the case, with its revelation of furtiveness, trickery and cheap devices for concealment, was a shattering blow for Parnell. He had been the man on a pedestal, not only for the Irish but for the English too, but now the aura of the man of mystery had been dispelled, and the *Times* could gloat that his love life was "a dreary monotony of middle-class vice over which M. Zola's scalpel so longingly lingers." The "fire escape" episode was the most unfortunate one since it exposed Parnell to merciless ridicule. This was not the life of the demigod but of Harlequin. It was parodied in the music halls and there was even a fire-escape toy. The squalor of the case, wrote Morley immediately, made it, in his view, impossible for any candidate to fight under a banner so tainted. But also involved was a breach of moral law and of man's law—and from a political standpoint, that was most serious in Victorian England.

The Queen noted in her journal that Parnell was "not only a man of very bad character but . . . a liar and devoid of all sense of honour or any sort of principle." What now was the reaction in her diary of the adoring Mary Gladstone? "He and she undefended and he had lived the life of lies all these years! A heartbreaking revelation. Blot out his name!"

VI

The story of Parnell's love life was not a tale of libertinism or sodden vice or "sensualism," as Davitt described it. It was a monogamous love characterized even by model uxoriousness. The one flaw in a life of middle-class morality was that he could not marry Katherine O'Shea because she was already married when he met her, married to a man who had long since adopted a life of his own. The revelation of the affair was followed by a burst of moral indignation which put an end to Parnell's leadership. But, it is interesting that it was the indignation and pressure of the English rather than the Irish, that was responsible for Parnell's fall, and it is more interesting because, far from being Puritanical, the English in Victorian times, behind a facade of morality, tolerated and practiced a loose code of morality. Disraeli told the story of what happened when he brought up to Queen Victoria the subject of legislation Parliament was considering to regulate brothels. The Queen recoiled in distaste. "Brothels in London!" she exclaimed. "Madame," replied Disraeli, "London is one gigantic brothel."

The very frankness about sex bespeaks the absorption in the topic. Even in Shakespeare's time travelers from the Continent were surprised to find in England anatomical talk of sex freely exchanged in mixed company. The first prime minister, Robert Walpole, said that he always preferred smut as a subject at the dinner table because it was the one subject in which all could join. British statesmen wenched with abandon and not much forethought. Swift told of walking with a minister, Bolingbroke, and, suddenly finding him gone, looked back to find him arm-in-arm with a whore. Charles James Fox, on his way to Parliament, would decide on the spur of the moment to stop at his favorite brothel. "We have all had our faults in this way," said William IV when his Prime Minister Melbourne was accused of adultery.

In Victorian days, there was a freer supply of *filles de joie* than ever, since it was elementary good sense to pleasing young maids that there was a better life available to them by the sale of their favors than the barbarities of the factory in the Industrial Revolution. Cyril Pearl, in *The Girl with the Swansdown Seat,* studied the subject and showed that Victorianism as a connotation of purity is humbug of the worst sort. "It was an age when prostitution was widespread and flagrant, when many London streets were Oriental bazaars of flesh, when the luxurious West End nighthouses dispensed love and liquor till dawn; when fashionable whores rode with duchesses in Rotten Row and eminent Victorians negotiated for the tenancy of their beds; when a pretty new suburb rose at St. John's Wood as a seraglió for mistresses and harlots and at popular pleasure gardens like Cremorne and Higbury Barn, prostitution was given a setting of woodlawn charm."

The Victorians were statistically inclined and did not overlook the prostitute population of London, which was estimated in 1860 at 80,000, or one in sixteen of the female population of all ages. With an average clientele per girl of twenty-five per week, the total clientage ran to 2,000,000 per week, compared with a total male population in London of 1,300,000 of all ages. The French historian Taine recorded on one visit to London that in Haymarket and the Strand in the evening "Every hundred steps one jostles twenty harlots." Patronage of the whores was widespread in all classes, since there was a prevalent belief that continence was bad for the health, and in a reverse proposition, Charles Dickens stated his belief that if a youth was chaste, it was a sign that he was in bad health. It was regarded as necessary to have a respectable income before marriage, which resulted in late marriages and then wives were continuously childbearing—thus, before and after marriage the men would sport.

The myth of Victorian morality was largely due to the novelists who subscribed to the convention that all men, that is, all gentlemen, are glandless, and women are unsullied by carnal thoughts. At a time when reading aloud was a popular pastime, the touchstone for acceptability was whether the book could be read aloud by a genteel man to a genteel woman. To make him acceptable, Thomas Bowdler unsexed Shakespeare in ten volumes—and gave us our word "bowdlerize." This convention in literature was enforced by the circulating libraries, without which no book could be a success, since these libraries were in the hands of strict-conscience Nonconformists.

The Parnell case occurred in a society that reeked with libertinism but which was wrapped in a pretense of morality, or, as someone put it, "Victorian morality reposed on the belief that if you could not be virtuous, you could at least be respectable." This shibboleth of morality was largely due to the influence of the Nonconformists, disciples of John Wesley, ardent church-goers and bawling hymn-singers, abnegators of the flesh. The hypocrisy of subscribing to that middle-class morality could be maintained as long as one was not caught. Gladstone was reputed to have said that he knew at one time or another eleven former prime ministers and that they were all adulterers, to a man—but they were not found out. Mrs. O'Shea wrote that Parnell's sin was that he had violated the Eleventh Commandment, "Thou shalt not be found out." That was a fatal sin at a time when the Nonconformist conscience ruled so heavily, particularly in the Liberal party. That the breach of morality was in the public scandal rather than in the adultery, she says, is quite evident since Gladstone had known from the first time he had met her in 1882 that she was Parnell's mistress.

The case of Sir Charles W. Dilke clearly foreshadowed the fate that was in store for Parnell. Divorce, except by special act of Parliament, had been impossible until it was legalized in 1857. Prior to that time, ecclesiastical courts dispensed decrees of judicial separation. Dilke was the first important political personality involved in a divorce case.

A Scottish lawyer in London, Mr. Crawford, received a letter, unsigned, which began, "Fool, looking for the cuckoo who has flown defiling your nest?" He showed the letter to his wife, who immediately confessed that she had broken her marriage vows; she had committed adultery on numerous occasions with Sir Charles Dilke, the Undersecretary for Foreign Affairs. She had met him at a rendezvous in morning hours, where she had been dressed by a maid, Sarah, who was a former mistress of Sir Charles. On one occasion, he had introduced into the bed another maid and former mistress, Fanny Stock, so that the three could perform French perversions together. Such was *la dolce vita* in the English aristocracy.

Crawford brought suit for divorce, naming Dilke as corespondent. Dilke recorded in his diary, "A sudden fall indeed. Such a charge even if disproved is fatal to supreme usefulness in politics." To a friend who cited the case of the Duke of Wellington, who had answered the threat of a blackmailing madame with "Publish and be damned," Dilke replied, "An aristocratic society then rather enjoyed a scandal. Today the middle classes rule and adultery to them is as bad as murder."

The trial took place in mid February, 1886, and Gladstone, then forming his government after the 1885 elections, omitted Dilke from it, his otherwise warm letter referring to a "recognition on my part of an external barrier." This was the first step in Dilke's downfall. In the trial, Mrs. Crawford's confession was introduced, but she did not go on the stand. It was expected that Dilke, to preserve his reputation, would take the stand, but he did not. Judge Butt granted the petition for a divorce but for lack of corroboration dismissed the case against Dilke, the legal absurdity thus being expressed that she had committed adultery with Dilke but he had not committed adultery with her.

The omission to take the stand is regarded far more seriously as a possible admission in English jurisprudence than it is in American law. Dilke frankly told his counsel and friends that he feared to be questioned about intimacies many years ago with Mrs. Crawford's mother, fearing that the salacious-minded public might think he had corrupted his own daughter—and, as a matter of fact, he was not at all sure that Mrs. Crawford was not his daughter.

William T. Stead, editor of the *Pall Mall Gazette,* pounced on the failure of Dilke to take the stand. Stead was a supreme egotist and a crusader for purity obsessed with sex, very much an Elmer Gantry type. He had carried on a campaign in his paper to raise the age of consent from twelve to sixteen, in the course of which he had carried off a girl of thirteen and had gotten a prison term of three months, to his great pride. Now he attacked Dilke as a shameless adulterer who was unfit for public office.

Dilke claimed that he had new evidence to refute the charge of adultery and persuaded the Queen's Proctor to bring suit to annul the decree nisi of divorce. On the stand Dilke badly botched his case, undoubtedly because Mrs. Crawford had told the truth. He did not produce Fanny Stock, as it was believed he could do. Mrs. Crawford, a pert-looking girl of twenty-three, gave a straightforward story which carried conviction. In the course of her testimony, she admitted that besides her affair with Dilke, she had had more extensive assignations with a young man named Forster, and there were other names raised who might have been her lovers in her short married life. Apparently there was no end of recreational opportunities for both Dilke and Mrs. Crawford.

The jury dismissed the suit of the Queen's Proctor in a few minutes and Dilke was disgraced. That year he lost his seat at Chelsea in the elections and was virtually ostracized. He returned to Parliament in 1892 but was never again a factor in government or politics, though Gladstone had once listed him as among the likeliest to succeed him as head of the Liberal party. Mrs. Crawford never remarried and spent the remaining sixty-two years of her life in social work, now the field of activity of John Profumo, War Minister in the Macmillan Cabinet who resigned in a sex scandal in 1963.

In a sidelight of the case Henry Labouchere told how Gladstone asked him to talk to Mr. Crawford and find out what inducement could persuade him to drop the suit naming Dilke. "Can nothing be done to prevent the ruin of such a pillar of liberalism?" Gladstone said. Labouchere reported back, "Crawford wants to be a judge but of course that's impossible," and Gladstone said, to Labouchere's surprise, "Why impossible?" Labouchere made further soundings and then had to tell Gladstone that Crawford had replied that nothing could induce him to drop the suit. It is interesting to compare Gladstone's desire and concern to extricate Dilke with the attitude he would take toward Parnell—even though Dilke's offense was far more heinous from a moral viewpoint.

VII

The overthrow of Parnell took place with such rapidity that his colleagues, even in writing about it in later years, seemed to gasp with incredulity that the unbelievable had occurred. As classical scholars, they used classical allusions, one citing the last lines of *Oedipus Rex* about the fragility of human fortunes, another pointing out that in ancient Rome, the Capitol, the scene of triumphs, was only a short distance from the Tarpeian Rock, from which state criminals were hurled to their death, and another quoting, *Fortuna vitrea est: tum cum splendet fragitur* (Fortune is of glass, it glitters just at the moment of breaking).

Yet the truth was that behind the facade of dictatorship Parnell's power had been declining for years. Fissions had appeared in the rock of his authority so that it required only a strong hammer blow for the rock to fall apart. The Church, of course, had looked on Parnell for years with suspicious toleration, Archbishop Croke being his only partisan in the hierarchy. The leftist element of the party, notably Davitt and to a large extent Dillon, had fiercely resented what it considered a sellout of the land program as the price of Parnell's release from prison, as revealed by O'Shea's bungling of the mission. The Galway affair had disgusted the idealists of the party, as well it should have. Again, Parnell's indifference to the Plan of Campaign had alienated the party zealots.

Due to his long neglect the machinery of the party had fallen into the hands of his lieutenants. Parnell had hardly been seen in Ireland for four years and had addressed no meetings. The lieutenants, notably Dillon and O'Brien in the Plan of Campaign, had won their independence and had built up their personal following. Every Caesar is the object of Cassiuslike envy, and certainly Sexton and Healy carried this in their hearts for years. Sexton had been shouldering the Parliamentary load for three years and undoubtedly had never received a word of thanks from Parnell. Sexton told Healy that after being absent from Parliament for almost the whole 1890 session, Parnell showed up on the day it was prorogued. Meeting Sexton, who was alone in the smoking room, Parnell took out a cigar and, with his back to the empty fire grate, said, "Sexton, never before have I known a session in which the Irish [budget] estimates were so perfunctorily discussed." "I might have said this was due to his absence," said Sexton to Healy, "but I was too disgusted to say anything."

In Healy's breast resentment was especially acute. In the early years of the dictatorship he had openly boasted that he was the real power, but at Galway he had been made to eat dirt. In the Special Commission he had been humiliated when Parnell had voided his brief. And now came the worst indignity: in the divorce case a letter was published written by Mrs. O'Shea in 1886 in which she quoted Parnell as saying of Healy, "it is better to put up with a great deal of abuse rather than retaliate, for it is ill fighting with a chimney-sweep." What an affront, to be called in public a "chimney-sweep"! Healy must have ground his teeth in rage.

And what of Gladstone? Could there have been some old score to settle? After the first day of the divorce trial Gladstone wrote to Morley, "Will he ask for the Chiltern Hundreds? He cannot continue to lead. The Pope has now clearly got a commandment under which to pull him up." It is unfair to censure Gladstone for hypocrisy, as Mrs. O'Shea and others have done, on the ground that he was well aware of the liaison. It was not the function of Gladstone to play Comstock to the private life of those about him—and in this field, who could escape whipping? Exposure was the hazard of the individual concerned, not that of Gladstone. It is, however, passing strange that before the divorce trial was even finished, Gladstone should have made up his mind that Parnell was unsuitable as a political ally, despite the fact that Gladstone had recognized more than once that the viability of the Irish Nationalist party, and hence of Home Rule, rested on Parnell.

"You know as well as I that he has always loathed me," Mrs. O'Shea quotes Parnell as saying to her. It is quite likely, but what could have been the wellsprings of this dislike? Was it formed in 1881 when Gladstone believed that Parnell was determined to destroy his land bill, which he believed to be the salvation of Ireland? Was it because of Parnell's frequent, belittling statements about him and his ill-concealed dislike? Was it because Parnell had been difficult to deal with during the fight for the Home Rule bill in 1886, when he threw Gladstone into a fury by threatening to withdraw support for the bill if Gladstone suspended further work on the bill for the session after the second reading? The eighty-one-year-old Gladstone certainly did not look forward to dealing again with this contentious personality on the next Home Rule bill.

The forces which clashed and interlocked in this tragedy of history were directed by fallible human beings who, while they acted at the conscious level on a strictly objective concept of the good to be served, at the subconscious level were driven by ordinary human prejudice.

VIII

All events seemed to converge to produce the tragedy. The 1891 session of Parliament was scheduled to start earlier than at any time in half a century, on November 25, or nine days after the divorce decree was granted. This chance circumstance caused events to move at a headlong pace, making any compromise solution of the problem difficult. Parnell himself acted boldly, and on the day of the court verdict he gave clear notice that as far as he was concerned his leadership was unaffected. He sent out a letter to all Nationalist members to be present on the opening day of Parliament, "as it is unquestionable that the coming session will be one of combat from first to last and that great issues depend on its course."

The reaction in Ireland surprised the English. Although divorce was absolutely banned for the great majority in Catholic Ireland and the code of morals was far stricter there than in England, its observance being more than the lip service and cant it was to so many in England, nonetheless the Irish (except for the clergy) rallied around Parnell. Such was the habit of obedience and the spell cast by his personality. Expressions of fealty came thick and fast. The *Freeman's Journal* stated that the issue as a political one would be judged by the Irish people alone and not by the English; it pointed out that Parnell was not a Catholic and cited the moral delinquency of many English leaders. It also made a rather piquant argument that was to be heard more than once: it blamed wicked Albion for Parnell's moral downfall. "It is living in England which has contaminated Mr. Parnell and were he living at home in Ireland he would never have fallen in with the O'Sheas."

On November 18, the General Branch of the Irish National League had a meeting in Dublin, and there was a stream of emotional expressions of loyalty and stigmatizations of possible desertions as high treason. Swift MacNeil said, "God forbid that he who led us in time of difficulty should be deserted by us in cloudy and dark days." John Redmond said, "If he were thinking of quitting, the Irish people would come as a man and entreat him not to desert them, but thank God no such danger exists."

On November 20, there was a gigantic meeting in Leinster Hall in Dublin attended by leading members of the party. The chairman was Justin McCarthy, who had written the day before to Mrs. Campbell Praed, "I think we ought to do nothing and take no notice," and then, blaming it all on Mrs. O'Shea, "He was a very young man when it began, she was considerably older than he even in mere years," which was inaccurate. Now, at the Leinster meeting, he said, "I ask you, suppose a man has gone morally wrong in some case, whatever temptation we know not, is that the least reason to excuse him from doing his duty to the people whom he is leading to victory?" The most notable speech was by Tim Healy, who would soon lead a merciless attack on Parnell. At this stage Mr. Healy found discretion the better part of rebellion, possibly chastened by the memory of his experience at Galway in 1886. "We must remember that for Ireland and for Irishmen, Mr. Parnell is less a man than an institution. We have under the shadow of his name secured for Ireland a power and authority in the councils of Great Britain and the world such as we never possessed before. I say it would be foolish and criminal if we, the seasoned politicians upon this occasion, at the very first blast of opposition, surrender the great chief who has led us so far forward." His concluding words were, "You are requested not to speak to the man at the wheel."

O'Brien and Dillon had been arrested for sedition on September 17 and released on bail on October 18. They had fled by yacht to France, then had gone to the United States on a fund-raising expedition, where they were joined by T. P. O'Connor, T. D. Sullivan and Tim Harrington. The Parnell crisis interrupted a tour that had been sensationally successful in raising funds for the Irish tenant farmers.

The immediate reaction of these leaders in America duplicated that across the sea. O'Brien in an interview said, "Mournful as has been his error, heavy and deplorable an affliction as it has brought upon our race, I say more deplorable and base it would be if in this hour of darkness for him we could forget for one moment the debt Ireland owes to his genius and his matchless qualities as a leader." Dillon in an interview said, "One cablegram from Europe reports me as saying 'Mr. Parnell will have to retire.' It is all moonshine. I do not think the priests will ask the people to abandon the movement if Parnell remains the leader of the party." A strong message of support was cabled to the Leinster meeting which had a profound effect on the audience there. There was one dissenter in America, however, the first. T. D. Sullivan of *The Nation*, the father-in-law of Healy, felt that Parnell had morally disqualified himself for leadership.

In a matter of days Healy, McCarthy, Dillon and O'Brien would be demanding Parnell's retirement. However cogent the arguments that would develop for this course, the swiftness of the *volte-face* is astonishing. The Leinster Hall meeting was the great watershed for Parnell's power—from that time on the descent would be a vertical one and the attack on him would answer to Goethe's remark "The Irish seem to me like a pack of hounds always dragging down some noble stag."

On the day of the Leinster Hall meeting, an influential and respected voice was heard with a call to arms against Parnell. Michael Davitt, who was infuriated at being deceived by Parnell, in the *Labour World* called for his retirement, at least temporarily, in order to deliver Ireland "from the deadliest peril to which it has yet been assailed." He asked Parnell to "make a sacrifice, a comparatively small one, in return for the many sacrifices which the most confiding and generous people, who have ever followed a political leader, have made for him."

In later years, William Butler Yeats wrote, "The Bishops and the party, that tragic story made," and James Joyce wrote that "the priests and priests' pawns broke Parnell's heart and hounded him into his grave." The culpability of the Catholic clergy in destroying Parnell has become a traditional view, but to put full blame, or even major blame there, is less than accurate. Had the impetus for an anti-Parnell drive not come from the Liberal party of England, the Irish people would have stood by Parnell and the Church would have been impotent to force a desertion from him.

The Church hierarchy was boiling with indignation. Archbishop Croke, who had always been sympathetic to the movement and to Parnell personally, wrote to Archbishop Walsh, "I have flung him away from me forever. His bust which for some time has held a prominent place in my hall I threw out yesterday." Cardinal Manning wrote to Archbishop Walsh, "There is now a great opportunity for the bishops to regain control of the movement. If ten years ago the bishops and priests had acted together, the movement would not have fallen into the hands of laymen." Both Archbishop Croke and Archbishop Walsh were doubtful and hesitant about launching an attack. They feared raising the specter of clerical control, and Dr. Croke thought that the clergy were regarded in the political arena as only "money-gatherers and useful auxiliaries in the movement." For the present, said Dr. Croke, after Leinster Hall, "Really I fear things must be allowed to take the direction given them by the Irish members, come what may." Cardinal Manning wrote regretfully, "Gratitude, blind loyalty and just anger at English violence will make the Irish people refuse to forsake Parnell."

After expressing surprise that the Irish bishops and priests had not risen up, Gladstone wrote to Morley in evident disappointment and referred to Parnell's summons to Parliament of Irish members, "But I think it plain that we have nothing to say and nothing to do in the matter. It is the Irish Parliamentary party and that alone to which we have to look." Morley told Gladstone, "I am pretty sure the Irish will stomach him though no priest will be with him on a platform for a long time to come!"

Then the Nonconformist conscience started to make itself felt. W. T. Stead started to lash out against Parnell in the *Pall Mall Gazette,* as he had against Dilke a few years before. A famous preacher, the Rev. Hugh Price Hughes, wrote in the *Methodist Times* that if the Irish retained Parnell they would be branded as "an obscene race utterly unfit for anything except a military despotism." A few days later, on November 23, he stated at a mass meeting in St. James's Hall that if the Irish retained Parnell the Liberals faced certain defeat in the next elections. This was a serious matter. The Nonconformists, as a matter of moral principle, had been solidly for Home Rule, and in northern England and Wales they formed the backbone of the Liberal party.

Reenforcing the serious political consequences in prospect was a report to Gladstone by Morley and Harcourt, who had just attended the annual meeting of the National Liberal Federation at Sheffield. The "absolutely unanimous feeling," they told Gladstone, was that the disgust against Parnell was so intense among rank-and-file voters as to make him an unbearable political liability in the next general election. Parnell would doom the hopes of the Liberal party and Home Rule for Ireland, hopes which had appeared so bright before the divorce trial.

IX

On November 25 there would be a sessional meeting of the Irish Parliamentary party to elect a chairman for the Parliamentary year, which had been a mere formality since 1883. At this meeting the party could have deposed Parnell with expediency and minimum ruckus by a simple vote. But this was not to be. From the start to finish this was destined to be a tragedy of errors. The wholehearted endorsement of Parnell at the Leinster Hall meeting without much forethought by the Irish leaders was a mistake. The failure of Gladstone to take adequate means to let his views be known by the Irish members before the sessional meeting was to be a second mistake. And the enthusiastic election of Parnell by his party was to be the fatal step which compounded the difficulties of the situation.

Gladstone, fortified by the Nonconformist reactions, had made up his mind that "It will nae do," as he put it. Parnell must step down. He rejected a suggestion from his advisers that he write a letter directly to the Irish party stating his views, since it would appear dictatorial, and, moreover, such a letter might make him appear to judge another man's morals, which "would make life intolerable." He therefore chose to adopt a circuitous method which was to fail. He asked Justin McCarthy to see him on November 24. He told McCarthy that he was amazed that he had had no communication from Parnell, since immediately after the Phoenix Park murders Parnell had written him offering to resign if in his judgment it would help the Irish cause. He then told him lugubriously that if Parnell remained as Irish leader it would, in his opinion, result in the certain loss of the next elections and the postponement of Home Rule to a day which he, Gladstone, would never live to see or participate in. Gladstone thought he had conveyed satisfactorily to McCarthy the thought that he would retire from Liberal party leadership if his advice were disregarded, but considering Gladstone's genius for circumlocution and the fact that the situation was a delicate one, McCarthy can be forgiven for not having grasped that point. It is clear that he did not.

Gladstone, after seeing McCarthy upstairs in his home, returned to the library and there conferred with John Morley, Arnold Morley, Granville and Harcourt. He said that he would write a letter to John Morley which might be shown to Parnell by McCarthy when they conferred. They were aware of McCarthy's timorousness, and the plan agreed upon was that John Morley would confer with Parnell, too, and would also show him the letter of Gladstone.

The intent of the Liberal leaders was to give a proud and sensitive man a chance to step down in a show of selflessness and patriotism, which he would find it contrary to his nature to do if subjected to pressure. As Morley wrote, "As anyone could see, its language was courteous and considerate. Not an accent was left that could touch the pride of one who was as proud as a man could be." The letter stated that Gladstone had acquainted McCarthy with his views. There were two vital sentences. The first included the words ". . . his continuance at the present moment in the leadership would be productive of consequences disastrous in the highest degree to the cause of Ireland." The last sentence, which was most crucial, stated that if Parnell remained, it "would render my retention of the leadership of the Liberal Party, based as it has been mainly upon the presentation of the Irish cause, almost a nullity."

This sentence, which was absent from the first draft, was inserted by Gladstone at Morley's suggestion that "You have not put in the one thing most likely to move him." This led to the belief stated later by William O'Brien (most probably a false supposition) that Gladstone did not really intend to threaten to resign and that Morley was the culprit in accomplishing Parnell's downfall by putting the thought in Gladstone's mind and then on paper.

Morley was not able to locate Parnell, and it has been said that Parnell's secretary, Henry Campbell, boasted that he had been instrumental in keeping them apart. McCarthy did manage to see Parnell. Whether he showed him the letter is disputed. In any event, Parnell told McCarthy very coolly that he intended to "stand by his guns." McCarthy did not carry the message further to the leadership.

The sessional meeting started at 2:45 P.M. The nomination of Parnell as leader was made by Thomas Sexton. "His praise and panegyrics were unusually fulsome," wrote Donal Sullivan to Healy, who remained in Ireland. The motion was seconded by Captain Nolan. He was then nominated by acclamation. A member who had succeeded Captain O'Shea from County Clare then asked Parnell if he would not retire for a short time, if only for a month. Parnell rose and made a short speech, as Sullivan wrote, "delivered coldly, calmly and bloodlessly," saying all that he ever had to say about the divorce. Notes were not taken, but members gave their accounts later. "I would rather appear to be dishonourable than to be dishonourable." Captain O'Shea and he had not been friends. "So long as I have known him he has pursued me with malice as a bitter and unrelenting enemy." In twenty-three years of married life, O'Shea had spent only four hundred days at home. He had never partaken of O'Shea's hospitality, never had a bite or sup or a glass of wine at his expense. He asked the members to keep their lips sealed until the proper time. He concluded by stating that he would remain to lead the party to victory.

It was an unsatisfactory explanation for the harassed members, the greatest number of whom were good, sober, family men to whom it was inexplicable how Parnell could have gotten into such a mess and remained in it for a decade. They had hoped that Parnell would offer a self-exoneration. His statement, such as it is, is an accurate reflection of what Parnell deemed an adequate defense based on moral grounds: when he met Mrs. O'Shea, her marriage had ceased to exist and he did not owe anything to Captain O'Shea. In characteristic *hubris*, Parnell had composed his concept of morality in place of the conventional one of society.

The election of Parnell was a long step toward disaster. Now any retirement by Parnell would seem to be surrender, and this would be hard for a man of his pride to endure. Later, in Committee Room 15, he would rebuke his erstwhile supporters, "Why did you encourage me to come forward and retain my leadership in the face of the world if you were not going to stand by me? Why did my officers encourage me to take my position on the bridge and at the wheel if they were going to act as traitors and hand me over to the other Commander-in-Chief?"

The news of Parnell's election with no dissent created consternation among the English Liberals. Not even a gesture to appease adverse public opinion!—Morley was taken aback. Meeting with Parnell, he showed him Gladstone's letter. Parnell showed his usual icy calm and detachedness. Morley urged temporary retirement on Parnell, reminding him that for two years he had been practically absent from active leadership. Parnell was unmoved.

Morley went to Gladstone's office, and in a few minutes Gladstone arrived. Even before closing the door and without taking off his coat and cape, he said eagerly, "Well, have you seen him?" Morley replied, "He is obdurate." Gladstone's vindictiveness toward Parnell would be unconcealed from that time on. He did not want to wait for the next day to have the letter published. "It is not too late, the *Pall Mall Gazette* can bring it out in a special edition." There was still some hope that if the Irish leaders were told about the letter privately they could prevail on Parnell to make a voluntary withdrawal. At this stage no one had in mind more than a temporary retirement by Parnell. Publication of the letter would destroy that last shred of hope, since Parnell would resist yielding to a public ultimatum.

Morley called Parnell from his seat in the House, and while they were walking side by side in the lobby he told him of Gladstone's decision. Parnell showed no emotion and, with his customary frost, said, "Yes, I think Mr. Gladstone will be quite right to do so. It will put him right with his party." At the time, the party whip, Arnold Morley, was already dictating the letter to William Pitt of the Press Association for publication on the morrow, and the Irish members were learning of it for the first time. They flocked around Morley while he was having dinner. Would the great English statesman retire from the leadership of the Liberal party unless Parnell retired from his leadership or was involuntarily retired? Yes, indeed, said Morley, that is what the letter means. And then consternation swept the Irish ranks. Gladstone had demanded Parnell's head as the price for leading the battle for Home Rule.

X

It was a very hard choice that faced the Irish members. To overthrow Parnell at Gladstone's request would be a humiliating surrender to the English. He had been the matchless leader who had commanded the confidence of all. Who could supplant him and do as well in command? Would not his deposal result in civil war? If they surrendered at Gladstone's word, would they not thereafter become a helpless tail to the Liberal kite? If Home Rule were morally right, why should it make any difference what kind of person Parnell was in his private life, particularly since English leaders had been notoriously lax in their private lives. As for virtue, as someone put it, "These English are the most extraordinary people in the world. You can never make out what virtue is or is not, except that virtue is always on their side, whatever that side is." In recent years the Liberals had condoned—if not encouraged— boycotting, outrages and a lot of other things that were criminal or idiotic, but now they had a fit of virtue about one man's divorce!

The argument to depose Parnell seemed far stronger. If Gladstone really meant to resign (and for some reason little thought was given to the possibility that he might not), then without his leadership, Home Rule had little or no hope in Britain. As far as abstract morality was concerned, since the argument for Home Rule was a moral one, how could the Irish object if a moral test were applied to Parnell? Moreover, Parnell's leadership was more than abstract— he would become the leader of the Irish Parliament if Home Rule were granted. However, more than a theory, a political reality was involved. Since 1886, all had waited and worked for the next elections, which would bring Home Rule, but now all would be lost if Parnell remained, and Home Rule would be postponed until the mythical calends. All gauges of sentiment among the electorate showed that disaster loomed ahead. In an election campaign, the caustic tongues of Salisbury and Chamberlain would tear Parnell apart. As an example, in an election meeting held the previous week, a speaker said from the platform, "Is there any price that Gladstone would not pay for eighty-six votes? What does Parnell want?" A voice from the audience called out "A fire escape."

Since the Man and the Cause were in collision, by this thinking, the Man, as a true patriot, must give way and be glad to make the sacrifice for the Cause.

The lieutenants undoubtedly believed themselves to be sincere in their new concept of the situation. Nonetheless, the speed of the reversal in the posture of their thinking was most astonishing. Lord Salisbury had a big laugh, saying that Healy and Sexton, in switching from Parnell to the Seventh Commandment, were like bettors at the race track hedging their bets when they heard something against the favorite. The *Times,* on the death of Parnell, commented about the "notable suggestion of cool calculation in the outburst of tardy indignation" by the lieutenants who must have had their own ambition in mind.

The next day, November 26, the Gladstone letter was published, and Sexton and McCarthy asked Parnell if he would hold a new party meeting, a request which Parnell curtly dismissed. John Barry and Arthur O'Connor, at Sexton's suggestion, then drew up a requisition for a new meeting which was signed by thirty-one members. This was equivalent to the Tennis Court Oath in the French Revolution as a step in the liquidation of Parnell rule. At first Parnell refused to heed the demand, saying that he would not be dictated to, but then yielded, since he had no choice.

At the meeting John Barry moved "that a full meeting of the party be held on Friday [two days later] to give Mr. Parnell an opportunity to reconsider his position." Parnell said little, listening glacially to a protracted discussion about himself. Sexton openly urged Parnell to retire, the first major party figure in open revolt. It was finally decided to have a further delay and hold the next meeting on December 1, the following Monday, and meanwhile to acquaint the absent leaders in America with the new turn of affairs and obtain their opinions.

Healy arrived the next day from Dublin. Parnell had received a wire saying, "Healy is going to London as your deadly enemy," and he cut Healy "stonily," as Healy put it, when they encountered each other. Healy had dinner with Sexton and canvassed the situation. "How did Parnell take the meeting yesterday?" he asked Sexton, who replied, "You know, if an intelligent foreigner had entered the room, he would have thought that *we* were being tried for adultery with *his* wife."

XI

The speed with which the revolt had taken shape was ominous for Parnell, as was the new turn of opinion of those in America. O'Brien released a cable he had sent (with which Dillon had agreed) suggesting that, in view of the common objectives of the Liberals and the Irish, "we earnestly recommend that the party immediately open negotiations with Mr. Gladstone." This would be somewhat supererogatory since Mr. Gladstone's thoughts on the matter were now all too clear. Another ominous development was that Archbishop Walsh had called a meeting of the Irish episcopacy to consider whether and to what extent the clergy would be able to support the party in the future as it had in the past.

The beleaguered Parnell, who throughout the fight was to show amazing ingenuity and generalship, decided that he would put his enemies on the defensive. "The old spider has nearly all my flies in his web. I think we shall have to fight, Queenie," he said to Mrs. O'Shea. "Can you bear it? I am afraid it is going to be tough work." He composed a manifesto "To The People of Ireland," which was published on November 29, three days after he had been asked to step down.

The document was an extraordinary one. It asked the Irish to believe that the Liberals were perfidious allies and that he had been deceiving them about Gladstone all the time. He clearly implied that to cheat them of their rights the Liberals were using the divorce as a pretext to get rid of the most formidable champion the Irish had. He started out by saying, "The integrity and independence of a section of the Irish Parliamentary Party having been apparently sapped and destroyed by the wire pullers of the English Liberal Party. . . ." Thus, the crisis was due to Liberal subversion, not to himself, and the dupes were old, trusted and hitherto loyal champions of Irish independence. Now he would give the facts "which will enable you to understand the measure of the loss with which you are threatened unless you consent to throw me to the English wolves now howling for my destruction."

The manifesto went on to say that in his conversation with Gladstone at Hawarden the year before, Parnell had learned that the measure of Home Rule the Liberals intended was altogether unsatisfactory. He asserted that the Irish representation in the English Parliament would be reduced from 103 to 32; the Irish Parliament would not be empowered to settle the land question and Gladstone would put no pressure on the English Parliament to settle it either; the Irish constabulary would be left under Imperial control indefinitely; appointment of Irish judges would be retained by the Imperial authority for a term of years. Among other charges, he said that Morley had proposed to him that he be Irish Secretary in order to undermine the independence of the party and had stated that the Liberal administration planned to do nothing for evicted tenants under the Plan of Campaign. "I conceived the idea of an Irish Parliamentary Party independent of all English parties. I believe the party will obtain Home Rule only provided it remain independent of any English party."

Parnell met five members of the party at the home of Dr. Fitzgerald in Chester Place to read the manifesto to them before its publication. When he had concluded, someone suggested that he should append a stirring Nationalist poem. Justin McCarthy, appalled at the manifesto, said in irony, "You can't do better than to take Grattan's statement when the Irish Parliament was dissolved by the Act of Union. 'I watched over its cradle and I am now following its hearse.' "

To McCarthy the manifesto appeared as it would to other Irish members, as a case of "Whom the Gods would destroy——." With one blow Parnell had smashed to bits the cornerstone on which he had built the Irish Nationalist cause during the last four years. The conversion of Gladstone, the great statesman and Parliamentary leader, to the Irish cause had been a monumental achievement for Parnell and for Ireland. Parnell had once gone so far as to call Gladstone "Our leader." In March, 1889, he declared that he wanted the Irish people to stand fast "until he [Gladstone] gets that chance which we hope and believe will be a near one, both for the sake of Ireland and the sake of England of again touching the great heart of his countrymen."

And now? McCarthy wrote, "The English people had been slowly growing into sympathy and affection for the Irish people. Suddenly the man who claims to be the leader of the Irish race breaks into a shrieking denunciation of the English people and the English leaders and does his very best to rekindle all the fierce and destructive forces of race hatred which we had all believed to be happily extinguished."

Gladstone was livid with rage when he read the manifesto. The unilateral breach of a confidential conversation was enough to put Parnell beyond the pale. Morley wrote to Lord Spencer, "His conduct in repeating confidential talks from Gladstone's dinner table and from mine reveals an infamy of character which I had never suspected." Harcourt, who had always talked of Parnell and his followers as Burke had talked of French Revolutionists, wrote his wife, "I feel some satisfaction in remembering that I have never shaken hands with him. . . . The blackguardism of the man is now patent to the world."

As for the substance of the conversation at Hawarden, we shall never know exactly what was said. It was merely a *pourparler,* and Gladstone might have talked, at best, in an exploratory way. He might have pointed out how the bill might have to be weakened to get approval of the House of Lords. What is most interesting is that Parnell neither raised a protest at the time nor expressed dissent afterward. Gladstone's memo of the conversation to his colleagues was that Parnell was "full of good sense from beginning to end" and "I did not press him to positive conclusions but I learned pretty well the bearing of his mind and ascertained that so far as I could judge nothing like a crochet or an irrational demand from his side was likely to interfere with the freedom of deliberations" when the time came for implementing the talks. It is noteworthy that Parnell left Hawarden for Liverpool, where in a speech he praised the "grand old leader" and said "my countrymen rejoice for we are in a safe path to our legitimate freedom and our future prosperity."

When the six fund raisers in America read the manifesto, they were thunderstruck. They received a cable from Sexton stating that the majority were prepared to repudiate Parnell and that "envoys [in America] supporting majority means practical unanimity." Five joined in a wire that the manifesto "convinces us that Mr. Parnell's continued leadership is impossible." They were Dillon, O'Brien, T. P. O'Connor, T. D. Sullivan and T. P. Gill; Tim Harrington would not join in but backed Parnell loyally. In his diary he noted, "With intense pain I hear both Dillon and O'Brien declare that on no account would they ever serve again under [his] leadership. I see the old daemon of Ireland's past misfortunes again triumphant. I find it quite impossible to control myself, the tears rush to my eyes and I can take no further part in the discussion."

The group traveled from Cincinnati to Chicago, where they drafted a countermanifesto. They were besieged by newsmen, who even listened in at the keyholes. In the countermanifesto they stated that Parnell's action was most lamentable and that he "has entered upon a rash and fatal path upon which every consideration of Ireland's safety as well as our own personal honour forbids us absolutely to follow him."

This declaration from America was a bitter blow to Parnell in view of the great prestige of Dillon and O'Brien, their dedication to the cause and their undoubted personal integrity. Equally ominous was the more forthright stand of the clergy. Dr. Croke wired to McCarthy, "All sorry for Parnell, but still in God's name, let him retire quietly."

XII

On Monday, December 1, the day after the countermanifesto, the Irish party reassembled, in accordance with their previous resolution, in Committee Room 15 in the Parliament building. It had been expected by the English that there would be a swift motion passed to depose Parnell, but they had not counted on the resourcefulness of Parnell nor on the manner in which Celtic emotionalism can rise to meet an occasion. The meeting was to last through the week, and words would flow in torrents, passions would flare, and moods would swing from earnest soul-searching to the roar of a barroom brawl. Since Parliament was in session, the English members could hear the noise of the fracas through the closed door, down the corridors and into the Library. The bloody internal struggle was also trumpeted *urbi et orbi* since the press had transcripts of the proceedings, and as far away as New York and Australia, the newspapers filled their front pages with the story.

The English Liberals were appalled. *"Qualis facies, qualis tabella est,"* Harcourt wrote to Morley, which is translated freely as "What a spectacle!" The Tories were delighted. One wrote in derision, "They have been engaged in a choice of President. With what coolness of demeanour, what dignity of bearing, what interchange of courtesy, this little matter is arranged by Irish gentlemen meeting in circumstances of their own conception arrangement and control, the world has been privileged to witness. What would College Green look like?"

Healy, who led the assault against Parnell, wrote of him in the crisis, "His genius showed like an upcast flame from an expiring light." The fiendish intelligence and cunning of the man and his iron will were on exhibit for all to see—there could be no doubt as to the talents which had made him master of the Irish party. Intimidated by his defiance, his opponents had asked him to set any form of compromise that would satisfy Gladstone—they had even proposed that the post of leader be left vacant and that he appoint a committee to run the party until a more favorable day. It would not be true to his nature, however, to accept any such proposal, since his pride could not admit even temporarily that he had bowed in defeat. The reckless gambler must play to the very end his luck and his belief in his destiny. So now he presided, as the *Times* said in admiration, "so imperiously, so implacably, so resourcefully."

The members assembled shortly after noon around a huge horseshoe-shaped table. Parnell was at the head, with his secretary Campbell at his left and McCarthy, the Vice-Chairman, on his right; beyond McCarthy were Healy and then Sexton. Almost seventy-five members were present in the room. A team of shorthand reporters from the *Freeman's Journal* worked in relays; when they left the room they read their notes to representatives of other papers. Parnell had taken his opponents by surprise; they had expected the meeting to be held *in camera*. However, since it was undoubtedly true at this time that the majority of sentiment in Ireland was for Parnell, he decided that he could intimidate some waverers who might be hesitant to have their remarks broadcast in their home constituencies.

The meeting opened with a reading of messages pro and con the

Parnell leadership, more pro than con. Then the anti-Parnell bloc were made to realize, if they did not realize before, what a wily foe they faced. The chairman announced that there was a motion pending before the body, namely the motion made by John Barry on November 26, "That a full meeting of the party be held Friday next to give Mr. Parnell an opportunity to reconsider his position." But, of course, this had meant Friday, November 28, which had passed. No, said Parnell, it must mean the coming Friday, December 5, since there had been a decision to adjourn until December 1. There was a shout of protest at this weird if ingenious ruling. Healy asked for a division and Parnell ruled that there could be no division on a point of order. Barry rose to request that his motion be withdrawn and Parnell ruled that in accordance with the rules of the House of Commons a pending motion could not be withdrawn except by unanimous consent. Would the chairman accept an amendment to the Barry motion? Yes, he would. Mr. William Abraham moved that Parnell be deposed. The chairman said amid laughter that that was not a proper amendment to the motion. He then accepted a motion by his supporter, Colonel J. Nolan, that the question of the leadership be postponed until the views of the constituencies be received and then a meeting be held in Dublin. Debate now proceeded on the Nolan motion.

It was now becoming evident that dislodging Parnell while he sat in the chair would be no easy matter. But there was a more serious complexion to the matter. The motion to secure a change of venue raised the suspicion that the manifesto, which had seemed so self-defeating insofar as winning over the party in Westminster, had a more diabolical purpose: it might be the first gun in a rabble-rousing campaign to appeal to the Irish people for support over the head of the party with the cry "We are betrayed." If so, this was only the first chapter in what could be a protracted civil war.

Sexton followed Colonel Nolan as first speaker for the insurgent faction. He defied Parnell to name the "wire pullers" of the Liberal party whom he had denounced in the manifesto, and Parnell answered vaguely that those whom he had in mind were self-evident. Sexton disavowed any such intrigue and proceeded to analyze the nature of the Liberal alliance that Parnell had built and the fatal consequences unless Parnell retired. "If the leader is to be retained, then in my judgment the cause is lost."

John Redmond followed. In later years he was to lead the united party, and this speech put him in the forefront of the Parnellites. To sacrifice Parnell would mean to sacrifice the independence of the party, which would become a discredited and powerless tool of the Liberal party. "When we are asked to sell out our own leader it seems to me that we are bound to inquire what we are getting for the price we are paying." Parnell here interjected, "Don't sell me for nothing. If you get my value, you may change me now." This was another delaying stratagem of Parnell, that he should be used now as a bargaining weapon with the Liberals.

Healy, with his penetrating mind, attacked the weak spots in the Parnell manifesto. Although Parnell attacked the Gladstonian plan for a Home Rule bill, the 1886 bill for which they had fought so hard had not given the Irish control of the judiciary or police and had provided for no representation at all at Westminster, yet it had been acceptable because it had established the Irish Parliament and the principle. Why had Parnell not taken issue with Gladstone? He discussed Parnell's speech at Liverpool after the Hawarden meeting and asked, "Why were these false words uttered at Liverpool? Either Mr. Parnell at Liverpool was false, or his manifesto was false." Parnell interrupted, "I will not stand an accusation of falsehood from Timothy Healy and I will call on him to withdraw." Healy did so "out of respect for the chair." Healy went on to say that Parnell's power was completely gone. "Place an iron bar in a coil and electrify that coil and the bar becomes magnetized. The party was that electric coil, there stood the iron bar. The electricity is gone and the magnetism with it."

Parnell rose to speak discursively. Why had the party appointed him as sessional chairman if it did not intend to back him up? He attacked John Barry as a professional "leader-killer" who had wielded the poniard against Isaac Butt as he was now doing against him. He spoke of Healy's ingratitude. "Who trained him? Who saw his genius? Who telegraphed him in America to come over? Who gave him his first chance to enter public life and got him a seat in Parliament? That Mr. Healy is here today to destroy me is due to myself."

Why had he not argued with Gladstone at Hawarden? "It was a question of dealing with a garrulous old gentleman who monopolized the conversation and with whom as everybody knows it is difficult to get a word in edgewise." Why had he spoken as he did immediately after in Liverpool? "My responsibility was enormous.

Was I at a single stroke without giving any time or opportunity to Mr. Gladstone to reconsider his position to denounce him on account of a half-completed programme?" He then told surprisingly that at his instance McCarthy had interviewed Gladstone and Harcourt the previous weekend to get assurances on the Home Rule bill and had failed. "I know very well what Mr. Harcourt will do for you, I know what Mr. Gladstone will do for you, I know what Mr. Morley will do for you. I know there isn't a single one of the lot to be trusted unless you trust yourselves." After excoriating the only men in sight who could bring about Home Rule, he concluded by saying, "I should like—and it is not an unfair thing to ask—that I should come within sight of the Promised Land."

McCarthy rose to expand on the abortive mission to Gladstone, which he implied was ill advised. He continued the attack on Parnell which had obviously been divided up with Sexton and Healy by asking why Parnell had continued to deceive the party for more than a year after the Hawarden talk. Even if Gladstone's remarks had been under the seal of the confessional, McCarthy would have have unable to keep the news from the party, particularly if he regarded it as the terrible news which Parnell professed it to be.

Lesser figures in the party took the floor to explain their positions. After a break of an hour for dinner the meeting continued into the night. Since there was no electricity in the room, candles and kerosene lamps threw eerie shadows in the room. Healy wrote his wife as the talk went on, "His phrases about Gladstone were in bad taste and will hurt his reputation. Barring that, though there was not much in what he said, he showed moderation. I cannot conceive of any other man going through such an ordeal with so much dignity. I feel sorry for him. He is, however, perfectly unscrupulous and would invent any lie or statement to help himself." At close to midnight the meeting adjourned after Healy wrangled with Parnell in an unsuccessful attempt to get a commitment that the debate would end the next day.

The next day the session resumed at noon. Before the opening, as he sat in the chair, Parnell was asked in a friendly manner how he was standing up to the ordeal. "Very well," he replied, "you may get another leader but you will never get one that will take so much killing." The first topic discussed was the countermanifesto, and there was a long debate about alleged backhanded and underhanded means used to produce it. In the afternoon there was a

z

continuation of the speeches of the members who wanted to state their views, accompanied by partisan cheers or groans.

Dr. Kenny said that his enemies were "hungry" for Parnell's blood, and Edward Harrington declaimed that the Irish would never surrender Parnell to be "decapitated" and have his enemies "lap up his blood." E. V. Knox, raising the moral issue, said that Parnell had wronged the "purest of nations"—an argument that suffered from the fact that with full knowledge of the divorce Parnell had been reelected to the leadership. A blind member, P. Mac-Donald, found no successor available for Parnell, since Dillon was too "self-centered," O'Brien was no Parliamentarian and Healy lacked the capacity for conciliation. Henry Harrison said that Parnell was needed to "squeeze" terms from Gladstone. J. F. X. O'Brien, the only living member who could claim the distinction of once having been sentenced to be hung, drawn and quartered, claimed that he had voted for Parnell as the sessional chairman because he had been deliberately misled by a *Freeman* representative that Parnell intended to resign forthwith. Alexander Blane, in a triumph of sophistry, wiped out the divorce issue completely —as a Catholic he was ignorant of the existence of divorce and as an Irish Nationalist he refused to believe the testimony of English witnesses.

Parnell presided with grave dignity and an elaborate show of impartiality, cautioning his followers to quiet down and give a hearing to the most bitter statements against him. In the midst of it Healy wrote his wife, "Charles II apologized for taking an 'unconscionably long time to die,' but our King Charles has no such sense of the proprieties. It looks as if we have raised a Frankenstein which is now about to destroy everything. . . . He feels exactly as you might expect a god to feel—that he could not be wrong and that anyone who would not obey him and follow him must necessarily be damned."

Except for a forty-five-minute break for lunch and an hour for dinner, the meeting had gone on continuously, the members not appearing in the House although an Irish land-purchase bill was being discussed. Now it was night and the candles and kerosene lamps had again appeared. Parnell, whose followers were obviously trying to prolong the proceedings with talk, turned to Sexton and said audibly, "I say, Sexton, are you fellows going to keep this up all night?" and laughed. The oratory finally came to an end at eleven o'clock, and the time had come for a vote on the Nolan motion for a delay of the decision and a change of venue to Dublin. Parnell asked for a voice vote and proclaimed, "The 'ayes' have it" amid derision and a challenge. Parnell then read the roll of names and announced that he had been defeated, the "ayes" being 29 and the "nays" 44.

XIII

Parnell would certainly be summarily ejected from the leadership the next day. So most thought, but another surprise was in store. The party met in secret session, and it was not until the close of the next day's session that the transcript was released. One of Parnell's supporters, J. J. Clancy, had offered a compromise solution, suggesting that since the recollection of Parnell and Gladstone differed on the vital points of the projected Home Rule bill, the whips of the Irish party should be instructed to obtain from Gladstone, Harcourt and Morley their views relative to these questions. If satisfactory assurances were given by the Liberal leaders, he was sure that Parnell would retire. Sexton raised the question as to who would judge the adequacy of the pledges made by the Liberals. The emotionally unstable Healy, in tears, pleaded with Parnell that if he would give an assurance that he would abide by the majority decision as to the adequacy of the Liberal pledges, "my voice will be the first at the earliest possible moment consonant with the liberties of my country to call you back to your proper place as the leader of the Irish race." Parnell asked for time to consider the proposal and the meeting adjourned.

By his political virtuosity, Parnell had turned everything upside down. Instead of being on the defensive, he was on the offensive. He had detoured the hostile majority onto a bypath of his own choosing. His version of the Hawarden conversation had been branded as demagoguery and arrant falsehood, "lies to catch gudgeons" in the words of Healy, but now he had been taken seriously enough that the party had accepted the idea of sending official emissaries to Gladstone and subjecting him to examination.

Newspapers in America solidly against Parnell were openly raising the question as to whether he had gone mad, the victim of hereditary insanity, and to *The New York Times* correspondent in Westminster this maneuver was convincing proof. "By a strange almost incredible freak of doubling up upon himself, Parnell has shifted the debate away from Mrs. O'Shea and concentrated it upon Gladstone's intentions to Ireland. The smartest lawyer could never have risen to such a height of inventive impudence. The feat is too weird and tricky for unaided genius. A strain of madness glistens in it."

Opening the meeting the next day, Parnell said that "my responsibility is derived from you to some extent but it is also derived from a long train of circumstances and events in which many of you have had no share. My position has been granted to me not because I am the leader of a Parliamentary party but because I am the leader of the Irish nation."

There was truth in this. He had formed the party himself under a mandate which he had conceived and which was ratified by the people, and now the servants were acting to depose their master and maker. This was attempted parricide. He went on to say that since the party was now trying to strip him of his responsibility, the very least that the party could do was to stipulate before conferring with the Liberal leaders their positions on the issues involved— and their stand must be that no Home Rule bill would be acceptable which would not confer immediate control of the police on the Irish Executive and which would not confer on the Irish Parliament full power to deal with the land question. "Gentlemen, it is for you to act in this matter. You are dealing with a man who is an unrivalled sophist."

Barry called out, "Which?" Parnell said, "The Grand Old Man." Disregarding Barry's "I don't believe it," Parnell went on, "You are dealing with a man with whom and to whom it is as impossible to give a direct answer to a plain and simple question as it is for me impossible to give an indirect answer to a plain and simple question." He then added a really good point, referring to Gladstone in 1885. "You are dealing with a man who is capable of appealing to the constituencies for a majority which will make him independent of both the Irish party and the Tory party at the next general election."

Healy said that these terms would put the deputation in a straitjacket and ensure its failure. "I regret you do not consider it a straight answer," said Parnell, "but it is my answer and upon that answer I will stand or fall before the country." "Then you will fall," retorted Healy. "What is the use of further debate?"

A Parnell supporter, Edward Leamy, said derisively, "Away with him, away with him!" John J. O'Connor followed with "Crucify him!" and Sexton appealed to Parnell not to permit blasphemy. Said Healy, "We will vote for Mr. Parnell's deposition be it today, Saturday or Sunday," and Colonel Nolan replied amid laughter, "Not Sunday, I'll not vote on Sunday."

A torrent of words came from Healy. He quoted Parnell on the Liberal alliance, speaking at his last birthday banquet, as an alliance that would endure and then asked, "What broke it off?" Parnell and Colonel Nolan called out, "Gladstone's letter," and Healy shouted out, "It perished in the stench of the divorce court."

Parnell's face froze. In rage, Healy pursued the attack. He would go to the people and state the real issues. "If you, sir, should go down, you are only one man gone. Heads of greater leaders have been stricken on the block before now for Ireland."

Parnell had fallen into melancholy thought, and John Redmond replied in his behalf. Was there any question that Parnell "is acting for the love of Ireland alone?" John Barry shot back, "I don't believe he is." Redmond said that in all cases where a leader is deposed, it is done to supplant him with a better man. Then, facing Parnell, he asked, "Who is the man to take your place? Who is the man who, when Home Rule comes to be settled, can discuss its provisions on an equal footing with the leaders of the English parties? There is no such man." Healy asked satirically, "Suppose Mr. Parnell dies?" and Parnell shaking off his pensive mood, retorted with spirit, "I don't intend to die."

Parnell then dropped the resolution he had offered at the start of the meeting, stating that he had only guidelines in mind, and the party voted to adopt Clancy's motion. A committee of four was picked to meet with the Liberal leaders with equal pro-Parnell and anti-Parnell membership, Redmond and Leamy for the pros and Healy and Sexton for the antis.

Parnell's strategy had obvious advantages for him. If perchance satisfactory assurances were given by the Liberals, he could retire temporarily in triumph; if they were refused he could proclaim to Ireland that this was proof of betrayal.

After the meeting, Parnell and the leaders sat around a table chatting quite amicably. "Parnell is as bland as ever," Healy wrote his wife, "as if we had done nothing to ruffle him. I don't know if the thing is a trick or if Parnell means to act honestly and retire." He and Sexton feared Gladstone's reaction, but on the other hand they feared the reaction in Ireland if they spurned the hope, albeit a slim one, for internal peace.

XIV

In this duel of wits and nerves, the Liberals had an opportunity to force Parnell's resignation or at least to put him in the position of one who had reneged on his pledge to resign. Parnell's acumen had led his party into a chimera of an argument about the terms of a bill that was scores of months away if the Liberals won the next election. Gladstone might have matched Parnell's astuteness, if not his unscrupulousness, by specifying his attitudes on the Home Rule bill in terms vague enough to satisfy the Irish, or, if he spoke forthrightly, there was time enough in the future for modifications, particularly since the bill would have to get through the House of Lords.

There was apparently no thought given to this course, since the Liberal leaders were out of temper with the Irish for their dilatoriness in ousting Parnell and were blinded by hatred and fear of him. Anything they said might be twisted by Parnell and used as a club to beat them. Harcourt refused to treat with the committee at all, regarding it as a "put-up job" to extract blackmail. A week before, he had written Gladstone, "It is a very dangerous thing to approach an expiring cat," and begged him to make no concession "to that man." Now he cited proof that the Irish were trying to victimize the Liberal leadership in a slick confidence game. "They are supping together like actors who have been murdering each other on the stage for the amusement of the audience." Also, there was Healy's amazing statement about welcoming Parnell back to leadership. "He will return long before you can bring forward a Home Rule bill and then you will have to deal with a man who has spoken thus of you." Morley spoke with dread to Gladstone of allowing Parnell "to cover his surrender." That is the scheme that the Liberals, in a calmer frame of mind, should have tried to devise, since they were well aware that the big stumbling block was always Parnell's pride.

These arguments carried weight with Gladstone, and he was exasperated with the Irish for having been led by Parnell into this cul-de-sac. At first Gladstone refused to discuss anything with the deputation, since the resolution passed by the party referred to a "difference of recollection" which he would not admit as an imputation on his honor. So another meeting of the party was held, at which the earlier resolution was rescinded and one acceptable to Gladstone was passed. But now when they met Gladstone, he set them back on their heels by telling them that he would talk of Home Rule legislation only "when the Irish party shall have disposed of this [leadership] question which belongs entirely within their competence." He confirmed this in a letter which was released to the press.

This futile bid to Gladstone took place on a Friday. That night, Healy and Sexton visited Parnell at the Westminster Palace Hotel and urged him to recognize the realities and for the good of Ireland to retire without protracting the debate and plunging Ireland into political civil war. Parnell said he would sleep on it, and the next morning he told them that his duty, as he saw it, proscribed such a course. They warned him bluntly that the anti-Parnellites would not sit in on the party meeting beyond that day. Parliament would soon rise for the Christmas recess, and they would not give him the excuse to shift the meeting to Dublin. As they went together to the door of the hotel, Parnell drew Healy aside to one of the pillars and extending his hand said, "Healy, let us shake hands for it may be the last time." And so the former comrades shook hands and parted company forever.

The meeting of the afternoon of December 6 was the last meeting of the unbroken party not only in the crisis but for years to come.

William Abraham, at the outset, rose to move that the leadership be vacated. Parnell ruled him out of order. The motion before the party, he said, was John Barry's original motion that he reconsider his position. Abraham threw a paper to McCarthy, who put on his spectacles to read it. Parnell, his nerves now frazzled to the breaking point, snatched it from McCarthy, rolled it into a small ball and put it into his trousers. Almost incoherently he spat out the words

"How dare you, sir, how dare you attempt to usurp me in the chair! You have been wanting to step into my shoes all the time. Until the party deposes me, I am chairman." Redmond and Leamy rushed to Parnell, as he appeared about to fall on McCarthy. Barry shouted to Parnell, "You are a dirty trickster." There were cries directed to Barry of "Shame, shame." Parnell calmed down in a few moments, smoothed out the paper, gave it back to McCarthy and soon was engaged with him in friendly conversation.

Parnell then recognized one of his followers, John J. O'Connor, who offered an amendment to the Barry motion expressing the regret of the party that Gladstone refused to enter negotiations unless Parnell should resign. While he was talking, Parnell sat sideways on his chair, reading the *Freeman's Journal*. John O'Connor said that if the party submitted to his dictate, Gladstone would be the party's new leader. Arthur O'Connor derided the argument, saying that Gladstone was not a member of the party.

John Redmond then corrected him with "The master of the party," and Healy hissed venomously, "Who is to be the mistress of the party?"

As the words left his lips, there was an uproar, as members called out, "Shame." Michael MacDonagh, a young shorthand reporter for the *Freeman's Journal* that day, afterwards wrote of the scene, as he saw it, in his book *The Home Rule Movement*: "A spasm of pain contracted Parnell's face. Twice he half rose from his seat and twice fell back again. Then grasping the arms of his chair, he raised himself up. He seemed so clearly bent on attacking Healy that his friends moved up and clustered about Healy. Arthur O'Connor said 'I appeal to the chair,' and Parnell replied 'Better appeal to your friend, better appeal to that cowardly little scoundrel there who dares in an assembly of Irishmen to insult a woman.' His fist was close to the face of Healy who did not quiver. He fell back in the chair exhausted and he was breathing hard through his nostrils and his thick beard could not conceal the twitching of his lips. The fiery glow in his eyes was quenched though there were no tears in them. It was to himself that he was crying, crying as if his heart would break."

The discussion continued. Mr. Abraham again tried to introduce his resolution deposing Parnell, this time as an amendment to the O'Connor resolution, but Parnell again ruled him out of order. It was now abundantly clear that while Parnell sat in the chair he would never permit a vote to be taken on deposing him. At four-thirty that afternoon McCarthy rose and said, "I see no further use carrying on a discussion which must be barren of all but reproach, ill-temper, controversy and indignity." He called on all who agreed with him to follow him out of the room, and forty-four members joined him. Twenty-six remained in the room with Parnell. The Irish Nationalist Party had split.

The talk in Committee Room 15 went on for a while, then in a flat, matter of fact tone Parnell said that the sergeant at arms had asked that the room be vacated by 5 P.M. Addressing his faithful followers, he adjourned the meeting, saying, "The men who have deserted from our party this evening have deserted on the eve of the day when we were about to return to our own country. It was this Irish opinion they wished to stifle, that they have recoiled from; and it was this Irish opinion they fled from when they fled from this room this evening. Gentlemen, we have won today. Although our ranks are reduced in numbers I hold this chair still . . . they stand today in the most contemptible of all positions—the position of men who having taken pledges to be true to their party, to be true to their leaders, to be true to their country, have been false to all their pledges."

Though he was left with a minority, it had been a brilliant maneuver on Parnell's part engineered by iron nerve to prevent his outright ouster. His opponents had not succeeded in stripping him of the mantle of leadership, and he could now brand them invidiously as deserters and seceders. According to an unnamed supporter who acted as a correspondent for the New York *Herald*, when he reached the street, Parnell exclaimed, "What a bunch of imbeciles! They could have deposed me by getting enough signatures to a declaration."

XV

Of those critical days, Mrs. O'Shea wrote, "I knew him too well to dare to take him from the cause he made his life-work; that even if it killed him, I must let him fight to the end." According to some, Parnell wavered at times before pleas that he make a self-sacrifice for the life of the cause, but he would go home to Brighton and the next morning his stand had become adamant again. Obviously, Mrs. O'Shea had stiffened him in his resolve to hold fast. It was quite natural that, for their future happiness, she would not want her love to have been the cause of his undoing, for which she would always be conscious of blame. There is another factor, too. An Englishwoman of her background would have little sympathy with the Home Rule cause. In her book she is concerned wholly with the fate of an individual—one can search in vain for any clue that she understood what her love affair meant to the life of a nation.

XVI

When informed of the Irish party breakup, Gladstone is reported to have said, "Thank God, Home Rule is saved." Lord Hartington, who at the time was living with a woman in adultery, told the Queen, "I never thought that anything in politics could give me as much pleasure as this does." As for the Conservatives, there was great joy in their ranks. Winston Churchill wrote in his later history that they had recovered in the divorce court the credit they had lost before the Special Commission. Lord Salisbury said, "Kitty O'Shea deserves to have a monument raised to her in every town in England," and one of his aides said that she was the first woman who had saved her country since Joan of Arc.

The press of London and England was almost solidly aligned against Parnell. One of the exceptions was the *Fortnightly Review*, edited by Frank Harris, which ran an unsigned article undoubtedly by him. Morality, he said, had nothing at all to do with the capacity to govern, and, indeed, chaste rulers like Charles I and Mary Tudor were far less successful as monarchs than those of loose morals like Elizabeth of England and Henry IV of France. Regarding Parnell's lie to Davitt, an American judge had very rightly remarked that a man who would not perjure himself when the character of a woman was concerned was not fit to be believed under oath on any matter whatsoever. (This was the same advice Harris had given Dilke with regard to the character of Mrs. Chapman, who, unfortunately for him, did not care to protect her character at all.)

The Irishman George Bernard Shaw championed Parnell in the British press. As far as morality was concerned, he said, the relationship between Parnell and Mrs. O'Shea was a perfectly natural one. "The whole mischief in the matter lay in the law that tied the husband and wife together and forced Mr. Parnell to play the part of clandestine intriguer instead of enabling them to dissolve the marriage by mutual consent." As for those who said that they did not mind the adultery but objected to the deceit, Shaw blamed the Coercion Law which forced deceit on the Irish to keep the Nationalist movement going—"the character of these reformers cannot be cut into two halves . . . the man who deceives a policeman will deceive his political followers . . . there cannot be two standards of morality, one for your conduct toward your sovereign and the other for your conduct toward your people"—a fair sample of Shaw's glib but superficial reasoning.

Yet, despite the elation among his opponents, there was disappointment that Parnell had fallen victim to a purely chance circumstance. The *Daily Telegraph* commented, "It is no satisfaction for us to feel that the political adversary, whose ability and prowess it was impossible not to respect, has been overthrown by an irrelevant accident wholly unconnected with the struggle in which he was engaged." The solicitor for O'Shea, Edward Clarke, said to the Liberal David Plunket, "I knew I was throwing a bombshell into the Irish camp, but I did not know it would do so much mischief," to which Plunket replied, "Ah, you did not know that when it burst they would pick up the pieces and cut each other's throat with them."

"A bubble and a squeak and it is all over," said a Liberal journal jubilantly. But Healy, Sexton, *et al.*, realized that the real fight was only beginning. Parnell, in the last days in Committee Room 15, had been building a foundation for an appeal to Ireland on the issue of betrayal by perfidious Albion, an emotional appeal that was bound to carry great weight. The *Freeman's Journal* was behind him, and its managing editor told Healy, "We've got the funds, we've got the press, we've got the organization, we've got the chief and we'll beat hell out of you."

And there was the magic of Parnell's name and the spell of Parnell's personality. The Irish people had worshipped him for so long that they would have to be educated out of the habit. At the outset, Healy wrote to his wife, "We are like pagans converted to Christianity being stoned for attacking our gods of yesterday." The young were more bewitched than their elders and would remain bewitched even after his death. A few weeks later Healy was assaulted by a group of boys in a city street in Ireland and wrote, "It appears as if we had the voters and Parnell had their sons." Tim Harrington, who alone of the deputation in America stood by Parnell, had the same observation to make. While he was in New York he wrote in his diary, "When I returned to my room [in the hotel] I found lying on the table quite a host of presents in the shape of cushions, packets of handkerchiefs, beads, etc. contributed by the Irish servant girls as proof of their admiration for my hold-ing by the leader." And when he left the hotel to return to Ire-land, "The servants—almost all Irish boys and girls—gathered in the hall or on the stairs or in the passages, and as I came by all cried out in voices broken by emotion 'Mr. Harrington, don't desert him, don't give in.' "

XVII

"Dublin will always be true to me," Parnell had said.

On December 10, Parnell returned to Dublin and received an ecstatic welcome from the time he got off the train. Parnell pro-ceeded directly to the offices of *United Ireland* and there advised the deputy editor, Matthew Bodkin, who under O'Brien's direction had been supporting the bolters, that he was fired. Bodkin said that he refused to be fired, but a mob surging through the offices influenced him to change his mind.

That night Parnell made a speech in the Rotunda, and it was a memorable night in the history of Dublin. A torchlight parade escorted him there, and a huge crowd waited for him, ten outside for every one who could get entrance. Katherine Tynan described the scene:

> It was nearly 8:30 when we heard the bands coming; then the win-dows were lit up by the lurid glare of thousands of torches in the street outside. There was a distant roaring like the sea. The great gathering within waited silently with expectation. Then the cheering began, and we craned our necks and looked on eagerly, and there was the tall, slender, distinguished figure of the Irish leader making its way across the platform. I don't think any words could do justice to his reception. The house rose at him; everywhere around there was a sea of passionate faces, loving, admiring, almost worshipping that silent, pale man. The cheering broke out again and again; there was no quelling it. Mr. Parnell bowed from side to side, sweeping the

assemblage with his eagle glance. The people were fairly mad with excitement.

I said to Dr. Kenny, who was standing by me, "He is the only quiet man here." "Outwardly," said the keen medical man, emphatically. Looking again, one saw the dilated nostrils, the flashing eye, the passionate face; the leader was simply drinking in thirstily this immense love, which must have been more heartening than one can say after that bitter time in the English capital. Mr. Parnell looked frail enough in body—perhaps the black frock-coat, buttoned so tightly across his chest, gave him that look of attenuation; but he also looked full of indomitable spirit and fire.

When Mr. Parnell came to speak, the passion within him found vent. It was a wonderful speech; not one word of it for oratorical effect, but every word charged with a pregnant message to the people who were listening to him, and the millions who should read him. It was a long speech, lasting nearly an hour; but listened to with intense interest, punctuated by fierce cries against men whom this crisis has made odious, now and then marked in a pause by a deep-drawn moan of delight. It was a great speech—simple, direct, suave—with no device and no artificiality.

While he was talking, *United Ireland* was retaken by anti-Parnellites who barred themselves in. After the speech Parnell was apprised of this. A pony trap was waiting for him outside the Rotunda, and with Dr. Kenny beside him, he sped through the mass of people, who gave way as if by magic. At the offices of *United Ireland* he jumped out, sprang up the steps and knocked. There was silence as the crowd stood hushed and expectant. There was no answer. He then called for a crowbar and the door yielded. He and others then entered through that door and another which was axed down. There was a scuffle inside, and then a window of the second story was opened and Parnell's face appeared, hair disordered, face and clothes covered with dust and plaster. There was a roar of triumph. Parnell said a few words, came down, got into the trap and drove to the railway station. Dublin would remember this night, as it was and colored by imagination.

To Mrs. O'Shea he wrote, "It was splendid fun. I wish I could burgle my own premises every day."

From Dublin he went on to Cork, where another great reception awaited him. But signs of his deteriorating health were now becoming visible to his friends. His frame, which had been somewhat portly in 1886, was now attenuated, as Miss Tynan noted. His skin was so pale that it seemed pearly white, as if reflecting the light. His long-time friend M. J. Horgan was appalled when he met him at the Victoria Hotel in Cork. "He looked like a hunted hind, his hair dishevelled, his beard unkempt, and his eyes wild and restless." From Cork, Parnell went to Kilkenny, where a by-election would take place on December 22 and his strength in Ireland would be first tested. The Nationalist candidate, Sir John Pope-Hennessy, an Irishman with a distinguished record in the Colonial service, had turned against Parnell in response to pressure from the clergy, and Parnell put up his own candidate, Vincent Scully. R. Barry O'Brien came to meet him in the hotel, and in the coffee room there "All spoke in whispers; waiters stole silently in and out. Every individual seemed anxious to make no noise. It was like the stillness of the sick room. Stretched on a number of chairs before the fire lay Parnell sleeping. To me he looked like a dying man. 'He has been very ill,' said J. J. O'Kelly."

He told Mrs. O'Shea on his return that he was feeling ill, but also said that he had to go on. The winter of 1890–1891 was an unusually severe one, and meetings in overheated rooms followed by exposure to icy winds would take its toll on his weakened constitution.

XVIII

The Kilkenny campaign was viciously fought on both sides since it was a crucial test. No less than seventy M.P.'s came into the district. All the big guns were trained on Parnell, the priests openly electioneered against him and emotions rose to the breaking point as Parnell, with his tremendous willpower, called on every resource of nerve and muscle in his fight for survival.

Katherine O'Shea was emerging as an absent participant in the fray. Healy charged that at Galway he and Biggar knew that Parnell "was prostituting a seat in Parliament to the interests of his own private intrigues," and again he said, "While William O'Brien was on the plank bed at Tullamore [jail], Mr. Parnell was on the fire-escape at Eltham." A procession came to a Parnell meeting carrying a woman's tattered undergarment on a pole, and the marchers called out, "Will the petticoat of Kitty O'Shea be the flag of Ireland?" The usually mild Davitt became most vindictive in his oratory. "False to friends, false to country, he now stands revealed as a tyrant the most unscrupulous that ever rode roughshod over the hopes and sentiments of a nation. Well may it be asked, 'Is Mr. Parnell mad?' That there are evidences of insanity in his actions, no one can doubt."

Parnell, his personality now becoming increasingly vulgarized by misfortune, answered with invective that was so out of keeping with his customary aristocratic reserve and dignity that it lent substance to the claim that he had lost his reason. "If I had ever made my position in Irish politics a personal one, there is no question that the miserable gutter sparrows who were once my comrades would not be in a position to come here today. But I will not waste my time on such miserable scum." He castigated Davitt as a "jackdaw," Dillon as a "sick raven" and "as vain as a peacock with about as much brains," Sexton as "uncertain and maudlin," and Justin McCarthy as "a nice old gentleman for a tea party and if you visit his hotel, you would find him with his feet in a mustard bath and with a jug of whiskey punch beside him." He accused Healy of being a "scoundrel who betrayed prisoners to the Crown when there was no more money to put in his filthy pockets"—a reference to a plea of guilty by prisoners represented by him in the Mayborough trial in 1888.

While he was making a speech a funeral procession passed in the rear. In view of the Irish reverence for the dead, John Redmond advised him to stop talking; instead, Parnell screamed out, "There goes the corpse of Pope-Hennessy." Even his most ardent supporters were shocked. Alfred Robbins of the Birmingham *Post* asked William Pitt of the Press Association on his return from Ireland how Parnell was doing. "He is not the Parnell you and I have known," Pitt answered, "That Parnell is dead."

In a working-class district of Kilkenny, Parnell attacked Davitt strongly and aroused the ire of many in the crowd. When leaving, he was spattered by something thrown at him—either lime or flour —which hit him near his eye. He blinked in time. For some time he wore a bandage around the eye. There was a difference of opinion as to whether it was flour or lime and whether Parnell was faking. Healy vigorously asserted that the latter was the case and that the "splendid comedian" was in his act. Journalists claimed that they saw him without the bandage and that there was no visible injury.

On election day Parnell's candidate was badly beaten, 2527 to 1362. As the English police counted the votes, Davitt said, "It reminds me of what you see in the Holy Land, Christians quarreling with each other over the Lord's tomb while Mohammedan soldiers look on and keep the peace." Gladstone, talking to Morley, also used a simile from the Holy Land. He said that the internal quarrel reminded him of the Jews quarreling among themselves while the conqueror Titus marched on to Jerusalem. The Kilkenny result gave Gladstone vindictive satisfaction. "It is a great gain, and yet sad enough to think that even here one-third of the voters should be either rogues or fools."

XIX

In the United States, O'Brien and Dillon waited eagerly for all the news from Ireland and chafed at their enforced absence from the battleground. O'Brien disliked Davitt, and both he and Dillon were strongly anticlerical and hated to see the growing intervention of the church. Whether or not Parnell was beaten at Kilkenny, they believed that Parnell was far from being done with and that it was imperative to find some compromise to avoid a fatal division of the party.

As O'Brien prepared to board a ship to France, Dillon wrote to him, "Healy is maddening. And I expect Davitt will be as bad. It infuriates me to read of Parnell being hounded by the priests." In his own diary, Dillon recorded gloomily, "I do believe the game is up, and unhappy Ireland must pass through the valley of death into which Parnell is dragging her." On board the ship, O'Brien wrote to Dillon, "Now I am wholly convinced that an understanding with him is our only salvation if the country is to be held together."

When O'Brien landed at Boulogne on Christmas Day, the victory at Kilkenny for the anti-Parnell forces had taken place. He was met by such leaders as Sexton and McCarthy to inform of that result and to urge him to abandon all attempts to salvage anything for Parnell. Archbishop Croke wrote him, "Parnell has hopelessly fallen. The bishops and priests and all good men are determinedly against him. How then can you touch him? What good can he do?" O'Brien replied to Dr. Croke, "Securing Parnell's retirement is one thing. Hunting him down like a wild beast and hacking him to pieces with all sorts of foul weapons is quite another thing."

On December 30, Parnell arrived in Boulogne. To O'Brien he

wore something of the pathetic air of a cedar struck by lightning but still erect and stately. At first he preferred to harangue O'Brien rather than to talk terms. He arraigned the Irish for giving in to Gladstone. "How am I to abandon the country to such a pack of sheep?"

The terms proposed by O'Brien were most generous and would enable Parnell to surrender the appearance of power but retain a substantial amount. The party would publicly express its gratitude to Parnell and acknowledge the informality of the election of McCarthy as the new chairman. There would be an effort made to secure the retraction by Archbishops Walsh and Croke of their manifesto and also to secure an acknowledgment by Gladstone that he was precipitate in publishing his letter. Parnell would continue as president of the National League, and if there were a committee appointed by the party to run affairs he could nominate half of the members.

Parnell seemed to accept the terms in a conciliatory mood, but he sprang a surprise. He proposed that O'Brien rather than McCarthy should be the new chairman of the party. When Dillon learned of the proposal, he immediately sensed the strategy of Parnell, that of detaching O'Brien from the rest of the party and perhaps from Dillon. He recorded in his diary, "Men here say that Parnell is mad but it seems to me that his astuteness is absolutely infinite."

On New Year's Day, Parnell, back in London, wrote to O'Brien and made another proposal, that for "consistency" and "regard for my responsibility" McCarthy should go to Gladstone and try to commit him to the terms of an acceptable settlement of the Home Rule question. Thus he resurrected the Clancy proposal made in Committee Room 15. If O'Brien and Parnell agreed that Gladstone's answers were satisfactory, Parnell would retire in good grace. Since Gladstone had previously balked at discussing terms until the leadership problem was settled and it now was settled, Gladstone would have no such out. As before, it was a strong card for Parnell to play. If the negotiations succeeded, Parnell could retire as the savior, if they failed, it was the convincing proof of the malignity of Gladstone. After more conferences, the parties on Parnell's and O'Brien's side agreed that Dillon, not O'Brien, should be the new chairman. O'Brien agreed that he and Dillon would actually take sides with Parnell in the struggle if Gladstone refused to give the requisite guarantees on the vital questions.

When Dillon learned the new terms by cable, he was stunned
with disbelief at O'Brien's naïvete. To O'Brien he cabled back,
"Proposed terms my judgment intolerable; not bona fide." He
would sail for France immediately. To his diary he confided, "He
[O'Brien] seems to have walked into the very trap into which the
party walked before. . . . Now the proposal is that I am to get
the chairmanship on terms such that I would rather earn an honest
living by blacking shoes than accept." There were further cabled
interchanges between Dillon and O'Brien in which the latter tried
to convince Dillon of Parnell's good faith. Dillon finally agreed to
the second official approach to Gladstone though he preferred that
all await his arrival in France. In his diary he wrote, "Parnell
seems to have captured him and I fear P. has succeeded in dividing
O'Brien from me."

Feelers were now extended to Gladstone. Morley wrote him that
"it is simply a terrific emergency" and that he and he alone could
save Ireland from anarchy, advising him that the moderate faction
who were asking him for help represented the best hope for Ireland.
"It is well enough for Healy to flourish the tomahawk but he has no
weight in Ireland; he is a mere gamin." Harcourt, on the other
hand, wrote Gladstone that this was "an infamous intrigue" and
wrote Morley that if the "Gaul of Eltham were bought off, he
will return upon us with *vae victis* and cast some other fire-escape
into the scale." Nonetheless, Gladstone decided to give to the
O'Brien-Dillon faction the assurances that they wanted.

On January 28, after extensive negotiations, Gladstone gave assurances that he favored Irish control over the police within five
years of the passage of the Home Rule bill and also favored giving
authority to the Irish Parliament to deal with the land question
if the Imperial Parliament did not do so within a brief time from
the Home Rule passage.

The terms were cabled to Parnell, and he arrived in Calais on
February 3, after two nights of traveling, weary and careworn.
O'Brien's account written in book form in 1910 must be accepted
as the authoritative account of what happened even though it is in
conflict with an earlier informal version he gave. Parnell now professed to be quite satisfied with all the conditions and guarantees
and wanted to talk over his withdrawal with Dillon if he should
come to Calais from Boulogne. He declined to accept the chairmanship of the National League, saying that he planned a year's holi-
day in the United States, where he was going to study many things,

which would not include political subjects. When Dillon arrived, Parnell was in good humor and talked of his retirement as an accomplished fact. He gave him advice from his own experience on running the party, such as that it would be unwise to saddle himself with a committee but he should rule alone. They started to discuss the management of the Paris funds, money of the party invested in securities which was used among other purposes to pay small stipends to party M.P.'s. Parnell suggested that there be two trustees, himself and Dillon. Dillon replied sarcastically, "Yes, indeed, and the first time I am in a fix leave me without a pound to pay the men!"

Parnell rose from his seat "white with passion, as pale as if a pistol had been fired into his face. 'Dillon, Dillon,' he gasped, 'that is not the kind of expression I had the right to expect from you.' " Then, as he always did, he recovered his blandness and reviewed the Liberal guarantees. But now it seemed unreal, like a physician talking about the cure for a patient already dead. He found more and more flaws in what Gladstone had had to say. When he embarked for England, his last words on the pier to O'Brien were "O'Brien, you had all but achieved the impossible. You and I could have done anything, but what are you to do with a man like that?"

The negotiations continued, but Parnell found that he had been put into a "humiliating and disgraceful position" by what he claimed to be a new condition that O'Brien alone should judge the sufficiency of the guarantees, and he also claimed that he had new information "of a most startling character" that Gladstone wanted the whole Irish membership to be retained in the Imperial Parliament, "the majority of the party of today having lost their independence and proved their devotion to the Liberal leaders." O'Brien wrote to Parnell's aide John Redmond, "The story of the new conditions is, of course, absolute rubbish—not a shadow of foundation for it," and to Parnell he wrote, "How unspeakably sad and tragic it seems to me that you should be gratifying your enemies by throwing away the last chance of saving us from the horrible state of things that is before the country."

But the efforts of the peacemakers had come to an end, and on February 12 O'Brien and Dillon crossed to Folkstone, England, where they were met by Scotland Yard detectives and escorted to prison to serve their six-month terms.

The agreement was indeed generous to Parnell, and Dillon in

later years insisted that Parnell understood clearly that his retirement would be only temporary. It was the belief of Dillon, as well as others, that Mrs. O'Shea at the critical moment, as always, had stiffened Parnell's resolve against any accommodation. For her part, in her memoirs, Mrs. O'Shea indicates that Parnell was playing a role and was never serious about reaching an accord. "Much against his wish, Parnell went over to Boulogne to see him [O'Brien] as the party was so anxious that he should go. He did not think that it would do any good, and feeling ill, he hated undertaking the extra fatigue." Later she says, "After the negotiations with Messrs. O'Brien and Dillon were brought to an unsatisfactory conclusion, my husband returned home to me and telling me of the result of his tiring journey, remarked, 'Ah, well, they are both out of the way for a bit!' . . . Parnell had always found Messrs. O'Brien and Dillon had a depressing effect on him, as he said it was hard to keep them to the difficulties of the moment while they were eagerly passing on to the troubles of to-morrow."

XX

"Ireland must have been a hell on earth to him," John Morley wrote of his last months. Every week he crossed the Irish Sea to visit a different area. After an exhausting trip he would come face to face with ever dwindling support, bolder clerical opposition and more outspoken vilification. "Three cheers for Kitty O'Shea," known as Tim Healy's battle cry, became familiar to him; from one end of Ireland to the other the name of Kitty O'Shea was sung in filthy rhymes or screamed out with obscenities. The fact, well known by now, that she was an Englishwoman intensified the hatred in Ireland for her name. A pamphlet, "Under Which Flag? or Is Parnell to be the Leader of the Irish People," with the author's name as "Gutter Sparrow"—believed to be Healy—referred to Parnell as a "putrefying political corpse," "a seducer of his host's wife," "a convicted adulterer," etc. At Mallow, County Cork, a crowd attacked his carriage, ripping the door panels and woodwork off, and Parnell and his companions tore away hat racks to defend themselves while a priest shouted through the window, "Down with libertinism."

To Mrs. O'Shea, Parnell said that there was one small solace, that no one close to Katherine ever knew her as Kitty. "It would really have hurt, my Queen, if those devils had got hold of your real name, Queenie, or even the Katie or Dick that your relations and Willie called you."

The kindly and venerable Justin McCarthy, though chairman of the seceders, remained on friendly terms with Parnell. Concerned with the visible inroads that the ordeal was making on his health, he said, "Charles, aren't you overdoing this? No constitution can stand the work you are going through." Parnell replied that it was the only anodyne he knew, that it was better than sitting alone and brooding.

The Healy-Sexton faction, as they steadily made gains, were setting up their own political apparatus. In early March, Healy started a new newspaper, the *National Press,* an organ designed to offset Parnell's powerful paper, the *Freeman's Journal.* They also launched the Irish National Federation, an organization designed to offset the Irish National League. In a speech at the inauguration ceremonies, Sexton, who had been in the past a most fervent idol-worshiper, declared, "We have had no representation, no democratic organization in Ireland in the last nine years, and I thank heaven for one thing here today, that I am helping you to bury forever the degrading idol-worship and one-man power in Ireland."

There was a second by-election test, in North Sligo, and Parnell and his opponents campaigned as hard here as in Kilkenny. The priests were now more openly active in behalf of the anti-Parnellite candidate than they had been before, Archbishop Croke having made the tongue-in-cheek remark "I hereby positively declare that I shall look on all my priests in exactly the same light whether they conscientiously denounce Mr. Parnell or support him—the latter, I think being impossible." His courtly reserve gone, Parnell now relied on billingsgate as much as on logical argument. Who could succeed him? he asked. "Can you select the foul-mouthed Healy? Can you trust in uncertain and wobbling Sexton? Or can you follow the hysterical Davitt who never belonged to a political party for twenty-four years altogether?" Gangs of rowdies, allegedly instigated by priests, drowned out Parnell's voice at meetings with noise-making devices. The anti-Parnellite candidate won, though by no overwhelming margin, 3261 to 2493.

Parnell, who was personally most conservative in philosophy, had been unsympathetic previously to the burgeoning labor movement and unionism, but in his desperation for votes he emerged as a friend of labor with proposals which were borrowed mostly from Davitt. In the workingmen's district of North Sligo he announced his slogan: "Eight hours' work and eight hours' play; Eight hours' sleep and eight shillings a day." Not long after the election the *National Press* was featuring news of a strike at Parnell's quarries in Arklow, where the men worked eleven hours a day for 3 shillings. It claimed that Parnell refused to discuss demands for a pay raise.

Healy was assaulted in Cork by a Parnell partisan. Four teeth were broken, his glasses were smashed and an eye injury necessitated a brief hospital internment, but this hardly moderated the fanatical campaign he was conducting. He was looking for issues and found one in an offer by Parnell on St. Patrick's Day that he and his fellow-member from Cork, Maurice Healy, should both resign and seek reelection. Healy immediately accepted the offer, but now Parnell wriggled out of it, saying that Healy must resign and seek reelection first before he would follow suit. "Oh, Mr. Fox," the *National Press* editorialized, picking up the famous Parnell alias. This argument led to a very sad scene in Westminster.

Parnell's attendance in Parliament was now more regular than it had been in years. He ignored the seceders, with the exception of McCarthy. T. P. O'Connor related that when he returned from America he extended his hand to Parnell and said cordially "How are you?" to which Parnell, ignoring the extended hand, said, "Better than you," and turned his back on him, a startling departure from his former stately courtesy.

Parnell retained his customary seat. He had never sat in the nearest corner to the Speaker on the first bench below the gangway as a leader should but had sat on the third bench, three seats from the head. Now Sexton and Healy sat on one side of him, Justin McCarthy on the other side, and they talked across him while he sat stony-faced, seemingly oblivious of their presence. On all bills he and McCarthy rose separately to state their respective positions, each holding himself out as the Irish leader.

On April 15, Parnell rose to speak against a bill to extend the Sunday closing of public houses to larger cities and towns. He said that he was against Parliamentary interference in a local question that Ireland should decide. "Make yourself sober first," said Parnell. Below him sat Maurice Healy, who then rose and said, "Neither on this or on any other question does the hon. gentleman represent the city of Cork. If the hon. gentleman wishes to test the truth of my remarks, let him resign." Amid the cheering, the baying "Hear, Hear" of Gladstone could be distinctly heard.

Parnell left his seat for a moment, and when he returned he found his bench entirely occupied, so he went up to the top bench. But the Healyites turned around and loudly jeered him and Parnell in self-defense had to leave the Irish bench and find a seat among the Liberals. Now that they had found him to be mortal, with the failings of a mortal, this was the revenge of the Irish members for the years of adulation that they had given him in the mistaken impression that he was a demigod. McCarthy, embarrassed, dropped his head into a newspaper, and Sexton's look of pain was quite evident.

In a few weeks there would be another humiliation, perhaps the most searing. Patriotism and idealism, as we have pointed out, were adulterated with a goodly dose of less noble motives, including envy, and in the case of Healy it encompassed envy about money. He had worked so hard for the party and how had he been rewarded compared with the slothful Parnell? With rancor he recorded in his memoirs that on the birth of his first child Parnell had intervened with O'Brien to get his writing contribution for *United Ireland* raised from all of two pounds to three pounds a week, and he added bitterly, "Parnell had been presented with a cheque for 40,000 pounds the day before," the Tribute. Healy had been accumulating evidence for some time as to the way money designated for the party had been finding its way to Parnell's pocket, and an opportunity was to come to spring this.

Archbishop Croke started a tour of his diocese in May and made speeches shedding any pretense of aloofness from the political contest. In a speech at Thurles he asked why the Irish had been united and were now divided. His answer was prominently featured every day in the *National Press*. "Our general has betrayed us. For his own miserable gratification he has sold the pass, preferring an ignoble and licentious life in London to the liberation and advancement of his too confiding countrymen."

Dr. Croke also raised the question as to how Parnell had the funds to travel through Ireland every weekend by special train. He told how two years previously he had suggested to Dillon that party funds should be audited for publication, how Dillon had passed this on to Parnell who promised to talk it over with Dr. Croke but had broken three successive engagements with him. After Parnell made an evasive reply, Healy went on the attack in the *National Press* starting on June 1 under the caption "STOP THIEF."

> On his native heath at Wicklow yesterday, Mr. Parnell shirked in the most cowardly and hang-dog fashion the terrible indictment of Archbishop Croke. We give elsewhere the alleged reply. As to the damning discourtesy with which the adulterer treated the metropolitan monitor no answer is attempted.
>
> The silence of Mr. Parnell now is the best explanation of his refusal to face in even five minutes "friendly conversation" with a powerful and determined Nationalist. Why? Because for years he has been stealing the money entrusted to his charge. . . . A wily thief is Mr. Fox. This charge if he fails to face it has come here to stay. It will haunt Mr. Parnell on the platform, in Parliament, in bed and board for the remainder of his career. We will force him to face it, or amidst the contempt of his own supporters "lash the rascal naked through the world."
>
> If Mr. Parnell debauched Mrs. O'Shea, one of the commandments delivered to us by Moses called this "adultery." If he appropriated the moneys left in trust with him—and we are prepared to prove that he did—the same old fashioned law-giver called that "theft."

The charge of theft or embezzlement related to a check for £5,000 from Cecil Rhodes to the cause which was not paid over to the party as a previous check for £5,000 had been; a check for £1,000 from one Morrogh which Parnell allegedly cashed himself; and £10,000 from the amount which was paid over to Parnell as a defense fund before the Special Commission and which seemingly remained after all expenses had been traced. Parnell never gave an answer to the charge, stating only as to the Cecil Rhodes donation that he had given it to O'Brien but "some of the balance I hold in my possession still and I shall continue to hold until the proper time comes." Every day the *National Press* announced that it was waiting for the writ for libel which never came.

As the autocrat of the party, Parnell was not a careful bookkeeper and undoubtedly kept for his own use money earmarked for the party. Dictators before and since have done that and probably on a mounting scale as their rule continued. Healy's conclusion in the *National Press* is a restatement of the famous Lord Acton apothegm, "Human nature decays and gangrenes like any other corruptible matter once the salt of criticism—which often in public serves for the sting of conscience—is removed." It must be added, however, in justice to Parnell, as to the particular expenditure of which Dr. Croke raised a question, that the expenditure of party funds by a party leader to suppress revolt within the party must be considered as legitimate.

To Parnell the indictment was a cruel and hurtful one and after his death, there were new words to the old rebel air:

> Who was it killed the Chief?
> Says the Shan Van Vocht
> Who was it cried "Stop Thief"?
> Says the Shan Van Vocht
>
> 'Twas Tim Healy's poisoned tongue,
> Our chieftain dead that stung,
> Better men than him were hung,
> Says the Shan Van Vocht

XXI

There was one joyous interlude before the curtain went down. On Thursday, June 25, 1891, Charles Stewart Parnell and Mrs. Katherine Wood O'Shea became man and wife before a registrar at Steyning. To throw newspaper correspondents who hung around the house off the scent, he had told his servant to wait a short distance from the house with his horse Dictator and the phaeton at 11 A.M. and that he would be required as a witness at the wedding. So the correspondents, misled as to the time, as Parnell had planned, were not prepared for an early morning ceremony. Parnell waked Katherine at 6 A.M., rapping on her door and saying, "Get up, get up, it's time to get married." In a fine mood, Parnell settled her in the phaeton, and though he usually did not notice her clothes, he said, "Queenie, you look lovely in that lace stuff and the beautiful hat with those roses! I am so proud of you!" Then, "They are after us. Let Dictator go!" So they raced the nine miles past fields of growing corn and hedges heavy with wild roses till they came to the registrar's house. While they were waiting for the maids to arrive by train, Parnell blew kisses to her in the mirror and said, "It isn't every woman who makes so good a marriage as you are making, Queenie, is it? And to such a handsome fellow, too." When the maids arrived the union was legalized.

When they returned to Walsingham Terrace, they had to run the gauntlet between waiting members of the press, but Parnell pushed them aside and the couple had their wedding breakfast together. An enterprising lady correspondent of an American paper broke in by climbing onto the balcony from the adjoining house, but she was evicted. Later Parnell gave an interview to the press to which all correspondents were invited except her. She retaliated by running an imaginary interview with the couple in her paper, illustrated by a sketch showing them seated in a room of the fluffy opulence of a Parisian demimondaine, with Parnell wearing a fur coat (in June) and Katherine in a diaphanous negligee attached to herself by diamonds. The news of the wedding filled the papers that afternoon, and the couple were bombarded with letters, telegrams and gifts, many of which were of a most insulting kind. The honeymoon was very short. After two days at the seashore, he returned to Ireland and the wars.

XXII

If Parnell believed that his marriage would blunt the sharp edge of the hostility toward him, he was doomed to disappointment. It had the opposite effect; the clergy regarded it as a "blatant flaunting of his sin" to take in holy matrimony a woman who was now denounced openly as a "convicted prostitute." Thus, the Bishop of Raphoe branded it as "the climax of brazened horrors." From then on the story is the melancholy one of repeated disaster.

His first concern after the wedding was the by-election at Carlow necessitated by the death at eighty-nine of the O'Gorman Mahon. Though he campaigned hard and was given a fairer hearing here than at Kilkenny and North Sligo, his candidate suffered a greater defeat, the vote being 3,775 to 1,559. The clergy was out in force against him, and it was charged that a priest had threatened to turn a man into a goat if he voted Parnellite. It was clear now that although Parnell had considerable strength in Dublin and the more populous centers, he was being overwhelmingly repudiated in rural areas by the "mud cabin" vote which he had fought to enfranchise in the electoral reform of 1884, when he counted on it as an accretion to the Nationalist vote. The moral code among these rural folk under the domination of their priests was very strict—so much so, said Katherine Tynan, that at that time if a young girl went wrong, she was literally thrown out by her family into the cold. Parnell could not complain that the English were being permitted to devour him. As James Joyce said in the

Piccolo della Sera, "the Irish did not throw him to the English wolves—they tore him to pieces themselves."

On July 2, a declaration of the full meeting of the archbishops and bishops, held a week previously, was published, citing "new and convincing proof that he [Parnell] is wholly unworthy of the confidence of Catholics and we therefore feel bound on this occasion to call on our people to repudiate his leadership."

On July 30, O'Brien and Dillon were released from prison and they lost no time in announcing that all previous hesitations were gone. They could not see how Parnell could continue as leader. O'Brien, on entering prison, had been regarded as highly sympathetic to Parnell, so this forthright declaration was a new blow. Parnell could only reply with scorn, "Some of the seceders have changed only twice, O'Brien and Dillon have changed four times."

The day of their release there was another serious reverse; Parnell lost the support of the all-important *Freeman's Journal,* which up to that time had stood by him in the face of all blasts. Edmund Dwyer Gray, Jr., son of the recently deceased Dwyer Gray and now the largest stockholder, came of age that year. He had lived in Australia, but on his return he had been deeply impressed by the declaration of the hierarchy, and now he stated that since Parnell's marriage made it impossible for the Catholic clergy ever to reverse its position concerning him, he must therefore reverse the position of his paper. Desertions multiplied. One night Parnell returned home unusually depressed, and Katherine did not press him to speak. After a long silence he said only one sentence, "O'Kelly has gone too."

Parnell's appeal for support, hollow in logic as it was, lost its force as his opponents mercilessly exposed it to ridicule. To Justin McCarthy, Parnell had improved on *"après moi le déluge"* with the battle cry "With me the deluge—hold to me and let us all be ruined together, cause, country and all." To Healy the appeal was so far removed from reality that it could be interpreted only as the comedian's greatest hour. He who had established the alliance with the Liberal party and had made it the sheet anchor of his policy was now denouncing it; he whose great achievement had been to convert Gladstone to Home Rule now proclaimed him Ireland's enemy; he who had led Ireland from the hopelessly futile counsels of armed revolt to the path of constitutionalism now sought to revive the spirit of irreconciliable Fenianism in an appeal to the "hillside men"; he who had fused unity from discord now sought to revive ancient feuds and differences; he who proclaimed himself Ireland's savior had split the party by refusing to accept any compromise; he who now endlessly preached the "independence" of the party ignored the fact that "independence" could bear no fruit since it required three Liberal votes for every Nationalist vote to win Home Rule; he who asked Ireland for a vote of confidence was now *persona non grata* to the Liberals and could accomplish nothing for Ireland since a vote of confidence in him would be fatal to Home Rule.

"He has gone mad" was freely said, as this Samson Agonistes seemed clearly bent on pulling down the roof of the temple and burying all under the rubble. It may well have been that there was a decomposition of Parnell's mental balance in line with the decomposition of his fortunes and the evident decomposition of his personality and physical well-being. Whether Parnell at this stage and earlier was mad, half mad or mad north-by-northwest, since it is a question of uncertain norms, can never be answered definitively. For years Parnell had been an eccentric, as Mrs. O'Shea herself gave testimony, yet the Victorian age somehow bred eccentrics, ranging from mild to wild. In a later year T. P. O'Connor wrote, "The truth is that for a period of ten years Ireland was led and consummately led by a madman of uncommon genius." The concept of the "mad genius" is very possibly a romantic one conceived to fit the Parnell legend which developed after his death.

Healy had long been a fascinated student of Parnell's behavior, and his opinion deserves great weight. In 1884 he had pronounced Parnell "half mad," influenced largely by Parnell's superstitions, which were truly pathological. However, in the late 1880s he had become convinced that Parnell was less a madman than an actor— in his opinion Parnell had read in the press that he was a man of mystery and therefore decided for his perverse delight to play the role to the hilt. In the last phase, Healy grappled with Parnell on a day-to-day basis, and in his letters of the time and his later account there is no hint that Parnell was mad—rather, he treats Parnell as one who had dropped his mask of impassivity and was now a wily, resourceful and unscrupulous foe, one who had exchanged the role of the strong man for that of the trickster.

Taking a long view of history, "rule or ruin" has not been an exceptional credo for military or political leaders who have remained faithful to a cause until they suffered personal frustration and then have turned against it, putting the salvation of their personal egos above the cause. Alcibiades and Benedict Arnold are examples of such military leaders. In the political field is there a more apposite case than that of Joseph Chamberlain, who became an enemy of Liberalism in a remarkable turnabout to Toryism, anti-Home Rulism and jingoism when his ambitions were frustrated in the Liberal camp? Was Theodore Roosevelt "mad" when he tried to wreck the Republican party in 1912 for what was undoubtedly less principle than personal grievance?

For Parnell there was every incitement to personal vindication and revenge. This proud man who had trod on the heads of men had been trampled upon in the most bitter humiliation, and the revilement heaped on him had included the woman he loved. He now fought to the death for his pride, which he miscalled his personal honor, and for the peace of mind of his beloved.

There will always remain the question of whether, aside from his passion for power, Parnell was ever inspired by any genuine devotion to Ireland's cause. Davitt, whose hatred for Parnell steadily mounted during the last phase, pointed out that Parnell, undoubtedly as the price of his release from jail, had pulled the teeth from the land movement; he had let the party go hang for months while he secreted himself with his mistress; he had rammed Captain O'Shea down the throat of the party as a favor to his mistress; he had comforted English landlords by sneering at the Plan of Campaign. While Davitt had endured unspeakable tortures for Ireland, Parnell had lived a life of ease even during his brief prison term, he had been showered with glory by his countrymen and had received a princely fortune to boot. Yet when the whole cause was at stake, Parnell had refused to make a small sacrifice by stepping aside only temporarily. Instead, he preferred to build a purely factitious case so that he might have a chance to hold on to power while his country's cause was ruined.

This is a burning indictment, and Davitt did not have the facts which came to light in Mrs. O'Shea's book—which would have made the case even stronger—such as Parnell's letter from Kilmainham that the people's idol in the land movement had only "disgust" with the whole thing, and Parnell's offer through Mrs. O'Shea to the Liberals in the 1885 general election that he would give them the Irish vote in four English constituencies if they would give the Captain a Liberal designation from Liverpool.

XXIII

In the last weeks he developed a jollity and a gregariousness that he had not exhibited before. In early September, he had a conference with Justin McCarthy about the Paris funds, and McCarthy wrote to Mrs. Campbell Praed, "We were as friendly and familiar as if nothing had happened to divide us, and we smoked at intervals of work and drank whiskey and soda—and I thought it dismal, ghastly and hideous, and I hated to have to meet him. But there was no help for it."

Patrick O'Brien, one of the seceders, told of dining with him one evening at Morrison's Hotel. At the next table a lady had a little dog to which she would say, "Now, tot, cheer for the Queen," and the dog would get on its hind legs and bark. Parnell winked at him and said, "I think that is intended for us." O'Brien invited him to the Gaiety Theatre, and to his surprise Parnell assented. "It is twenty-five years since I have been to the theatre and I would like to go." The performance was on when they arrived, but a murmur swept the audience when he entered the box and eyes were fixed on him all through the show. When it was over, the crowd assembled around the theater and blocked all passages, so that the management had to get him out by a secret exit. Afterward they had a private supper, and at 2 A.M. O'Brien walked him back to Morrison's Hotel. Then Parnell insisted on walking O'Brien back to the National Club, and then O'Brien returned the compliment by walking him back to Morrison's. When Parnell proposed to walk O'Brien back again, O'Brien said, "If you do so, we will be walking the streets till daybreak," and so they parted company.

He was thinking of the future in long terms. In a conversation with R. Barry O'Brien he said, "Gladstone will be satisfied if he gives us any kind of Parliament. He is an old man and cannot wait. If we do not get it this year or next, I can wait for half a dozen years." (That he had written off Home Rule as a near-term objective was something Parnell had not dared to state publicly.) When O'Brien suggested that if both he and Gladstone should depart this life then Home Rule might be gone for a generation, he answered, "I will not go. I am a young man and will not go."

However, the nervous reserve on which he had been drawing was now close to exhaustion. The ceaseless grind, the griefs and anxieties were bringing life's journey to a close. While his speeches were as forceful as ever, it was noticeable to observers how he sagged in his chair afterward. In his last letter to his mother he wrote, "I am weary, dear mother, of these troubles, weary unto death, but it is all in a good cause." Katherine found him looking so ill and worn that she was thoroughly alarmed. "I saw as I sat watching him while he slept that the tired, grey shadows were growing deep upon his beautiful face and that in sleep he had that absolute stillness which one only finds in very healthy children or in the absolutely exhausted sleep of adults."

XXIV

He was scheduled to speak at Creggs, a town close to Roscommon, on Sunday, September 27. He left Brighton on Friday in good spirits and sent wires to Katherine from Euston Station, Holyhead and Dublin, but after he arrived in Dublin he wired her that he was feeling ill. He was complaining of a pain, seemingly a rheumatic pain, in his left arm. Dr. Kenny put it into a sling and advised him to cancel his engagement of the following day. However, he insisted on going, saying that he did not want to disappoint his people.

It was raining during the meeting that day and Parnell, arm in sling, spoke bareheaded in the downpour, refusing the offer of an umbrella. He spoke haltingly, so slowly, in fact, that his words could be taken down in longhand. In opening his speech, he apologized for the lameness of his delivery, saying that his doctor had advised against his coming there. "However, I do not think that any very material harm will come to me from this meeting. If I was to allow the suggestion of such a thought, we should have our enemies throwing up their hats and announcing that I was buried before I was dead."

The little bag that Katherine always packed for him with a change of shoes and socks was left at his host's home by mistake, so Parnell had to spend a few hours with his feet soaked. He felt a chill. On the return trip to Dublin he stayed up through the night with the *Freeman's Journal* reporter, saying that he did not want to be alone.

He stayed in Dublin for a few days working on plans for a new newspaper, the *Irish Daily Independent,* to support him in place of the *Freeman's Journal*. This enterprise would require money, which may explain why his last letters to Katherine from Ireland concerned details of mortgage transactions to raise money. Since he was feeling more pain, Dr. Kenny urged him to remain in Dublin, but he said, "No, I want to go home, I must go home." He left that Wednesday night, stating to Dr. Kenny that he would return a week from the following Saturday. This was a promise that would be kept within a few hours. Dr. Kenny had been fortifying his strength with brandy and had given him some champagne to drink, which made Parnell quite nauseated as he set out for home.

Alone, worn-out and dispirited, wracked with pain that drove from his mind the cares which beset him, the dying Parnell, the "Uncrowned King of Ireland" a scant year before, journeyed for the last time across the Irish Sea to England. How often he had made this journey—as a boy to attend school and later the university—in the flush of youth to attend the embassy balls in Paris and to woo the beautiful Miss Woods—to take his seat in Parliament at the age of twenty-eight—filled with ambition to plan new attacks on the perfidious English and to win increasing recognition as Ireland's new hope—after the great electoral triumph of 1880 to take his place as the Nationalist leader—in the midst of the Land League campaign to break off and return suddenly to England so he could catch only a glimpse of Katherine, but in vain—released from prison, hungry to be reunited with his mistress and to look upon his first-born child—loaded with honors and with all the adulation that Ireland could bestow on one man, to find comfort and joy with his secret love and his secret children.

Then followed the turn of fortune's wheel and the retreats to Brighton, hurt and bruised, seeking balm after the increasing rebuffs and disgrace, as Ireland took back what it had given. And now, as the career of Ireland's discrowned king had run its course, his life was spent also.

When he reached London, after the long, twelve-hour trip, he went to a Turkish bath, hoping that it would ease the pain in his left arm, which had spread to his shoulder, but this was ill advised, since it sapped his strength further. By this time, as Sir Henry Thompson later advised Katherine, he was beyond all medical help. "A blow had been struck—not so heavy—apparently a light one, but his worn-out constitution, of late fearfully overtaxed by a spirit too strong for its bodily tenement, had no power to resist and gave way, wholly unable to make any fight for itself against the enemy." A buggy met him as usual at the Brighton station, and as she helped him out Katherine saw how weak he was. She made him a blazing fire, though the weather was warm. He had a good dinner, but afterward could not walk without assistance and painfully made his way up the stairs.

The next morning he felt better. Instead of summoning Sir Henry from London, which he was loath to do on account of the expense, he wrote to him about his illness, revealing his identity. He sat up in bed, smoked a cigar, prepared notes for a new speech and worked on the mortgage he was going to put on Avondale. He became worse that night and could not sleep, and the next day, despite his protests, she sent for a local practitioner. He did not sleep again that night, and a superstition came to his mind, an old one, that if he did not sleep two nights in a row he would die. He asked her to lie beside him and put her hands in his so he could "feel" that she was there. He asked that his old dog, Grouse, stay in the room with him. He did not sleep again that night and the next day, Tuesday, he was very feverish, with bright color on his usually white face. After the doctor gave him some medicine, he lay quietly, just smiling if she touched him. During the evening, he dozed and she heard him mutter "the Conservative Party."

Late in the evening he suddenly opened his eyes and said, "Kiss me, sweet wifie, and I will try to sleep a little." She lay down by his side and kissed the burning lips he pressed to hers for the last time. As she slipped her hand from under his head he gave a little sigh and became unconscious.

The time was a quarter to midnight and the date was the 6th of October, the month Parnell had always said was his "unlucky" one. He was three months past his forty-fifth birthday. The official medical verdict was "rheumatism of the heart."

XXV

He had passed away as noiselessly as the passing wind. "The breaking of so great a thing should make a greater crack," said Octavius Caesar when informed of the death of Anthony. The world was caught by surprise. It had been watching with bated breath a Homeric struggle on a stage of nations, and the sudden disappearance of the principal character, offstage, was an interdiction by fate that did not fit the scenario, an anticlimactic ending, disappointing even to his enemies.

John Horgan, the son of Parnell's friend M. J. Horgan, was nine years old at the time and wrote in later years of the reception of the news in Cork. All business shut down after noon, and he saw men crying openly in the streets. His father came home utterly broken down. "I had never seen him cry before and it was terrible to behold." When *United Ireland* arrived, the boy had to read it to his sobbing father. "He is dead. The Leader whom it was our glory to follow shall never again rally all that is true in Ireland. . . . Slain, sacrificed by Irishmen on the altar of English Liberalism, he, the greatest chief that this land has known in the stuggles of centuries against English domination, has been murdered by the men whom he dragged from obscurity and who hated him even whilst they fawned upon him because they could never repay all that he had done for them. Murdered he has been, as certainly as if the gang of conspirators had surrounded him and hacked him to pieces."

The news had spread over London by word of mouth before the papers carried it. James J. O'Kelly heard it when he checked into a hotel on his return from Paris, and he immediately went to Brighton. Later, Henry Harrison, the "Oxford stripling," felt stabbed as by an icy wind when he saw the newsboys' placards. He wired Mrs. Parnell and offered his services; without waiting for an answer he took a train to Brighton, where he took charge of the funeral arrangements and was to act as an adviser to the widow for the next few months. John Redmond, Edward and Tim Harrington, and Colonel Nolan were later arrivals.

Katherine lay prostrated in her room, and all communication had to be conducted through her devoted daughter, Norah O'Shea, then nineteen years old. Because of the high fever, decomposition set in immediately, no death mask could be made, and he was quickly put into a lead coffin. Mrs. Parnell consented, somewhat reluctantly, that the body be transported to Ireland for a public funeral and interment in his native soil. At a quarter past twelve on Saturday afternoon, through a heavy rain, the hearse, followed by three mourning coaches, made its way to the Brighton station three miles away.

At Holyhead there was a long wait for the arrival of a steamer from Ireland carrying many dignitaries, including the Lord Mayor of Dublin and family members, Mrs. Emily Dickinson, Henry Tudor Parnell and Alfred MacDermott, widower of Sophie. It was not until 3 A.M., two hours late, that the mailboat set out across the stormy Irish Sea. On the pier at Kingstown a huge crowd was waiting, among them was the twenty-six-year-old poet William Butler Yeats, who was there to meet his friend Maud Gonne. The somber scene would remain always in his mind—the packed mass of humanity, the dim morning, the pelting rain, the muttering and curses against Tim Healy, the low moan when the coffin was carried down, the rows of heads all bared to the rain. Another huge crowd was at the Westland Row station in Dublin, and when the wooden boards enclosing the coffin were thrown off before it was put into the hearse, there was a wild melee of people fighting to tear away a fragment of wood as a memento of the great man.

After a brief service at St. Michan's Church, the coffin was moved to the City Hall, where it was laid down close to a statue of Daniel O'Connell. It was draped with the flags of the Irish Volunteers of Grattan's day, taken from the walls of the Avondale home; at the foot of the coffin was a wreath from the absent wife "To my true love, my husband"; at its head was a Celtic cross six feet high composed of lilies with chrysanthemums and ferns, from thirty-two Parliamentary followers. By one side was a mass of wreaths four feet high—one from the Parnell Leadership Committee of Belfast had at the top the word "Murder" worked in flowers and at the bottom "Revenge"; another large wreath had the inscription "Murdered by the priests." After thirty-five thousand had passed the coffin, the funeral procession began at one-thirty. The rain had stopped and the sun had come out.

The *Times,* reporting the funeral, conceded that the crowds were the greatest since the funeral of Daniel O'Connell and explained it away thus: "The Irish masses are fond of pageantry in every shape and form but especially when it combines political excitement with an appeal to sentiment." It was estimated that there were thirty thousand in the procession and a hundred and thirty thousand spectators. No priests were to be seen and they had urged their parishioners not to attend. Sir Joseph Ridgeway, the Irish Undersecretary, wrote to London, "Parnell dead has done what Parnell living could not do. He has struck a staggering blow to priestly domination." Delegations had come from all over Ireland—a thousand from Cork and eight hundred from Limerick. Leading the procession was the

honor guard of five hundred strapping young men of the Gaelic
Athletic Association, then the City Marshal on horseback, then a
long line of vehicles led by the Lord Mayor followed by a carriage
carrying the two old Fenians James Stephens and John O'Leary.
There were one hundred and sixty vehicles in all, followed by delegations and trade associations on foot. The hearse was close to the
rear; after it came a funeral car filled with wreaths. Next, Parnell's
old black horse from Avondale was led, Parnell's riding boots,
reversed, attached to the stirrups, the historic symbol of the fallen
leader since the days of Genghis Khan.

As bands played Chopin's "Funeral March" and to the accom-
paniment of prayers, dirges and laments from the spectators as
the hearse passed by, the procession moved slowly to Glasnevin
Cemetery. It was not until early evening that the coffin was beside
the open grave in the "poor section" and brief services were held.
As the coffin was being lowered into the grave, according to the
testimony of many, a strange phenomenon appeared in the sky—a
meteor or a falling star. Standish O'Grady wrote to Yeats, "I state
a fact. It was witnessed by thousands. While his followers were
committing Charles Parnell's remains to the earth, the sky was
bright with strange lights and flames." A witness, Katherine Tynan,
wrote a poem, commencing:

> That night our chief we laid
>   Clay in the ice-cold sod
> O'er the pale sky sped
>   A strange star home to God.
>
> Ran the East sky cold
>   The bright star glistened and went
> 'Twas green and living gold
>   That lit the firmament.

Many years later Yeats wrote a poem, "Parnell's Funeral," which
began:

> Under the Great Comedian's tomb the crowd.
> A bundle of tempestuous cloud is blown
> About the sky; where that is clear of cloud
> Brightness remains; a bright star shoots down.

The falling star in the heavens; his was a strange life. Could a
dramatist have devised a more fitting omen for the passing of that
life into legend?

EPILOGUE

I

THE CRUEL BLOW prostrated me, almost irrevocably left me for dead. Anger kept me up enough to see two or three reporters to tell what I thought. I would rather have died than not denounce poor, poor Charlie's murderers and call down vengeance on them. Gladstone will suffer for his knavish brutal wickedness to his dying day. The Roman Catholic organization has become an abomination to men and God. The widow—the mother is heard in heaven. Your brother's blood cries aloud for vengeance.

THUS wrote the aged, grief-stricken mother of the dead leader to her son John.

She returned from Bordentown to Avondale, which had been taken over by John as heir. Charles had left it in his will to Katherine and his two children by her, but since the will had been made before his marriage, it was invalid. At any rate, the estate was so loaded with debts that John had to fell trees and almost denude the woods around the mansion to raise money to pay the workmen on the estate and defray current expenses. In time he had to dispose of it, and he sold it to a Dublin butcher for £8,000.

Two years after Charles' death, on the morning after a gay dinner party at which Mrs. Parnell had denounced England and all things English in her old style, her clothing caught fire while she was sitting before a log fire in her bedroom and she died that evening of the burns. She was buried beside her son in Glasnevin Cemetery, and in 1940 a stone was set over the two graves with the simple inscription "Parnell." The widow of Parnell never visited the grave; the Englishwoman did not set foot on Irish soil in her lifetime.

The chief problem faced by Katherine Parnell when she got back on her feet was that of money, since her inheritance from Aunt Ben was tied up by the probate fight. A settlement was made with the contesting relatives under which she received half the estate. Out of this, however, a large sum was reserved in trusts for her children and she gave a few thousand pounds to Captain O'Shea, who, according to Harrison's account, extorted money from her in exchange for relinquishment of custody rights over the two girls who he now well knew were Parnell's children. After legal fees, O'Shea realized so little that he wrote Chamberlain, "When a gypsy of Cordova has exhausted every other curse upon his enemy, he finishes with the most direful of all 'May you have lawsuits and win them.'" His contact with Chamberlain now was most occasional, and the conclusion is inescapable that Chamberlain, having no further use for the tool, had shunted him aside. Captain O'Shea died in 1905.

Parnell's widow lived until 1921, reaching the age of seventy-five. She outlived her second-born child by Parnell, Clare, the wife of a physician, who died in childbirth in 1910. Of the younger child, Frances, there is no reliable information. Katherine had financial problems for a good deal of her life after her husband's death, since the solicitor to whom she entrusted her funds speculated with them and lost most of the money. Her memoirs, published in 1914, must have been as painful for her to publicize as they were to Parnell's admirers to read, but they were undoubtedly dictated by the financial exigency. A strange feature of her widowed life was that she moved from home to home restlessly as she and Parnell had moved from home to home in his last years. There were twenty-one on the list of homes she occupied, and the list might not be complete.

As she lay dying, her daughter, Norah O'Shea, wrote to Henry Harrison. "She has the happy delusion that Parnell comes to her at night, when things are worst, and draws her out of the black waves."

II

"I do not remember any such sudden catastrophe of change taking place in the fortunes of a man, a political party and a national movement."

Thus wrote Justin McCarthy in the *North American Review* in February, 1891. It is an interesting statement by a distinguished historian. More than that, it is significant that eight months before the death of Parnell, while Gladstone was exulting about Parnell's defeat at Kilkenny, the more perceptive McCarthy sensed that the

man and the cause were indissolubly linked and that they were
going down together. So it was to be.

The death of Parnell was succeeded by bitter months in which
Parnellites and anti-Parnellites assailed each other with hatred and
vituperation, a political civil war such as had never been seen before
in Ireland. In the general election of 1892 the Parnellites suffered
a sharp defeat, winning only nine seats out of eighty-one. But the
majority became split between Healyites and Dillonites, and the
monolithic party under Parnell was now divided three ways, each
faction as bent on the other's destruction as on the advancement of
Ireland. William O'Brien lamented anew, "It was never the Sas-
senach that lost the battle for the Gael but the Gael that lost it for
each other."

The Liberal vote fell far below Gladstone's expectations, and he
was able to command a majority only with the support of the Irish
Nationalists. In August, 1892, the "old, wild and incomprehensible
man of 82-½," as the Queen referred to him in a letter, became
Prime Minister for the fourth time. In 1893, Gladstone guided a
Home Rule bill through 85 sittings of the House of Commons. Irish
opinion about the bill was divided—John Redmond, leader of the
Parnellites, accepted it as "provisional," describing it as "like the
toad, ugly and venomous, which yet wore a precious jewel in its
head."

The bill passed the third reading by 43 votes but was overwhelmingly defeated by the House of Lords. The bill was then abandoned,
Home Rule was dead for the century and the book was closed on
the era of Irish agitation which had opened in 1877 when Parnell
joined Joseph Biggar in "obstruction." The emotional upheaval
surrounding Parnell was succeeded by apathy in the public at large,
including Ireland, where the young had become disillusioned with
the Parliamentary party. The political intervention of the clergy
against Parnell convinced Ulster more than ever that "Home Rule"
meant "Rome Rule," and many in the Liberal party agreed, as well
as being disgusted with the dissension in the Irish party. It was the
verdict at the time, as well as the verdict of historians since, that
the Parnell-O'Shea affair had wrecked what would otherwise have
been the certainty of Home Rule.

Gladstone resigned in March, 1894. R. Barry O'Brien interviewed
him for his book in early 1898, soon before his death. "I cannot tell

you how much I think about him [Parnell]," he told O'Brien. Evidently his vindictiveness toward Parnell had given way to compassion. "Poor fellow. Ah, if he were alive today I would do anything for him."

In his years of retirement Gladstone must have turned over in his mind many times the hectic events in November and December of 1890 which had resulted in the dismal failure of what he had planned to be the crowning achievement of his life. He may well have regretted his precipitate decision to publish immediately his letter to Morley with its ultimatum to Parnell and the Irish party; he may well have regretted the stubborn refusal on his part a week later to give assurances on the Home Rule bill that might have given Parnell the chance for a graceful exit. It was clear in retrospect and should have been clear at the time that the expulsion by force of Parnell from the Parnell Movement would more likely wreck Home Rule than would defiance of the protest against Parnell's flouting of the moral code. Gladstone could have met that protest in most statesmanlike fashion by stating that true democratic process under the principle of Home Rule was to leave to the Irish in Ireland the determination of who was morally fit to be their leader.

A storm of emotion had unseated cool and reasoned good judgment. The Conservatives in glee had tried to pour oil on the flames, but privately they were confounded. Thus, the Irish Undersecretary, Sir Joseph Ridgeway, during the crisis, wrote to Balfour, "How could the G.O.M. have been such a fool! It seems grotesque that a great policy should be thrown away because Parnell had carnal relations with Mrs. O'Shea. What fools the Parnellite majority has been. If they had only stood by Parnell, the storm of cant would have passed over and the G.O.M. would have had him again at Hawarden."

A reasonable explanation, one to which we have previously adverted, is that resentments smoldering beneath the surface in the case of the Liberal leadership and the Parnell lieutenants were ignited, and the issue presented by the divorce became an opportunity for settling scores with Parnell, although the motivation may not have been a conscious one.

The "terrible tragedy," as Gladstone put it to R. Barry O'Brien, was in his mind more massive than the tragedy to one man. The tragedy of Parnell has rightly been called a "stupendous calamity" in world history. Self-government was denied for a generation. Beyond that, although it is not absolutely certain that Parnell's objective of nationhood by gradualism and without tears could have been achieved, it is reasonably certain that Home Rule in Parnell's time would have averted the loss of Irish and British blood before the Irish Free State was established. It presented the best opportunity for solving the Ulster problem and thus averting the present partition of Ireland which keeps a third of the population under British rule. Home Rule, granted as an act of magnanimity by Britain, would probably have averted the grave problems that Britain had to face in two wars because of Irish disaffection, most importantly the catastrophic loss of life and treasure that resulted from the denial of Irish bases in the second World War.

The population of Ireland in 1890 was 5,200,000—today, including Northern Ireland, it is 4,300,000. The population of Great Britain has risen from about 30,000,000 to 50,000,000, and populations have soared all over the world. Thus, Ireland's retrogression is unique, a reflection of diminishing economic opportunities, high emigration, late marriages and a low birth rate. Parnell has been accused of being a statesman of limited vision—yet it is clear from various statements he made that his next goal after achieving political stabilization under Home Rule would have been to press for tariff protection and an infusion of British capital to industrialize the country. Whether Parnell's program could have turned the economy of Ireland in the direction of growth is highly conjectural, of course, but it is an intriguing speculation.

III

"This man cannot be forgotten," wrote T. P. O'Connor on Parnell's death. "He was a portent, a great and tragic exception to nature's ordinary laws, like an eclipse or an earthquake."

Parnell lived after death with a stronger flame than his admirers or detractors could have predicted. Many years after his death, the writer Lady Gregory (Isabella Augusta), in a place on the sea near Galway, saw an old man on a rock addressing a small crowd. "Tha sa beo, tha sa beo," he chanted. "What is he saying?" she asked. " 'He is living, he is living,' " was the answer. "He says that Parnell is alive yet." The theme became a recurrent one in Irish literature.

In Joyce's *Ulysses,* in the midnight talk, the cabman says, "One morning you would open the paper . . . and read 'Return of Parnell.' "

In a strange way the drama of Parnell caught the imagination of the young, and by myth and legend the real Parnell underwent a remarkable transmogrification. The "Parnell shock" provided a focus and a stimulus for the Irish cultural renaissance which flourished in the nineties and included romance, poetry, the theater, ancient Celtic literature and the revival of the Gaelic tongue. William Butler Yeats wrote, "It was the death of Parnell which convinced me that the moment had come to work for Ireland," since the young would turn now from the frustrations of politics to the more rewarding field of letters.

It was even stranger that as the Parnell myth evolved it bore overtones of the sacrifice of the Messiah. Herbert Howarth has made a notable contribution in a study of the Parnell influence in *The Irish Writers,* and he says therein of the mythology, "The Irish committed the crucial act of killing their prophet, and the guilt, the belief that his sacrifice sanctified, the belief that the sacrifice assures rebirth, gave them irresistible vigor in the next generation. . . . The young gradually integrated his memory into their hope of an ancient, powerfully imaginative, physically powerful and audacious Ireland. A literary movement found symbols and the language for the dream. The literary movement inflamed, half-consciously, the militant movement."

The Messiah sacrifice symbolism runs through Yeats' poem, "Parnell's Funeral," of which we have given the first few lines. It continues:

> What shudders run through all that animal blood?
> What is this sacrifice? . . .

Emmet, Fitzgerald and Tone had been murdered by the English, and the Irish watched as on a "painted stage."

>   . . . But popular rage,
> *Hysterica passio* dragged this quarry down.
> None shared our guilt; nor did we play a part
> Upon a painted stage when we devoured his heart.

In 1914 the Parnell mystique got a rude jolt with the publication of Katherine O'Shea's memoirs. Sir Roger Casement told Wilfred Blunt that if the book had appeared a few years before, there would have been no Parnell statue in Dublin. James Joyce had been a Parnell worshipper since childhood—his first publication, at the age of nine, financed by his father, had been *"et tu Healy."* Mrs. O'Shea's story gave Joyce something of a shock, though his future writings would continue to reflect the Parnell influence.

It was not so much the political revelations in her book, such as the Kilmainham letters, which did much to deglamorize Parnell as the selfless patriot. It was more a feeling of alienation on the part of a true-blooded Irishman from one who had little in common with the Irish. He was shown as a frigid Englishman who could read through *Alice's Adventures in Wonderland* without cracking a smile, who detested the Irish green, for whose English recreation his English mistress had set up a shooting range and a small cricket field at Eltham, who preferred puttering around the home at Eltham to keeping his speaking engagements with waiting Irish audiences, who referred to his Irish associates as "rabble" and viewed Home Rule as a gift that he as an Englishman would condescendingly grant the Irish, about whom he said, "I am not as they for they are among the world's children. I am a man and I have told these children what they want and they clamour for it. If they let me I will get it for them."

There is a great deal more to mar the image of the "romantic" hero who gave all for love and consequently was dragged to the dust and torn to pieces by the vulgar mob led by bigoted priests. No doubt Parnell was caught in the toils of love. However, it must be borne in mind that both Parnell and Mrs. O'Shea were thirty-four years old when they met and embarked on adultery. Neither was in the heyday of the blood and both had responsibilities which might be expected to sober them—one to his party and country and the other to her three young children. Moreover, through the long love affair the tale is not one of the compulsions of the grand passion but rather a sordid tale of the compulsions of the lust for money—Mrs. O'Shea was unwilling to get into the divorce court for fear of losing Aunt Ben's fortune and persuaded Parnell to that course. So the trickery of her husband by the shabbiest devices continued for years while Aunt Ben lived on. If the suit had occurred years before, the squalid details, which were the worst part of the scandal, would have been absent.

And the matter cuts deeper than that; more is involved than some priggish view of sexual morality. It is not too much to ask that one who aspires to be a leader of society should respect the basic institutions of society; if in his arrogance and contempt for society he chooses to flout those rules, he has no cause for complaint if he forfeits his leadership. Nothing in society is more basic than the integrity of the marriage bond. As nature has designed the human organism to function for self-protection and reproduction, so society in macrocosm functions under man-made rules for self-protection and perpetuation. For that continuity of life the marriage bond is vital since, if it is respected, a man is sure who his children are and he is legally and morally bound to love and protect them. Otherwise, biology being what it is, the rearing of a new generation would be most difficult since no man could know for certain his own children.

Parnell's offense was rank since it exposed the vice of adultery at its very core. He fathered three children by Mrs. O'Shea, of whom two survived. Captain O'Shea was considered the father by society and they bore his name. This is the situation that marriage is designed to prevent, a gross and unnatural situation. In all literature is there any uglier story than Dostoevski's *The Eternal Husband*? In this short novel, a couple invite to be their guest a bachelor who proceeds to have an affair with the wife. When she learns that she is pregnant, she sends away her lover, has relations with her husband and tells him that she is to bear his child. The unsuspecting husband dotes on the child for years until he learns the truth on his wife's death. Filled with anger, he wreaks his vengeance on the innocent eight-year-old girl, tormenting her to her death.

While Parnell answered grievously for a grievous offense, should not his accomplishments nonetheless be celebrated by his country and the world? He was only human in loving not wisely but too well, and his love affair became trammeled in the rules of society. Had he been a wanton libertine he probably would have gone scot free. In his political life, his human ego may well have been such that he played a synthetic role from the beginning, as the Great Comedian performing on his own painted stage, to the wonderment and applause of the multitude. It may well be that he thirsted for glory and power. If so, he was not much different from most great leaders in history, to whom glory for country gradually becomes transmuted to their own self-glory.

Let him be judged by the real test: his accomplishments achieved within the span of a handful of years. From the Land Act of 1881 and by successive land purchase acts, his leadership of the land movement resulted in the transformation of the landholding structure of Ireland from great feudal baronies held by English landlords into small proprietorships held by Irish farmers, a veritable social revolution. He picked up the Home Rule cause when it was regarded as a farcical failure, and by forming the Irish Parliamentary party and unifying the moral resources of Ireland, he brought it to the verge of realization. Though the dream of national freedom was shattered in his personal tragedy, it remained alive to be realized in the next generation. His success was achieved not only by his undoubted political genius but also by qualities of character, high courage, reckless self-confidence and contempt for English public opinion—qualities which unfortunately were carried over to his personal life and proved his undoing.

The English journal *Punch* paid him this tribute on his death:

> Let the laurels hang
> About his tomb, for, with whatever fault,
> He led with valour cool a fierce assault
> Upon a frowning fortress, densely manned
> With strong outnumbering enemies. He planned
> Far-seen campaigns apparently forlorn.
> He fronted headlong hate and scourging scorn,
> Impassively persistent. But the task
> Of coldly keeping up the Stoic mask
> O'ertaxed him at the last; it fell away, and lo!
> Another face was bared to friend and foe.

BIBLIOGRAPHY

THE BASIC SOURCES for this book have been the accounts of Parnell by those who knew him. Concerning his early life, we have used the book by his older brother, John Howard Parnell, *Charles Stewart Parnell* (1916) and the one by his sister Emily M. Dickinson, *A Patriot's Mistake* (1905). The book by his brother is far more informative and reliable. Charles had a warm affection for his brother, and John was in a position to give an intimate and authentic picture of Parnell in his youth. The most intimate account is that of his wife, who wrote of her life with Parnell in 1914 under the name of Katherine O'Shea, *Charles Stewart Parnell; His Love Story and Political Life*. She was a strong-minded and intelligent woman, and the theory that she had the collaboration of her son, Gerard O'Shea, in the interest of Captain O'Shea's reputation does not seem tenable, though she undoubtedly had a collaborator for the political part of the work, which occupies a large section. Her greatest contribution was the inclusion of the letters Parnell wrote to her, which are almost the only Parnell letters we have. She also included, in a mass, Captain O'Shea's letters to her, which, when separated by time and related to events, are most illuminating.

Whether due to the fascination of the man to his colleagues or the public interest in Parnell after his death, there were a large number of memoirs of Parnell written by his close associates in the Irish Nationalist Movement, though they often appeared under a different rubric. Thus, Frank Hugh O'Donnell wrote *The History of the Irish Parliamentary Party* (1910), which for the most part is the story of Parnell, of whom he had a close-up view in the early days of his political career. The history reflects the same traits that O'Donnell displayed in his own political career: a highly acute mind but great vanity and some highly eccentric viewpoints. *Letters and Leaders of My Day* (1928), by Timothy M. Healy, though it carries the story of Healy's life through 1922, is devoted in greater part to the twelve years he knew Parnell. Except for his animadversions to Parnell's sexual morals, it is an honest account and historically is most valuable, since we have a running account through his letters to his brother, Maurice, and his wife. *The Fall of Feudalism in Ireland*

(1904), by Michael Davitt, although the topic is ostensibly the land movement, is in substance a memoir of Parnell and is scholarly, objective and thoughtful.

Among his associates, T. P. O'Connor almost made a literary career of writing about Parnell. In the latter part of Parnell's life, he wrote for the American market, probably in his role as the party's publicity director, *The Parnell Movement* (1891) and *Gladstone-Parnell; The Great Irish Struggle* (1886). Capitalizing on the immediate interest after Parnell's death, he published in that very year *Charles Stewart Parnell; A Memory*. In 1929, his *Memoirs of an Old Parliamentarian* appeared, which is mostly about Parnell, the most important personality of his life. William O'Brien supplied valuable insights into Parnell at various periods of his career in *The Parnell of Real Life* (1926), and his *An Olive Branch in Ireland* (1910) tells of his abortive efforts to find a compromise during the critical year of 1891. Justin McCarthy shows a good deal less absorption with Parnell than the others, but he gives revealing material in his *Reminiscences* (1899) and, with Mrs. Campbell Praed, *Our Book of Memories* (1912).

Then there are the works of those who were on more distant bases with Parnell, ranging from moderate to slight acquaintance. R. Barry O'Brien was a party follower who had close contact with Parnell during the last year, when Parnell was most in need of friends. In 1899, he published the first formal biography, *Life of Charles Stewart Parnell*. O'Brien was not a deep student of politics, had few documents to work with and knew little of the love affair. He concentrated mostly on the personality and used to great advantage the interview technique, the results of which give his book prime historical importance. Henry Harrison, a young M.P., was a worshipful follower, probably from afar. In 1931, forty years after Parnell's death, his book *Parnell Vindicated, The Lifting of the Veil* appeared. By a judicious use of selected letters and events and unsupported statements made to him by the widow, he constructed the thesis that Captain O'Shea consented to, if he did not connive at, the adultery of his wife. His book, seven years later, *Parnell, Joseph Chamberlain and Mr. Garvin* advances the more plausible thesis that Joseph Chamberlain and his desire for revenge furnished the key to Parnell's ruin. Gladstone's lieutenant John Morley built his personal recollections of Parnell into his books *Recollections* (1917) and *Life of Gladstone* (1903).

Two journalists knew Parnell professionally and wrote of him. Sir Alfred Robbins, Parliamentary correspondent of the Birmingham *Post*, wrote *Parnell; The Last Five Years* (1926), and Frank Harris, *My Life and Loves* (1925), which, divorced from the overblown amatory experiences, gives an excellent view of the period and personalities in it. The writer Katherine Tynan and Margaret Leamy, wife of the editor of *United Ireland*, had some acquaintance with Parnell and gave their impressions of the last phase in *Twenty-five Years; Reminiscences* (1913) and *Parnell's Faithful Few* (1936), respectively.

Biographies of Parnell's political associates have been most useful. They include: F. Sheehy Skeffington, *Michael Davitt: Revolutionary Leader and Labour Agitator* (1908); Michael O'Hara, *Chief and Tribune: Parnell and Davitt* (1919); Liam O'Flaherty, *The Life of Tim Healy* (1927); H. Fyfe, *T. P. O'Connor* (1934); D. R. Gwynn, *Life of John Redmond* (1932); and Michael Macdonagh, *Life of William O'Brien* (1928).

Biographies of figures in English political life have been equally useful. *Life of Joseph Chamberlain* (1932), by J. L. Garvin, is indispensable for the study of Parnell's life since it contains the facts about the Chamberlain-Captain O'Shea alliance and the correspondence between the two. Weymyss Reid, in *Life of the Rt. Hon. W. E. Forster,* discusses the Irish land movement from the point of view of the Gladstone government. Deserving of note are several other biographies: Winston Churchill, *Lord Randolph Churchill* (1906); A. L. Thorold, *Life of Henry Labouchere* (1913); Philip M. Magnus, *Gladstone* (1954); A. G. Gardiner, *Life of William Harcourt* (1923); Blanche E. C. Dugdale, *Life of Arthur James Balfour* (1936); and Roy Jenkins, *Sir Charles Dilke* (1958).

There have been two biographies of Parnell in this century, *Parnell* by St. John Ervine in 1925 and *Parnell* by Joan Haslip in 1937. Since that time some scholarly works have appeared that cover Parnell's career and influence. On the eve of World War II, John L. Hammond's *Gladstone and the Irish Nation* was published. This massive work, a great advance over Lord Eversley's *Gladstone and Ireland,* was based in part on an exhaustive study of the Gladstone papers, which, incidentally, revealed his extensive correspondence over a period of years with Mrs. O'Shea. *Parnell and His Party* (1937), by Conor Cruise O'Brien, analyzes the composition of the party and the party pressures which Parnell had to avoid or to which he had to respond. *The Fall of Parnell* (1960), by F. S. L. Lyons of Trinity College, is based in large part on an examination of the papers of those concerned, principally those of John Dillon and Sir William Harcourt. A recent meritorious contribution, of which the title is self-explanatory, is Herbert Howarth's *The Irish Writers: 1880–1940; Literature under Parnell's Star* (1958).

Other books which have been consulted with profit are: David Anderson, *Scenes in the Commons* (1884); James Bryce, *Studies in Contemporary Biography* (1903); Joseph Chamberlain, *A Political Memoir* (1953); Edward Clarke, *Story of My Life* (1918); L. P. Curtis, Jr., *Coercion and Conciliation in Ireland: 1880 to 1892* (1964); Mary [Gladstone] Drew, *Her Diaries and Letters* (1930); Robert D. Edwards, *The Great Famine* (1956); Joseph Hone, *W. B. Yeats: 1865–1939* (1943); J. J. Horgan, *Parnell to*

Pearse (1948); Shane Leslie, *Studies in Sublime Failure* (1932); Elizabeth Longford, *Queen Victoria: Born To Succeed* (1965); Sir Henry Lucy, *Diary of the Salisbury Parliament* (1892); Michael Macdonagh, *The Home Rule Movement* (1920); Patrick S. O'Hegarty, *A History of Ireland under the Union: 1801–1922* (1952); Cyril Pearl, *The Girl with the Swansdown Seat* (1958); Bernard Shaw, *The Matter with Ireland* (1962); Charles C. Tansill, *America and the Fight for Irish Freedom: 1866–1922* (1957); P. J. Tynan, *The Irish National Invincibles and Their Times* (1894); Cecil Woodham-Smith, *The Great Hunger* (1962); William Butler Yeats, *Autobiographies* (1926).

Articles which have been used include: T. M. Healy, "The Rise and Fall of Mr. Parnell," *New Review*, March, 1891; Charles de Key, "Intellectual Phenomenon," *Critic*, November, 1899; J. L. Garvin, "Parnell and his Power," *Fortnightly Review*, December 1, 1888; Justin McCarthy, "The Deposition of Mr. Parnell," *North American Review*, February, 1891; T. W. Moody, "The New Departure in Irish Politics," in *Essays in British and American History* (1949), by H. A. Cronne, T. W. Moody and D. B. Quinn; T. W. Moody, "Parnell and the Galway Election of 1886," *Irish Historical Studies*, March, 1955; William O'Brien, "Was Mr. Parnell Badly Treated?" *Contemporary Review*, November, 1896; Frank Hugh O'Donnell, "Revelations of Parnell's Widow," *Living Age*, June 27, 1914.

Newspapers of the period were consulted, notably the London *Times*, which had a full report of the divorce trial in November, 1890, with the correspondence between Captain O'Shea and his wife, much of which has appeared in this book. The *Freeman's Journal, National Press* and *United Ireland* were consulted in the National Library in Dublin. The hearings of the Special Commission in 1888 and 1889 were utilized and frequent use was made of Hansard's Parliamentary Debates.

INDEX

INDEX